BIRDING ON THE GREEK

by Richard Brooks

Inside cover paintings by Ernest Leahy

Bird illustrations by Steve Cale and Ernest Leahy

With additional sketches by Kelvin and Mary Thatcher

All photographs by the author

Brookside Publishing

CONTENTS

This book is dedicated to the people and wildlife of a wonderful island. Long may it remain a haven of tranquility.

ISBN 0 9527249 2 8

Printed by the Lanceni Press Fakenham Norfolk
First published December 1998 by Brookside Publishing, 24 Croxton Hamlet, Fulmodeston, Fakenham Norfolk NR21 0NP   01328 878 632

BIRDING ON THE GREEK ISLAND OF LESVOS

LESVOS - THE STORY SO FAR

I first visited Lesvos in May 1991 on the recommendation of a birder I met in Northern Majorca the year before. He assured me that it was an unspoilt island with a variety of habitats, friendly people and a wonderful mix of birds. Moreover, the whole island and its birds were far more accessible than, say, Majorca; where several tracks had recently been closed and 'Private' or 'Privado' signs had begun to proliferate - partly due, I imagine, to the increasing pressures of tourism.

Here then was the chance to explore a new area, acquaint myself with its birds and hopefully capture a selection of them on film. I was not to be disappointed and the initial trip of one week so exceeded my expectations that I have returned every year since (sometimes twice). In fact, the attraction of the island, far from diminishing, seems to grow stronger with each visit, and I find myself on my return pining for its quiet spots, its friendly people and, above all, its obliging birds! In short, I couldn't wait to get back there, and I can honestly say that no two trips have been the same.

After three trips, all in May (there being no direct flights after late October until early May, and precious little accommodation either at this time), I decided that I was well enough qualified to offer Lesvos as one of my slideshow topics. In the course of various talks throughout East Anglia and the South East I was gratified by how much interest the island generated and by the loyalty and enthusiasm that existed amongst those who visited it; often, like myself, on a regular basis.

Although information on Lesvos and its birds could originally be gleaned from Steve Whitehouse's *Lesbos Compilation* and from Marjorie Williams' *Birdwatching In Lesbos*, covering some of the best sites and the birds likely to occur there; I felt that there was a need for much fuller coverage of the island and exactly what it has to offer the birder. After another two week trip in May '94 I found myself lecturing on the subject at the British Birdwatching Fair at Rutland Water in August; where I again found much interest being generated. Some BTO staff were running an unofficial ringing trip there in September, and I began to think about its autumn potential. I was also lucky enough to meet John Bannon of Hobby Publications, who encouraged me in this direction and also expressed interest in the idea of a book. In addition, *Birdwatch* ran my Lesvos article in its October issue (No. 28) and again a lot of enquiries resulted; so it seemed logical to take the project further.

A two week trip from late September to early October was quickly arranged, with some sponsorship being obtained from the Greek Tourist Board to defray at least my accommodation expenses and a week's car hire. This proved very enlightening, and an appeal for the records of visiting birders soon followed in both *Birdwatch* and *Birding World*. The response to this was especially encouraging and gave me several species new to the island. Though biased in favour of the usual spring migration period, there was nevertheless a good scattering of records through from summer to late autumn (ie the end of October). The gap in knowledge for the winter months and detailed information on Lesvos' special breeding birds was filled by Dr. Filios Akriotis - one of that rare breed; a dedicated and enthusiastic Greek birder with an impressive scientific and academic background. Other winter records could only really be obtained from local hunters, who gave me a list of the 'quarry' species available at that time - valuable nonetheless. I am also indebted to Dr Peter de Knijff, whose wealth of information on, and up-to-date censusing of the current Cinereous Bunting population and distribution proved absolutely invaluable.

Another more extended trip via Athens took place from 10th April to 25th May '95, (made possible by free accommodation, arranged through the Greek Tourist Board). This enabled me to fill in many gaps in the early spring period, and to witness the transition from winter to spring birds. Prior to this, for example, it was assumed that wintering Kingfishers had left by February or March - in fact they are still widespread in mid-April, along with Green Sandpipers. A different base in Mytilini for two weeks also enabled me to check out some new sites. The result of all this was the publication in December '95 of the first edition of *Birding In Lesbos*, which was given good coverage in *Bird Watching* magazine especially, and thankfully received generally favourable reviews in most of the birding press..

April '96 found me back on the island again (based in Skala Kalloni for a month from 21st April), and following this trip certain changes to sites and new bird species discovered led to the publication of my *Lesbos Spring '96 Update*. Now that visiting birders at last had a 'yardstick' to help them evaluate the scarcity or otherwise of their sightings, things really started to gather momentum; and I was soon deluged with enough trip-lists to cause me to contemplate the possibility of revising the book sooner rather than later!

Hand in hand with this there developed an increasing awareness amongst some of the more far-sighted individuals on the island that this trend towards some form of sustainable green tourism, in the Kalloni area especially, was just what the island needed at a time when several tour operators were pulling out or cutting back their operations, and the long-term future of its tourist industry was somewhat uncertain. Perhaps also, by extending the season at times when 'normal' holidaymakers would be less likely to visit, the growing numbers of off-season birders might teach those in high places the importance of conserving its abundant wildlife and unspoilt places for future generations to enjoy.

To promote both these aims and to make people aware of just what the Kalloni area had to offer in April I organised a stand at the Rutland Bird Fair in August '96. Made possible by generous sponsorship from the Mayor of Kalloni, I was successful in tempting 70 odd individuals to make the trip from 19th April '97 (travelling with Olympic Airways via Athens). In spite of one of the coldest springs for 40 years, most seemed to thoroughly enjoy the experience, and many logged over 170 species in their two week stay (with the spectacular display of wildflowers proving an added bonus). I actually stayed from 18th March to 20th May, and came away with 212 species to my credit. This was the first time the true scale of migration in April had been witnessed by so many birders, and it was inevitable that a further flurry of records would result. If I'd been in any doubt before about the need to update the book I certainly wasn't any longer; and the whole project was greatly helped by the publication that year of *The Birds of Greece* by George Handrinos and Filios Akriotis, which finally enabled me to set the occurrence of all the various species in an overall context, and also gave me a yardstick against which to measure the records I had accumulated.

With over double the number participating in the mid-April '98 trip (during which conditions were thankfully warm and sunny almost throughout), and increasing co-operation from the hoteliers of Skala Kalloni (especially my friend George Capsalis of Malemi hotel) towards promoting such ventures, it seems likely that April trips will now be ongoing (especially if interest for '99 is anything to go by!); and it may be possible to extend the season even further if there is sufficient interest. Certainly the prices being offered for accommodation and car hire at this time (together with a special group fare from Olympic Airways) make this a very attractive financial proposition (not to mention the wonderful migration and wildflower spectacle on offer in early spring); and anyone interested is welcome to contact me for further details. Hopefully both The Wildlife Photofair and the Rutland Bird Fair will continue to act as a vehicle for this, as they did once again in July and August '98 thanks to generous sponsorship from the Malemi hotel.

This whole process has also been aided by Malcolm Rymer's excellent video *Lesbos In Spring*, compiled over two April trips and detailing most of the best sites around Skala Kalloni and their associated birds and wildflowers. Apart from a promotional video for the Bird Fair, Malcolm has also produced two new 'video diaries'. Entitled *The Lesbos Journals Part One and Two* (Malcolm doesn't yet share the now generally accepted 'classical' spelling for the island!). Part one goes under the heading *Orioles to Orchids* and part two *Peonies to Pratincoles*; and all three videos should prove popular both with those intending to visit, and as an evocative reminder for those who have - see later for further details. I am also indebted to my friends Dennis Buisson and Paul Denning for their help at these events - their enthusiasm for, and knowledge of Lesvos is second only to mine! Moreover, anyone who can share both a car and a room with me for a period of 2 weeks or more deserves both congratulations and sympathy!

Information gathered over the last few years tells me that Lesvos has the capacity to produce good birds at virtually any time of year (even high summer), and often when you would least expect them - this was borne out by a three week trip in January '98 courtesy of Olympic Airways, during which I was able to investigate the island's midwinter potential, (and also regrettably to witness the shooting season for the first time). In spite of unseasonably mild weather I still recorded over 90 species, with several new to me (and also to the island), some impressive counts of certain species, and one or two surprises - not least the fact that it was probably warmer and sunnier than early April '97! All this I was able to utilize for another article in the December '98 *Bird Watching*. One day I hope perhaps to realize my aim of spending a whole year on the island (assuming of course I could secure enough rolls of film for this eventuality). Even then it may be necessary to spend several years to complete the overall picture - or pictures I should say! Meanwhile I shall have to content myself with a modest couple of months or so, though in '98 another two month stay from 22nd March through to 20th May (my 10th visit) resulted in a near three month presence on the island that year!

These then are my aims. Though of course there is always a chance that in sharing my experiences, particularly of such an idyllic island, I may run the risk of making it simply too popular as a destination, I sincerely hope that this does not happen. I feel in the end that the best way of securing the survival of such beautiful places is to make sure that they are not despoiled through ignorance; and if I can succeed in this aim at least then my efforts will not have been wasted. I recently received some encouraging news that would suggest that the Mayor of Kalloni and others appear to have taken some of these ideas on board; and a large sum of money has now been earmarked through EU funding to enhance the important wetlands around Skala Kalloni. Though it is not yet clear how this can best be done, it does at least recognise some sort of commitment, and therefore represents a positive step forward - bearing in mind that the ICBP and WRB included 12,000 hectares of the area known as Kolpos Kallonis (Kalloni Bay) in the shadow list of wetlands of international importance, as defined by the Ramsar Convention way back in 1975!

Although those who bought the original *Birding In Lesbos* in '96 will be familiar with much of the text, I hope they will nevertheless appreciate (as I did) the need to produce a new guide incorporating the wealth of new site information, the species new to Lesvos and the changes in status of a good number since more complete coverage of the island was obtained. This is particularly important in the early spring period, when we can now see a much clearer picture of migration through the island. Being there in January and mid-March as well as October also helps clarify the situation regarding winter visitors (much of which was, by necessity, fairly sketchy in the first book); and a good number of midsummer and early autumn records helps to piece together previously much needed information on the island's breeding birds. Regular ringing trips by Dawn Balmer and Jeremy Wilson of the BTO (in conjunction with the Hellenic Ornithological Society) every September since '94 (barring '97, when an April trip was made) have also greatly increased our knowledge of migration through the island at a time when many species would otherwise be overlooked. Their results are summarized at the end of the book, and I would like to take this opportunity of thanking

Dawn for making this and other information readily available to me - not to mention her meticulous note keeping during a shared trip in April '98, and finally her help and moral support with a much needed revamping of some of my sketch-maps and records.

As a result of all this, there is now a danger of incorporating too much rather than not enough information - you only need to compare the records for Bittern in the systematic list to see the difference three years can make! Moreover, some of the new records received for early spring go back as far as '84 - giving us a full 14 year coverage to work with, and ensuring that a reasonably accurate picture emerges. Of course, even then we are going to miss something, but that is going to be the case with any publication; and I felt I owed it to all the people who have given me their support and enthusiasm (and records of course!) over the last few years to try and produce the best testament yet to this wonderful island.

I felt little need to change the section on some of the history, culture and mythology connected with Lesvos, nor that describing its geography. However, certain subtle changes may be apparent in the description of habitats and birds throughout the seasons, (together with current site guides), and also in the systematic species by species status guide. I have also removed some information that I felt may be too current and not likely to stand the test of time - particularly some relating to existing tour operators, car hire details etc, which experience has taught me are inclined to be prone to sudden changes. I have also bowed to pressure in giving the island its true 'classical' spelling of *Lesvos*, rather than anglicizing it as many still do. Certainly this pronunciation is more popular with the Greeks, so since it is their island I thought it only fair to follow their wishes!

Finally, I thought it just worth mentioning some of the changes that are taking place on the island. Now that we can look back over 14 years, it is inevitable that even a comparatively unspoilt island like Lesvos is going to witness some changes - obviously not all for the better - though the new reservoirs at Petra and the Potamia Valley (when wet - see later) are certainly of positive benefit for those visiting in autumn especially - when such sites prove a magnet not just to wildfowl and waders but to a host of others exploiting such an abundant food source. In spite of the fact that it has only really been a tourist destination since '85, some who visited the island even before then have, however, noticed a deterioration in some of the wetland habitats in Skala Kalloni - connected as much as anything with hotel development around Kalloni Pool and a general encroachment of buildings in the direction of East River. Whilst any such development is regrettable, it is still fairly low-key, and is unlikely to be very noticeable to those who hadn't visited in these early years.

Nevertheless, agricultural 'improvement' and the draining of wet, flower-rich meadowland was catalogued at Sigri and around Kalloni Salt Pans as far back as '85; and this extended to a loss of old meadowland and the mosaic of small olive groves and hedges around Kalloni East River - due in part to the Common Agricultural Policy, but also to the effects of a very severe winter with several weeks snow cover between '85 and '86 causing farmers to switch more to cereal production in this area. By '92, moreover, hotel construction on the north side of Kalloni Pool destroyed an area of old olive and fig trees, and the building of a dirt track on the east and north sides of the pool also led to increased disturbance. The process was accelerated when this track was tarmaced and lit on the seaward side, and more hotels were built between Kalloni Pool and West River - all causing the pool outlet to become blocked and no longer subject to tidal influences. Finally, the building of a disco and various chalets between Skala Kalloni Square and East River (with EU *Leader* funding) caused some fragmentation of an excellent area of coastal heath.

I am writing this to prevent any of us becoming too complacent. Although these changes are scarcely evident to the majority of visitors (who still consider the island largely unspoilt), the importance of areas like Kalloni Pool and East River cannot be overstressed, and if there remains even the remotest chance that the former could still be drained to make room for more hotels, then visiting birders should be aware of it, and keep up the pressure on people like the Mayor of Kalloni to safeguard the future of this vital area indefinitely (also mentioning the issue of rubbish dumping at Kalloni West River and Parakila Marsh at the same time!). Of course, EU funding is evident in other ways, with the continuing impovement of the island's road network a prime example. This is somewhat of a 'mixed blessing'. On the one hand birders appreciate being able to get about more easily, and visit far-flung destinations with the minimum of hassle; but on the other hand many feel that the island is in danger of losing some of its underlying peace and tranquility if too many of its dirt tracks and small by-ways are replaced with tarmac. This is a difficult issue to address, but hopefully the right balance can be struck to ensure that Lesvos retains its integral charm well into the 21st century.

After reading the previous few paragraphs some may be forgiven for thinking that Lesvos is going the same way as so many other holiday destinations, but the fact remains that in comparison with accelerating change elsewhere (the UK especially) it still remains a paradise, with its roots firmly in the past and lagging perhaps 40 years behind us in many ways. Many of its wetlands are still largely pristine, and its underlying rural traditions remain basically unaffected by the pressures of modern life. Where else could you find yourself at one moment cursing and another marvelling at the flocks of sheep being shepherded along the main road by a small boy and his sister, or maybe by a moped rider with an open pick-up truck to the rear, complete with its cargo of goats or a tethered horse trotting along behind! The sole reason that the majority of these people care so little about their natural heritage (albeit wildflowers, birds, reptiles or butterflies) is that it always seems to have been there. They know little of the huge losses sustained by our impoverished flora and fauna, and it's partly up to us as visitors to try and make sure that they don't repeat our mistakes - at least through ignorance. This, ultimately, is the value of *green tourism*; and we shouln't lose this opportunity of helping shape the island's future - in however small a way.

CULTURE

This is an area I do not intend to dwell on; but suffice it to say that Lesvos has long been renowned for its cultural development and as a base for the fine arts. It was home to the great philosopher Theophrastus, born in Eressos in 372 BC and well versed in logic, rhetoric and metaphysics; but especially the study of plants (of which there are no shortage in a wet spring!) In fact, the beauty of the island has for long served as an inspiration to poets like Alcaeus and Sappho, who presided over Lesvos' cultural peak in the 7th and 6th Century BC The former, distinguished in all forms of lyric poetry, was the originator of the metre bearing his name; and the latter, born in Eressos in 612 BC, was described as the greatest female lyric poet of all time. She is considered as unrivalled even now in the passion, sensitivity and subtlety of her poetry. She regarded women as individual and independent beings; and her poems were therefore directed mainly at the female sex. This is the actual origin of the term 'lesbian' - sorry it wasn't more exciting! In Sappho's day, Mytilini was perhaps the most advanced and civilized city in the ancient world: it was prosperous, had a remarkable intellectual life, and was a considerable sea-power.

Aesop, the great storyteller, was a native of Lesvos, and the musicians Terpandros and Arion also came from the island, together with the Homeric hero Palamides, the inventor of numbers and letters; Matriketas the astrologer and Mysilos the historian and others too numerous to mention. Lesvos has since enjoyed a sustained cultural tradition through its writers, poets, painters and musicians right up to the present day (with Theophilos the painter, born in Vareia in 1873, the Nobel prize winning poet Elytis and the writer and poet Myrivilis being but a few recent examples). The musician Kakourgos, too, can still be found playing the santouri (a dulcimer like instrument) in the cobbled streets of Agiassos - though, like Kruper's Nuthatch, he can't be guaranteed!

MYTHOLOGY

The long tradition of producing many highly creative people, though strongly borne out by its history, actually has its roots in mythology; (though the two are often intertwined). According to myths, Lesvos was first peopled by descendants of Makareus, son of the Sun; and it is from his children that the principal towns on the island take their names. His son-in-law, Lesvos, is claimed to have given the island its name; (though the word is also supposed to mean an island of lush vegetation and enchanting beauty).

Lesvos certainly figures in Homer's Epics, when Achilles apparently attacked the island many times and captured the beautiful Brysiida, flying into a rage when Agamemnon took her from him; and was only appeased when offered seven of Lesvos' most beautiful women, who, it was claimed, 'surpassed in beauty the entire race of women.' This especially applied to the village of Dafia near Kalloni; and the very word Kalloni actually means beauty. Another version of events states that Achilles stopped off on Lesvos with Odysseus en route to the Trojan Wars, and was offered the seven women as an incentive. At all events the end result was the same!

The earliest ornithological link can be traced back to the myth of Orpheus; and again there are two slightly differing versions. Both agree that he was so skilled a musician that 'even the animals and stones were moved by his songs'; but the first states that inhabitants of Thrace were so overwhelmed by his music that they left their wives to stay by his side and listen to it continuously. This infuriated the Maenads so much that they killed him and threw his dismembered body into the Evros River, which carried his remains out to sea. His head and lyre were washed up on the shores of Lesvos, close to what is now Gavathas; from where they were retrieved by the local inhabitants and buried with full honours.

The second version has it that the part played by Orpheus in helping Jason capture the Golden Fleece (he played a lullaby to send to sleep the fearsome dragon that was guarding it) endeared him to Dionysus, the god of wine, who entertained in his court the Maenads; some particularly wild women who became positively lethal after a few glasses of wine! Orpheus, meanwhile, fell in love with and married Eurydice, who was unfortunately fatally bitten by a serpent on their honeymoon. Totally inconsolable, he resolved to visit the Underworld, ruled by Pluto, Zeus' brother; to try and bring her back to earth (strictly forbidden for a mortal), and he only succeeded in his quest by charming first the guards and then Pluto with his music. Their safe return was conditional on Orpheus not looking back over his shoulder to check Eurydice's progress; but regrettably curiosity got the better of him and she was lost for ever.

In consequence he made the decision never to play another note, and the Maenads, in their fury, killed him and cut up his body. Again, the end result was the same; and it is claimed to this day that the reason the Nightingales in Lesvos sing 'with a sweeter song than anywhere else on earth' is because of the gift of music that Orpheus brought to the island. Logic dictates that this should also apply to the Orphean Warbler! Arion, the son of Poseidon the sea god, was another great musician from Lesvos; who it was claimed, after winning gold and jewels in a musical competition in Italy, was thrown overboard by the greedy crew on his return trip, but was rescued and returned home by the music-loving dolphins which followed the ship - rather a fishy story this one, in all senses of the word!

HISTORY

To return now to historical fact; archeological excavations suggest that Lesvos has been inhabited since at least the Neolithic period, and by the early Bronze Age had already developed an extremely advanced civilization, very similar to the Mycenean and Trojan; influenced as it was by its geographical closeness to Troy.

From 1100-1000 BC Mytilini flourished and gradually extended its commercial and colonizing activities to the shores of Asia Minor. The people of the island were mainly engaged in agriculture and shipping, and for a considerable period were a major naval power. This eventually brought them into conflict with the Athenians, who in 427 BC conquered the island and divided it up. It was later conquered by the Spartans, the Egyptians in 323 BC, and in 88 BC by the Romans, under whose rule it flourished and was even able to preserve its political autonomy. The town of Mytilene, especially, was greatly improved and traces of a Roman aqueduct can still be found in Moria to the north of the capital.

After the break-up of the Roman Empire in 300 AD and its division by the Emperor Constantine into East and West, Lesvos was incorporated into the Eastern Byzantine State. This period greatly influenced the island ideologically, especially its art and churches; and the symbol of the period, a double-headed eagle (another ornithological link) purports to stand for the equal power of Church and State. This symbol can still be found in the church at Agiassos and the Limonas monastery amongst others.

The island was later conquered by the Saracens in 1084, and plundered by the Venetians and Crusaders, becoming part of the Latin Empire, before returning to Byzantine rule in 1261. In 1354 Lesvos was ceded as a dowry to the Genoese nobleman Francesco Gattelusi, and things began to improve. His benevolent rule gave support to commerce, literature and the arts; whilst also showing an interest in the well being of the island's inhabitants. (Above the castle gate in Mytilini you can still see a shield bearing the Gattelusi coat of arms, together with the two-headed Byzantine eagle). Unfortunately, he was killed by an earthquake in 1401, which also destroyed the town of Mytilini. In 1445 the Bulgarians destroyed the flourishing town of Kalloni, and in 1462 the island was overrun by the Turks under Sultan Mohamet the Second, resulting in terrible destruction. The majority of the population were exterminated or deported (the population shrank from 100,000 to 30,000), crippling taxes were levied on all non Muslims and most cultural and economic life ceased; with the spirit of resistance only being kept alive through the churches and monasteries - dark days indeed.

Though this situation remained for over 400 years, Lesvos nevertheless took on importance as a centre for the Turkish navy, and in the late 1700's a shipyard was built in Mytilini employing hundreds of islanders. The Turks also built Sigri Castle in 1757 to protect the area from raiders. The 19th Century, too, saw the development of a strong economic base to the island; in spite of another severe earthquake in 1807 which caused much material damage and loss of life. In 1893, too, Lesvos acquired an extensive road network.

However, as a result of the cruel suppression of uprisings against Turkish rule elsewhere in Greece, culminating in the public execution of the Patriarch (the leader of the Greek Orthodox Church) in Constantinople (modern Istanbul); revolutionaries on the island, inspired by Papanikolis (whose statue stands on Eressos sea front) gradually acquired the upper hand; and the last Turks were driven from the island in 1912. In 1914 Lesvos was finally ceded to Greece by the Treaties of London and Athens, and the Treaty of Lausanne in 1923 officially recognized the fact. This state of affairs has remained ever since (barring its occupation by the Germans between May 1941 and September 1944).

It is hardly surprising, therefore, that the tension with Turkey, situated so close to its shores, remains strong - witness the military bases dotted around the coastline and elsewhere (where binoculars and telephoto lenses should be used with caution) - take it from one who knows! It is in fact, a tribute to the people of Lesvos that their culture, tradition and language has survived such turbulent historical events. If anything it has probably strenghtened their love of music, dancing and general good humour which is so evident today. In short, they are genuinely nice people!

CUSTOMS

For those visiting the island not totally preoccupied with its birdlife, it is, perhaps, useful to know of certain customs and traditions, and even some of the annual festivities (if only to avoid the area at such times!).

For a long time, Lesvos, because of its access to underground water supplies, has been associated with hot springs and their so-called restorative powers. Those at Thermi, Geras, Polichnitos and Eftalou, in particular, being recommended for easing a variety of complaints, including rheumatism, arthritis, galistones and certain 'female problems'; not to mention the more likely ones of 'photographer's shoulder,' 'scoper's neck' etc, brought on by an excess of birding; or, in my case, up to ten hours of daily bodily contortions in a car, in order to pursue my 'art'! These pools range in temperature from 39.7 to 87.6 C at Polichnitos (claimed to be the hottest in Europe) and date back to mediaeval times and beyond.

Agiassos, too, is home to an icon claimed to be one of six painted by St. Luke and brought to the island around 700 AD by St. Agathon after fears for its safety at the height of the Iconoclastic period. A tradition of miracles associated with this has meant that, since early times, Agiassos has become a place of pilgrimage. This also resulted in a number of craftsmen moving to the area (potters to make flasks for the spring waters with their 'miraculous powers', and wood carvers to make and sell copies of the icon) - a good place to visit, then, for lovers of ceramics and wood carvings (but only after Kruper's Nuthatch has been ticked!).

Plomari also has, in the Church of Ayios Nikolaos (1847) an association with icons (those of Ayios Dimitrios and the Archangels Michael and Gabriel), and this culminates every year in a large religious festival and procession on December 6th. It is also customary for the Bishop to throw his wine glass to the crowd (after drinking it, of course!). In fact, Plomari is best known as the main centre on the island for the production of ouzo; and the locals are claimed to be somewhat affected by its liberal consumption.

Moving from drink to food, various feast-days are also celebrated, such as the Feast of St. Ignatius, from 13th to 14th October, starting in Skala Kalloni and continuing uphill to the Limonas Monastery five kilometres beyond Kalloni. This monastery was an important refuge during the four centuries of Turkish occupation; and the significance of the feast dates back to the building of a monastery and school by St. Ignatius of Kalloni; granted permission to do so by a Turkish Sultan in gratitude for allegedly curing his deformed son with his 'healing powers'. The most famous feast day is that of the Virgin Mary, held on August 15th and celebrated especially in Petra and Agiassos; accompanied by much eating, drinking and dancing. On a musical theme, there is also a folk festival, held at the Church in Filia sometime in May, which also sees a celebration of the founding of the Ipsilou Monastery in the hills above Andissa by Theophanus around 800 AD; and here again, six Byzantine icons take pride of place. Christmas is also observed, with a long celebration leading up to New Year's Day, though an olive branch is often hung outside doors instead of a Christmas tree. In some cases this is also done in the hopes of ensuring a good supply of olive-oil.

Some of the annual celebrations, though often spectacular, are not always for the squeamish, and usually involve the slaughtering of a bull. One such event is held at Mandamados (a village best known for its unusual pottery), whose Church holds an icon of the Archangel Michael, the patron saint of the region, and indeed, of Lesvos. According to legend, the icon was originally fashioned out of rudimentary materials by a grateful monk, the sole survivor of a raid on the Monastery by Saracen pirates. He put his salvation down to the divine intervention of the Archangel, and to this day the Church celebrates on the third Sunday after Easter with a large religious and commercial fair; including the slaughtering of a bull, from which a dish called 'keskeki' - a mixture of meat, herbs, onions and wheat - is shared out, after first being blessed. Not much to celebrate for the other 99% of the Monastery, though!

A similar dish is served at the 'Feast of the Bull', held every year since 1774 at Agia Paraskevi on the first Sunday of the last ten days of May; (and believe me, that's a lot of bull!) This, again, has its roots in pre-Christian tradition, and legend has it that, during the Turkish occupation, a local farmer, in chasing after his runaway bull, inadvertently wandered into a forbidden area during the curfew; and though spotted by a Turkish soldier, disappeared from the latter's view on each occasion that he raised his rifle to shoot him. This so-called miracle impressed the Turks to such an extent that they gave the villagers special permission to hold an annual festival. This starts with them riding up to the Church on the Saturday night and holding an all night celebration; followed by horse races and a lot of colourful costumes on the Sunday afternoon (not to mention the obligatory bull slaughtering). Apparently the local women use its blood to make the Sign of the Cross on their children's hands. This, and the contact made with the animal prior to its demise is meant to dispel magic and treat disease - though it doesn't do much for the bull; which is said to 'wait placidly with no resistance' (rather a local euphemism here I feel!).

Of course, this apparent Greek disregard for the finer points of animal welfare is just as evident when encountering donkeys left out in the hot sun with a front and back leg tied together to stop them wandering too far; or dogs tethered to old abandoned cars etc in the middle of nowhere, with only a bowl of water and maybe a few scraps or an old bone in the vicinity. They usually wag their tails hopefully on your arrival, and the soft-hearted may care to carry a packet of biscuits around, or some leftovers from breakfast (probably preferable, as biscuits are somewhat expensive!). Though this all appears fairly distasteful to animal lovers, we must remember ultimately that it is their island, and we are only visitors, who often wander at will over their land and private domain, without occasioning any animosity on their part.

Indeed, I well remember one occasion, whilst photographing near a Middle Spotted Woodpecker nest site in the middle of an olive grove, using the car as a hide. When the owner duly appeared, my apprehension and feeble attempts at communication (pointing at a bird book etc) were met with the standard reaction to birders - amused resignation, imparted with a smile and a shrug of the shoulders. It was only then that I realized he had come to switch on his sprinkler system, and several thousand pounds worth of lens was in imminent danger of a soaking. Needless to say, I took hasty action, but at least got a free car wash!

This leads us usefully on to a short section on language, which, for those patient enough (unlike myself) might make for better communications and help impress the locals - though I do tend to find that those of us with binoculars or long lenses are usually treated with a certain amused benevolence, as being almost a race apart: as indeed we are! (This, however, does not apply near military bases!). Finally, those, like myself, staying in Skala Kalloni and wishing to observe the locals, in turn observing the antics of the local courting couples and generally taking the air, could do worse than visit Skala Kalloni Square on a Sunday evening, when they take their local promenade or sit outside the bars chatting. This scenario can be repeated almost anywhere on the island, down to the smallest mountain village; and this is really the essence of the place. As a famous person once said : all human life is here!

LANGUAGE

No phrases seem to be listed for the exclusive use of birders, though requests to be towed out of a marshy quagmire or a deeper than expected ford are usually self-evident! Indeed, a local on a moped once rolled up his trousers and waded enthusiastically into a swollen river, moving rocks aside left, right and centre without any prompting, on seeing my predicament (though this could have had something to do with the fact that I was blocking the ford at the time!).

Most tourist books tend to list mainly words connected with food and household requirements - hardly surprising, I suppose. I intend here just to list a few courtesy words, which may help impress the locals if you are somewhere you shouldn't be (which I am most of the time!) A simple 'yassoo' covers most general greetings, though technically,'good morning' is 'kalimera', 'good evening' 'kalispera' and 'goodnight' 'kalinichta'. Phoenetically spelt, 'thank you' is *'F Harry's Toe'*, 'please' *'parakalo'* and 'where is?' *'poo eenay?'*

For car drivers, the following may be vaguely useful :

left	aristera
right	dexia
straight	efthia
mechanic	mihanikos
petrol	venzini
unleaded	amolivthi

(Be warned - some hire cars designed to run on unleaded have been converted to run on super, and this can confuse some of the smaller garages, especially as the pump nozzle is occasionally a different size).

The age-old question 'how much?' is 'poso kanee?' Staying with money matters, 'bank' is 'trapeza'. Some more useful words are listed below, though will hopefully not be needed.

airport	aerodromio
bus-stop	stasis
chemist	farmakio
post-office	tahidromio
telephone	tilephono
dentist	othondoyiatros
doctor	yiatros

Finally, the subject of food is almost unavoidable, and some of the following may just stave off the risk of starvation!

bread	psomi
butter	voutiro
cheese	tiri
chicken	kotopoulo
chips	patates
chops	brizola
egg	avgo
fish	psari
fried	tiganito
Greek salad	horiatiki
ham	jambon

honey	melee
ice-cream	pagoto
lamb chops	paithakia
liver	sikoti
lobster	astakos
(without) meat	(horis) kreas
milk	gala
minced meat	kima
octopus	oktapothi
oil	lathi
olives	elies
pepper	piperi
pork	hirino
prawns	garithes
rice	risi
salad	salata
salt	alati
sugar	zachari
water	nero
wine	krassi
yoghurt	yaourti

To assist with the consumption of any of these items, 'ehete' means 'do you have?' Those in further doubt should consult a guide book. Of course, the most important phrase : *I'm only looking at the birds*, I have been informed by Filios Akriotis, is *Kitazo ta poulia* - but he pointed out that, even if you were to say it, the locals still wouldn't understand why you were watching them!

GEOGRAPHY, FAUNA AND BIOTYPES

Lesvos was originally joined to the coast of Asia Minor, but was detached by powerful geological disturbances, which gave it its current intriguing shape, likened by the poet Elytis to the leaf of a plane tree (of which, incidentally, several mature specimens up to 500 years old or more, adorn some of the village squares, in Agra, Plomari and Messotopos, for example).

It is the second largest of the Greek Islands after Crete (if one discounts Evia, which is technichally a peninsular), and is more than double the size of Corfu. Situated within 5-8 miles of the coast of Turkey, it is 70 kms long by 45 kms wide (approx 40 by 25 mls), with an area of 1630 sq. kms. It has 2 large bays, Kalloni and Geras, both with narrow entrances. Kalloni Bay measures approx. 19 by 6.5 kms (12 by 4 mls) and Geras 10.5 by 4 kms (7.5 by 2.5 mls). Though there are no permanent large rivers with a steady flow of water, there are abundant springs, and water-courses in winter and spring at least - whilst some of the river mouths and pools are semi-tidal and never dry out, even in autumn.

Indeed, strong winds in the right direction at this time of year can whip up the sea and send it some way up the river mouths. Such areas include Kalloni East and West Rivers, the Chalandra River Skala Eressos, and the inter-tidal rivers and pools at the area known as 'Derbyshire'. Moreover, the island's 2 sets of salt pans, certainly those at Skala Polichnitos, usually remain wet (unless deliberately drained, of which more later). Although the main Kalloni Salt Pans have been known to dry up in the past, this is less likely in the future now that they are being regularly worked again, and in any case there is always some water in the surrounding channels.

The main marshes and flatlands, then, occur around Kalloni, Skala Eressos and Sigri-Faneromeni; and the hilliest areas are in the west around Eressos, to the north around Molivos, and to the east around Agiassos; and the nearby Mount Olympus, peaking at 3500 ft, is the highest point on the island after Mount Lepetimnos, actually one metre higher! These uplands are usually cloaked mainly in pines and holme oak, with olives on the lower reaches, and, around Agiassos, some stands of deciduous woodland, including sweet chestnut (though the mountains around Eressos are probably the barest and most rugged on the island, and it is no coincidence that they play host, amongst others, to one of its special birds - Cinereous Bunting). There is also much oak woodland to the west and north-west of the island (especially between Skoutaros and Vatoussa) and this area plays host to several specialized species not always easy elsewhere - Nuthatch and Hawfinch for example.

Around the coast especially there are large areas of low-lying scrub and grassland, often with a profusion of wildflowers in spring. The most rugged coastline (with scattered cliffs and offshore islands) tends to occur on the north and north-east coast (roughly from Anaxos east to Thermi) and also to the west and north-west from Skala Eressos upwards. For this reason birds like Shag, Eleonora's Falcon and Alpine Swift are most regularly recorded offshore here in the summer months. Further inland, dried-up river beds (for example just up from Skala Eressos and at Faneromeni) offer similar arid scrub with its own special birds - like Rufous Bush Robin.

Olive groves, though, predominate on the island, and there are 11 million trees, yielding approx. 20,000 tons of olives - about a quarter of all those grown in Greece. These trees, many of them very old, are extremely productive for insects, and hence, of course, birds like warblers, Hoopoe, Masked Shrike and Middle Spotted Woodpecker; and their continued production is due in no small measure to the temperate climate. Snow, though not that rare, is usually short-lived, and settles mainly on the higher ground, whilst more sunshine hours are recorded than practically anywhere else in Greece, or even the Mediterranean come to that.

The 1971 census recorded a population of 97,008, reducing slightly to 88,601 in 1981. and 86,907 in '91; and this trend seems likely to continue. Of these, about 25,000 live in the capital Mytilini; and this is, incidentally, about the only place on the island one is likely to encounter traffic jams! Apart from tourism, (which you should realize by now is fairly low-key on Lesvos) most are employed in small-scale agriculture, with some, of course, in the military; and a few in the fishing industry (Kalloni, especially, being famous for its sardines - always, annoyingly, out of season when I'm on the island, though I did finally score on my January '98 visit, when local mushrooms were also on offer).

To sum up then, the basic geography of Lesvos, together with its size and location so close to the Turkish coast, mark it out as an area of varied habitats, with some good wetlands, likely to prove extremely attractive to spring and autumn migrants; wet enough to keep a fair variety of wintering wildfowl, waders etc; yet also playing host to a good mix of breeding birds - some of them, like Cinereous Bunting and Kruper's Nuthatch, quite outstanding. For this reason it could be argued that it has more in common with Turkey than Greece (at least in the ornithological sense) - but don't let the locals hear you say that!

Before moving on, just a word or two of advice at this stage - to make access easier, and to minimize disturbance to the birds, a car is recommended. Birds generally feel far less threatened, and in consequence are far more approachable than if viewed on foot or by bicycle. (This, of course, applies especially to photographers like myself). Please think twice about approaching a parked car if it is occupied, and it looks as if the occupant might be attempting to photograph something - it could be me!

THE BIRDING YEAR

It has to be said that spring is best, and most birders used to visit in May, when direct flights to the island commence. However, now that my own experiences have given me an increased awareness of the island's attractions outside this period (especially the migration spectacles on offer in March and April) and even the potential of a midwinter or autumn visit, I thought it might be beneficial at this stage to give a rundown of Lesvos's bird potential on a month by month basis - bearing in mind that this is only a rough guide and is very much weather (and observer) dependent.

January-February - The severity of the weather very much affects the species and numbers present at this time, though even during mild weather Great Crested and Black-necked Grebes, Cormorants, Mergansers and the occasional Black-throated Diver are usually present on the sea or river mouths in varying numbers, along with wintering Sandwich Terns. Dominant birds on the wetlands are Greater Flamingos (salt pans, sometimes river mouths and 'Derbyshire'), Great White Egret, Grey Heron, Little Grebe, wintering Avocet, Redshank, Curlew and Snipe, Shoveler, Shelduck, a few Teal, Pintail and perhaps Pochard, with Coot, Water Rail, Kingfisher, Water Pipit and White Wagtail widespread (with smaller numbers of Grey Wagtail likely). Wintering gulls include Black-headed, Mediterranean and usually a few Lesser Black-backed and Little. The banks of Kalloni East River, Chalandra River Skala Eressos, and other lowland areas and farmland are good places to locate mixed flocks of Corn Bunting, Skylark, Woodlark, Goldfinch, Greenfinch, Linnet and Serin feeding on seeds. These may be joined by the odd Yellowhammer in harsher weather, and at all events are likely to attract the attentions of wintering raptors like Hen Harrier, Buzzard and Sparrowhawk - the latter being especially widespread.

Reedy areas (and especially Dipi Larssos Reedbed) also sustain small numbers of wintering Marsh Harrier, which often join other raptors like Peregrine, Goshawk and the occasional Merlin to predate the large winter Starling roost which occurs there. This is also an excellent area for Water Rail, Stonechat (along with Sardinian Warbler much commoner in lowland areas at this time), Cetti's and wintering Moustached Warbler and Reed Bunting. Other birds frequently encountered throughout at this time in a variety of habitats (especially olive groves) include Robin, Black Redstart, Chiffchaff, Blackcap, Blackbird and Song Thrush - whilst flocks of Hawfinch and Siskins can occur in varying numbers. This partly depends upon the severity of the weather, but if temperatures plummet, there may also be an influx of ducks, wild swans and even geese from nearby Turkey, whilst Lapwing, Golden Plover, Redwing and Fieldfare can all occur with varying frequency at such times.

March-early April - Between the first and second weeks of March there is usually some evidence that migration is already underway. Garganey, Ruff, Black-tailed Godwit, Yellow Wagtail, and Wheatear are amongst the first arrivals, soon followed by the first Swallows, House Martins, Common and Alpine Swifts. Later in the month Night and Purple Herons begin to appear in favoured wetland areas, where they may be joined by the first returning Black and White Storks, Black-winged Stilts, Little Ringed Plover and Avocets (in addition to the wintering birds) and a marked passage of Marsh Harriers, Marsh and Green Sandpipers, White Wagtails and Sedge Warblers. Kingfisher and Water Pipit numbers are thinning out and Black Redstarts and Chiffchaffs are gathering in preparation for their departure. By the month's end the first Little and Spotted Crakes should already have been seen, the first of many calling Quails heard, the passage of Bitterns should have commenced and that of Mediterranean Gulls will have peaked (try Dipi Larssos or Mytilini and Skala Sikimmia harbours), along with that of Garganey, Shoveler and Pintail - often seen sharing the flooded field behind Kalloni Salt Pans with good numbers of Ruddy Shelduck. The first

Wrynecks and good numbers of Tree Pipits and Red-rumped Swallows should have put in an appearance. Black-eared Wheatears, Lesser Kestrels and Short-toed Eagles will also be more visible in the upland areas, which on fine days will resound to the display flight and song of the Woodlark.

By early April the first Cuckoo is eagerly awaited and the first bursts on Nightingale song should be audible, along with that of Subalpine, Orphean and Ruppell's Warbler where scrub predominates and the penetrating call of Cetti's and the 'zit, zit, zit' of Fan-tailed in the damper reedy areas. Returning Cretschmar's Buntings will soon outnumber the singing Cirl Buntings, passage Whimbrels may be seen alongside Curlew, and Hoopoe and Stone Curlew will have arrived from Africa - although the latter will not be in evidence much before mid-month, by which time Cinereous Bunting too should be singing, and Ortolan Bunting passage should have begun in earnest. Great Reed Warblers should be particularly noticeable in wetland areas (with the odd Savi's somewhat less so), and the first Citrine Wagtails should have been picked out amongst the army of Black, Blue and Grey-headed - whilst numbers of Glossy Ibis and Little Egret which have been steadily increasing since late March should be building up well. Flocks of migrating Gull-billed Terns should also have appeared anytime from early April. In the raptor line winter visitors like Sparrowhawk will have thinned out dramatically, whilst the passage of Pallid Harriers will probably have peaked by mid-month, alongside a smaller passage and exodus of Hen Harriers and the beginnings of the Montagu's Harrier passage. Hobbies are now also an increasingly frequent sight, along with passing Osprey, occasional Black Kite and displaying Long-legged Buzzard and Short-toed Eagle. Little Owl will be very visible in daylight around their nesting sites (as are calling and prominently perched Western Rock Nuthatches and 'nasal' Rock Sparrows), and the first Woodchat Shrikes in early April will soon be followed by the first arivals of Masked Shrike mid-month.

Mid-April - early May - Mid-April onwards is probably the peak passage time for both numbers and variety of birds, and it would be almost impossible to mention all of them in this section. Nonetheless, the movement of Collared Flycatchers (often involving a few Semi-collared and reasonable numbers of Pied Flycatchers, Redstarts, Whinchats and Wood Warblers) is often an obvious feature, as is that of Rollers and Golden Orioles a little later. Returning to the wetlands, Squacco Herons start to become very obvious from mid-month, where they compete with other herons and crakes for the wealth of food on offer. This also attracts Common and Wood Sandpiper (by far the commonest spring wader), Greenshank, Spotted Redshank and Little Stint, and by now the first of several spring Spur-winged Plovers may already have been logged, along with Ferruginous Duck if you're lucky! Great White Egrets, Green Sandpipers and White Wagtails are now becoming scarce after an early April peak and a few Kingfishers may linger late into the month. Now is a good time to locate daytime roosting Scops Owl in the Eucalyptus grove at Papiana before they start nesting in earnest in the water tower - where Barn Owl are also visible (and vocal) at night. Mid-month also tends to produce large mobile and extremely noisy flocks of Spanish Sparrow gathering or passing through! Isabelline Wheatear will also have returned to their breeding grounds in the west of the island and may be indulging in their moth-like flight display. Throughout the month good numbers of shearwaters (especially Mediterranean) may be passing offshore, particularly during northerly winds. Audouins Gulls, too, may be looked for - usually off the north coast.

The third week of April sees the arrival in earnest of birds like Olivaceous Warbler, (whose song will soon be a familiar sound in many wetland areas by the month's end) and Olive-tree Warbler, that much sought after but frustrating guttural songster whose short and often intermittent bursts of song can be responsible for many a long sojourn in the Potamia Valley! Migrants like Barred Warbler are also best looked for now before they disappear to skulk in the rapidly greening vegetation. Little Bittern numbers start to build, and continue doing so well into May. The first Eleonora's and Red-footed Falcons (the latter such an obvious feature of the spring migration period) now start to appear given suitable weather conditions - usually about the same time as the marsh terns (that other great spring migration spectacle). Also about now the first of many flocks of migrant Bee-eaters should have been heard (if not seen) - heralding a major arrival of returning birds by the month's end. Lesser Grey Shrikes are also becoming more obvious, though Red-backed numbers have yet to peak in early May. The end of April will have seen the peak of the Montagu's Harrier passage, but Collared and a few Black-winged Pratincole, Turtle Dove, Red-throated Pipit, Short-toed Lark and Spotted and Red-breasted Flycatcher usually attain their maximum numbers about now, along with returning Little and Common Terns. Rufous Bush Robins also start to arrive, about the same time as the first few Black-headed Bunting, whilst Greater Flamingo numbers at both sets of salt pans will have declined dramaticaly, along with Cormorant, Great Crested and Black-necked Grebe numbers offshore.

Early-late May - Little Stint and Curlew Sandpiper numbers usually peak about now, and (resplendant in their summer plumage) they are usually joined by similarly gaudy Turnstones and a few Sanderling which pass through later in the month. Noisy and often aggressive breeding Black-winged Stilts and more localized Avocets are also an obvious feature at this time. Early May, too, is a good time for semi-rarities like Thrush Nightingale, River Warbler, Calandra Lark and (for the lucky few) perhaps White-throated Robin! Numbers of White-winged Black and Whiskered Terns are often at their highest now and may be accompanied by a few Black Terns in the right weather conditions - not to mention attracting the unwelcome attentions of local Peregrines or Lanners which regularly patrol Kalloni Pool and Salt Pans (where they may have been harassing the large Ruff flocks since early April). Weather also governs the peak numbers of Red-footed Falcons, which may be joined increasingly in their feeding flights by insect hawking parties of Eleonora's - especially over Kalloni East River and Salt Pans. Honey Buzzards and Levant Sparrowhawks too (both locally returning breeders and passage birds) are likely to be more obvious at this time - though probably first recorded from mid-late April. By the end of the first week of May Kruper's Nuthatch at their now regular breeding site near Achladeri will usually have fledged young from fairly near the picnic area, and although the family parties tend to linger locally for a week or so they become progressively harder to locate and rarely compare with the stunning views usually achieved earlier on. Local Middle Spotted Woodpeckers should, however, be easier to see as they usually continue feeding young almost to the month's end (and are at their most visible and vocal in the process). The same applies to breeding Hoopoes, though nest sites are usually more tucked away in olive groves and oak woods, and birds even then often tend to be more heard than seen.

Although numbers of Red-backed Shrike and returning Black-headed Bunting can still be spectacular, and Little Bittern, Squacco and sometimes Night Heron numbers still impressive (especially when feeding on the glut of tadpoles then available at sites like Faneromeni ford), the main migration spectacle on offer from mid to late May relates to colourful and noisy passage flocks of Rose-coloured Starlings - often pausing to drink or bathe at places like East River ford, or gathering to feed in nearby Mulberry trees (where they can be surprisingly well concealed!).

Late May-July - Late storms and unsettled conditions at the month's end may replenish water levels and lead to a few lingering marsh terns, herons and waders (the latter often into early June - eg Greater Sandplover in '98!), but the end of the Rose-coloured Starling passage at the beginning of June effectively marks the close of the spring migration period and sees a time of consolidation. By now, locally breeding Little Grebes will be much less obvious (though most should have well-advanced young). Red-backed Shrikes will be scarce and the few pairs of breeding birds remaining (mainly to the west of the island) will be much less obvious and need seeking out. The song of the Nightingale, Olivaceous Warbler and Black-headed Bunting will still be fairly widespread, but some may decide to visit the Sweet Chestnut Woodland above Agiassos or the oak woodland near Skalochori for the more localized song of Eastern Bonelli's Warbler, Chiffchaff, Song Thrush or Robin - all suspected of breeding above Agiassos. Others may wish to look out for the crepuscular activities of the Nightjar (which breeds in good numbers around 'Derbyshire', the Potamia Valley, and many of the western and northern resorts) Though present since late April or early May, birds are now really churring and displaying in earnest and usually repay the small investment of time necessitated. Most Buntings, Larks, Western Rock Nuthatch, Masked Shrike etc will be moving around in family parties and be fairly visible by early June, whilst both Black-eared and a few pairs of Northern and Isabelline Wheatear should also have fledged young and be conspicuous. July, though usually fairly quiet, can often produce good views of locally breeding raptors like Honey Buzzard, Goshawk and occasional Hobby or Levant Sparrowhawk - not to mention gatherings of Eleonoras (which are now only just starting to breed) joining flocks of Alpine Swift on offshore islands to the north and west.

July-August - Return wader passage is now well underway, though on a reduced scale compared to spring numbers and obviously very much dependent on water levels at the various sites - which can also be responsible for a redistribution of summer and breeding birds like Black-winged Stilts and Avocets as particular sites dry out. August is usually the peak month for Broad-billed Sandpiper records - with particularly approachable birds normally present in the Kalloni area, either at West River or the Salt Pans, and sometimes on Kalloni Pool if wet (as in August '98). Other waders like Green and Wood Sandpiper, Greenshank and Little Stint are now being increasingly seen from mid or late July onwards around Petra reservoir, which is a real magnet for wetland species at this time of year - also being responsible for regular Garganey records (a bird only originally recorded on spring passage) and for attracting small feeding flocks of Eleonora's Falcon and predatory Peregrine, Lanner etc if good numbers of prey species are present. Even waders like Black-tailed Godwit, Ruff, Spotted Redshank, Temminck's Stint etc and the odd Purple Heron, Glossy Ibis, and marsh tern etc (all thought of as rare autumn birds) can be recorded at this time if water levels permit, as they did in the case of Kalloni Pool in late summer '98 and usually do with the semi-tidal pools at 'Derbyshire' and Kalloni West River (and East River and Chalandra River to an extent). Kingfishers, too, start to arrive in good numbers at most wetland sites, and are also regularly seen offshore.

Bunting numbers usually peak from late July to mid-August, and flocking is usually evident as the 3 summering species prepare for departure - with Black-headed usually being the first (closely followed by Cinereous and Cretzschmar's). Wheatears and shrikes may linger a little longer. The month of August can also be good for the odd wandering raptor (perhaps commuting from Turkey), like the occasional Golden Eagle, Black Kite etc most likely along the north coast - whilst Honey Buzzard passage usually starts from mid-month on a larger scale than spring, and the peak passage of both Black and White Stork also occurs.

September-October - Red-rumped Swallow numbers begin to decline and the passage of many common migrants like Turtle Dove, Whinchat, Spotted Flycatcher and Red-backed Shrikes usually peaks in early September, when large concentrations of birds (including larks, pipits, wagtails, warblers, hirundines, wheatears shrikes and lingering buntings) are often present in fields of crops like alfalfa and frequently gather to feed, drink and bathe around irrigators in the Faneromeni, Kalloni and Skala Polichnitos areas particularly. Usually dominant in these flocks will be Willow Warbler and Yellow Wagtail (often occurring literally in hundreds), with smaller numbers of Tree Pipit, Short-toed and Crested Larks etc. The true extent of the numbers often can't be guaged unless they are flushed from the high crops by a passing raptor or some similar threat. Clearly a lot of birds regularly occurring at this time (including Wryneck, Barred Warbler and Thrush Nightingale) are likely to be overlooked because of their skulking habits. Although Lesser Grey, Masked and Woodchat Shrike numbers will have declined dramatically, Red-backed (mainly immatures) are still present in considerable numbers at least to the end of September. Flocks of migrating Bee-eaters and large gatherings of Alpine Swifts are also regular throughout the month (especially over wetland sites like Kalloni Inland Lake and Petra reservoir). Flocks of the latter can often be seen mobbing en masse a passing raptor - likely to include Osprey, Eleonora's, Hobby or the beginning of a small autumn/winter influx of Buzzards. Petra reservoir will by now be hosting an impressive number of Little Grebes and Coot (with perhaps the odd returning Black-necked Grebe); whilst Flamingo numbers also start to build up at the two sets of salt pans, along with flocks of wintering Black-headed and Mediterranean Gulls and perhaps a few Little.

By late September or early October winter visitors will also be starting to return - amongst them being Sparrowhawk, White Wagtail, Skylark, Black Redstart, Robin, Song Thrush, Chiffchaff and Blackcap - the latter two especially often being difficult to separate from passage migrants. Unsettled weather at this time (and earlier in September) can also be responsible for small falls of birds like Redstart and the *ficedula* flycatchers - though not in the same numbers as spring. The same applies to Red-throated Pipit, small numbers of which may stay to winter in certain circumstances. By mid or late October, too, numbers of wintering Great White Egret, Grey Heron, Curlew, Redshank, Snipe and ducks like Shoveler, Shelduck, Pintail and Teal will have joined the Flamingos around both sets of salt pans and Kalloni West River, whilst wintering Great Crested and Black-necked Grebes will be becoming more visible offshore and birds like Woodlark and Corn Bunting are likely to be flocking and joining concentrations of Crested Lark and Skylark in stubble fields and other favoured feeding areas. Siskins too should be arriving.

November-January - Colder and wetter weather in this period is likely to see an increasing build-up of duck, including Red-breasted Mergansers on the sea and river mouths - to which Cormorants and Sandwich Terns will now have returned in good numbers. The odd Black-throated Diver may now start to appear, and wintering Pygmy Cormorants might also be looked for amongst the now fairly obvious and vocal Water Rails at Dipi Larssos - which will also be hosting small numbers of wintering Marsh Harrier, Moustached Warbler, Stonechat and Reed Bunting. Great White Egrets, Flamingos, and hunting Hen Harriers, Buzzards and Kestrels will be much in evidence around the salt pans, and areas like Kalloni Pool, Inland Lake and Parakila Marsh should now be home to good numbers of Little Grebe, duck (especially Shoveler), Coot, gulls and Kingfisher, together with Water Rail, White Wagtail, Chiffchaff and Black Redstart. A family of Mute Swans or even the occasional Whooper Swan or rarer duck could return to Kalloni Pool in hard weather or during irregular influxes. At this time Petra reservoir is clearly worth a look for diving ducks like Pochard, Tufted Duck etc which are scarce elsewhere, and Mytilini harbour may produce an interesting gull roosting on the groynes *en route* to the airport - eg the island's first recorded Great Black-backed Gull in January '98!

Favourite quarry species with the local hunters at this time (apart from duck) include Woodcock, Blackbirds and Thrushes - all widespread in this period. Colder weather should also see larger numbers of Lapwing, Golden Plover, Redwing and smaller numbers of Fieldfare. Moreover, the island may just be due for another Waxwing invasion! At all events things have now gone full circle and the whole process begins again!

WHEN TO VISIT - CONCLUSION

The first two weeks of May are certainly a good time to visit the island, both for migrants and breeding birds - all of which should have appeared by mid-month (with the possible exception of Rose-coloured Starling). Even then, however, the weather is not guaranteed - I have experienced several cold, dull days, rain and even hail in the mountains; though generally the bad weather doesn't last for long, and the sun soon breaks through. The display of wildflowers, though probably peaking in late April, can still be quite spectacular; especially after a wet winter. Autumn is another possibility, with quite a wide range of birds (see P240 for tables of autumn ringing totals), though in smaller numbers and with several marsh species largely missing. The advantage, though, is that the weather is extremely settled, with quite warm nights still, often right up to the end of October; and swimming conditions are still perfect, unlike spring.

For those taking a family holiday, summer may be the only available time; and there are still a good number of breeding, if not migrant, birds to be seen. Moreover, return wader passage starts in July, and by mid-August migrants are starting to appear again. Obviously, it is much drier then, and birding also tends to be less productive in the heat of the day, but positioning yourself close to a water source (albeit even a small puddle) can pay dividends.

Anyone feeling more adventurous, and willing to get to the island via Athens could always, accommodation permitting, try a week or two between late October and late April; to search out Lesvos' wintering birds and early spring migrants. As mentioned earlier, this is something I have done myself several times - the earliest being a January trip, which I found to be very enlightening and graced with a largely excellent spell of weather (the so-called *halcyon days* after Christmas that the islanders refer to). The only other drawback here is that one may have to witness some of the shooting which thankfully is not allowed at other times. Certainly I have rarely witnessed or had reports of any transgressions, though they may, of course, occur amongst the irresponsible few - such as the character I saw at Faneromeni in late March '98 roaring around on a motorbike with a gun on his back and a belt strapped to his waist containing several freshly shot Garganey!

Since my spring '95-'98 trips, I have to say that it really is worth the effort of getting there in April, (or even late March) when the weather is often extremely pleasant (sometimes more settled than May), and the migration season well underway (certainly from mid-month); with late winterers still on view, and plenty of water still to draw the birds. As mentioned earlier I can usually help with travel arrangements at this time.

In conclusion, then, although mid-April to early May is likely to be most productive, I would just stress that no two years are exactly the same, and in spring '95, for example, migration seemed about ten days earlier than the year before, and was consequently over that much earlier. On the other hand, April '98 enjoyed such a spell of settled weather compared to May (which was mainly cool, overcast and showery at times) that the migration period was quite protracted, and some species peaked much later than usual and in smaller numbers to April '97 - when cooler unsettled conditions and northerly winds some days caused some truly spectacular 'falls'. Obviously the weather plays an important part in all this, and it's worthwhile remembering that at migration times good settled weather rarely produces the bird spectacles we often associate with this period on the island - so please don't blame me if things are not quite as you expected! Often a good overnight storm, with torrential rain and contrary winds is just what's needed - so long as it doesn't last too long of course!

In short (leaving aside the matter of how you get there) most periods have something to commend them - dependent partly on the special interests of the observer in question. Clearly migration periods are likely to be the most productive overall (with early spring, as mentioned) being my own personal favourite, but those who can only travel in summer should still connect with a reasonable number of the breeding species at least. At this time (and also in autumn) a knowledge of the local water sources would certainly pay dividends, though the heat experienced at the middle of the day is usually best avoided - and water sources like your hotel swimming pool would be more beneficial! Certainly those who dislike meeting too many other birders would find such periods generally quieter (witness my January '98 trip when they were, hardly surprisingly, non existent!); but there are others who appreciate the 'camaraderie' and exchanges of sightings. Either way the choice is yours - the main thing is to go!

WHERE TO STAY

Tourism on Lesvos is still relatively new, and hardly geared to the masses; and for this we should be grateful. The tourist industry originated in Molivos in 1985, and didn't really spread to Skala Kalloni until 1989. (The first hotel there wasn't built until 1987). In fact, most hotels on the island are no bigger than 50-60 rooms, although a hotel recently built in Skala Eressos boasts all of 300 rooms. (Prior to that, the biggest on the island, in Molivos, contained 250). In consequence, there are only a handful of recognised locations to stay. Of these, by far the best, in my opinion, is **Skala Kalloni** - it is quiet, central and has two good rivers, marshes and a set of salt pans within easy reach; and even, dare I say it, in walking distance! Also, there are five hotels and several apartments within viewing distance of the Kalloni Pool; which can be an excellent site for herons, waders, duck, crakes, marsh terns etc (water levels permitting), and also a good focal point for birders to gather and exchange information. **Kalloni Two (phone 0253 23334/7 / fax 23386)** and **Aegean** Hotel **(0253 22309 / fax 22827)** are both very friendly, pleasant and in excellent locations with the potential for some good 'balcony ticks', (Kalloni Two also possessing a particularly spacious dining and lounge area), whilst the nearby Hotel **Pasifai (0253 23156 / fax 23154)** boasts good facilities and is quite popular with groups. The smaller, more intimate Hotel **Malemi (0253 22594 / fax 22838)**, which has the advantage of being family run (by George and Effy Kapsalis), boasts excellent home cooking and a friendly 'ambience' - and also has heating in many of the rooms (which might interest those wishing to visit earlier in the year). Moreover, it even has a thriving Spanish Sparrow colony in the tamarisks which border it! Finally there is the neighbouring Hotel **Pela (phone / fax 0253 23530)** which also enjoys a quiet location and is clean and comfortable - regrettably it is the only one of the five I haven't stayed or eaten at, though I found the bar more than acceptable! Suffice it to say that all the hotels have something to commend them and enjoy similar standards, and a lot comes down simply to personal preference. I have not touched on the self-catering apartments, as I have little experience of them and most will be dealt with in the travel brochures anyway.

For those who like a bit more life, and an excellent selection of restaurants in a superb location steeped in history and with good views of the Turkish coast (with the old castle as a backdrop), **Molivos** could be the answer. The only drawbacks are the rather steep gradients of some of the streets, (especially after a few ouzos!) and the rather tedious drive southwards to Kalloni, with lots of hairpin bends and slow lorries and coaches; often almost impossible to overtake. Its 'suburb' of **Petra** is also becoming a very popular resort, boasting a good beach and some wonderful sunsets and still possessing 'olde worlde' charm. In common with the nearby expanding resort of **Anaxos**, (which shares good views of 'Rabbit Island') it has a good selection of eating places also. Though Molivos boasts the largest number of hotel rooms on the island (1401 in 1993), Petra and Anaxos can lay claim to the largest number of rooms to rent (2103 in 1993). Bird-wise, this whole area, though lacking any real permanent water (with the exception of a 100 hectare reservoir just outside Molivos, which was completed in '96 and is now already fulfilling its early promise - especially in autumn) and consequently not having the wide variety of species found in the Kalloni area, is still good for many upland species - with many excellent and productive walks amongst local hillsides and olive groves. It also acts as a gateway to the north-east coast, with its wonderful scenery and attendant raptors around its mountain range (the highest on the island). For these reasons, perhaps a half-hour or more's drive to the Kalloni area is not too high a price to pay.

Another possibility would be **Eressos** or **Skala Eressos**. Though a bit more remote, with limited accommodation (especially earlier in the season), and harder to get to the other sites from, it has a good beach (nudist in one section, so take care with long lenses!), a good river for marsh species, and is in the heart of Cinereous Bunting country. The coast road and river valley between it and Sigri I rate just about the best on the island for visible migration, not to mention the Lesser Kestrels offshore. If one likes things even quieter, then the small nearby fishing village of **Sigri** could be considered. Although the area beyond it to Faneromeni beach and beyond is productive for migrants and some marsh species (water at the nearby ford permitting), the surrounding area is more mountainous and some of the roads from it more tortuous. It is also rather 'out on a limb' - being a good one and a half hour drive from Kalloni.

The same criticism could be levelled at the growing resort of **Vatera**, situated on the south coast below Polichnitos. Though quite handy for those salt pans, and having a good area of beach, some interesting dunes and quite a productive river mouth, it still necessitates a long drive to the north and west of the island. It also tends to be popular with Germans later on in the season - not that I'm implying this is a criticism!

Another alternative, especially out of season, would be to stay in **Mytilini**, and this I have done myself but would be rather loathe to recommend. In spite of quite a pleasant and sometimes productive harbour and nearby headland, and one or two reasonably pleasant looking hotels near the airport, the location is hardly ideal for accessing the rest of the island - not to mention the tedious drive in and out of it, and general noise and traffic problems. Otherwise, nowhere on Lesvos is really that far from a good birding site. The roads can be surprisingly good in places, and from Kalloni now right up to Messotopos and beyond is all tarmacked; though this has only happened in the last few years. There are no doubt several smaller places I haven't mentioned where accommodation should be available, but probably not to book in advance; so you would need to possess a certain spirit of adventure.

In short, though, wherever you stay on Lesvos you are unlikely to be too disappointed (or to be too far away from good bird sites), but taking all things into consideration the Skala Kalloni area still remains the best base, from which all other areas can easily be covered, and the greatest number of bird species realized. But do remember that my comments are angled from a birder's point of view: the only proviso being that one would really need a car to do justice to most of them. Otherwise ones experiences are likely to be limited.

HOW TO GET THERE

I apologise in advance for those reading this book outside the UK, for whom this section is likely to be of no help whatsoever - unless they are willing to fly there via our shores! Regrettably any further information is simply beyond the scope of the book.

For the '99 season **First Choice** feature a variety of locations including Anaxos, Petra, Molivos, Vatera and Skala Kalloni (currently the only operator now using the resort). **Manos Holidays** feature Anaxos, Petra, Molivos and Vatera; with **Kosmar** also covering the first three, and **Direct Greece** concentrating on Sigri and Eressos in the west. **Thomsons, Airtours,** and **Inspirations**, however, now all pulled out of the island, though they may subsequently decide to feature it again.

Ironically, although several tour operators appear to be cutting back their operations on the island, many specialist bird tours (too many to list here!) are now featuring it. It would almost be easier to list those that don't! Though obviously a more expensive option, these tours include virtually everything in their price. Of course, not everyone likes to be quite so organised, and the fact remains that there is so much to see on Lesvos, that anyone with a car and a rudimentary knowledge of the best bird sites should have no trouble, at least in spring, in mustering a trip list of 150 species or more.

Do remember, though, that holiday companies can change their venues from year to year (often in response to demand - or lack of it), and it is always worth checking with your local travel agent to see what is currently on offer. There could certainly be changes afoot, depending on how tourism on the island evolves; so please don't hold me responsible if the above information becomes out of date! As mentioned already, however, I can usually give help or advice to those contemplating travelling outside the main holiday season and wishing to base themselves in Skala Kalloni - so long as they are prepared to travel with Olympic Airways via Athens and pick up a 40 minute connecting flight to Lesvos.

DRIVING ON THE ISLAND

A word of warning here - car hire is not especially cheap (though petrol is currently slightly cheaper than here), so shop around and look for good deals; and it isn't really worth hiring for less than a week. Make sure you get unlimited mileage, and consider hiring when booking the holiday if a favourable offer exists. Minibuses are gradually becoming more readily available on the island, but nine-seater models are currently limited and some others are only six-seaters (including driver). Coaches are also posible but can be restrictive in some of the more sensitive sites with limited access, and success may also be partly dependent on the English fluency of the driver! I can usually help with car hire arrangements (especially in early spring) if contacted in advance.

Don't worry too much about needing a four-wheel drive, by the way (which is often nearly double the price). So long as conditions are not too wet, most roads and tracks are usually driveable with care - though unexpectedly heavy rain or flash flooding can sometimes present problems on the 'dirt tracks' in early spring. Ground clearance is often an important consideration here. Subarus I find extremely good, and my only warning would be to try and avoid the colour red if possible - some birds simply don't like it!

Finally in this section; a few words about the island's roads. In many cases, these can be surprisingly good, and with EU grants being made increasingly available, several sections of road have either been recently improved, or are soon due to be - and even roads to what were basically just small fishing villages like Tavari have now been upgraded. The section, for example, between Parakila and Messotopos has improved out of all recognition over the last couple of years, and is now fully tarmacked almost to Eressos- as are many roads in the middle of the island, and along the east coast. Up to spring '95, the worst roads (apart from the coastal stretch between Eressos and Sigri - which is truly stomach-churning!) were probably along the north coast, between Molivos and Skala Sikimmia, and Skoutaros and Skalochori. The latter, though still rough in places, has been greatly improved from the Anaxos end (as has the road from Vafios right through to Sikimmia - which is now tarmacked, along with much of the Stipsi-Clio route). The former is now much better, but has only been resurfaced with earth and hardcore, and winter flash-flooding could cause further deterioration.

Moreover, even on the tarmacked roads, one can encounter the odd totally unexpected pothole, which may be present from one year to the next. I well remember an occasion along a section of road between Filia and Anemotia, when I was overtaking a car on a seemingly good, straight stretch of road; when it suddenly pulled out without indicating to avoid a series of very deep potholes - so be warned! Of course, some of the tracks are a different story again. But just remember - without these potholes, there would be far fewer puddles to attract birds, and the recent tarmacking of the Vafios to Argennos road, for example, has destroyed an excellent roadside puddle where drinking Hawfinch were regular, and parties of Red-rumped Swallow frequently came to collect mud. So it isn't just their loss but ours also, and some people would bemoan what they consider an overall loss of the island's character. Clearly you can't always please everyone, and accelerating change could soon make much of this section already out-of-date!

WEATHER

Lesvos enjoys a relatively mild climate, and though the winters (ie from late October to the end of February) can be quite wet, the temperature rarely falls below 50 degrees F. At all events, the weather starts to improve by late March, though it can still be unpredictable up to May (and even beyond). The year can best be summed up as follows :

January and February
The coldest months, but mainly bright (especially the 'halcyon' days often experienced in the first half of January) - some rain, and outside chance of some freezing conditions (though unlikely). Less cold from mid-February.

March and April
Unpredictable. Showery months, but temperatures gradually improving, and often quite bright. April can prove a more settled month than May.

May
Less rain - perhaps only an hour or so all month. Warmer and sunnier, but northerly winds can still cause temperature drops and cloudy spells.

June to September
The hottest months, especially from late June to late August. Weather extremely settled, though strong winds from mid-July to September are possible, and can cause sea water to be pushed upriver.

October
Normally dry, but outside chance of a little rain towards the end. Still quite warm, especially the early part of the month.

November
From about 15th to 20th rain is likely, perhaps for 3-4 days at a time. Temperature drops.

December
Rain is likely throughout, and the chance of snow (perhaps 2 years out of 3 - but usually short-lived, and confined mainly to high altitudes). Rather cold nonetheless.

For those interested in the average monthly temperatures and rainfall, the following list of climatic data collected from the Mytilini Weather Centre may be useful. Prevailing winds, incidentally, are predominantly northerly, and on approximately 40 days exceed 6 on the Beaufort scale.

	Av. Temp.	Av. Rainfall
January	10.2 C (50.4 F)	131 mm (5.16 ins)
February	10.6 C (51.1 F)	93.0 mm (3.66 ins)
March	11.5 C (52.7 F)	71.9 mm (2.83 ins)
April	15.7 C (60.3 F)	53.1 mm (2.09 ins)
May	20.1 C (68.2 F)	29.0 mm (1.14 ins)
June	24.8 C (76.6 F)	9.9 mm (0.39 ins)
July	27.7 C (81.9 F)	3.0 mm (0.12 ins)
August	27.1 C (80.8 F)	2.0 mm (0.08ins)
September	23.1 C (73.6 F)	0.9 mm (0.03 ins)
October	18.9 C (66.0 F)	56.9 mm (2.24 ins)
November	14.3 C (57.7 F)	149.9 mm (5.90 ins)
December	11.6 C (52.9 F)	142.0 mm (5.59 ins)

Yearly Average   18.0 C (64.4 F)   **Total**   751 mm   (29.57 ins)
Average Spring Temp.   15.9 C   **Average Winter Temp** 10.4 C

THE SHOOTING SEASON

A local hunter told me that, apart from the shooting of Turtle Doves in August and September, and the Chukar from November to March, the main quarry species are Quail (especially in autumn) and various thrushes and Woodcock in winter. He claimed the period officially extends from the beginning of October to 20th March, and that for grey geese from December to February. But neither geese nor duck are regular in Lesvos in winter in any numbers; except in severe conditions. There have been occasions of protected species like pelicans and flamingos being shot and ending up at a taxidermist in Kalloni, but thankfully, such transgressions are becoming less common, as far as we know; though it is perfectly normal, for example, for wintering blackbirds and thrushes to be shot - which we tend to find rather offensive. Moreover, the scarcity of such species as Kestrel and Buzzard could be related to this practice. Certainly it used to be very popular to have a stuffed bird of prey, heron or gull for decoration; but those that still adorn various restaurants and tavernas on the island seem to be fairly old; so the fashion is hopefully declining.

During my January '98 visit to the island, much of the shooting appeared to be centred on the olive groves (often near dusk for Blackbirds and thrushes returning to roost), but also the damper, scrubby hillsides where dogs were often used to flush Woodcock. Regrettably, although both sets of salt pans are supposed to be protected, there was a regular traffic of gun-wielding moped riders using the beach approach track to Skala Polichnitos Salt Pans, Dipi Larssos Reedbed and the large flooded sheep field behind Kalloni Salt Pans - all of which were littered with shotgun cartridges by early spring. Apart from this I saw no wholesale shooting of duck - though this may have been more to do with the mild weather than anything.

Otherwise the only transgressions I have witnessed are of another gun-toting motorbike rider with Garganey hanging from his belt at Faneromeni in late March '98 (already mentioned earlier), a dead Bittern by the side of the track there in mid-April that year (which could conceivably have been hit by a car) and various disturbing records from the Lesbian Wildlife Hospital (also involving a Bittern shot in winter - but thankfully treatable), a few injured Long-legged Buzzards and Marsh Harriers (cause usually unknown), a Golden Oriole presumed shot in late September '98, and an unrelated record of a Goshawk picked up in early May '98 near Vatera - also presumed shot. Not a perfect record by any means, but better than witnessed on some of the other Greek islands like Crete, Corfu and especially Cyprus - and much better than some of the other Mediterranean 'blackspots' like Italy and Malta. Nevertheless, local claims that the practice is gradually dying out and largely confined to the older generation was not entirely borne out by my own experiences whilst watching some decidedly youthful participants. I also got the impression from certain conversations that general boredom may play a part in the practice at this time!

For those who are interested, the official shooting season in Greece is from 10th Sept to 28th Feb, except for :

Chukar, Rock and Grey Partridge and Pheasant (3 days per week from 16th Sept. to 28th Dec).

Quail, Woodpigeon, Turtle Dove, Skylark, Song and Mistle Thrush, Redwing and Fieldfare (for which the season opens on 20th Aug, but only in limited so-called 'migratory zones' - ie most lowlands). A current list of the legal game species in Greece is as follows:

Wigeon	*Anas penelope*	Coot	*Fulica atra*
Gadwall	*Anas strepera*	Lapwing	*Vanellus vanellus*
Teal	*Anas crecca*	Jack Snipe	*Lymnocryptes minimus*
Mallard	*Anas platyrhynchos*	Snipe	*Gallinago gallinago*
Pintail	*Anas acuta*	Woodcock	*Scolopax rusticola*
Garganey	*Anas querquedula*	Rock Dove	*Columba livia*
Shoveler	*Anas clypeata*	Woodpigeon	*Columba palumbus*
Pochard	*Aythya ferina*	Turtle Dove	*Streptopelia turtur*
Tufted Duck	*Aythya fuligula*	Skylark	*Alauda arvensis*
Chukar	*Alectoris chukar*	Blackbird	*Turdus merula*
Rock Partridge	*Alectoris graeca*	Fieldfare	*Turdus pilaris*
Grey Partridge	*Perdix perdix*	Song Thrush	*Turdus philomelos*
Quail	*Coturnix coturnix*	Redwing	*Turdus iliacus*
Pheasant	*Phasianus colchicus*	Mistle Thrush	*Turdus viscivorus*
Moorhen	*Gallinula chloropus*		

MAJOR HABITATS AND TYPICAL BIRD SPECIES

WETLANDS

Probably the most productive habitat on Lesvos, certainly in spring, is its wetlands; and these include the two sets of salt pans (at Kalloni and Skala Polichnitos), Kalloni Pool, Kalloni Inland Lake and ditches, Kalloni East and West Rivers, Potamia River and Chalandra River Skala Eressos, Dipi Larssos Reedbed and the area known as 'Derbyshire', east of Kalloni; and Parakila Marsh, west of Kalloni. There are other rivers (for example approaching Sigri and at Faneromeni Beach) which can be equally productive, but the latter isn't always sufficiently wet.

Although Dipi Larssos is the only reedbed of any size on the island (and with its scattered pools is consequently important as a breeding site for Little Bittern, Water Rail, Fan-tailed and Reed Warbler - not to mention as a wintering site for Marsh Harrier, Moustached Warbler, Reed Bunting and occasional Bittern; and a roosting site for hirundines, wagtails and Starlings) there are also several fairly extensive stands of reeds nearby (especially the low-lying area south of it towards Perama), and smaller areas around Faneromeni, Kalloni Salt Pans and West River.

Apart from the two new reservoirs at Petra (good for winter duck and grebes and waders and water dependent birds in late summer and autumn) and the Potamia Valley (potentially similar but currently undergoing 'repairs' and more often dry than wet since spring '97), the island's wetlands, by their very nature, are likely to be most productive in spring, and some, like Parakila Marsh, Kalloni Pool and a large section of Kalloni East River, are often dry from early summer. The most typical spring birds to be encountered here are Black and White Stork (several pairs of which nest), Little Egret, Glossy Ibis, Grey, Purple and Squacco Heron (of which the latter is by far the most widespread). Little Bittern can be extremely numerous (especially around the Kalloni and Faneromeni wetlands, where they are often surprisingly visible and regularly feed in the open). Night Heron too, occur quite widely, but may be overlooked because of their earlier passage and more secretive habits. This applies to crakes too (both Little and Spotted) - though with a little patience they can prove very confiding.

Many wader species are to be found (of which Black-winged Stilt and Avocet usually nest - water levels permitting; together with Little Ringed and Kentish Plover). In order of frequency, Wood, Curlew and Common Sandpipers all occur, together with Little and Temminck's Stint, Spotted Redshank and large numbers of Ruff. Rarer waders like Marsh and Broad-billed Sandpiper, Spoonbill and Spur-winged Plover are always worth searching for at the Kalloni Salt Pans, where Stone Curlew can also be encountered with a little patience (usually a nesting pair or two). Other nesters here and along the East River are Bee-eaters, which can often be seen perched along riverside bushes, accompanied by singing Nightingale, Savi's, Cetti's, Great Reed and Olivaceous Warbler and four possible Shrike species in passage (Red-backed, Woodchat, Lesser Grey, and occasional Masked), with omnipresent singing Crested Lark, Black-headed and Corn Bunting everywhere.

The main duck species here in spring are Ruddy Shelduck (which, though it does breed, is a very wary species here - possibly because of shooting) and Garganey; whilst Water Rails can sometimes be located with careful searching. However, it is really for marsh terns that the island's wetlands can prove most spectacular; and the sight of a large mixed flock of White-winged Black and Whiskered Terns, together with lesser numbers of Black and Gull-billed, and regular Common and Little can prove memorable. Pratincoles, mainly Collared, may also occur with these, not to mention assorted hirundines and swifts and a profusion of various races of Yellow Wagtail and good numbers of Red-throated Pipit in spring.

Finally, raptors also figure in these movements, with a good spring passage of Marsh and Montagu's Harriers (the two sometimes in almost equal numbers) and smaller numbers of

Hen and Pallid earlier on; with large parties of Red-footed Falcons in season, especially around the Kalloni Salt Pans. Long-legged Buzzard, Short-toed Eagle and passage Osprey also occur, together with numbers of Eleonora's Falcon from late spring.

The autumn brings a good wader passage, though with marsh terns, Little Bittern and Squacco Heron, for example, largely absent. Greenshank and White Wagtail, though, seem much more common; and Kingfishers appear in good numbers at most wetland sites from mid to late July until March or April (presumably a post-breeding dispersal from Turkey or Eastern Europe). Wintering Flamingo numbers, too, build up at the two salt pans, which also host several Great White Egret and small numbers of duck (mainly Pintail and Shelduck, with a few Teal). Woodcock and Snipe can also be found then, and in really severe weather larger numbers of duck, and, perhaps, White-fronted Goose, Whooper and Mute Swan may also appear; though obviously with winter shooting quite widespread, such species are unlikely to settle for long, and are probably only a small part of the flocks regularly following the Turkish coast at this time.

COASTAL HABITATS

Away from the low-lying, fairly flat coastal areas around Kalloni and Geras Bays, the coastline to the north, north-east and parts of the west can be quite rugged, with cliffs and several small rocky islands offshore from Anaxos, Agios Stephanos, Sigri and Makara for example. Here birds like Shag, Lesser Kestrel, Eleonora's Falcon and Alpine Swift all breed offshore, and Shearwaters and gulls (including the odd Audouin's) are often seen feeding, whilst Peregrine, Blue Rock Thrush, Rock Nuthatch and occasionally Crag Martin and Rock Dove frequent the steeper cliffs. Those that are less precipitous and with scattered scrub (between Petra and Molivos and Thermi and Madamados for example) may host nesting Ruppell's, Orphean and Subalpine Warblers, together with Cretzschmar's and Cirl Bunting. They may also be popular with hunting Short-toed Eagle and Long-legged Buzzard.

The coastal dunes around Kalloni Salt Pans, Skala Eressos, Dipi Larssos and Skala Polichnitos to Skala Vassilika (apart from being excellent for wildflowers) are important for larks, pipits, wagtails, wheatears, and Hoopoe. Stone Curlews also nest and harriers regularly hunt such areas - whilst Red-footed Falcon may gather to feed on passage (particularly in adverse weather).

CULTIVATED FIELDS AND GRASSLAND

These areas usually occur alongside rivers and river valleys, where water is generally easier to obtain (often being pumped direct from the river). This applies particularly around the Plain of Kalloni, and also at Skala Eressos and Faneromeni Beach. The attraction of these fertile areas is obvious, and apart from playing host to good numbers of larks, as well as Corn Bunting (often in large flocks in autumn and winter), they also attract a variety of migrant shrikes, chats, flycatchers, large numbers of wagtails and warblers, pipits, shrikes and buntings - especially in autumn when irrigators are regularly in use. Grassland is generally unsprayed, and in consequence holds a wealth of plant and insect life - so its appeal to birds is obvious; and in addition to the above species, look out for Stone Curlew, Little Owl, Marsh and Montagu's Harrier, Lesser Kestrel and Red-footed Falcons in season (often hunting for insects from overhead wires or low bushes, especially near cattle).

ARID SCRUB AND DRY RIVER BEDS

This habitat, together with dried-up river beds (good examples being the one crossed just before entering Skala Eressos on the road from Messotopos, and also the area beyond

Faneromeni ford) is quite widespread - especially by autumn. Although it occurs inland, some of the best places to locate its associated warblers (Subalpine and Ruppells being dominant), together with shrikes and chats, are probably along the coastal strip between Petra and Molivos, the headland from Agios Stephanos to Palios (excellent for Sardinian Warbler) and the coastal road from 'Derbyshire' to Achladeri. The latter is particularly good for Red-backed, Woodchat and Lesser Grey Shrike, Nightjar, chats and Cirl Bunting.

In addition, the dry river beds also regularly hold Rufous Bush Robin, Nightjar and occasional Stone Curlew in season, and are good for migrant flycatchers, warblers, shrikes etc - with the slim chance of migrant White-throated Robin in early May.

OLIVE GROVES

Extremely widespread habitat on the island, both at low altitude and on the lower mountain slopes, the variety of food to be obtained from these often ancient trees makes them very attractive to birds. Special species here include nesting Masked Shrike, Middle Spotted Woodpecker and Olive-tree Warbler. Naturally, other warblers, chats, shrikes and Cirl Bunting are also likely; and look out for hawking Bee-eaters, migrant Rollers and Golden Oriole in passage - and good numbers of thrushes, Blackbirds, Robins and Blackcap in winter feeding on the fruits.

UPLAND PINE AND OAK WOODS

These make up a large proportion of the island, as any aerial view would soon show you. Though at first glance birds may appear fairly thin on the ground, it is an important area for Sombre Tit, (which is mainly an upland species here) - Jays and Middle Spotted Woodpecker are widespread, and Short-toed Treecreeper and Serin also occur in the pinewoods, together, of course, with one of the island's star birds - Kruper's Nuthatch. Although most people used to look for this on the wooded hillsides above Agiassos (which also contain a sizeable area of deciduous woodland and sweet chestnut -over which soaring raptors like Sparrowhawk, Goshawk and Buzzard can sometimes be spotted), several other suitable sites undoubtedly exist; like the now well-known Achladeri site and the road to Vatera. A stop at the picnic site here might produce Long-Tailed Tit, Wren, Dunnock or wintering Goldcrest - all quite rare and localized birds on the island; though taken for granted at home.

Oaks, of which there are two kinds on Lesvos, are always productive for birdlife, and a wealth of small birds are likely to use them and be attracted by the numerous insects they hold. Hoopoe, tits, finches, warblers, shrikes, flycatchers and Golden Oriole are a few possibilities, and Buzzard, (mainly Common, but also a few pairs of Honey - especially to the east and north of the island) are the commonest raptor here, sharing the airspace with a few pairs of Short-toed Eagle and Goshawk. Scattered oak woodland to the west and north-west of the island (especially between Skoutaros and Vatoussa) is also the haunt of the localized Nuthatch, Hawfinch and Bonelli's Warbler, and sometimes (where they mingle with Olives) Olive Tree Warbler.

BARE UPLANDS

The final habitat type consists of the barer, boulder-strewn uplands that one encounters most often in the west around Eressos and Sigri, but also east and south of Molivos. These areas are the stronghold of the Western Rock Nuthatch and Black-eared Wheatear, and also of the Rock Sparrow and Blue Rock Thrush. Raptors are always worth searching for here -

Peregrine, Eleonora's Falcon, Lanner, Lesser Kestrel, Long-legged Buzzard and Short-toed Eagle for example (with Bonelli's Eagle always a possibility).

Although Cretzschmar's Bunting are abundant in this sort of habitat (especially where a few scattered bushes or scrub can be found), it is probably for Cinereous Bunting that these hills, (especially around Eressos) are best known. Chukar, too, are thinly distributed, and Little Owl seem as much at home here amongst the rocks as in the lowland areas; and it is back to these lowland areas that we now go in commencing my selection of the island's best bird sites and how to reach them.

WHERE TO WATCH BIRDS IN LESVOS - A BIRDER'S SITE GUIDE

As anyone who has visited Lesvos will be aware, the island has many prime bird sites; and good birds can turn up almost anywhere. Moreover, depending on weather, wind direction and winter rainfall, no two years are exactly the same. This, of course, is part of the attraction; but it means that no site guide can be 100% accurate. The following guide, therefore, cannot claim to be exhaustive, but gives a fair idea of the birds one might reasonably expect to see in certain places at particular times of year. Because it is based largely on my own observations, and records sent to me, it is obviously biased in favour of spring (i.e. April-May) and autumn (i.e. September and October) - these being the most productive times, when most people visit. However, I have tried to list a selection of what may be encountered (epecially at some of the wetland sites) in winter - based largely on my January '98 visit and several March records.

Some sites (like Kalloni Salt Pans for example) may have something of interest all-year-round, whilst others may only deliver their full potential in spring; and this fact should be remembered when visiting, if one is not to be too disappointed. One should also be aware of numerous different spellings for the same place, so please bear that in mind before accusing me of mis-spelling place names! Since I usually stay in the Kalloni area, where probably the largest concentration of birds on the island is to be found, I intend to start with a run-down of sites in that particular area. For simplicity, all site maps are located together between P226-239.

1) KALLONI POOL AND SKALA KALLONI HARBOUR *(See Map 1, P226)*

Those staying in Skala Kalloni are likely to make this pool their first port of call, besides which it is only a few hundred yards from the Square. Because of its location and comparatively small size, it is likely to suffer some disturbance; but I don't find this to be a major problem, and most birds seem used to people - though marauding dogs can be a problem at times in the nesting season! Obviously, though, it is best visited either early morning or late afternoon; and in any case, the latter is my favourite time, as the light then is ideal for viewing and photography from the hotel side. It is really a spring location (usually being dry by summer - except in '98), and while the bird species present can vary according to water levels, there is often a constant changeover in spring, from day to day, or even hour to hour on some occasions!

Garganey and Black-winged Stilt are almost permanent features here in spring, and there are usually good numbers of smaller waders and marsh terns and regular Glossy Ibis. Raptors like Peregrine and Marsh Harrier are often attracted by these gatherings and may well do observers a favour by flushing birds from the well vegetated area at the back - best viewed from the short track running parallel to the beach road just behind the buildings. Herons, Little Bittern, Water Rail, crakes and various races of Yellow Wagtail (including occasional Citrine) are also likely, whilst the perimeter and surrounding scrub plays host to the inevitable Crested Lark, and various warblers. Both Little and Barn Owl are in the area (though the latter is more often heard than seen) and Nightjar is sometimes also possible after dusk in late summer. On the seaward side, look out for the large Spanish Sparrow colony in the Tamarisks at the back of the main beach, and check the sea for Great Crested and Black-necked Grebes in spring, and Black-necked again in autumn. In stormy conditions in winter and early spring grebes may well shelter in the harbour, Red-breasted Merganser are possible and gulls and terns are always worth checking for. For several years now the harbour area has been hosting a 'tame' White Pelican 'adopted' by local fishermen and even provided with its own house on the beach. If it remains *in situ* only personal conscience will dictate whether or not it is tickable!

Winter and early spring sees a good build-up of Little Grebe, duck, Coot, gulls, Water Rail, Kingfisher etc, with numbers of Chiffchaff and Black Redstart in the area (including the beach tamarisks) and attendant raptors like Buzzard and Sparrowhawk.

SPRING - Little Grebe, Black-necked Grebe (scarce offshore), Bittern (occasional), Little Bittern, Night, Squacco, Grey and Purple Heron, White Stork, Glossy Ibis, Garganey, Shoveler, Ferruginous Duck (scarce), Peregrine, Marsh and Montagu's Harrier, Hobby, Water Rail, Coot, Black-winged Stilt, Little and Temminck's Stint, Curlew and Wood Sandpiper, Little Ringed and Kentish Plover, Spur-winged Plover (erratic), gulls, Whiskered, White-winged, Black and occasional Gull-billed Tern, Kingfisher (to early spring), Grey and Black-headed Wagtail, Citrine Wagtail, hirundines, Short-toed Lark, Sedge, Olivaceous and ocasional Moustached Warbler.

AUTUMN (if wet) - Chance of various herons, Glossy Ibis, Garganey, Water Rail, Black-tailed Godwit, stints, sandpipers (including Broad-billed), Spotted Redshank and Greenshank.

WINTER-EARLY SPRING - Little Grebe, Black-necked Grebe (offshore), Grey Heron, possible Mute Swan (rarely Whooper's), Shoveler (common), Mallard, Teal, Pochard, Hen Harrier, Buzzard, Sparrowhawk, Water Rail, Coot, Redshank, Dunlin, Black-headed, Mediterranean, Little and possible Slender-billed Gull, Kingfisher, Water and Meadow Pipit, White and Grey Wagtail, Chiffchaff, Black Redstart, Stonechat, Reed and Cirl Bunting.

PS The threat to this area by way of draining it for a 1000 room hotel development appears to have receded for the moment in the face of intense opposition from a number of quarters (for which I have to take some credit!). However, there is still no room for complacency and it is important that as many visitors as possible continue writing to the Mayor of Kalloni voicing their concerns for the future well-being of this vitally important site.

2) KALLONI WEST RIVER *(See Map 1, P226)*

Easily observed when crossing the bridge over the main Kalloni to Parakila road (just beyond Skala Kalloni) this river can be explored both sides of the road, though its appearance (with piles of rubbish dumped at random on both sides) can be off-putting. Depending on how wet a spring it is, some of the tracks alongside it may be driveable with care, but recent changes, together with further rubbish dumping and the fencing off of the main rubbish tip on the eastern side have limited vehicle access somewhat - though this track (which skirts back to Kalloni) can usually be followed by simply lifting (and then replacing) the rather crude sheep gate and carrying on to the pool area close to the tip - regrettably being gradually encroached on by rubbish dumping. The river is surrrounded by a low-lying area of saltmarsh and brackish pools, and bordered by fields and some scrub. Varying water levels can greatly affect bird numbers encountered; but this river, being largely tidal, is always wet, and it can also hold some good species in autumn.

Look out especially for a pre-dispersal autumn gathering of Stone Curlew on the landward side, in the fields or dry saltmarsh around the rubbish-tip. In spring, the odd pair may be found nesting either side of the road, along with a few pairs of Black-winged Stilt in the pool near the tip, and several breeding pairs of Little Ringed and Kentish Plover (especially in the pools just east of the road bridge - though this area by the road has now been degraded somewhat to the point where it almost resembles a large car park!). The landward track on the opposite bank is usually your best bet, and you should be able to access it by vehicle for several hundred metres at least. These pools (often invisible from the road) can turn up a good selection of close waders (especially Green and Wood Sandpiper), and I have also had Citrine Wagtail here amongst numerous Black-headed. The field just beyond the bridge (ie on your left as you drive up the track) is usually flooded in early spring and may hold good numbers of Ruff and even Glossy Ibis, together with other waders, pipits, wagtails etc.

Though not as easy to work as the East River, this location is still worth checking out, as it tends to turn up regular Black Stork and other localized birds on the island, like Grey Plover and Curlew - mainly around the saltings near the river mouth. This area can be especially productive for herons, egrets, gulls, terns etc and can also be observed by walking (or driving if conditions allow) towards the river mouth from Skala Kalloni beach. Black-necked Grebe and duck like Pintail and Merganser may well be present just offshore, Great White Egret often linger into late spring and Flamingos may also feed here in good numbers during winter and passage times in certain conditions - often dependent on water levels. Look out also for the large shrew colony at the river mouth that may sometimes attract raptors. Alternatively you can view the saltings by simply driving along the track past the Aegean Hotel that connects with the main road.

SPRING - Great Crested and Black-necked Grebe, Little and Great White Egret, Grey Heron, Black Stork, Spoonbill (scarce), Ruddy Shelduck, Marsh, Montagu's and occasional Pallid Harrier, Common and Long-legged Buzzard, Oystercatcher, Black-winged Stilt, Avocet, Stone Curlew, Collared Pratincole, Little Ringed, Kentish and Grey Plover, stints, Curlew Sandpiper, Dunlin, Ruff, Snipe, Whimbrel (scarce), Curlew, Common and Spotted Redshank, Greenshank, Green and Wood Sandpiper, gulls, terns, Little Owl, larks, pipits, Yellow, Citrine and White Wagtail, chats, Wheatear, Fan-tailed Warbler, Black-headed and Corn Bunting.

AUTUMN - Black-necked Grebe, Little and Great White Egret, Grey Heron, Black and White Stork, Ruddy Shelduck, Teal, Osprey, Stone Curlew, Grey and Ringed Plover, stints, Broad-billed Sandpiper, Snipe, Redshank, Greenshank, Green and Common Sandpiper, Black-tailed Godwit, Curlew, gulls, terns, swifts, Kingfisher, hirundines, Yellow and White Wagtail.

WINTER-EARLY SPRING - Little, Great Crested and Black-necked Grebe, Cormorant, Great White Egret, Greater Flamingo, Grey Heron, Hen Harrier, Buzzard, Pintail, Teal, Merganser (river mouth), Coot, Oystercatcher, Lapwing, Dunlin, Snipe, Curlew, Redshank, gulls, Sandwich Tern, Kingfisher, Skylark, Water Pipit, White Wagtail, Black Redstart, Stonechat, Reed Bunting.

3) KALLONI EAST AND UPPER EAST RIVER *(See Maps 1 & 2, P226-7)*

With the exception, possibly, of Kalloni Salt Pans, this has to be the best value birding spot on the entire island; and what helps make it so easy to work is the raised levees for at least 3 kms either side of it. This makes the viewing of most of its birds by car a very viable proposition; and the best way of keeping disturbance to a minimum. It can be approached in several ways - either, from Papiana, just outside Skala Kalloni (turn right immediately before the church with the Stork's nest on the roof) or from the main Kalloni to Mytilini road which crosses it. An even more direct route from Skala Kalloni is to take one of several tracks from the Square - and either follow the one nearest the beach (which comes out at a recently cleared area behind some apartments), or turn right off the Papiana road in a hundred metres or less, along a track immediately opposite the football pitch. (The surrounding area is often favoured by Barn Owl at night, and along with Little Owl it can sometimes be seen flying over the Square). This track takes you past a small marshy area with an open culvert to your left and a pool on your right in the triangular area between two converging tracks (the other being the one mentioned above). By mid-May or thereabouts, this area may be largely dry, except for the culvert. Nevertheless, when wet it can be a magnet for bathing or drinking birds (including White Stork, Wood Sandpiper and other waders, pipits, wagtails, and buntings) and Swallows and House Martins especially come here and to other nearby puddles to collect mud.

You either bear left or right here (right from the beach track and left from the football pitch track) and carry on past the new disco building, watching out for a very deep pothole (which on one occasion caused my head to make severe contact with the roof of the car!). Carry on past the new buildings on the beach and the now fenced off area on your right leading to the river mouth (where regrettably you may see some rubble and other rubbish dumped) and up a steepish gradient to the river bank. You may still be able to obtain access to the river mouth from here depending on the purpose of the new fencing. Certainly it used to be possible to drive right to the river mouth and may still be. If not, walking should still be possible, or the river mouth can be accessed on foot from the other side - though this may well disturb many of the herons, gulls, terns etc usually resting on the sand-bank. The total distance from Skala Kalloni to the river is slightly less than 1km. This can obviously be walked, but please remember that the very accessability of this area is putting it under increasing pressure from birders at a time when several birds are attempting to nest. Bee-eaters especially are then at their most vulnerable - so please don't be tempted to linger too long in sensitive areas.

The East River is best divided into three sections (or four if you count the Upper East River described later) - the first being that to the left of the main road just by the garage and looking towards the large grain silos. This area can be accessed on both sides and includes an old broken, (but just driveable) ford, ideal for waders and marsh terns, not to mention Little Bittern and Squacco Heron. There is always a big gathering of Yellow-legged Gulls here and further upriver, and waders, wagtails and warblers often rest or feed on the small mud-spits, and vegetated islands either side of the ford. The river here is flanked on both sides by olive groves with nesting Middle Spotted Woodpecker, Hoopoe, shrikes etc, but is totally dry by the summer. In spring, do watch out for numerous tadpoles and froglets of the Marsh Frog if crossing by car! Further along the left-hand bank past the large new house with the Greek flag flying, towards the obvious grain silos, one reaches, after about 0.5 km, a small stone building with a dripping tap. Looking to the left here, up a small gulley beyond a fence (where there was another small stone building in the process of being demolished) often produced a pair of Rufous Bush Robins in spring '95-7, and continuing further along on foot (across a rough ford over the river) also provided many people with good views of a pair of nesting Ruppells Warbler, and even of singing Cinereous Bunting once higher ground was reached. These may all be regular, but are not what I would consider typical birds of the East River, so are included instead under the heading of Upper East River which follows - those associated with the river and immediate environs inland from the bridge being held back for inclusion under the rest of East River.

Upper East River - This is the area reached by turning off to the left before the small building with the dripping tap to the grain silos and then doing a right (with the same ditch that feeds Kalloni Inland Lake on your left) and following the track up into the hills (past a farm or cattle pen on your right) for several kms. You very shortly reach a fork where you have the chance of doing a left towards the valley (where sheep are often grazed) or bearing right and carrying on for several more kms with some excellent views until the track eventually terminates at a small pit which your nostrils tell you long beforehand is used for dumping local goat and sheep casualties! Certainly local Buzzards and Ravens approve, even if we don't!

The whole area bordering the track is scrubby and fairly boulder-strewn, and the section between the farm or glorified goat pen first described and the junction of the two tracks and a little way above is excellent for displaying Rufous Bush Robins in spring, with

Cirl Bunting and Western Rock Nuthatch at all times (the latter having a very obvious nest plastered to the side of a large rock just past the cattle pen on your right) - being joined by White and Grey Wagtail, Black Redstart and mixed finch, sparrow and Corn Bunting flocks feeding around the livestock in winter. As mentioned above, on your return simply carry straight on past the grain silos (checking the ditch on your right all the way) for a km or more, and you then come out at a concrete bridge and some shops which signal you are back in Kalloni Square. This small section is one way until you rejoin the main road opposite the school, where a right will take you out on the main Molivos road or a left back through the town towards Skala Kalloni.

SPRING - Short-toed Eagle, Common and Long-legged Buzzard, Goshawk and displaying or migrating raptors (including Booted and possible Bonelli's Eagle), Hoopoe, Woodlark, Tawny Pipit, Rufous Bush Robin, Stonechat, Black-eared Wheatear, Blue Rock Thrush, Subalpine, Sardinian, Ruppell's and Orphean Warbler, Sombre Tit, Western Rock Nuthatch, Red-backed and Woodchat Shrike, Raven, Linnet, finches, Cirl, Cretzschmar's and occasioal Cinereous Bunting.

WINTER-EARLY SPRING - Buzzard, Goshawk, Sparrowhawk, Kingfisher (ditch area), Skylark, White and Grey Wagtail, Robin, Black Redstart, Stonechat, Blue Rock Thrush, Song Thrush, Sardinian Warbler, Blackcap, Sombre Tit, Rock Nuthatch, Raven, Serin, Linnet; Cirl, Corn and possible Rock Bunting.

On my spring '95 trip I was made aware of plans to dam the river about 0.5 kms upstream from the road bridge and create a reservoir. The implications of this may sound horrendous, but Filios Akriotis reassured me to some extent by pointing out that it would be designed to catch surplus rainwater which may otherwise simply flow out to sea. It would also be designed to overflow back into the river; and would, in any case, probably be 20 to 30 years away (if, indeed, it ever happens at all). He also pointed out that it may even prove to be advantageous by encouraging more wintering duck (like Tufted, for example -which normally require deeper water than Lesvos has to offer). Nevertheless, I still remain sceptical!

Lower East River - The second section is that to the right of the road, about 2 kms up to the next concrete ford (which is always driveable). This obviously has a greater selection of birds, especially Little Bittern, herons, storks, Glossy Ibis, crakes, waders, wagtails etc in the river, and numerous singing Black-headed and Corn Bunting, regular Nightingale, Bee-eater, passage shrikes and a wealth of singing warblers in the riverside tamarisks. In early spring, check the overhanging willows 0.5 km inland from the ford on the Skala Kalloni side for the chance of roosting Night Heron, which usually peak around mid-April, after which the trees are starting to come into leaf and they are not so easily seen in any case. They are usually best looked for from the opposite bank. Squaccos can also be abundant here on passage, and I once counted 17 along this short stretch in late April '95! Bee-eaters nest in the steeper river banks, and are usually present in good numbers during late spring and summer, when their liquid calls are a familiar feature of the area.

Though still mainly wet in late spring, this section of river can have shrunk to just a short stretch alongside the ford, or maybe no more than a few pools, by the autumn. (In fact, the river is usually mainly dry by early July, and full again anytime from mid-October, but certainly by the end of the month, when the worst storms of the year often occur). As in late September '94 though, sea water can be whipped up by strong winds (anytime between July and September) and forced further upriver, making it an easy food source for egrets, waders, Kingfisher and Water Rail. The ford itself and the stand of reeds on its inland side and scattered rocks on its seaward side, in spite of regular disturbance (both from birders and commuting local farmers and smallholders) can still be a good place for close Little Bittern, crakes, waders (particularly stints and sandpipers), Kingfisher, and warblers - especially in early morning and late evening, when it can also play host to late spring parties of Rose-coloured Starling pausing there to drink and bathe. In autumn it can be superb for Kingfisher and the odd confiding Water Rail.

Finally, the last section from this ford to the sea is always wet. Though bird-wise it is only a shadow of its former self by autumn. It has a large shingle spit just beyond the ford, and another in the form of an island just before it joins the sea; (and this is often a good place for nesting Stone Curlew; and also worth checking for pratincoles and terns in passage). Access by car is still possible about 75% of the way here, and the river mouth can be a wonderful spot in spring for watching migrating wetland species and attendant raptors. This section (especially the riverside tamarisks along the bank furthest from Skala Kalloni) is probably the best area to view singing Olivaceous and Great Reed Warblers soon after they arrive from mid to late April; again before the vegetation becomes too rampant. Short-toed Larks, buntings and the odd Hoopoe are also likely along here; and this is usually one of the best sites to encounter returning Black-headed Bunting in late April. In winter mixed feeding flocks of larks, finches Serins and Corn Buntings often attract Hen Harrier, Sparrowhawk, Merlin etc.

Apart from the various tracks between East River and the Salt Pans (described in the next section) there are numerous small tracks criss-crossing the olive groves in both the Skala Kalloni and Kalloni directions - either coming out on the main road or at the back of the Kalloni loop road where the supermarket is situated. There really are too many to describe, but they are certainly worth checking out - especially for birds like Wryneck and various warblers. To sum up, possible birds likely anywhere in the East River area are almost too numerous to mention, but should include the following :

SPRING - Little Grebe, Little Bittern, (also occasional Bittern in early spring), Night Squacco, Grey and Purple Heron, Little and Great White Egret, Glossy Ibis, Black and White Stork, Water Rail, Garganey, Honey Buzzard, Marsh, Hen, Pallid and Montagu's Harrier,

Goshawk, Sparrowhawk, Levant Sparrowhawk, Common and Long-legged Buzzard, Osprey, Red-footed and Eleonora's Falcon, Hobby, Lanner and Peregrine, Quail, Spotted and Little Crake, Moorhen, Black-winged Stilt, Stone Curlew, Collared and Black-winged Pratincole, Little Ringed, Kentish, Golden, Grey and occasional Spur-winged Plover, Little and Temminck's Stint, sandpipers, Ruff, Common and Great Snipe, Marsh Sandpiper, Greenshank, gulls, Gull-billed and occasional Caspian Tern, Sandwich, Common, Little, Whiskered, Black and White-winged Black Tern, Turtle Dove, Little Owl, swifts, Kingfisher (scarce after mid-April), Bee-eater, Hoopoe, Wryneck, Middle Spotted Woodpecker, Short-toed Lark, hirundines, Tree Pipit, Yellow, Citrine and White Wagtail, Nightingale, Redstart, Whinchat, Northern Wheatear, Cetti's, River, Savi's, Sedge, Marsh, Reed, Great Reed, Olivaceous and Icterine Warbler, Common and Lesser Whitethroat, flycatchers, Golden Oriole, Red-backed, Woodchat, Lesser Grey and Masked Shrike, Rose-coloured Starling, Spanish Sparrow, Cirl, Ortolan, Black-headed and Corn Bunting.

AUTUMN - Little Grebe, Cormorant, Little Bittern (very scarce), Grey Heron, Black and White Stork, Honey Buzzard, Levant Sparrowhawk, Common and Long-legged Buzzard, Red-footed and Eleonora's Falcon, Hobby, Water Rail, Little Ringed and Kentish Plover, Little Stint, Dunlin, Broad-Billed Sandpiper, Snipe, Greenshank, Green and Common Sandpiper, Turtle Dove, swifts, Kingfisher, Bee-eater, Hoopoe, hirundines, Tawny and Tree Pipit, Yellow, Grey and White Wagtail, Whinchat, Northern, Black-eared and Isabelline Wheatear, Cetti's, Sardinian and Willow Warbler, Blackcap, Spotted Flycatcher, Red-backed Shrike, Cirl, Ortolan, Cretzschmar's and Black-headed Bunting.

WINTER-EARLY SPRING - Little, Great-crested and Black-necked Grebe (river mouth), Cormorant, Pygmy Cormorant (scarce), Great White Egret, Grey Heron, Greater Flamingo and Pintail (both river mouth), Hen Harrier, Goshawk, Sparrowhawk, Buzzard, Water Rail, Moorhen, Green Sandpiper, Snipe, assorted gulls, Sandwich Tern, Kingfisher, Woodlark, Skylark, Meadow and Water Pipit, Grey and White Wagtail, Robin, Black Redstart, Stonechat, Song Thrush, Cetti's and Sardinian Warbler, Blackcap, Chiffchaff, Starling, Serin, finches, Linnet, Cirl and Corn Bunting.

4) POTAMIA VALLEY *(See Map 3, P228)*

This area is, once again, found just inland from the Kalloni to Parakila road, where one turns right a few hundred yards past the West River. As the main road does a sharp left, take the second of two adjacent tracks and follow the directions as described in the map. For the Potamia Valley simply bear left - this track eventually takes you past olive groves, (and the new embanked reservoir to your right), by a stone bridge just beyond an old footbridge over the Potamia river, and uphill almost as far as one cares to go, (skirting the river for a while and ignoring the track to the left). Approx 3.5 kms from the main road, you eventually come, after two small white buildings on your left, to an area where the olive trees are interspersed with oaks, and this is as good a site as anywhere on the island for breeding Olive-tree Warbler - though they can be rather frustrating and are more often heard than seen.

Orphean Warbler, Masked Shrike, Sombre Tit and Cirl Bunting are also regular. Look out too for Woodlark and overhead swifts, raptors and Bee-eaters etc. In spring and summer, churring and hawking Nightjars are likely, especially in the area before the river is crossed. Moreover, I have received some good reports of the area surrounding the large dead tree about 1km up the track from the two neighbouring bridges. Apparently Goshawk, Levant Sparrowhawk and Eleonora's Falcon have all been seen well here - sometimes perched on the dead tree (even in summer), whilst Nuthatch has also been present calling from the very same tree! Finally, if you wish to press on further up the valley there is plenty of scope to do so, and you should encounter some fairly impressive scenery and vertical rock faces *en route*. You also cross one or two fast flowing rivers with some mini-waterfalls (assuming these are still flowing by May).

It was on one such exploration that a couple in mid-May '98 located a singing and obviously territorial Finsch's Wheatear! They described the site as approx a half hour walk beyond the Olive-tree Warbler site (ie probably as far again as the distance from the main road to the two stone bridges) with a deep ravine and sheer cliffs both sides, where a stone bridge crosses a fast flowing section of river here running over a shallow open area with rocks. It was there on a rocky outcrop that the bird appeared, and was later verified by other birders. It may well reappear in subsequent years. As this Upper Potamia Valley is very underwatched it may well have been present previously and simply overlooked amongst all the Black-eared. At all events this area may be worth exploring (singing Icterine Warbler were also apparently present, and certainly has good raptor potential. I did once try to find a way out at the upper end of the valley (which eventually levels out into a small plain with fields and some sort of habitation suggesting another way in), but a steady deterioration of the track caused me eventually to admit defeat and return the way I had come!

Although there is so far no evidence to suggest that they occur, the rocky crag just after the valley entrance looks like it ought to be ideal for Eagle Owl. A visit early in the spring about half an hour before sunset to listen out for their call could just produce something. (But so could countless other far-flung sites on the island; so please don't hold me to it!). Instead of returning direct to the main road some may wish to visit the Inland Lake from here, and this route is described in the next section which follows the list of bird species.

SPRING - Black Stork, Short-toed Eagle, Goshawk, Sparrowhawk, Levant Sparrowhawk, Common and Long-legged Buzzard, Lanner, Peregrine, Rock Dove, Turtle Dove, Nightjar, Bee-eater, Roller, Hoopoe, Wryneck, Middle Spotted Woodpecker, Woodlark, Crag Martin, Thrush Nightingale (scarce), Nightingale, Redstart, Whinchat, Black-eared Wheatear, (also check for chance of Finsch's), Blue Rock Thrush, Marsh, Olive-tree, Sardinian, Orphean and Barred Warbler, Whitethroat, Blackcap, flycatchers, Sombre Tit, Nuthatch (occasional), Western Rock Nuthatch, Red-backed, Woodchat and Masked Shrike, Raven, Serin, finches, Linnet, Cirl, Corn and possible Rock Bunting.

AUTUMN - Wandering raptors (including Honey Buzzard, various eagles, Hobby and Eleonora's Falcon), Rock Dove, Turtle Dove, swifts, Crag Martin, Red-rumped Swallow, Red-backed and Woodchat Shrike, Wryneck, Middle Spotted Woodpecker, Redstart, Whinchat, wheatears, Sardinian, Garden, Wood and Willow Warbler, Spotted Flycatcher, Sombre Tit, Rock Nuthatch, Raven.

WINTER-EARLY SPRING - Buzzard, Lanner, Peregrine, Rock Dove, Middle Spotted Woodpecker, Robin, Black Redstart, Stonechat, Blue Rock Thrush, Song Thrush, Sardinian Warbler, Blackcap, Chiffchaff, Raven, Serin, Hawfinch, Cirl, Corn and possible Rock Bunting.

5) KALLONI INLAND LAKE *(See Map 3 P228)*

There are several possible approaches to Kalloni Inland Lake. It is easiest here to describe first how to access it via the track from the Potamia Valley. If returning from the latter simply do a left not far beyond the reservoir, with an olive grove on your right and keep going straight on, past the junction with the other track by the small white building where you originally came in off the main road over West River. Before this junction is reached, there is another track which leads off uphill to the left; and if this is followed for about 1km, (driveable with care) one can obtain some unrivalled views of the whole Kalloni Plain and its associated wetlands (and even the Salt Pans). This is one of the occasions where birds may take second place to scenery! You can actually see the lake far below you from this vantage point. Carrying on towards the lake you are in a good area for shrikes (especially Masked and

Woodchat) and there are several large poplar and plane trees on your left at the T junction of the 2 tracks with the small white building to your right (where you carry straight on - the same as turning right as described below.) The tangle of bushes and damp vegetation behind them can be excellent for warblers and singing Nightingale, and these plane trees hosted a feeding party of at least 30 Hawfinches in early April '97.

An alternative approach to the lake (obviously easiest if coming from Skala Kalloni) is to follow the first of the two adjacent tracks at the sharp bend in the main road between Kalloni West River and Potamia River, bear right at the T junction past the farm (with the small white building on the left where you would have come out on the track from the Potamia Valley as described above) and follow the main track until, after 0.8 km and about 0.2 km past a small stone ruin on your left, you come to a little stone bridge with wet ditches to either side of you (virtually dry in autumn). Do a left here, at a small staggered crossroads, and then almost immediately (after 0.1 km) right over another small culvert for the lake - or carry straight on in spring and check the ditch for Little Bittern, Night Heron, Nightingale, Olivaceous and Cetti's Warbler etc. The lake itself (which you skirt for about 0.3 km) produces similar species (check the adjacent tamarisks on the far side for roosting Night Heron) but also holds nesting Little Grebe and attracts Purple and Squacco Heron, Garganey, marsh terns, hirundines, swifts etc - whilst assorted raptors, Rollers, shrikes and Golden Orioles are often seen. Apart from birds, it is a particularly good spot for observing terrapins at close range - both the common Stripe-necked and the rarer European Pond often show very well in the ditch area (the former often in considerable numbers). I also regularly encounter Tree Frog here.

If you wish to follow a circular route all you need do is to carry on along the track (leaving the lake on your left), checking the reedy, scrubby borders to your left for warblers etc as you go. After 0.3 kms you come to a T junction with a steep, rocky ridge in front of you, where you do a left (looking out for the Western Rock Nuthatch nest plastered to a large rock after 0.1 km to your right, and checking the water trough by the small white building just beyond it), and keep going for 0.8 kms (checking the fields for migrants) until you come to a small flat area on your left with a drystone wall. Do a sharp left here over the small stone bridge which crosses the same ditch you saw on your way into the lake. On this route you will have passed two turn-offs to the right. Both are dead-end tracks through fields marked Metochi and Ag. Anargyron and end up in a fast-flowing boulder-clad section of the Upper West River - Dipper would be a nice find here! The second and more major one goes for 1 km and the first peters out after 0.3 kms at a chapel approached by a small stone bridge. They may be worth exploring if time permits.

Returning to the approach to the lake, the above route is ideal in the late afternoon for viewing the ditch on your left (Little Bittern, crakes, Kingfisher and warblers especially can be encountered on this productive 0.4 km stretch) - or in the early morning for the main lake. In either case the sun will be behind you and you will be looking to your left. Apart from several marsh species, warblers etc here, there is also an opportunity to locate various upland species or raptors soaring over the ridge; whilst the fields and hedgerows passed just before returning to the ditch via the small bridge can also be productive for migrants. There are many other possible tracks you could take to extend this route, which some may wish to explore for themselves. One is to go straight on over the bridge on reaching the ditch instead of turning left, and this takes you past a small rough area with brambles on your right which always looks promising for migrants, and then heads towards the Potamia Valley, with an olive grove and a small ditch to your left. This peters out by a ford just past a small farm, but the whole area is worth further exploration, and the rocky crag ahead is often good for Long-legged Buzzard.

If you wish to combine the Inland Lake with a visit further afield (especially the west) it may be worth knowing that all you need to do on leaving the lake behind you on the first route described is to do a right instead of a left at the T junction and follow this track below the ridge as far as it goes unti it meets a tarmac road (actually the back of Dafia). Then it's simply a matter of doing a staggered straight across at the blue Metoxi sign up another (rather bumpy) track for 0.3 kms and turning left on the main road to Filia - which puts you en route to Sigri. This is ideal for those who wish to view the lake first thing (when the light is right) and then head off west without retracing their steps. Conversely, when returning from the west you may want to check out the ditches in the late afternoon / early evening before returning to Skala Kalloni - in which case you need only take the track to your right off the main road between Filia and Dafia mentioned above (at the blue sign saying *Metoxi and Ag. Anargyron 3*) and retrace your steps to repeat the process. Then the ridge will obviously be directly above you to your right.

For those wanting to combine a trip to the Inland Lake with a visit to Kalloni East River or Salt Pans, it's quite a simple matter to leave the lake the way you first came in, but instead of doing a right past the stone ruin back towards the Potamia Valley simply turn left over yet another stone bridge and follow the ditch on your left all the way back to Kalloni for 2 kms. You need to do a left by Bookshop Eirmos when you reach the first narrow street (which is one way). Take the first right and then right again at the large church (which occasionally produces Little Owl sat at a hole in the brickwork!). You are then back in the main Kalloni Square and only need to do a right and a quick left on the main Mytilini road past Arisvi to access East River via the main road bridge or reach the Salt Pans slightly quicker by continuing along the main road a little further. To reverse this process just leave Kalloni Square by the narrow road just mentioned (which has a kiosk immediately to its right). Bookshop Eirmos (where you turn immediately left) should be clearly visible from the main road. There is also an excellent fast food outlet serving freshly made up rolls etc on the main road between where you turn off and the road you return on! At this point you may wish to head on straight to East River or Kalloni Salt Pans via the main Mytilini road (see below).

The Inland Lake is unusual in that it is one of those few locations which can actually be more productive in autumn, when it still contains a fair bit of water; but the edges have dried up sufficiently to make it particularly attractive to migrant waders and wagtails. It is also a magnet to hirundines, swifts and Kingfishers at a time when water inland is so scarce (though it is often pumped out for irrigation purposes at this time, and may start to form into several separate pools). Kingfishers actually remain in the area until the second or third week of April (sometimes later), which is also a good time for locating crakes, before the vegetation gets too rampant and the ditches dry up. Of course, high water levels on the lake in autumn usually make for a dearth of waders, whilst the ditches will normally be bone dry at this time.

A word of warning here - when covering Kalloni Inland Lake, especially in spring, you are likely to be very close to the birds (by the ditch particularly); so if at all possible, do try and work the area from a car, or you will simply flush everything on your arrival, and spoil it for everyone else (not to mention the birds, of course!). Upland species listed below may only be encountered along the main ridge behind the lake.

SPRING - Bittern (scarce but regular in early spring), Little Bittern (often in considerable numbers), Night, Squacco, Grey and Purple Heron, Garganey, Black Kite, Short-toed Eagle, Marsh and Montagu's Harrier, Goshawk, Long-legged Buzzard, Booted Eagle, Osprey, Hobby, Little and Spotted Crake, Moorhen, Common and Green Sandpiper, Whiskered and White-winged Black Tern, Kingfisher, Alpine Swift, hirundines, Roller, Wryneck, Hoopoe, Nightingale, Thrush Nightingale, Whinchat, Black-eared Wheatear, Blue Rock Thrush, Cetti's, Savi's, Sedge, Marsh, Great Reed and Olivaceous Warbler, Common and Lesser Whitethroat, Western Rock Nuthatch, shrikes, Rose-coloured Starling, Spanish Sparrow.

AUTUMN - Little Stint, Ruff, Greenshank, Kingfisher, Bee-eater, Wryneck, Sand and Crag Martin, Red-rumped Swallow, Yellow, Grey and White Wagtail, Thrush Nightingale, Whinchat, wheatears, Cetti's and Willow Warbler, Blackcap, Whitethroat, Spotted Flycatcher, Cirl Bunting.

WINTER-EARLY SPRING - Bittern, Mallard, Goshawk, Sparrowhawk, Buzzard, Water Rail, Coot, Moorhen, Green Sandpiper, Snipe, Kingfisher, Crag Martin, Black Redstart, Blue Rock Thrush, Cetti's Warbler, Blackcap, Chiffchaff, Rock Nuthatch, finches (including possible Hawfinch).

6) KALLONI SALT PANS *(See Map 4, P229)*

Although most people's first view of these is usually on the journey from the airport, a few miles before reaching Kalloni, you can also reach them from Kalloni Inland Lake via Kalloni Square and thence on the main Mytilini road as described above. Personally I prefer to approach them along the tracks closest to the East River stone ford (i.e. the seaward one). This obviously makes sense if coming from Skala Kalloni, and also has the advantage of producing good birds all the way from one prime habitat to another!

In fact, the tracks linking the two are quite driveable, though they can be a bit wet on occasions - especially after heavy rain in early spring. They are likely to hold Little Owl, (usually around the two small stone buildings almost opposite each other), singing Corn and Black-headed Bunting, shrikes, (Lesser Grey especially), Cuckoo, wagtails and possible Red-footed Falcon on the wires in season. The surrounding fields can play host to quite large numbers of Collared Pratincoles in spring passage; and when wet are good for certain waders (especially Ruff, stints and sandpipers - with Black-tailed Godwit and Curlew often quite numerous in early spring). Herons and Egrets may also feed in these wetter areas. Red-throated Pipits, too, are likely, and I have regularly heard Quail here. As you come out on the tarmacked road which skirts the Salt Pans channel you will be aware of the imposing new water treatment works on your left. This was popular with wintering Black Redstart in January '98 and also with a nesting pair of Northern Wheatear that spring, which utilized an old pipe dumped outside!

When the Salt Pans proper are reached, all these birds are still likely; but a lot more also become possible and the main channel alongside the road to the salt works (once again best viewed from a car - pedestrians or cyclists often tend to flush the birds), apart from all the usual herons, egrets, storks, pratincoles, waders, terns, hirundines etc, has also produced scarcer migrants like Spoonbill and Spur-winged Plover. Both Bee-eaters and Stone Curlew nest here, and passage raptors include all four harriers, Hobby, Eleonora's and Red-footed Falcon (the latter often in sizeable numbers), with regular sightings of Common and Long-legged Buzzard, hunting Short-toed Eagle, Peregrine and sometimes Lanner harassing the waders and passage Osprey always a possibility. Furthermore, this is a good part of the island for nesting Lesser Grey Shrike; quite often seen here along with the commoner Red-backed.

The water levels on the actual Salt Pans beyond the channel (after not being worked for three years prior to '96) were prone to considerable fluctuations from year to year - sometimes being dry in autumn, and occasionally even in spring. Numbers of migrating and breeding waders were therefore very variable. Now that the whole area (covering 263 hectares in all and capable of producing 10,000 tons of salt per year) is again in operation, there are plans by the owners (Hellenic Saltworks) to manage it in a more 'ecological' way - ie better control of year-round water levels, provision of observation facilities and the creation of islands to assist the breeding of 'protected' species like Avocet and Black-winged Stilt. It will be interesting to see when or if any of this happens (knowing the Greek time scale is somewhat dissimilar to ours!). Nevertheless, one must remain optimistic. The surrounding channel is normally fairly brackish, and its main purpose is to drain rainwater and prevent it inundating the main Salt Pans. These are normally drained about mid-April to enable salt production to get underway, and by early May the channel is at its most attractive to waders - with the optimum food supply available in the form of developing crustaceans. This situation applies again in August, when the main return wader passage occurs. With regular water levels, good numbers of Avocet and Black-winged Stilt will hopefully breed successfully - though past records have shown them all too often failing, as did all 13 pairs of Avocet in spring '95 when the pans dried out too early.

In addition up to 30 Great White Egret, and several hundred Greater Flamingo winter, and Common Gull is also a winter visitor in small numbers. (Because the pans are considered as a 'scientific area', no shooting is allowed there, at least officially - so wintering birds are relatively secure, so long as they don't wander too much from the main pans!) Regrettably, as a photographer, I tend to consider the views obtained on these main pans rather too distant for my taste! Certainly a 'scope would be necessary here, but bird numbers can be impressive, especially in early spring when Ruff and Black-tailed Godwit numbers peak.

Otherwise I find that the pools and marshy areas on the other side of the road yield some very good birds - and fairly close as well. Carrying on after the tarmac finishes by the actual salt workings can also be productive. Good numbers of Bee-eaters, pipits, shrikes, buntings etc perch on the perimeter fence, falls of Cuckoos, Whinchats etc often occur from early to mid-April and the flooded fields to the right are a likely spot for egrets and storks, Glossy Ibis, assorted waders, Red-throated Pipit, Yellow and possible Citrine Wagtail. In April and early May, Marsh and Montagu's Harrier are usually regular here, (with Hen and Palid Harrier peaking by early April and Red-footed Falcon numbers from late April onwards often quite staggering - though perhaps only for a few days). However, do remember that these fields may already be dry by early or mid-May, depending on winter rainfall.

After passing over the first channel you pass a low scrubby area just to the right of the track as you look over towards the old wooden jetty on the beach. Here and on the perimeter fence is a good place to observe singing and displaying Rufous Bush Robins (best from early May - when up to 2 pairs are normally present). Birds can also sometimes be seen singing from rocks on top of the spoil-heap to your right. Any such heaps of soil at the side of the track are also likely to prove attractive to nesting Bee-eaters, Tawny Pipit or Wheatear.

You can continue on from here to the shore, where a small concrete headland built up with rocks provides an ideal vantage point over the sea and the channel to your left. Provided you stay in the car, you can usually obtain excellent views of fishing terns and close-up waders, which from mid-May onwards often include groups of Turnstone and Sanderling in full summer plumage - a truly stunning sight! Whilst you're here, of course, it's always worth a quick scan out to sea for the chance of Black-necked Grebe, and the odd Godwit or Curlew feeding on an inlet or resting on the shoreline (which is viewable for some distance from here). This is also a gathering point for Little Gull in spring, and there's always the possibility of one of the rarer gulls or waders turning up here. Just before this headland is a likely spot for Stone Curlew, and the small stone bridge across the channel just before it overlooks a large marshy field with grazing cattle and several pools, at least up to early May.

This whole area, (which backs on to an otherwise unseen section of the Salt Pans) is certainly worth a look. Although there is usually a crude wire gate across it to keep the livestock from wandering, and I wouldn't wish to condone trespass, things are so laid-back in Lesvos that I don't think a quick wander would do any harm. Again, I tend to stay in the car, as straying too near any of the pools is simply likely to flush everything and be largely self-defeating. From the track up the middle of this field, in April and May '95, I was able to obtain mega views of Red-throated Pipit (very numerous), Stone Curlew, Collared Pratincole, Black, Blue and Grey-headed Wagtails feeding in large numbers amongst the sheep, Short-toed Lark, Montagu's and Marsh Harrier, and more distant, (but still very acceptable) views of Black and White Stork and regular flocks of up to 30 Ruddy Shelduck (apart from 'Derbyshire' probably the most reliable site on the island to see them). Since then I have regularly connected here with Calandra Lark, and more recently (April '98) with Richard's Pipit and Citrine Wagtail. In fact this field has now become something of a 'must' for all those visiting the Salt Pans - yielding excellent views of all four harriers in April and May '98 (at one time all on view at once!). Rose-coloured Starlings also favour the area on their migration from mid-May onwards, and when really wet in late March and early April it can host considerable gatherings of Garganey, Shoveler, Pintail and Ruff especially. If you follow the field as far as you can go you actually come to a river (the Mylopotamos) which feeds the Salt Pans. This appears to be always wet, and some of the hidden pools just before it also tend to stay wet late into the spring, and consequently harbour a good concentration of herons and storks at times.

Part of the Salt Pans can also be viewed from the main Mytilini to Kalloni Road, as I mentioned at the beginning; and the channel also continues all the way round. This road is not easy to stop on, however, and a lot of the area is hidden from view; so some waders are likely to be overlooked. Certain distant views can still often be had of Stone Curlew (especially when massing in late summer), Avocet and Black Stork along this channel, and a pool here exactly 1 km before 'Derbyshire' from the Salt Pans (part of which is visible from the road) regularly held up to 6 Black Storks, the odd Glossy Ibis, and occasional Spoonbill in May '95, when the bulk of the main pans were dry. Finally, before leaving the Salt Pans I should really mention the small but often extremely productive pool situated just opposite the main road entrance to the pans. Because it is situated to the left of the main Kalloni-Mytilini road almost opposite the Shell garage I shall in future refer to it as 'the main road garage pool'. The road here is just wide enough to be able to pull up right alongside it and view birds like egrets, Garganey, Wood, Green and Marsh Sandpiper, Spotted Redshank, stints and wagtails (including Citrine) at exceptionally close range at times. Success here is largely dependent on the amount of water present, since as it dries out (usually in early May but sometimes later) the waterline gradually recedes further from the road and makes viewing more distant. Certainly in winter it is a good spot for viewing normally wary Great White Egrets, which seem to become more accustomed here to people and traffic.

There is also another track down to the Salt Pans from the main Kalloni-Mytilini road, and (coming from the Kalloni direction) this involves doing a right at a small loop road (actually the course of the old road but now a glorified lay-by) shortly before the conventional tarmac turn-off. This takes you along past a red corrugated iron building with a ridge on your right and good views of the pans below to your left. Several reedy pools are passed (a good area for harriers and for displaying Fan-tailed Warbler - anywhere between there and the main road end of the tarmac approach road); and Little Owls are regular on the buildings. As you carry on past some vines the track bears to the right and then crosses a small concrete ford before eventually coming out at a T junction where doing a right through potentially damp fields takes you back to East River, but turning left along a sometimes quite wet section of track past a small olive grove on your right brings you out on the track which skirts the obvious channel at right angles to the main Salt Pans road. This is the one you first see on your left just just past the new treatment works when accessing the area from the East River tracks. This may all sound complicated, but in actual fact is really very straightforward, and gives you a variety of possible routes to get the best from this fascinating and extremely productive area.

From all these descriptions and the list that follows, you will once again see that the Kalloni Salt Pans are really a place to be in spring, when the spectacles on offer can be truly stunning given the right conditions. Autumn can be quite interesting, (especially with the early wader passage) but can never really recapture the pure magic of watching hundreds of waders, marsh terns, hirundines and pratincoles wheeling together as one when a Lanner suddenly appears in their midst, or the late afternoon sun picking out the wonderful greenish-brown sheen on the backs of a large party of feeding Glossy Ibis. Add to this hordes of Red-footed Falcons hovering in unison by the side of the road, and you may get some idea of its potential! Compared to this an autumn visit may be a slight anti-climax, though I found the area rewarding for wintering birds during my January and March '98 visits. Just one further word of advice - when viewing the pans and channel late afternoon is best; as you then have the light behind you (and this is a must if photographing).

SPRING - Great Crested and Black-necked Grebe, Cormorant (all mainly offshore), Squacco, Grey and Purple Heron, Little and Great White Egret, (the latter declining from mid-April), Black and White Stork, Glossy Ibis, Spoonbill, Greater Flamingo, Ruddy Shelduck, Shelduck (scarce after mid-April), Pintail, Shoveler, Garganey, Short-toed Eagle, Marsh, Hen, Pallid and Montagu's Harrier, Common and Long-legged Buzzard, Osprey, Kestrel, Red-footed Falcon, Hobby, Eleonora's Falcon, Lanner, Peregrine, Quail, Corncrake (scarce), Oystercatcher (irregular), Black-winged Stilt, Avocet, Stone Curlew, Collared and Black-winged Pratincole, Little Ringed, Ringed, Kentish, Golden, Grey and Spur-winged Plover, Lapwing (the latter two both scarce), Sanderling, Curlew Sandpiper, Dunlin, Ruff, Snipe, Black-tailed Godwit, Whimbrel (to late April), Curlew, Spotted Redshank, Redshank, Marsh Sandpiper, Greenshank, Green, Wood and Common Sandpiper, Turnstone, gulls (including

Mediterranean, Lesser Black- backed, Little and occasional Slender-billed), Gull-billed, Sandwich, Common, Little, Whiskered, Black and White-winged Black Tern (with occasional Caspian and Arctic), Great Spotted Cuckoo (scarce), Cuckoo, Little Owl, Kingfisher, Bee-eater, Hoopoe, Roller, Short-toed and occasional Calandra Lark, hirundines, Richard's Pipit (scarce), Tawny, Tree and Red-throated Pipit, Yellow, Citrine and White Wagtail, Rufous Bush Robin, Whinchat, Northern Wheatear, Fan-tailed Warbler, Lesser Whitethroat, Whitethroat, Golden Oriole, Red-backed, Lesser Grey and Woodchat Shrike, Rose-coloured Starling, Spanish Sparrow, Ortolan, Black-headed and Corn Bunting.

AUTUMN - Grebes as above, Cormorant, White and Dalmatian Pelican (scarce), Great White Egret and Little Egret, Grey Heron, Black and White Stork, Spoonbill (scarce), Short-toed and possible Bonelli's Eagle, Osprey, Hobby, Kestrel, Red-footed and Eleonora's Falcon, Hobby, Avocet, Stone Curlew, Little Ringed and Kentish Plover, Little Stint, Dunlin, Curlew, Redshank, and Greenshank in good numbers, other waders possible in much reduced numbers - though Broad-billed Sandpiper more likely. Black-headed, Mediterranean Little and Common Gull, marsh terns possible in much reduced numbers, Cuckoo, swifts, Kingfisher, Bee-eater, Hoopoe, Short-toed Lark, Skylark, Meadow and possible Red-throated and Richard's Pipit, Tawny and Tree Pipit, Yellow Wagtail, Whinchat, Stonechat, Isabelline, Northern and Black-eared Wheatear, Willow Warbler, Red-backed and Lesser Grey Shrike, Ortolan, Black-headed and Corn Bunting.

WINTER-EARLY SPRING - Little, Great Crested and Black-necked Grebe, Cormorant, Bittern (irregular), Great White Egret, Grey Heron, Greater Flamingo, Ruddy Shelduck, Shelduck, Teal, Pintail, Shoveler, Hen and occasional Marsh Harrier, Goshawk, Sparrowhawk, Common and Long-legged Buzzard, Kestrel, Merlin (scarce), Peregrine, Oystercatcher, Avocet, Kentish, Golden and Grey Plover, Lapwing, Dunlin, Snipe, Curlew, Redshank, gulls as above + possible Slender-billed, Kingfisher, Skylark, Meadow and Water Pipit, Grey and White Wagtail, Dunnock, Robin, Black Redstart, Stonechat, Fieldfare (hard weather), Fan-tailed and Sardinian Warbler, Chiffchaff, Rook (vagrant), Starling, finches, Reed and Corn Bunting.

7) 'DERBYSHIRE' AND ACHLADERI AREA *(See Map 5, P230)*

Carrying on towards Mytilini leaving the Salt Pans behind to your right, you come, after 6 kms to a right-hand coastal fork to Achladeri, just by a new bridge (with the remains of old bridge still visible to the left of the main road). This takes you almost immediately onto a now fully built up and tarmacked road with a very visible rocky outcrop to your left, a large pool beyond it, and further small pools to your right. From here until the next bridge over a tidal river is the area known as 'Derbyshire' - presumably because of its passing resemblance to a microcosm of the Derbyshire Peak District.

For quite a small area, this can hold some good birds; some of which are quite localized on the island, or at least not always easy to see (and these include Short-toed Lark, Tawny Pipit and Rufous Bush Robin for starters). Although, once again, spring is best; because the river and pools (to a degree) are largely tidal, there is water here even in autumn, though it doesn't tend to attract as many birds then - with the exception of wintering Great White Egret, Grey Heron, Kingfishers etc. It is, moreover, sometimes prone to disturbance from passing army convoys *en route* to and from the nearby base at Achladeri, and is also used at times by motorbike scramblers - which can be rather tiresome, not to mention somewhat noisy and dusty!

As a spring site it can be excellent for Ruddy Shelduck, (being mainly found on the pool beyond the rocky outcrop - this held 45 or more by late May '95, together with up to 8 Black Storks, and a Terek Sandpiper mid-month!). It can also be good for Red-footed Falcon - attracted by the overhead wires and low bushes bordering the track, and no doubt helped in their food quest by the sizeable herd of grazing cattle usually in evidence around the outcrop; which is also the best place to check for Rufous Bush Robin (up to 2 nesting pairs). Most other specialities should be seen at reasonably close range from the car - only Bush Robin seekers really need to walk! Rollers are also likely here in passage; and the area beside the old bridge you pass on the main Kalloni to Mytilini road is as good as anywhere. The marsh here on the landward side of the road - skirted by a track - can also hold some good waders, Glossy Ibis, occasional Bittern (as in April '98) and even Citrine Wagtail on occasions.

The whole 'Derbyshire' area is again good for Bee-eater, (with several pairs nesting and regularly perched on rocks, spoil heaps or posts alongside the road), Tawny Pipit (usually near the tidal river), Short-toed Lark, Wheatear etc, and the pools regularly attract Avocet, Little Egret and Great White Egret, Stints, Black and White Stork etc. Since this road was made up in spring '95 and raised by several feet (presumably as protection against flooding), although one can still park and pull over, one is unable to drive off to the side as one could before: with the result that the birds are now that much further away. Also, some of the roadside habitat was degraded, and Tawny Pipit (which had previously nested) was absent that year. Though still likely to produce some good birds, the overall effect of these works makes the area somewhat less attractive and less easy to work.

When carrying on over the Krioneri river towards Achladeri (where once again the new and the old bridge are juxtaposed) one should not neglect the track immediately to the left by the small stone army building. This leads for several kms up the hillside through a scrubby area interspersed with rocks which may produce Rufous Bushchat and Rock Nuthatch and is certainly excellent for Subalpine and Orphean Warbler, Red-backed and Woodchat Shrike, Cirl Bunting etc. There is also a late spring bonus here in the form of good numbers of churring and hawking Nightjar. Usually when taking this road to Achladeri (now synonymous with Kruper's Nuthatch) I tend to carry on via the coastal route to Skala Polichnitos Salt Pans - only a modest 30 minute drive if you don't get lost! This is a pleasant and fairly direct route, with several spots worth checking out on the way - as you will see from Maps 5 and 6. Any of the coastal scrub is likely to be good for Subalpine Warbler, Cirl Bunting, and, of course, shrikes. Remember to check the coastal pool on your right approx 2 kms from 'Derbyshire' before the next river (actually the River Vouvaris) for regular Black Stork and Ruddy Shelduck, which you look down on from the road through a wire fence - but I can assure you they are wild! There is also a collection of pools and old flooded workings of some sort just before the river, but these are possibly too deep to be especially productive.

The river itself is bordered by pines and a small picnic area, and this spot sometimes holds roosting Night Heron, though not easy to see. (Long-eared Owl has also been flushed twice from this site, so keep your eyes open!). Other herons and various warblers are also likely here, and the jangling of Serins and the song of Nightingales is all around; whilst the ridge to the left is worth scanning for Blue Rock Thrush, Rock Nuthatch and hunting raptors like Short-toed Eagle or Long-legged Buzzard. A track to the left by the Vouvaris river is driveable for a distance, but leads eventually to some houses with one or two tiresome barking dogs! Some of the riverside trees and scrub has also been fairly recently cleared for some strange reason. Nevertheless, this is an excellent area for flycatchers and warblers, with nesting Black-eared Wheatear further down.

The next section (known as Achladeri Plain), comprising small fields, mainly of grass, surrounded by brambles and barbed-wire fences, can be excellent in spring for Whinchats, resident Stonechat, Cuckoo, Subalpine Warbler, wheatears, and up to 4 shrike species. As you approach the Achladeri pinewoods (with a sandy track regularly used by the army heading off through the trees to your left looking promising but rarely producing anything unusual) you come to some isolated scrubby trees either side of the road, with a well-concealed sheep pen and stone wall to your right (0.25 km before the Kruper's track). This is all good shrike country (especially for Masked) and Orphean Warbler are also regular. As you approach the beachside taverna on your right on a bend in the road you first reach (0.3 km earlier) the now disused white army buildings clearly visible a short distance along two obvious tracks into the pinewoods. The first (and longer of the two) can be walked for several kms, but the second (no more than 0.1 km beyond it on the bend) needs hopefully only to be driven up a short distance to connect with the island's star bird - Kruper's Nuthatch. Simply drive past the disused white shower block and latrines and the old rusty oil tank just beyond it and reverse back to the pile of shingle currently at the end of this track and you may be lucky enough to be able to eat your sandwiches in the shade whilst watching Kruper's feeding young at the nest in a nearby pine. Certainly this has been the case for the last three years - up to and including the '98 season.

Because the area is a regular picnic site used by locals and also the army on special occasions, the birds seem well acclimatized to human activity - especially if you remain in the car. Middle Spotted Woodpeckers are also regular nesters, but are generally more wary. Short-toed Treecreepers, Subalpine Warbler and Serin are also widespread, and localized birds like Long-tailed and Coal Tit, Mistle Thrush and Wood Pigeon can usually be located with patience. Overhead look out for locally breeding Buzzard, Goshawk and possible Sparrowhawk, with Nightjar present in late spring and various flycatchers in passage including Collared. Just remember that Kruper's usually fledge young round about 7th May, and although there may be up to three pairs nesting in the immediate area and some may be a little later, the family parties only tend to stay local for a few weeks before dispersing - after which they become much harder to locate other than perhaps by sound. Of course, the exact time of dispersal may be dependent on the availability of water in the small rocky stream that runs (at least in early spring) between the two tracks.

Continuing beyond Achladeri, (and remembering to keep a low profile around the army base 0.5 kms further on!) you have the choice of bearing left at the avenue of cypress trees (towards the main Mytilini to Polichnitos road) or skirting the coast and checking out a few small pools and inlets (mentioned in the next section) *en route* to Skala Polichnitos via Alikoudi Pool (a sort of mini Salt Pans that has recently proved an excellent value site and very easy to work). This spot where you leave the avenue of conifers seems a good cut-off point to assess and list the bird species posible so far - bearing in mind that Kruper's is obviously localized and wetland species only occur at 'Derbyshire' and around the Vouvaris river and asociated marshy areas.

SPRING - Little, Great Crested and Black-necked Grebe, Little and Great White Egret (latter to approx mid-April), Black and White Stork, Night, Squacco, Grey, and Purple Heron, Glossy Ibis, Common and Ruddy Shelduck, Honey Buzzard, Black Kite, Short-toed Eagle, Hen, Marsh, Pallid and Montagu's Harrier, Goshawk, Sparrowhawk, Common and Long-legged Buzzard, Osprey, Kestrel, Red-footed Falcon, Hobby, Eleonora's Falcon, Peregrine, Black-winged Stilt, Avocet, Little Ringed, Ringed and Kentish Plover, Little Stint, Curlew Sandpiper, Dunlin, Redshank, Greenshank, Common, Green, Wood and Common Sandpiper, gulls, Caspian Tern (scarce), Sandwich, Common and Litle Tern, Woodpigeon, Turtle Dove, Cuckoo, Long-eared Owl (scarce and localized), Nightjar, Kingfisher, Bee-eater, Roller, Hoopoe, Middle Spotted Woodpecker, Short-toed Lark, Tawny and Tree Pipit, Yellow and White Wagtail, Mistle Thrush, Rufous Bush Robin, Redstart, Whinchat, Stonechat, Northern and Black-eared Wheatear, Blue Rock Thrush, Fan-tailed, Subalpine and Orphean and Barred Warbler, Blackcap, Whitethroat, Lesser Whitethroat, Wood and Willow Warbler, Spotted, Red-breasted, Collared and Pied Flycatcher, Long-tailed and Coal Tit, Kruper's and Western Rock Nuthatch, Short-toed Treecreeper, Red-backed, Lesser Grey, Woodchat and Masked Shrike, finches, Serin, Cirl and Ortolan Bunting.

AUTUMN - Little and Great White Egret, Black and White Stork, Honey Buzzard, Goshawk, Sparrowhawk, Buzzard, Osprey, Hobby, Dunlin, Little Stint, Redshank, Greenshank, Kingfisher, Middle Spotted Woodpecker, Skylark, Tawny Pipit, Yellow and

White Wagtail, Redstart, Whinchat, Stonechat, wheatears, Mistle Thrush, warblers, flycatchers and tits as above, Rock Nuthatch, Short-toed Treecreeper, Red-backed, Woodchat and Lesser Grey Shrike, finches, Serin, Cirl Bunting.

WINTER-EARLY SPRING - Little, Great Crested and Black-necked Grebes (river mouth), Cormorant, Great White Egret, Grey Heron, Greater Flamingo (irregular), Shelduck, Ruddy Shelduck, Red-breasted Merganser (offshore), Hen Harrier, Buzzard, Goshawk, Sparrowhawk, Merlin (scarce), Peregrine, Oystercatcher, Redshank, Green Sandpiper, Snipe, gulls, Sandwich Tern, Kingfisher, Skylark, Meadow and Water Pipit, White and Grey Wagtail, Black Redstart, Mistle Thrush, Sardinian Warbler, Goldcrest, Long-tailed and Coal Tit, Stonechat, Short-toed Treecreeper, Serin, Cirl Bunting.

8) SKALA POLICHNITOS SALT PANS AND SURROUNDS *(See Map 6, P231)*

As mentioned above, to approach these I prefer the coastal route from Achladeri which takes you along the shoreline past the avenue of cypress. There are several stands of reeds and a couple of small river mouths on this first section - which can produce various warblers including Fan-tailed, and obviously have the potential to turn up a lot more in season. Once you turn off inland by the (blue) taverna at Skala Vassilikon and the new blue sign for Skala Polichnitos you find yourself driving through olive groves with a water trough reached shortly on your left worth checking out en route. Anywhere along this route Rollers, Golden Oriole etc are possible in spring. A little over 1km later you turn right onto a tarmac road and after a brief spell of 0.4 kms on this road you turn right amid olive groves just past a sharp right bend at a small, rather old rusty Greek sign (which may of course be updated in the near future). After this the signs to Skala Polichnitos should be quite clear, so long as you remember not to turn off right at the small crossroads to Skamioudi but to bear straight ahead and then not turn right for the Salt Pans until after you've crossed the rather suspect looking bridge over a rather foul-smelling river! Although you then bear right you ignore the first right turn until the actual pans are sighted and you see the blue sign 'Glaros' (or beach).

One exception you may care to make, however, is to turn off right slightly more than 1km before the pans (shortly beyond Skamioudi) just past the Vassiliki apartments at a currently half-finished building at a small crossroads with a sign in Greek which translates 'Alikoudi beach'. In the unlikely event that you miss it, there is another track after a few hundred metres which gives more obvious views of this wetland area, but access is not nearly as good. It is best, therefore, to access via the first track - though this can be wet and quite deeply rutted at times. The technique here is to make sure you keep at least one wheel of your car in the middle of the track as you go - since a wheel each side may bottom it! I can assure you that it is likely to be well worth the effort, since this 'mini wetland' is capable of turning up as good a selection of waders at close range as almost anywhere else on the island. You can drive along the track between the pool and the beach (though lighting looking left is not ideal before early evening). Nonetheless, there are also waders possible on the beach (including Turnstone), and in mid-April '98 I encountered several large 'falls' of several Yellow Wagtail species posing beautifully amongst the wildflowers in company with various chats, Tawny Pipit etc. Although you can't circumnavigate the pool by car because of the presence of a small channel, you can easily turn round and drive along the beach for some distance in the other direction - where Stone curlew would look a distinct possibility and anything may be possible. The presence of a large pile of gravel and a digger here in spring '98 looked slightly ominous, since such tracks are only normally made up if there is an obvious financial benefit in doing so - let's hope I'm proved wrong! This really is too good a site to lose.

You could also have driven to the beach beforehand via Skamioudi, and this area (though the track eventually peters out on the shoreline at a small river mouth) can also be excellent for migrants during a good 'fall' - like almost anywhere on Lesvos. It really depends how much you really want to divert from your route! But returning to the access to Skala Polichnitos Salt Pans on the route already described you pass one final dead-end track on the seaward side. Although it doesn't go as far as the beach it does seem to be a good spot for Lesser Grey Shrike, and it seems likely a pair may breed nearby. Between here and the nearby pans the damp area of tussocky grass is home to Fan-tailed Warbler, is regularly hunted in spring by harriers and frequented by wagtails, chats and Tawny Pipit. As mentioned, the pans are best approached via the track skirting the perimeter fence with the blue 'Glaros' (beach) sign. You will notice a small channel on your right which runs to the beach and is crossed by a concrete bridge leading to a house. This area is worth checking out, as it held a pair of Citrine Wagtail in mid-April '98! You can also drive along the beach past this house for a fair way in the Alikoudi direction until the track again peters out at a small river mouth. Flowers can be excellent here in early spring and migrants and Stone Curlew may turn up.

Otherwise, if you turn left at the track along the beach (also excellent for wildflowers in April especially, for migrant Grey Plover and Sanderling on occasions, and for an ultra-confiding Whimbrel in late April '98) you should be able to drive alongside the pans nearly all the way to the workings,-just before which there is an obvious area of higher ground like a small gravelly ramp which you can drive up to view the waders from your car without the necessity to flush anything. This is ideally done in late afternoon when the light is behind you, but because of the distance sometimes involved a 'scope might be helpful. The only drawback here is that occasionally the track can be partially flooded towards the end if the channel overflows, but there is a small 'loop' track alongside it which is usually OK. Nonetheless, I have at least twice got stuck on this beach trying to turn round, and had to be dug out by some rather bewildered locals! You should also remember that both Kentish and Little Ringed Plover frequently nest on the beach (sometimes on the track itself), so do be careful not to inadvertently destroy their nests. Stone Curlew is another regular nester, so if you flush a bird please try not to linger too long in the vicinity, as you may be keeping it off eggs. Using the recommended technique these pans can be viewed fairly quickly and the minimum of disturbance caused. Because of their rather remote location in relation to other bird sites on the island, and the fact that most people, in any case, tend to stay around the centre or north of the island; they tend to be rather neglected, and overshadowed by the Kalloni Salt Pans. They have the potential, however, to turn up just as impressive a list of waders, ducks etc, and are well worth a visit or two - sometimes coming into their own in autumn, when they can be much wetter than those at Kalloni, and hence attract some better birds. (A visit in April '95, however, found them almost totally dry!). They also tend to be a reliable wintering site for birds like Greater Flamingo and Great White Egret, not to mention Pintail and Black-necked Grebe. In addition, they are the main stronghold for Redshank on Lesvos, ironically not an easy bird to get to grips with in these parts! The large gull roost here is, incidentally, always worth checking for something more interesting than the usual Yellow-legged Gulls.

A perimeter track also skirts the landward side of the pans, and this is perfectly driveable, but best done in the morning, when the light is behind you. Also you need to be patient - as from this side lots of waders can lurk unseen under the numerous banks and walls that criss-cross and divide these pans; making them not that easy to work if time is limited. The surrounding area, too, can be good. Check the wires here for possible Roller at the right time - in April '95 I also had a large fall of Cuckoos on these wires, and some migrating Golden Orioles nearby. The grassland on the landward side of the encircling track can often be wet, and hold lurking Purple Heron and Golden Plover to give just 2 examples. Moreover the fairly brackish area within the pans (more on the lines of a saltmarsh), surrounded by a partially broken chain-link fence, has produced Spur-winged Plover at least once. So do spare the area a thought. You never know; you might turn up something new here, and have it all to yourself - while all the other birders are busy checking out the Kalloni Salt Pans!

If you continue on the landward side of the pans in the Skala Polichnitos direction you pass a strip of rough ground in varying degrees of wetness (sometimes almost dry) with wooded slopes above which are frequented by Buzzards - after which you simply bear left past the workings and find yourself in the small coastal resort of Skala Polichnitos. You then have various choices (depending on the time of day). You may wish to continue inland to Polichnitos and return to Kalloni on the main road via Vassilika (taking a left through pinewoods opposite Mikri Limni wetland signposted Achladeri) and hence back again to 'Derbyshire'. I have reliable reports of Kruper's along this road (actually drinking from a trough about 0.5 km after the turn-off from the main road), and it would seem to be a regular site for them and other drinking and bathing birds well into the summer and autumn, when other water sources may well be dry. In early spring, however, I have usually found it disappointing. Otherwise it is mainly woodland birds like Short-toed Treecreeper, Coal and Long-tailed Tit that occur on this route. I shall mention this area again in connection with a visit to Agiassos and surrounds, which one may want to combine with a visit to Skala Polichnitos Salt Pans via main roads.

There is another alternative on leaving the pans, and this is to do a right on the coastal track to Nifida well before Polichnitos is reached. Because this takes you eventually to some reedy pools which may produce different birds to the area already described I shall hold it back until dealing with the Vatera area due south of there, and with which some overlap of species occurs - especially at its eastern river mouth. To sum up then, some of the potential birds of the Skala Polichnitos area (including Alikoudi pool and approaches) would include :-

SPRING - Little and Great White Egret, Squacco, Purple and Grey Heron, Black and White Stork, Glossy Ibis, Spoonbill, Greater Flamingo, Pintail, Garganey, Shoveler, Short-toed Eagle, Marsh, Hen and Montagu's Harrier, Common Buzzard, Red-footed Falcon, and Eleonora's Falcon, Hobby, Quail, Stone Curlew, Collared Pratincole, all waders as for Kalloni Salt Pans (including Whimbrel), Little, Mediterranean, Lesser-black Backed and Yellow-legged Gull, all terns as for Kalloni Salt Pans, Turtle Dove, Cuckoo, swifts, Kingfisher, Bee-eater, Hoopoe, Roller, Middle Spotted Woodpecker, Short-toed Lark, Tawny, Red-throated and Tree Pipit, Yellow and Citrine Wagtail, Redstart, chats, Northern Wheatear, Fan-tailed, Orphean, Icterine and Willow Warbler, shrikes, Golden Oriole, Ortolan, Black-headed and Corn Bunting.

AUTUMN - Black-necked Grebe, Little and Great White Egret, Black and White Stork, Greater Flamingo, Grey Heron, Pintail, Wigeon, Teal, Osprey, Eleonora's Falcon, Kentish, Ringed, Little Ringed and Grey Plover, Dunlin, Little Stint, Redshank, Greenshank, Marsh Sandpiper, above gull species, Kingfisher, Yellow and White Wagtail, pipits, wheatears, Willow Warbler, Chiffchaff.

WINTER- EARLY SPRING - Black-throated Diver (scarce offshore), Black-necked Grebe, Great White Egret, Grey Heron, Greater Flamingo, Shelduck, Wigeon, Teal, Pintail, Shoveler, Red-breasted Merganser (offshore), Hen Harrier, Sparrowhawk, Common Buzzard, Kestrel, Merlin (scarce), Peregrine, Water Rail, Oystercatcher, Avocet, Golden and Grey Plover, Lapwing, Dunlin, Snipe, Curlew, Redshank, gulls as above, Sandwich Tern, Skylark, Meadow and Water Pipit, Grey and White Wagtail, Robin, Black Redstart, Stonechat, Sardinian Warbler, Chiffchaff, Starling, finches, Reed and Corn Bunting.

9) VATERA AND SURROUNDS *(Map 7 P232)*

This is actually an area I only recently checked out after receiving some interesting reports from one or two people who have stayed there. Apart from an extensive beach and dunes with some associated scrub which looks especially attractive to migrants, it also possesses some interesting wooded areas and two promising river mouths - one at its eastern and one at its western end.

Because it is situated just due south of and fairly close to Skala Polichnitos (on a good road) it seems fairly logical to combine it with a trip there. Alternatively, if you're feeling brave enough to take the long and winding road via Ambelikon (which is now fully tarmacked in its latter stages and gradually being extended) you could possibly work it in with a trip to Agiassos - described in the next section. Anyway, assuming for the moment that you are approaching via Skala Polichnitos, it may be worth a quick diversion to the right just out of the village well before Polichnitos is reached. This takes you onto a small road (clearly sigposted Nifida) which skirts the coast for a couple of kms before petering out in a small bay - which can prove good for viewing shearwaters in the right conditions. Moreover, the headland beyond (known as the Bogat headland) produced Cinereous Bunting in the first week of May '97, and this may prove a regular site. The whole road up to there is now surprisingly good, and this may well be because some development of the beach is planned - especially since shower buildings have now miraculously appeared!

Anyway, it makes a pleasant drive, with possible close views of grebes offshore (also Black-throated Diver and Red-breasted Merganser on my January '98 trip), and there are a couple of reasonable sized reedy pools just off to the left about three quarters of the way along. If you turn off alongside a white wall you are upon them almost immediately, and can usually do a circuit of both if the surrounds are not too wet. Although there are several houses in the vicinity, and therefore the likelihood of fairly regular disturbance, in April '98 they certainly proved good for Garganey, waders like Black-winged Stilt, Little Ringed Plover, Greenshank and Wood and Marsh Sandpiper, plus numbers of hirundines, pipits and wagtails. Crakes and Kingfisher would also seem likely, and probably Little Bittern and herons also, not to mention various gulls and terns. Clearly they deserve further scrutiny, but it's difficult to say how long they might remain wet, so success is by no means guaranteed. However, for such a short investment of time, it's worth giving them a try.

Having retraced your steps, carry on to Polichnitos - no doubt pausing to check out (or perhaps photograph) the stork's nest on the tall chimney just to your right at the road junction. This is usually occupied (even in January '98!), so it seems this particular bird may be resident. Anyway, carry on at a staggered straight across to Vatera via Vrissa - which should be clearly signposted. This takes you along a good road with some pleasant views (especially as you drop down through wooded slopes past Vrissa to Vatera). Before this, however, you skirt a river to your left with a concrete ford parallel to the road and bordered by a scrubby, rocky gulley. The same river is crossed again in a couple of kms. The area always looks promising (especially for raptors), and the ford area is always a good bet for warblers and other migrants in season. My last stay there was, by necessity, rather brief - owing to the stench emanating from a dead sheep which had presumably drowned in the river!

As you reach Vatera beach you come across probably the biggest proliferation of local signs on one board possible anywhere on the island; and this testifies to the resort's growing popularity as a tourist resort! However, in April and early May it is still virtually deserted, so don't let that put you off. The best plan is to do a quick right first and check out the reedy river mouth and disused ford in that direction (either following the inland track which skirts it for a while, or carrying on over the bridge on a dirt road for 2 kms to the harbour or a short seawatch at Agios Fokas headland before returning along the beach road and checking out the dune area and the virtually deserted river mouth to the east of the town - see map 7 for further details). There are also numerous tracks off to the left through pines, scrub and olive groves, often with some promising looking clearings - albeit with the odd old building or rusting tank left over from some army manoeuvres! The river mouth itself is fairly gravelly with little vegetation, but is favoured by wagtails, Little Ringed Plover etc. There is also quite a deep reedy pool to the left, much favoured by terrapins, but also attracting Little Bittern and Crakes in season. There may also be one or two puddles on your left just before it, and these may be used by Red-rumped Swallows and Crag Martins (which nest on the nearby rock-face beyond the river mouth). Of course, any migrants, warblers and buntings that are present in the area are also likely to drop in to drink or bathe, so it may be worth a short vigil here.

Alternatively, you could explore the area to the left - which consists of a small flat area interspersed with rocks and bordered by riverside scrub, with a small farm and a few fields beyond. This area produced Stonechat, Ruppell's and Orphean Warbler, several Lesser Whitethroat, wheatears, and good numbers of Serin on an early April visit; so should be even more productive later on. The other side of the river there appears to be a new hotel under construction, and although it doesn't seem to have advanced much beyond a shell in the last year or so we have to assume it will eventually be finished! This may well change the nature of what is currently a very quiet area. It will also necessitate some means of crossing the river, which is currently often too deep even for me to chance driving through! We shall have to see what develops, but at present this area is still well worth a visit, and according to recent reports has the potential to turn up a fair proportion of the species recorded in the Kalloni area in spring - even down to a couple of pairs of breeding Rufous Bush Robins. Since the area has only really been covered in spring this is the only period for which I shall list sightings, though the river mouths and beach area should surely produce something in autumn.

SPRING - Cory's and Mediterranean Shearwater, Shag, Cormorant, Little Bittern, Night and Squacco Heron, Little Egret, Purple Heron, Garganey, Short-toed Eagle, Marsh and Montagu's Harrier, Common and Long-legged Buzzard, Lesser Kestrel, Red-footed and Eleonora's Falcon, Hobby, Peregrine, Little and Spotted Crake, Black-winged Stilt, Little Ringed and Grey Plover, Snipe, Greenshank, Wood Sandpiper, Mediterranean, Audouin's and Little Gull, Gull-billed, Common, Little and White-winged Black Tern, Turtle Dove, swifts, Bee-eater, Hoopoe, Middle Spotted Woodpecker, Woodlark, Crag Martin, Red-rumped Swallow, Tawny and Tree Pipit, Yellow and White Wagtail, Rufous Bush Robin, Nightingale, Whinchat, Stonechat, Northern and Black-eared Wheatear, Blue Rock Thrush, Cetti's, Fan-tailed, River, Reed, Great Reed, Olivaceous and Olive-tree Warbler, Common and Lesser Whitethroat, Blackcap, Orphean, Subalpine, Sardinian and Ruppell's Warbler, Spotted Flycatcher, Sombre Tit, Western Rock Nuthatch, all four shrikes, Spanish Sparrow, Serin, finches, Linnet, Cirl Bunting, Cinereous Bunting (Bogat headland only), Cretzschmar's, Black-headed and Corn Bunting.

10) ABOVE AGIASSOS VIA VATERA AND SKALA POLICHNITOS *(See Map 8, P233)*

As mentioned earlier, you may wish to visit the area above Agiassos from either Vatera or Skala Polichnitos - taking either the main road or the minor road (currently being improved) through Ambelikon. The latter can be rather hard going initially, and also passes through fairly uniform olive-clad hills until the pinewoods are reached and the road improves. Let us assume therefore that you are approaching Agiassos from the main Polichnitos road, which you would do in any case if you came from the Kalloni direction via Achladeri (another road in the process of being made up in sections). Between Polichnitos and Vassilika, a good aerial view of the Salt Pans can be obtained on your left, after which you carry on until, opposite the Achladeri road junction, you see an obvious wetland to your right, largely hidden on one side by pinewoods - with a dirt track skirting the side opposite the road junction. This is known as Mikri Limni (or small lake in English) - as opposed to Megali Limni (or large lake) reached further along on your left just before the Ambelikon turn-off.

Mikri Limni can be a difficult site to view, because of the amount of emergent vegetation and the fact that it is bordered to a large extent by pinewoods, with only a few gaps (mainly near the road) through which to view it. However, the end nearest the road is more open, and can also be skirted by car if conditions permit. At this end I obtained good views of a pair of Ferruginous Duck in late March '98 and a group of Marsh Sandpiper in early April.

Little Grebe also appreciate the amount of cover here, and almost certainly breed - whilst Kingfisher should be regular in winter and early spring (at which time Bittern have also been recorded). Snipe and crakes undoubtedly occur, though the site may not be open enough to produce good numbers of waders. Otherwise the pinewoods turn up the usual Coal and Long-tailed Tits, Goldcrests in season and also Kruper's Nuthatch - which have recently been encouraged by the provision of nestboxes in what is otherwise an area of rather uniform woodland with few old or decaying trees to provide natural nest sites. Of course, most of this area is home to breeding Goshawk, which I have seen several times between here and the picnic site just past Megali Limni.

The latter area also turns up Kruper's around its borders (where I have recorded them feeding amongst mixed tit flocks in winter and early spring). However, although more extensive and containing several stands of reeds, Megali Limni has clearly been drained to a fair extent for small scale agriculture and (apart from regular feeding parties of White Stork) doesn't really seem to live up to its potential - especially for raptors (eg harriers), waders and duck. To be fair though, it can only be viewed from a few places, and there is no proper access; so it may well have been underwatched and not yet realized its potential. At all events it is best viewed from its south-eastern end, nearest the Ambelikon turn-off. Here a track goes off left through pine trees alongside a culvert and water course, which leads to a small farm or similar. There is often an area of standing water here up to early spring, which regularly attracts Red-rumped Swallow, various warblers, Serin etc - with Black-eared Wheatear and flycatchers (including Collared) often flitting around the barbed wire fence and small stone buildings that border Megali Limni. Hoopoe are also likely here, together with most of the typical woodland birds seen around the picnic site on the corner of the Ambelikon / Vatera turn-off *en route* to Agiassos. Apart from here Kruper's have also been seen about a km down this road before the signposted turning up to the summit of Olympus. Although there is a radar station of sorts with a likely army presence at the top, you may wish to drive up this winding road which always looks good for raptors, Kruper's and just possibly Rock Bunting. Certainly the views are impressive!

Returning to the main road between this and the Agiassos turning (actually after 1.5 kms), a fast-flowing, boulder-strewn river skirts the road for a while on your left (though sometimes some distance below it). Here, where you suddenly start to drop steeply through a series of sharp hairpin bends, is the most reliable site I know on the island for breeding Grey Wagtail, and one can often be heard calling from roadside rocks, or even perched on the crash-barrier to your left! (Sometimes they can also be seen around or flying over the car park just before Agiassos). Anyway, carrying on to Agiassos, take the clearly marked turning to Agiassos and Plomari on your right and then take a left on the Plomari road (actually signposted in Greek) as opposed to carrying straight on into Agiassos on a cobbled road (not to be recommended!). By all means, take the time to explore the town, with its delightful narrow, cobbled streets and wealth of tourist shops - but only after locating Kruper's - which in itself is no mean feat.

This location has been well described in virtually any literature on Lesvos and its birds, by virtue of the fact that it used to be the most reliable spot to find the island's star bird. However, now that Kruper's is known to be so regular at the Achladeri site (at least in the breeding season) fewer people tend to make this pilgrimage - myself included! In some ways this is a pity, since this area is more or less unique on the island. The Sweet Chestnut Woodland (with its localized bird species, wildflowers and orchids) can be a magical place, and well worth the investment in time that a trip necessitates.

By far the most reliable technique to score with Kruper's used to be to take an extended lunch-break parked a short distance from the Sanatorium (about 4 kms from the town centre sign and 2 kms beyond the little chapel on your left), where a cracked pipe leaked water across the road and formed a small puddle, regularly visited by Kruper's and a wealth of other birds in autumn '94. Unfortunately, this now appears to have been repaired, and was dry in spring '95 and in subsequent years. However, it was then discovered that Kruper's had taken to drinking from the water storage container a little further on! This structure (in white stone, with broken pieces of wood laid across the top and situated about a third of a km past the sanatorium on the left, just before the drinking fountain) used to leak water out of the wall near the bottom, and the area was betrayed by the presence of patches of green algae. Clearly listening out for the bird's unusual call would often help locate it. Described in the various books as 'a harsh *schwee* or a single soft *pwit* recalling the ticking of Great Spotted Woodpecker,' there is also the more familiar rippling sound as made by Common Nuthatch - but the former sounds are more useful in betraying its presence. Once heard, it wasn't usually too long before it could be seen hanging on the side of this wall extracting moisture from the bricks - quite an amazing sight!

However, this water tank now seems to have fallen into disrepair and to have dried up, so unless fixed or refilled the area would seem unlikely to produce the birds on such a regular basis again. It may be worth trying the drinking fountain just beyond on the right - certainly in summer or autumn. In spring there is usually sufficient water around for them not to need to visit this regularly - though Crossbill have been recorded here in spring '97 and summer '98. In spring '95 Kruper's were nesting near the top of a dead pine almost opposite the water tank- so observation was relatively easy. But nest sites have not been located since the discovery of the nest site near Achladeri in '96 (at least to my knowledge), so who knows what future years may bring?

After checking out this area anyone feeling more adventurous can drive all the way to Plomari from here; and, apart from sampling the local ouzo, there is also the possibility of a boat trip to the nearby Garmias Island, which I'm told can be good for both shearwaters, Eleonora's Falcon and close dolphin sightings. A large area before Plomari was burnt out round about '94 and appears fairly slow to recover, and there is also a large army camp on the ridge to your left with regular guards on patrol and several prominent 'No Photography' signs! In practice, therefore, I tend to turn back soon after the Sweet Chestnut woodland, which is a wonderful area for a walk in early spring; with masses of wild flowers, and bird song everywhere. This is one of the few areas on the island where the song of Mistle Thrush, Wren, and the occasional Song Thrush, Robin, and Willow Warbler can be heard, mingling with the ever-present Nightingales, the monotone call of the Hoopoe and the resonant trill of Eastern Bonelli's Warbler. Short-toed Treecreeper seem to appear on almost every tree trunk at times; and the whole spectacle is a peculiar mixture of the familiar and the totally unfamiliar - all very strange, but well worth investing the time (especially in April and early May, before the trees come into full leaf). These, incidentally, are riddled with Middle Spotted Woodpecker holes and are also home to numerous Persian Squirrels.

Further on, anywhere to the right where a good view can be obtained over the mixed woodland (a large part of which - rather unusually for the island - is deciduous), may produce sightings of the odd soaring raptor, especially Sparrowhawk or Goshawk. But Red-footed Falcon, Common Buzzard, and Bonelli's Eagle have all been seen here, and Honey Buzzard almost certainly breeds and is fairly regularly seen in late spring. Finally, all Middle Spotted are worth checking out for the slim possibility of Great Spotted (which has been recorded here). Claims of Syrian or White-backed should be treated with caution, since the most reliable island records are all from lower elevations.

Similarly, Common Nuthatch has been reported, but is not regular (preferring the oakwoods to the west of the island). It is certainly a good area to check for other relatively scarce and localized woodland species on Lesvos, like Coal and Long-tailed Tit, and wintering Goldcrest. In spring singing Nightingale and Subalpine Warbler are everywhere - even if Kruper's aren't! But don't despair, you should locate them eventually with time and patience. For those wishing to get the best out of the area at this time (botanists especially) the circular walk described below (reproduced with grateful thanks to Simon Gillings and Su Gough) may prove useful.

Circular flower walk around Agiassos (c.5kms)

Flowers likely to be encountered in late April/early May include:

Wild Paeony *Paeonia mascula*
Wild Tulip *Tulipa orphanidea*
Orchids incl.   Lax-flowered *Orchis laxifolia*
      Green-winged *O. morio*
      Provence *O. provincialis*
      Toothed *O.tridentata*
      Sword-leaved Helleborine *Epipactis longifolia*
      Violet Limodore *Limodorum abortivum*
Wild Fritillary *Fritillaria pontica*
Giant Arum *Arum elongatum*
Peacock and Crown Anemones *Anemone pavonia* and *coronaria*

This area is also excellent for woodland birds, scarce on the rest of the island, such as song thrush, robin, wren and chiffchaff.

Park at lower end of Agiassos – take the right hand fork on approaching the town which leads to an obvious parking area before the hill starts to climb.

1.   From car-park walk up the main street in town, past a yellow post box and large grey and red building on your right. Go right at the staggered junction (left to visit the church and market). Go past the church of 'Zoodchion Rigis' in its sunken courtyard on left. The road climbs and swings to the left. (Another street comes in from above right.) Stay with the cobbles as they swing round to the right – there's a number of garage doors in front of you.

2.   At a fork by a trekking sign (man with rucksack and stick!) and memorial spring dated 1995, go right uphill. Follow the clear path with its 'kalderim' surface intact in places as it climbs up. At a clear junction the kalderim swings left, follow this. (The straight path continues up the hill with Mt. Olymbos on your right.) Your path runs along the hillside, under the Sweet Chestnut.

3.   As the path starts to drop towards a shady streambed look for a little walled enclosure on the opposite bank. Cross the stream here and go to the left of the enclosure on woodland path. Stick to the most obvious path as it bears around the hillside towards a second stream. Paeonies here! The path crosses 4-5 wet flushes.

4.   On reaching the second stream you should see 4 young trees along the opposite bank, the middle two have obvious red marks on their trunks. Cross the stream here. The path heads left and up away from the streambed. Follow this until you reach a junction with a broad kalderim track (that leads up to the sanatorium). Go left and down an initially wide and paved kalderim. Wonderful view of Agiassos ahead! Reach a small pink church with nearby leafy spring. Continue to the right, past a second pink church. Further still a 3rd church.

5.   Cross the stream by bridge at this church and bear right down a concrete road. After a few minutes this brings you back to the cobbled street you initially walked up.

SPRING - Honey Buzzard, Short-toed Eagle, Goshawk, Common and Levant Sparrowhawk, Bonelli's Eagle, Hobby, Eleonora's and Red-footed Falcon, Peregrine, Turtle Dove, Cuckoo, Hoopoe, Wryneck, Middle Spotted Woodpecker, Red-rumped Swallow, Grey Wagtail, Wren, Robin, Nightingale, Redstart, Black-eared Wheatear, Blue Rock Thrush, Song and Mistle Thrush, Icterine, Subalpine and Barred Warbler, Lesser Whitethroat, Whitethroat, Garden Warbler, Blackcap, Eastern Bonelli's and Wood Warbler, Chiffchaff, Willow Warbler, all five flycatchers, Long-tailed and Coal Tit, Kruper's Nuthatch, Short-toed Treecreeper, shrikes, Raven, Serin, Crossbill (sporadic), Siskin, Cirl Bunting, Rock Bunting (occasional).

AUTUMN - Honey Buzzard, Goshawk, Sparrowhawk, Common Buzzard, Bonelli's Eagle, Turtle Dove, Middle Spotted Woodpecker, Wryneck, Wren, Robin, Redstart, Blue Rock Thrush, Song and Mistle Thrush, warblers, flycatchers and tits as above, Kruper's Nuthatch, Short-toed Treecreeper, shrikes, Raven, Serin, Cirl Bunting.

WINTER TO EARLY SPRING - Goshawk, Sparrowhawk, Common Buzzard, Peregrine, Middle Spotted Woodpecker, Wren, Robin, Black Redstart, Blue Rock Thrush, Song and Mistle Thrush, Redwing (sporadic), Chiffchaff, Long-tailed and Coal Tit, Kruper's Nuthatch, Short-toed Treecreeper, Raven, Serin, Siskin, Cirl Bunting, Rock Bunting (occasional).

11) DIPI LARSSOS REEDBED AND SURROUNDS *(See Map 9, P234)*

This is likely to be one of the first sites glimpsed en route from the airport, being situated on your left about 9 kms outside Mytilini on the main road to Kalloni. It is the only reedbed of any size on Lesvos, so really shouldn't be neglected. Moreover, this site holds a massive roost of *feldegg* wagtails and hirundines at peak times, and is the main breeding site on the island for Little Bittern and Reed Warbler and is reliable for wintering Moustached Warbler, Marsh Harrier and occasional Pygmy Cormorant. Since from the other direction it is only about 35 mins drive from Skala Kalloni on the main road, you may wish to combine it with a trip to Agiassos (see above). Alternatively, you may decide to follow on and explore the Bay of Geras as far as you can go - ie just below Pyrgi. This route is described below.

Views of the reedbed from the main Mytilini to Kalloni road are limited except for a few pools visible when the main road skirts it just before you turn off to reach it as detailed below. However, traffic here can be quite heavy and there is nowhere to pull of and view it. To access the reedbed, therefore, do either a left from the Mytilini direction or a right off the main road from Kalloni just by the garage and opposite the obvious rocky crag onto the road leading to Perama and Plomari. This road actually skirts the whole of the southern shore of Geras Bay, and makes for quite an interesting drive (see later).

A track off to the left after 0.3 kms just before the river and leading to the shore provides the only real access, though a raised flattish area with a few spoil heaps opposite a garage just before it provides a reasonable vantage point. This track is via a gate (never so far locked and usually open), but which it may be necessary to open to gain vehicle access. This is usually driveable (albeit sometimes a bit wet and rather bumpy), but it can be very worthwhile, as in the course of the short drive to the beach an open area to the left with scattered scrub and several pools (whose perimeter may well be driveable if conditions are not too muddy - check first) often affords close views of waders, Garganey, Water Rail, chats, displaying Fan-tailed Warbler and hunting Marsh Harrier. In fact in dry conditions it is usually possible to drive as far as the large reed-enclosed pool with the obvious ruined stone building alongside it. The track skirting this traverses a small section of the reedbed and comes out further along the beach.

After continuing on to inspect the area around the river mouth (where a small inlet on the beach and the large sandspit just offshore can both be interesting for herons, egrets, waders, gulls, terns etc, not to mention chats, wheatears and larks - occasionally Calandra - on the beach) it may be worthwhile to park just as the track narrows and walk a short distance along the beach before picking up this track to the left through the reedbed and walking as far as the stone building. Although the reeds here are high and views limited, you may pick up some good warblers (Moustached for example) or the odd crake at close range. Some of these enclosed pools are also favoured by Pygmy Cormorant in winter or early spring - at which time the whole area can also be good for Marsh Harrier, Goshawk, Sparrowhawk, Buzzard and Peregrine (often attracted by the large Starling roost), for fairly scarce and localized winterers like Moustached Warbler and Reed Bunting and for a usually sizeable and often spectacular gathering of Mediterranean Gulls at the river mouth - peaking in late March (when you may also pick up the odd Oystercatcher here).

On leaving the reedbed and turning left on the Plomari road you cross the bridge over the river. This river has driveable tracks to the right on both sides, which lead, after 2.8 kms, to another bridge which brings you back on the main road to Agiassos, just before Keramia. Rubbish dumping is a major problem here, much of the water may be stagnant and views of the river are not good, owing to rampant vegetation and bushes alongside it. Nevertheless, apart from being a short-cut to the Agiassos road, the riverside scrub and willows can be excellent in season for warblers (including Whitethroat, Cetti's and Barred), and especially for Nightingale (which is often heard here before anywhere else), shrikes and flycatchers. The low-lying fields nearest the Plomari road as you first join the track are also often flooded in early spring - when they can produce good numbers of waders and considerable flocks of feeding Starlings. You can also follow the river along both banks on the other side of the Agiassos road, until extensive olive groves are reached - this also affords better views of the river, often sometimes alive with hirundines, various waders, a few egrets and storks, regular Hoopoe etc, with Short-toed Eagle and other raptors likely overhead.

Assuming, however, that one wishes to double back here and continue on the original road either to Plomari or Perama, it is worth just pointing out that the reedbed skirts this road for a further 1.5 kms, and that after a few hundred metres beyond the bridge, by another petrol station, various small tracks give some restricted views (eg one to the right just past a sharp bend after a small bridge near the end of the reedbed. This borders a run-down industrial area and is very dusty; but the small stream alongside it, though polluted with the run-off from nearby olive presses, holds a thriving population of terrapins, and is very good for Cetti's Warbler. It also proves attractive to gulls in winter).

If you follow the road through olive groves for a little over 3 kms, you can either bear right for Plomari, or carry on to Perama. Assuming you do the latter, you can turn off almost immediately left towards Napi (opposite some poplars with a large lone eucalyptus to your left) on a small reed-fringed track by the sea, with a reasonable sized pool to your right. Several early spring visits here have produced Little Grebe, Garganey, Little Ringed Plover, Kingfisher, Cetti's Warbler etc, and the track can be followed for just over 2 kms along the shoreline - possibly affording some good views of Kingfisher and the odd Black-necked Grebe in the bay or the small harbour before it eventually peters out. It is skirted by reeds for most of its length, and usually has several puddles which are likely to attract hirundines, warblers and other migrants. Another small reedbed and a deeper pool to the right of the coast road after another 1 km, has produced Buzzard and a fine adult male Marsh Harrier (probably wandering from Dipi Larssos), together with various sandpipers, Snipe etc and the strong likelihood of crakes and some good warblers if you explore further. Similar promise is held by the boggy, reedy area bordering the road for nearly 4 kms before you approach higher ground, and here a large pool is visible on your right just before the port of Perama is reached (at the end of yet another run-down industrial area). The sea and various small inlets along this stretch are always worth checking for gulls, terns and the odd wader, egret etc.

Just one word of warning - there is an army camp here alongside the beach just past Perama. Although it has 'No Photography' signs these are on the seaward side and not that obvious until you encounter them on your return. This is something I found out recently to my cost, when I stopped to photograph a nicely posing group of Sandwich Terns on the beach - only to have an armed guard in full combat gear running towards me shouting and gesticulating wildly! I took this to mean I should clear off, which I did - but on my return from Pyrgi an hour or more later I was flagged down, interrogated and (in spite of numerous protestations and bird books being waved in front of their faces) eventually had to accept confiscation of my film. Since I had just changed one and it was totally blank it was not too much of a loss! They later returned the processed films to my hotel with apologies, but be warned anyway! Just past the army camp to the right there is a further area of boggy ground with a small grassy, fairly open inlet skirted for a little way by a track to the right of it. This always looks promising, though I have not recorded anything stunning here. You can continue to skirt the coast in a southerly direction beyond Pyrgi, but the track gradually deteriorates. However, there are some quaint houses and olives and other trees stretching right down to the shoreline on one stretch - which ought to produce some migrants with a bit of luck and the right conditions. Otherwise my main sightings here have been of Great Crested and Black-necked Grebe and ever-present Kingfisher in early spring.

On your return you may wish to bear left at the port of Perama for Pappados and then on to Plomari. Indeed, when I took this route I fully intended to drive right through Plomari, and do the complete circuit, returning via Agiassos. However, be warned - you need nerves of steel to negotiate some of the narrow, cobbled and almost vertical streets (often petering out in a virtual sheer drop), with no alternative but to reverse back and try the next one! Signs appear to be virtually non-existent; and I was forced in the end to return the way I had come. Perhaps you might do better, but don't say I didn't warn you!

The list that follows omits this last area entirely, concentrating on Dipi Larssos Reedbed itself and the nearby river, coastal pools and shoreline (the reason being that on my only trip here, it poured with rain, and it simply proved impossible to locate any birds - traumatized as I was with the effects of trying to negotiate Plomari!). Moreover, I'm not too sure I should be encouraging people to linger for too long anywhere near the army camp at Perama - just in case they suffer the same fate as me!

SPRING - Little, Great Crested and Black-necked Grebe, Bittern (scarce), Little Bittern, Little Egret, Night, Squacco, Grey and Purple Heron, Garganey, Short-toed Eagle, Marsh Harrier, Goshawk, Buzzard, Long-legged Buzzard, Osprey, Kestrel, Hobby, Eleonora's Falcon, Peregrine, Water Rail, Spotted and Little Crake, Coot, Oystercatcher, Little Ringed, Kentish and Grey Plover, Little and Temminck's Stint, Ruff, Snipe, Curlew, Spotted and Common Redshank, Marsh Sandpiper, Greenshank, Green, Wood and Common Sandpiper, gulls (including Mediterranean and Slender-billed), all eight tern species possible, swifts, Kingfisher, Hoopoe, Calandra and Short-toed Lark, hirundines, Tawny Pipit, Yellow and White Wagtail, Nightingale, chats, wheatears, Cetti's, Fan-tailed, Moustached (to early spring), Sedge, Reed, Great Reed, Olivaceous and Barred Warbler, Common and Lesser Whitethroat, flycatchers, Red-backed and Woodchat Shrike, Starling (to early spring).

WINTER-EARLY SPRING - Grebes as above, Great White Egret, Grey Heron, Marsh Harrier, Goshawk, Sparrowhawk, Buzzard, Kestrel, Peregrine, Water Rail, Coot, Oystercatcher, Snipe, Curlew, Redshank, Green Sandpiper, gulls as above, Sandwich Tern, Kingfisher, Skylark, Water and Meadow Pipit, White Wagtail, Wren, Dunnock, Black Redstart, Stonechat, Cetti's, Fan-tailed and Sardinian Warbler, Starling, Reed Bunting.

12) MYTILINI AND SURROUNDS

Though this bustling and rather noisy town may, at first glance, seem a place to be avoided, it does have several redeeming features. Both accommodation and food here is quite cheap, and once you master the one-way systems and traffic-jams (virtually the only ones you are likely to encounter on the island!) you tend to view the place in a slightly more favourable light. Apart from the castle the harbour is an obvious plus point; and in addition to being quite picturesque in its own right (especially at night) it can also play host to a few wintering Great Crested and Black-necked Grebes, Kingfishers and Sandwich Terns, with Black-throated Diver possible and Great Black-backed Gull with other roosting gulls on the new breakwater in January '98 being an island first!

Both Scops and Barn Owl have been seen and heard in the middle of town, (the latter presumably making use of some of the old derelict buildings, as does the odd pair of Blue Rock Thrush some years). I have even seen Stone Curlew on the beach between the town and the airport, although it was probably a migrant. Finally, the small fertile strip of greenery bordering the road from the airport can prove attractive (especially in autumn) to a variety of migrants - wagtails, pipits, larks and wheatears for example.

Two additional sites are here worthy of mention, largely for those finding themselves near or at the airport with time to kill - a situation that is not unknown! Firstly, the headland south of the airport holds the usual Subalpine Warbler, Common and Black-eared Wheatear etc, and the sea is always worth a look for any lingering grebes in spring or migrants along the shore. Moreover, as you head south of Kratigos towards Haramida the road is particularly good for Chukar. You may wish to have a look at Haramida Reedbed, situated in a small bay, just to see why it is so productive as a ringing site - though it may only be wet in early spring. Having gone so far you may decide to carry on to Loutra and back to Mytilini that way.

Even closer at hand, there is a site within easy walking distance of the airport. On approaching from Mytilini, a track is visible bordering a stream just before a no entry sign at the start of the airport perimeter fence. This has a few stands of reed surrounding it, and acts as a magnet to birds at the appropriate times! Though it can only be followed for a few hundred metres, it may be well worth the effort. Of course, it is only wet in early spring, though the reeds may hold a few birds at other times. My first visit there in mid-April '95 produced a wealth of hirundines, *feldegg* wagtails, Wood Sandpiper, and singing Sedge, Olivaceous and River Warbler - not bad for a site almost within spitting distance of the main terminal building!

Finally, the castle itself, to the north of the town is worth a look when in the area or heading up the east coast. Being surrounded by pine trees it is home to good numbers of Serin and finches, migrant Collared Flycatcher etc, whilst both Black-eared Wheatear and Blue Rock Thrush nest in crevices in the walls, where Little, Scops and Barn Owl are also undoubtedly present. Swift flocks are regular, and include Alpine and Pallid. Finally, the coastline here and further north to Moria is good for grebes, possible Black-throated Diver in season and various gulls, Cormorant and Shag.

13) EAST COAST BETWEEN MADAMADOS AND MYTILINI (*See Map 10, P235*)

This section is described on the assumption that you are heading south from Madamados to Mytilini, largely because I prefer to view the coastline on my left - in case of a quick photo opportunity! This is also more logical because in the afternoon (when you are most likely to do this journey) you will then have the light behind you and not be looking out to sea in the glare of the sun. But this is a personal choice, and you may wish to do the journey the other way round rather than on your return from Skala Sikimmia. Either way this eastern coastal section of the island has few specific sites which attract birds, but is an easy and pleasant drive with some lovely coastal scenery; and as the small coastal islands come into view soon after Madamados, it is worth keeping an eye out for Eleonora's overhead. Short-toed Eagle and Buzzard are also likely, and the narrow section of scrub between the road and sea a little further on has one of the highest densities of scrub-loving warblers anywhere on the island, with singing Subalpine, Ruppell's and Orphean being quite obvious in spring.

If you have time on your hands, and don't mind a lot of potholes, try turning left just past Madamados (incidentally, there is a promising looking pool, before that - near Klio - which always holds plenty of gulls, the odd White Stork etc, but is unfortunately situated right next to an occupied army post; so I don't advise lingering with binoculars!). Anyway, the turning you are looking for is a minor road (or rather track) to Agios Stefanos and Palios just about where the main road from Madamados joins the coast. Though quite jarring on the back at times, this coastal headland can be good for Chukar, Short-toed Lark, warblers (especially Sardinian) wheatears and Red-rumped Swallow, and in spring various pools just before Palios can produce close views of Ruddy Shelduck, which apparently breed in some numbers in the nearby bay. It also seems a good area for reptiles, and suffers very little disturbance - not too surprising considering its rather remote location and the state of its roads!

Carrying on towards Mytilini, in fact about 11 kms before it, and 1.5 kms before the turning to Thermi, there is an obvious bridge over a small river, where it joins the sea; and a concrete ford to the right. You can drive along one bank of it on a track leading to olive groves. I visited this site several times in mid-April '95, and found it good for Kingfisher, Green, Common and Wood Sandpiper, superb for hirundines, and absolutely outstanding for wagtails, (both for White and just about all the races of Yellow Wagtail in huge numbers). Little Crake was an added bonus, and a Moorhen on eggs was actually my first breeding record for the island! Hoopoe was also very vocal in the nearby olive grove, and the call of Marsh Frogs was deafening. A week later, however, things had quietened down considerably, and by mid-May the river was down to a trickle and was largely deserted. No early spring visit since has been as productive, and it now appears rather overgrown and choked with rubbish. This all goes to show the importance of timing, and how water levels are so critical in predicting what birds you are likely to see at a given site.

On the last leg of the journey south to Mytilini, the sheltered bay near Pamfilla is ideal for close-up views of grebes (both Great Crested and Black-necked) and Shags, also, regularly fish close offshore. Before entering Mytilini, you pass the impressive ruined castle on your left, which has already been covered in the above section on Mytilini. Because this whole east coast is generally fairly non-productive and unlikely to turn up anything not possible (and easier) elsewhere, I feel there is no need to list possible species other than those mentioned above.

14) NORTH-EAST COAST VIA PETRA AND MOLIVOS (*See Map 10, P235*)

For anyone staying in the north (ie Petra, Molivos, Anaxos or Eftalou) this route is literally on their doorstep, but even from Kalloni it is only about a 40 minute drive to reach the north coast - though this particular road is full of hairpins, and can be rather tiresome if stuck behind coaches or cement lorries! Because it is not easy (and sometimes positively dangerous!) to stop on, I am not including any detail on the section from Kalloni to Petra - although I shall mention one or two worthwhile sites for the return journey. All I would recommend is that you stop at the petrol station on your right just before Petra, where you are always served with a smile and usually get your windscreen cleaned into the bargain - with a bit of coaxing this can often extend to the back and side windows as well!

Just out of the village towards Molivos you cross a small river mouth, but (like the one crossed just before Molivos) I have never encountered anything stunning here - though others have recorded breeding Kingfisher here in early June, so there is obviously potential. Though quiet in April, by mid-May this coastal stretch of road seems to be constantly heaving with commuting holidaymakers wishing to spend their time in Molivos, but finding themselves billeted out in the annexe resort of Petra. Since many of these are on foot, it can be rather frustrating trying to sit quietly in a car in either of the two coastal lay-bys (see map) which are best for viewing Ruppell's Warbler (with Peregrine and Blue Rock Thrush thrown in as a bonus). However, this is one of the most reliable places on the island to locate them, and there are some wonderful views along the coast, looking down towards Molivos and its picturesque castle on a hill (which can be an excellent spot for Alpine Swift, calling Scops and Barn Owl at night, and watching for migrants along the north coast, including the chance of a few raptors - up to 400 Red-Footed Falcons spent a day or two here in early May '95!).

Eleonoras are possible over the sea here, but the pair of Peregrines which breed on the nearby cliffs are more likely to appear while you are waiting for the Ruppell's. The first lay-by is difficult to miss, since it is situated almost opposite a strange reddish-brown amphitheatre-like structure with a mast on the top - purporting to be a disco! If the birds aren't showing well here, or singing from the bushes and wires opposite (or further up the hillside track which can be accessed only on foot) then proceed about 0.5 kms further on to the next one and try your luck there. As there are several pairs in the area they may also be found a little further on at a third lay-by, where Orphean also regularly sing (as they do sometimes from the second lay-by). To avoid the crowds, and also to get the sun directly behind you, early morning is best; though this is not quite so crucial with the second lay-by, where you have a wider angle of view. The birds tend to become progressively less active as the season advances, and disperse over a much wider area once the young are fledged - although 2 broods are quite likely. (You may then need to scan or walk the track to the landward side of the road). To get the male at its most territorial, therefore, an April or early May visit is recommended. Singing Blue Rock Thrush, Cretzschmar's and Black-headed Bunting are also likely here, and the cliff-top is often enlivened by the sight (and sound!) of a family party of Western Rock Nuthatch at close range.

Moving on from here, and assuming you don't wish to visit Molivos (which is best left to the evening in any case) you can then do a right before the town is reached. You have two choices here - either to take the first road marked to Vafios and Sikimmia, or the second to Eftalou and Skala Sikimmia. If time is short, I would suggest the first option, since it enables you to return to Petra on a track (fairly rough in places) located on your right, 1.5 kms from the main coast road. This takes you back past 'Petra Dam', a 100 hectare reservoir completed in '96 and (in spite of its fairly steep plastic sides) proving something of a magnet to duck, waders, Bee-eaters, swifts, hirundines, warblers, hunting Eleonora's and Peregrine - especially in late summer and autumn when water on this part of the island particularly is at somewhat of a premium. I also achieved my first island record of Tufted Duck here amongst numerous Little and a few Black-necked Grebe in January '98. Anything may therefore be possible, and certainly the nearby stone buildings hold Little Owl (which is rather scarce on this part of the island), and also recently hosted a Western Rock Nuthatch nest - check the far side wall of the last roadside building which overlooks the perimeter fence.

This track wends its way back to Petra for 3.5 kms, giving some superb coastal views on the way, and also the chance to connect with Orphean and Subalpine Warbler (the latter very common here), together with various raptors and the usual shrikes, buntings etc. Moreover, in spring '95, a pair of Bush Robins were present in a small triagular patch of scrub to the right, between two converging tracks just before the reservoir is reached - an area also popular with Sardinian Warbler. The only proviso with this track is that it sometimes tends to suffer disturbance from pedestrians taking a short-cut from their apartments to the beach - so again, early or mid-morning (by which time they should have completed their journey) is best. The same applies in reverse later on, and the ideal, of course, is to visit it in April or early May, before the main holiday-makers arrive! The only snag then is that it may be turned into a quagmire by heavy rain in early spring. Whilst access to the reservoir is usually possible from the Vafios end in most circumstances, I have heard fairly disturbing recent reports that the other end towards Petra is now scarcely driveable. Of course, this may well change, but at present I would suggest treating it with caution and perhaps trying it on foot to check it out.

It is also worth checking the small river which crosses the Vafios road at the junction with this track and wends its way towards the reservoir. Its scrubby surrounds can often be alive with warblers and other migrants in season, and if you continue a few kms in the Vafios direction you come to a track on your left with a yellow Greek sign, which leads after about 0.1 km to a ford - which can sometimes be good for drinking and bathing pipits, warblers and buntings, and is also the only place on the north of the island that I have so far connected with Little Bittern.

If, however, time is no object, and you have most of the day at your disposal, I would suggest the second option, which is to take the road marked Eftalou and Skala Sikimmia. You will also notice a sign 'Kastro', for the castle, which is approached by bearing left soon after the coast road. It may well be worth a stop for close-up views of nesting Black-eared Wheatear and Blue Rock Thrush, not to mention the chance of Alpine and Pallid Swift overhead, with possible raptors including Lesser Kestrel, Red-footed and Eleonora's Falcon. There are also some wonderful views to be had of Molivos and the surrounding coastline, and it is a good place to escape to in the heat of the day, when its cool recesses (and the attractions of its terrace bar!) may tempt you. At night, morever, it is all floodlit, and could provide you with views of Little, Scops and Barn Owl - all have been seen well framed in the floodlights - the latter even with young! There is also the option of exploring the fields and headland to the north-east of the castle, where (running down from the crag with a monument on the top and down the field below to the road) there is an area of surface water (certainly wet in early September '97) which is bordered by an area of greenery for about 3 metres on either side. Obviously this can prove particularly attractive to hirundines, pipits, wagtails, warblers, shrikes, buntings etc - in autumn especially, when it may well repay some time spent (assuming, of course, that it doesn't dry out in the meantime!).

Carrying on from here to Eftalou and beyond makes for a very pleasant (and scenic) coastal trip, with the road skirting the shoreline for a while before suddenly climbing quite steeply and giving more wonderful views of the sea and cliffs. Several trees and stunted bushes on the seaward side can be good sites for Northern and Black-eared Wheatear, Sombre Tit (quite regular on this stretch), singing Cirl and Cretzschmar's Bunting, and even Ruppell's Warbler. Hoopoe can usually be heard, and raptors can be surprisingly visible on occasions, with several Short-toed Eagle in the area (sometimes hovering for long periods along the cliffside), and Buzzards regularly displaying over the deciduous woodland to the right. There is also always the chance of a Peregrine, Lanner, Hobby or passing Eleonoras Falcon to liven things up! One or two small, scrubby river gulleys crossed on this route may be worth lingering at for various warblers, shrikes and other migrants - though the small army huts on the cliffside just before Eftalou definitely are not! You are very close to Turkey here don't forget, and once again I speak from painful personal experience!

Before moving on it may just be worth mentioning (especially for those staying in this location) the area known as 'Eftalou Valley', accessed by a dirt track off the tarmacked Eftalou road just before the brow of the hill on the approach to the Molivos Two hotel. The valley is situated directly behind the hotel and is accessible via a good track for 1.5 kms before a somewhat rougher 'goat track' leads into the hills. Here an olive grove at the bottom gives way to areas of boulder-strewn rock-face interspersed with trees and bushes, and a good selection of raptors, warblers, shrikes, buntings and other upland birds is possible.

But returning to the main coastal route, anywhere between here and Skala Sikimmia, (by which time the road has again dropped down to follow the shoreline) it is worth scanning the sea for wandering parties of Cory's and Mediterranean Shearwater, which can be quite numerous up to early May, and again in autumn. Shags and sometimes a few Cormorant are also likely to be seen and parties of Mediterranean Gull can often be spotted offshore between Eftalou and Skala Sikimmia up to mid or late April. Small numbers of Audouin's Gull are now also regularly being seen here (mainly from April-May but also August-September, when the odd Lesser Black-backed may appear and small numbers of raptors may commute from nearby Turkey). Moreover, the last narrow steep-sided gulley and water course heading inland just before Skala Sikimmia has been known to hold White-throated Robin in the breeding season!

This road, though very rough in places prior to spring '95, was then being 'improved', though it is currently still not tarmacked, and its condition (though usually perfectly driveable) is largely dependent on the severity of winter flooding and further remedial works - which are always difficult to predict. At all events, once the charming little fishing village of Skala Sikimmia is reached, you are quite likely to want to linger at one of the tavernas overlooking the harbour for a snack, or perhaps just a cool drink, before heading off inland again. At this point, you actually have 3 choices (apart from returning the same way you came - which is not very original!). You can either carry on past Sikimmia and Madamados, and follow the east coast down almost to Mytilini, before turning inland to Kalloni via either Moria or Thermi (see last section) or you can take either of the two shorter routes (back to Molivos via Lepetimnos and Argennos and Vafios, or rejoining the main Kalloni to Molivos road via Pelopi and Stipsi).

Which route you choose will obviously depend on the time available, but of the latter two, I rather favour the shorter route through Vafios. For a formerly minor road, this is now surprisinly good (having recently been fully tarmacked along its entire length), and produces some excellent scenery *en route*. Apart from being excellent for Subalpine, singing

Nightingale, Cirl and Cretzschmar's Bunting, it also passes the highest point on the island (Mount Lepetimnos), where both Bonelli's and Golden Eagle have been claimed and the odd pair of Rock Bunting may possibly breed. Other raptors are obviously worth looking out for, and these include Short-toed Eagle, Buzzard, Peregrine, Lanner, Eleonora's Falcon and Hobby. However, this road really scored with the discovery in mid-May '96 of 3 Hawfinches regularly drinking from a puddle 3 kms east of Vafios. This site was easier to find approaching from the Molivos end, because it was alongside the fifth culvert beyond Vafios where the ground falls away sharply to the left and the slopes are clad with a mixture of oak and plane trees. Regrettably, since the making up of the road this puddle has disappeared, and although birds were seen in nearby treetops in April '97 their drinking site was not discovered - it may have been one of the several water courses that run through here. However, in spring '98 they were only seen on one or two occasions, so don't appear to be as regular as initially hoped.

In contrast, the route via Stipsi (having been recently tarmacked at both ends, but not yet quite meeting in the middle - hopefully by '99!) whilst looking promising for raptors especially, doesn't seem to produce a great amount. Having to drive through some several villages, though quite interesting, does make it seem a bit more laborious. However, Western Rock Nuthatch is quite common on this road, and one redeeming feature is the presence of a very obvious nest plastered to the side of a roadside hut on the left 0.5 km before the 'Pelopi' sign is reached coming from Skala Sikimmia! These birds often remain faithful to the same site, and it may well still be in use in future years! Around Stipsi is also a good area for singing Cirl Bunting.

Whichever route you take, you end up back on the main Molivos to Kalloni road, which may well produce the odd good raptor on your return journey to Skala Kalloni, usually at a time when you are least able to stop! Exactly 5 kms south from the Stipsi turn-off you pass some sort of electricity sub-station to your left, with 2 largish and quite deep pools in front of it usually containing water. There are also tracks both sides of the road through pinewoods, which may be worthy of exploration - where warblers, flycatchers, Serin an other woodland birds may be present. Otherwise the final descent towards Kalloni is also good for Western Rock Nuthatch, singing Cirl and Cretzschmar's Bunting, and the view looking down to Kalloni Plain is wonderful. Finally, the raised picnic cum 'bandstand' site to your left with a small lay-by alongside about 5 kms before Kalloni may well be worth a stop. Apart from being an excellent vantage point for viewing any movement of raptors, this site has also produced nesting Ruppell's Warbler and singing Cinereous Bunting, along with more regular Cretzschmar's. It might therefore be a good place to enjoy your sandwiches or afternoon drink in a shaded location with some fine views - what more could you ask, even if the lure of Kalloni Salt Pans nestling below you may be strong?

Summing up possible birds for the whole north-east area so far described is obviously difficult, but is likely to include the following (with the sighting of birds like Rock Bunting, Bonelli's and Golden Eagle being the exception rather than the norm).

SPRING - Little Grebe (reservoir), Cory's and Mediterranean Shearwater, Cormorant (early spring), Shag, Honey Buzzard, Black Kite, Short-toed Eagle, Goshawk, Sparrowhawk, Levant Sparrowhawk, Common and Long-legged Buzzard, Bonelli's Eagle (scarce), Lesser Kestrel, Kestrel, Red-footed and Eleonora's Falcon, Hobby, Lanner, Peregrine, Chukar, Coot (reservoir), Mediterranean, Audouin's and occasional Lesser Black-backed Gull, Sandwich Tern, Woodpigeon, Turtle Dove, Cuckoo, Barn Owl (castle), Scops (castle, Petra and Molivos), and occasional Little Owl, Tawny Owl (Petra), Nightjar, swifts, Bee-eater (localized), Roller, Hoopoe, Middle Spotted Woodpecker, Red-rumped Swallow, Tawny Pipit, Rufous Bush Robin (reservoir), Nightingale, Stonechat, Northern and Black-eared Wheatear, Blue Rock Thrush, Icterine, Subalpine, Ruppell's, Orphean and Barred Warbler, Common and Lesser Whitethroat, Blackcap, Eastern Bonelli's and Wood Warbler, flycatchers, Sombre Tit, Western Rock Nuthatch, Golden Oriole, Red-backed, Woodchat and

Masked Shrike, Rose-coloured Starling, Hawfinch, Cirl, Ortolan, Cretzschmar's and Black-headed Bunting.

AUTUMN - Little Grebe (reservoir), Cory's and Mediterranean Shearwater, Cormorant, Shag, Garganey (reservoir), raptors as above (except for Red-footed Falcon), Chukar, Coot (reservoir), waders including Black-winged Stilt, stints and sandpipers, Redshank and Greenshank (reservoir), gulls as above, occasional marsh terns (reservoir), Woodpigeon, Turtle Dove, Cuckoo, swifts (Alpine especially), Kingfisher, Bee-eater, Roller, Hoopoe, Middle Spotted Woodpecker, Sand and Crag Martin, Red-rumped Swallow, Tawny Pipit, Isabelline, Northern and Black-eared Wheatear, Blue Rock Thrush, warblers as above, flycatchers, Red-backed and Woodchat Shrike, Hawfinch, buntings as above (rarely beyond August).

WINTER (reservoir) - Little and Black-necked Grebe, Pochard, Tufted Duck (irregular), Buzzard, Kestrel, Lanner, Peregrine, Coot, gulls, Water Pipit, White Wagtail, Robin, Black Redstart, Stonechat, Blue Rock Thrush, Song Thrush, Sardinian Warbler, Chiffchaff.

15) NORTH-WEST COAST VIA PETRA AND ANAXOS *(See Map 11, P236)*

Although this area is not one of my regular haunts, it is one in which many birders booking package holidays often find themselves based; and in consequence I have been sent a good number of interesting records that suggest it really has very good birding potential. Though short on wetlands, apart from the odd small river mouth (eg along the coast road just before Petra, plus the small water-course opposite the football pitch) and the reed-fringed pools on Anaxos beach (which nevertheless seem to turn up some good birds like Thrush Nightingale and Moustached Warbler) it has some productive olive groves and an offshore island (known as 'Rabbit Island') and also excellent areas of oak woodland between Skoutaros and Skalochori, with its own associated bird species like Nuthatch and Hawfinch - quite localized elsewhere.

Pleasant as Petra may be as a resort (with its bustling market and attractive chapel built on a large rock where Wallcreeper was claimed in '96!) I normally tend to leave the beach (with its collection of sun loungers and heaving flesh!) behind me as quickly as possible and head out on the now excellent and recently tarmacked coastal route to Anaxos. The cliffs here looking out towards 'Rabbit Island' usually produce noisy feeding parties of Jackdaws, whilst Eleonora's and Alpine Swift can sometimes be seen in good numbers - especially later into the summer. At night this stretch of road (like the approaches to Molivos) regularly turns up Nightjar in spring and summer, which find the scrubby hillsides much to their liking. In fact they can even be seen hawking insects from the taverna on Anaxos beach! You can also witness some stunning sunsets in this location, and it may be worth turning down the short road to the main resort just to check out the reedy pool already mentioned. It seems to be surrounded by hotel encroachment, and may not stay wet too far into the spring, but is obviously worth a few visits if you're staying in the area.

Otherwise I would tend to press on, perhaps checking the small river that briefly skirts the road after 1 km before heading inland past Skoutaros (through some potentially productive olive groves and on a still excellent road with a promising ridge to your left). Here you carry straight past the village with a sheer drop to your right and a steep ridge with poplars below. At the same time there is a river course parallel to the road on your right, which you then cross before doing a sharp right on the track to Skalochori, by now (at least up to spring '98) visibly deteriorating and full of potholes. However, after exactly 2.5 kms from the start of this track is where I struck gold in May '98 with the discovery of a new site for Olive-tree Warbler! If you are coming from the other direction this site is 3.6 kms from Skalochori, and it consists of a mixture of oaks and olives (particularly favoured by this species) with a drystone wall at the side of the track on which brushwood has been placed. This will be on your left coming from Skoutaros, though the birds may be singing or perching either side of the road - but especially on the brushwood (see picture 49).

Judging by the amount of activity here in May '98 there must have been at least 7 territories in the area, and this is confirmed by others. Even if Olive-tree Warbler were not present (or are not active later in the season or not yet arrived earlier in April) this is still an outstanding area for some otherwise fairly locally distributed or difficult birds - eg Hoopoe (5 calling birds), Nuthatch and Hawfinch (2 seen). Masked Shrike also breed nearby, together with Orphean and Subalpine Warbler, Whitethroat, Cirl Bunting etc with Stonechat likely and Short-toed Eagle, Goshawk, both Buzzards, Eleonora's Falcon and various raptors possible overhead. This is also near to the site where White-backed Woodpecker was reported - albeit back in '87! All in all it may just be worth braving a few potholes for such goodies!

Carrying on to Skalochori it's always worth checking the drystone walls for churring Nightjar (sometimes audible during the day) and just before the village is reached you pass a more fertile area bordered by ditches and usually with a few pools - one especially to your right looking fairly permanent and inhabited by a good number of terrapins. Shrikes are regular along here and Red-rumped Swallow is also likely. A dirt track heading off to the right just before the village is marked to Ancient Andissa and Gavathas, and it ought logically to be possible to do this route and then rejoin the main Kalloni to Sigri road at Andissa. In practice I failed dismally to complete the circuit and found it fairly rough and dusty - but things could change, and there is the odd river mouth and valley to explore for the adventurous. Nevertheless, I think on balance I prefer to rejoin the main road at Skalochori - which is actually quite straightforward if you just keep straight on through the village and square on a concrete road and don't deviate at all - famous last words those! Of course, you can do an even shorter circuit by rejoining the main road at Filia from the Skoutaros direction, and not do a right on the rough track at all - but you might miss an awful lot by so doing, and who knows, they may make up another section of it soon!

Anyway, depending on the time of day you can either do a left back to Kalloni or head on west to Sigri, which is the only area still to be covered after a quick rundown of some of the bird species posible on the route so far described (spring coverage only).

SPRING - Shearwaters, Cormorant, Shag, Honey Buzzard, Short-toed Eagle, Goshawk, Sparrowhawk, Levant Sparrowhawk, Buzzard, Long-legged Buzzard, Lesser Kestrel, Red-footed and Eleonora's Falcon, Chukar, Nightjar, swifts, Roller, Hoopoe, Wryneck, Middle Spotted Woodpecker, Woodlark, Red-rumped Swallow, Tree Pipit, Thrush Nightingale, Nightingale, Stonechat, wheatears, Blue Rock Thrush, Mistle Thrush, Moustached Warbler (Anaxos), Olive-tree Warbler, Icterine, Subalpine, Sardinian, Orphean and Barred Warbler, Common and Lesser Whitethroat, Blackcap, Eastern Bonelli's and Wood Warbler, flycatchers, Sombre Tit, Common and Western Rock Nuthatch, Golden Oriole, Red backed, Woodchat and Masked Shrike, Jackdaw, Hawfinch, buntings.

AUTUMN - Most of above possible.

16) POTAMIA RIVER *(See Maps 1 & 3, P226 & 228)*

This follows on from Kalloni West River 1.7 kms to the west of it - so (along with Parakila Marsh) is certainly worth a quick look on any trips to the west of the island.. It is driveable to its seaward side on one bank, but disturbance from lorries using the adjoining aggregate works is tiresome, and high vegetation makes visibility difficult. If you ignore the tethered, barking guard dogs at the small depot you can actually drive much further alongside the river - where a track leads to a small house. You can then explore the river mouth, beach and small pools to your right on foot if you wish - the area certainly looks promising. Bee-eaters usually nest (judging by the holes in the bank) and the usual species can occur near the river mouth, including Stone Curlew and Black Stork. On its landward side, it is driveable along both banks; and this is less disturbed (excepting occasional locals on mopeds and traffic of sheep!) and easier to observe. It usually seems to have water, even in autumn, though spring is obviously more productive. It also holds nesting Little Grebe, and can be good for hirundines, Yellow Wagtails, Little Bittern and Squacco Heron in season. The side beyond the bridge from the Kalloni direction is usually more productive and less rough, and is also easier to turn round on - it leads to a farm after about 1km or less. The river can also be accessed from various bridges or concrete fords further up the Potamia Valley, but here tends to be narrower, faster flowing and less productive - except perhaps for feeding Black Stork. Maybe a Dipper will turn up one day!

SPRING - Little Grebe, Black and White Stork, Squacco, Night and Grey Heron, Little Bittern, Marsh and Montagu's Harrier, Little Crake, Stone Curlew, Green, Wood and Common Sandpiper, gulls (mainly Yellow-legged), White-winged Black and Whiskered Tern, Kingfisher, Bee-eater, Hoopoe, hirundines (often *en masse*), Yellow and White Wagtail, Cetti's, Olivaceous, Sedge, Reed and Great Reed Warbler, Cirl, Ortolan, Black-headed and Corn Bunting.

AUTUMN - EARLY SPRING - Little and occasional Black-necked Grebe, Bittern (scarce), Great White Egret, Hen Harrier, Buzzard, Green Sandpiper, White Wagtail, Kingfisher, Crag Martin, Sardinian Warbler, Chiffchaff, Serin.

17) PARAKILA MARSH *(See Map 12, P237)*

This is reached by continuing west along the above-mentioned road from Kalloni to Parakila. It is situated approx 10 kms from Kalloni and about 4 kms beyond the Potamia River (about 1km before the sign to Parakila village). The marsh, easily seen to the right of the road, is only really worth a visit between winter and late spring, after which it rapidly dries up. To help matters, it is bisected by a rough, but perfectly driveable track and is also skirted by a track on the Kalloni side which leads up to a farm. If conditions are not too wet it may be possible to drive in via one and back by the other. It's usually only the small area by the gate at the end of the middle track that can sometimes be a little tricky to negotiate. Of course, you can walk round, but this usually flushes everything almost immediately, so isn't entirely recommended! To my knowledge, the area has not produced any stunning rarities, but always merits a quick look when one is passing (which one is bound to be at some stage). The whole marsh is nowhere near as open as it used to be, and for this reason viewing (especially from the middle section where locals regrettably still sometimes go to dump rubbish!) is not straightforward. Skulking species like crakes (though common enough on passage) may well require a bit of patience to connect with - though birds like Marsh Harrier are obviously much easier (unless perched of course!). Several pairs of Black-winged Stilt nest, and often get up to mob raptors like the above - which can be helpful, and sometimes very spectacular!

There is also a small river outlet and pool on the beach just before the marsh starts. This is conveniently situated at the end of a lay-by so that you can pull over and observe it. Although this may be already virtually dry by the end of April and possibly overgrown, in the right conditions it can turn up waders like Little Ringed Plover and Common Sandpiper, together with wagtails and pipits. I have also had Ortolan Bunting here, so anything may be possible. Finally, the fields immediately before the marsh are usually wet at this time, and the ditches, pools and reedy areas here regularly attract quartering Marsh Harrier and occasional Bittern in early spring. You may also want to take a last look at the sea here for close grebes etc before heading off inland towards Agra.

SPRING - Little Grebe, Bittern, Little Bittern, Night, Squacco, Grey and Purple Heron, Little Egret, Glossy Ibis, Garganey, Shoveler (early spring only), Marsh Harrier (usually present), Hobby, Little and Spotted Crake, Water Rail, Black-winged Stilt, Avocet,

Little Ringed and Kentish Plover, Little Stint, Wood, Green and Common Sandpiper, swifts and hirundines, Fan-tailed, Savi's, Sedge, Reed and Olivaceous Warbler.

WINTER-EARLY SPRING - Little Grebe, Shoveler, Hen Harrier, Marsh Harrier, Water Rail, Coot, Moorhen, Water Pipit, Fan-tailed Warbler, Stonechat, Reed Bunting.

18) SOUTH OF PARAKILA - 'DEVIL'S BRIDGE' *(See Map 12, P237)*

Continue on the coast road by-passing Parakila (but pausing in early spring to inhale the wonderful intoxicating scent of orange blossom!) and you pass an old ruined minarette on your left after 0.4 kms - from which one lucky observer once recorded Barn Owl emerging at dusk, and where Sombre Tit has also been found nesting. After another 0.4 km there is a sharp bend to the left by a small bridge or culvert. Pull in to the right, at a small lay-by with a green bench and drinking fountain, and you will see some steps, leading up after about a hundred metres to a small chapel. Apart from a site inland from the East River, (which may or may not be a regular one), this is the nearest place to Skala Kalloni to connect easily with Cinereous Bunting, which can often be observed singing from the top of a large tree just left of the chapel - the dead poplar it used to frequent has regrettably blown down! There are also several other buntings present, and Nightjar has occasionally been flushed here. In short it is quite a good area to get a taste of upland birds when heading west, being pleasantly shaded in places and therefore making an ideal lunch venue.

SPRING - Short-toed Eagle, Goshawk, Long-legged Buzzard, Eleonora's Falcon, swifts, Hoopoe, Red-rumped Swallow, pipits, Black-eared Wheatear, Blue Rock Thrush, flycatchers, Sombre Tit, Western Rock Nuthatch, Golden Oriole, Cirl, Cinereous, Cretzschmar's and Black-headed Bunting.

19) WEST OF THE ISLAND - ERESSOS AND APPROACHES FROM KALLONI
(See Map 12, P237)

I have saved the west of the island until last because, after the Kalloni area, it is my personal favourite. It is certainly a wilder area, and though rather isolated as a base, it holds a good mix of birds (some fairly localized); and makes for an excellent and fulfilling day out. There are two ways of reaching Eressos from Kalloni - one is on main roads up the middle of the island (tarmacked but full of hairpin bends and not always easy to stop on). The other is the partly coastal route via Agra and Messotopos (now fully tarmacked to the latter and beyond - with further improvements due, if not already carried out.) For the purpose of simplicity I shall deal with the former on the return journey to Kalloni, though you may wish to do it the other way round. Either way both routes are productive and have various areas worth investigating on your way - which you must be aware by now applies to almost anywhere on Lesvos!

This latter route tends to be a more pleasant and relaxing drive, with less traffic, and more opportunities to stop at short notice and has already been documented beyond Parakila Marsh and up to and including 'Devil's Bridge' (see site guides 17 and 18 above). Between there and Agra (a distance of about 16 kms) the road becomes more winding, with some impressive scenery and increasingly open, rocky terrain. Throughout, upland birds like Black-eared Wheatear, Cinereous, Corn and Cretzschmar's Bunting, Western Rock Nuthatch and Rock Sparrow tend to predominate, with the odd raptor possible almost anywhere.

Just a km or so beyond 'Devil's Bridge' there is a surprisingly good track off to the left by a pool and culvert signposted Apothikes and Makara (on what is currently a fairly small and basic sign). However, it is virtually the only turning off the main road, so can hardly be missed, and is also situated just beyond an impressive elevated view of the mouth of Kalloni Bay, with a noticeable wetland area and river mouth below which always looks promising - though often appears strangely devoid of birds. This track actually boasts a near lunar landscape in places, which is much appreciated by Western Rock Nuthatch, Sombre Tit, buntings and passing raptors such as buzzards, occasional eagles and Eleonora's Falcon. Anyway, after 1.3 kms it bends left to the small fishing village of Apothikes and you may wish to carry on and explore that area (excellent in places for Western Rock Nuthatch) and the river mouth mentioned above.

Various rocky tracks radiate out from the village skirting the coast (some being rougher than others - eg the one to your left which briefly follows the coast and then looks down on the inlet and sandbars already mentioned). Undoubtedly this could be productive at times, but my chief memories of the area are somewhat clouded by an extended stay in a local fisherman's abode whilst frantic phone calls were being made to get my car towed back to Kalloni after its driveshaft somehow became disconnected in a particularly remote spot on a bitterly cold early April evening! In spite of the language barrier they made me extremely welcome and refused any money for phone calls etc. After several hours and the harrowing experience of being towed back along hairpin bends in the dark with no steering and only the prospect of a glass of five star Metaxa to warm me on my return to keep me going, I can somehow never bring myself to view that track in a totally objective way again!

The alternative route is to do what I normally do and take a right to Makara. This takes you past some fairly uniform rocky terrain with a few larger outcrops to the left (potentially good for breeding Sombre Tit) and some small buildings later on your right (often holding fairly prominent Little Owl!). A riverbed is then visible below to your right, bordered by a small cultivated area of olives, figs etc with a few more scattered buildings. Rather bizarrely you then pass on the seaward side an old abandoned tank in a ramshackle wooden housing (which of course may eventually be removed - though this so far seems unlikely!), after which, just beyond a small stony beach the river mouth and ford are reached. There is also an old bridge here, and this is a good point at which to pause and view the river - which is certainly still wet into May most years. I have recorded good numbers of Alpine Swifts and hirundines feeding over the river mouth and bay in April, together with a large flock of migrating Night Heron in early May '98 and a reasonable selection of waders. Some have also observed movements of shearwaters and gulls here heading up the gulf, and there is clearly migration potential for various wagtails, larks, pipits etc. Moreover, it is possible to proceed a short distance along the track the other side of the river leading up to a small farm; and here is an excellent scrubby area for warblers and shrikes. Lesser Grey was showing particularly well here in late April '98, as was Rufous Bush Robin on one or two ocasions - to give just two examples. However, if time is short and you wish to reach the Eressos area sooner rather than later, then simply retrace your steps the 4 kms back to the main road and press on to Agra - perhaps pausing to check the rocky gulley and watercourse with scattered trees that you cross a couple kms before Agra for possible warblers, flycatchers etc.

Just remember, after entering Agra, to do a left to Messotopos just past the ancient plane tree in the square. This used to be signposted in Greek, but the sign may by now have changed. Either way it is a very obvious left, leading out of the village on a road with pine clad slopes which very soon opens out just past some ancient stone fortifications into some distinctly rugged terrain with some sheer drops to your left. This used to be just a dusty track, but has now been greatly 'improved' over the last few years - although possibly with a certain loss of character. The scenery now starts to become even more spectacular as you head further west, though the immediate surroundings can be a bit barren at times.

The area 3 kms beyond Agra is worth a look for a good chance of Rock Sparrow in the breeding season. Here, alongside a concrete culvert on your left with a line of 4 red and black broken markers (ie like a half finished crash barrier) and a dilapidated building just beyond with a corrugated iron flat roof with rubbish on it, there is a large mound about 10 metres beyond the culvert with a large rock on top stained white with droppings at its base.

With a bit of patience this should produce calling Rock Sparrow (which presumably nest just below the culvert) and also singing Black-eared Wheatear and possible displaying Rufous Bush Robin - with both Cretzschmar's and Cinereous Bunting present in the area. In fact this whole route to Messotopos is good for most of the upland species mentioned above, and also for regular roadside sightings of Little Owl - rather surprising in such bleak terrain.

Although Messotopos (reached after 8kms) is by-passed, you may wish to make yet another deviation here and turn off left on the coastal route to to Tavari and Kroussos. This used to be a very rough and dusty track, but has now been dramatically improved along most of its length (rather illogically from the coast working back and not the other way round!); so presumably the beach area here is scheduled for some sort of development - once again the magical wooden shower cubicles have appeared! Nonetheless, at present it is still a very quiet and potentially productive area with several fords and two river mouths (at Tavari and Kroussos) worthy of exploration. To reach this area simply take a left at the signpost saying 'Eressos 12' on leaving Messotopos (ie the town sign with a cross through it). This will be marked to Tavari, Kroussos (sometimes spelt Crousos) and Podaras. Then bear right at a blue sign to all three on a wall to your left, and after 2.7 kms of fairly rugged terrain you reach another blue sign to Kroussos or its alternative spelling on your right.

Immediately below here is a ford over the small river which skirts the right hand side of the road, and this is Tavari ford - a scrubby watercourse with rocks and a drystone wall above. The ford itself is very shallow, and may be down to barely a trickle by mid or late May, but it can act as a magnet to birds from the surrounding area wishing to drink and bathe. These include various wagtails, warblers, shrikes, finches and buntings, and both Rock Sparrow and Rufous Bush Robin can be regular - so it may well be worth viewing for half an hour or so whilst having lunch or whatever (in spite of sometimes rather tiresome disturbance from commuting locals in pick-ups who seem to insist on hooting as they drive through!).

There is a circuit you can do here which involves crossing the ford and heading off on the track to Kroussos. You then come to a second ford after 1.2 kms, with 2 farms on the right just before a rocky area with some old buildings, and then yet another ford (which may well be dry) after a further 0.3 km with a large oak opposite. There are actually a fair number of scattered oaks on this section of rocky, fairly sparsely vegetated hillside - which should produce warblers, shrikes, buntings etc, with Hoopoe likely and Little Owl possible on the farm buildings further on to your left. At this point you find yourself climbing steeply,and about 2 kms beyond the third ford you do a left seawards at a blue sign for Tavari (pausing to check out the cattle drinking pool to your right on the corner). There is an especially promising bush to your right here which always looks good for shrikes, and actually produced both Red-backed and Lesser Grey at the same time in late April '97!

After another 0.8 kms you come to some cliffs, which may produce Crag Martin, the odd Kestrel or other raptor and the inevitable Little Owl! After this point you drop down steeply and follow the coast until after a further 0.8 kms you come to Tavari river mouth and harbour - where you will encounter what (to women at least) is a particularly welcome sign in blue- 'Toilets here!' Apart from a few wagtails and the odd Little Ringed Plover I haven't personally recorded too much here, but others staying nearby have done much better for waders etc. Either way it's a nice spot to have lunch before turning back inland on the road you first came in on. This shortly takes you alongside the river which you originally crossed at Tavari ford, and this section parallel (and close to) the road on your left is obviously worth checking - although fairly narrow and rocky. Just remember shortly before rejoining the main road to Eressos to bear left at the blue Greek sign to it (amongst other destinations), or you will find yourself ending up back in Messotopos.

From here on through to Eressos, once you have crossed a small bridge over a river with poplars to your right the area gradually becomes more fertile, especially once you begin your descent to the Eressos Plain (a mosaic of small fig and almond orchards, olives, oaks, scrub and cultivated fields, often, like elsewhere on the island, still farmed in a largely traditional manner). Before you finally drop down to the large bridge over the Chalandra River you will pass a ridge with a radio mast which can often be good for raptors moving through. I have several times had Honey Buzzard here (being 'escorted' by resident Long-legged), and Hobby, Eleonora's Falcon and several unidentified eagles into the bargain. The steep oak covered hillsides you will have passed on your left can also regularly turn up Golden Oriole. However, it is in the area of Eressos Plain that you can really score with migrants in good 'fall' conditions, and the roadside fences and bushes (together with an obvious pool to your right a couple of kms or so before the Chalandra River) are likely to prove productive in spring for perched shrikes and Whinchats (often quite numerous), together with Bee-eaters pipits, warblers, flycatchers etc. Whilst passing through this cultivated and fertile area, it used to be worth checking a small pool (or rather a large puddle!) on your left a little way before the river bridge. This was often used by wagtails, pipits etc, and by Common and Red-rumped Swallows as a source of mud - though in recent years this appears to have been dry.

Anyway, as already mentioned, 10 kms beyond Messotopos, and 1 km before the main Eressos to Skala Eressos road junction is reached, a bridge takes you across the Chalandra River, which at this point (depending on winter rainfall and time of year) may be almost dry, especially to the right of the bridge. The first bank to the right is driveable, with care, for about 1km, but after that it is probably better to walk (and if I say that it must be rough!). To find the main quarry species here (Rufous Bush Robin), it may be necessary to walk as far again up the dry river bed. Of course, there are other things to see here as well - it is a good area for shrikes and flycatchers, there is usually a small Bee-eater colony to the right in some sandbanks; and from late April to late May, the whole area is heavy with the scent of Jacantha (or Spanish Broom). You can also drive along the river both sides to the left of the bridge, and follow it to Skala Eressos. If you encounter any obstacles on one side it is usually possible to cross on one of the concrete fords to the other side and continue your journey.

Whilst this river may not have a great flow of water, there are usually one or two productive stretches, and apart from Little Egrets, occasional Night Heron, Little Bittern etc and a reasonable selection of waders, this section between the two bridges also produced a pair of Citrine Wagtail on several occasions from mid-April to early May '98. Morever, the riverside trees hosted a good number of Pied, Collared and even a few Semi-collared Flycatchers during the big 'fall' of *ficedula* flycatchers in late April that year. Finally, the track to the left was also notable that year for producing nesting Nuthatch sharing a dead poplar with a Middle-Spotted Woodpecker just a few hundred metres from the Messotopos road bridge. Amazingly (and even after 10 visits) this was a new island bird for me - so this area has clearly gone up in my estimation!

If you had carried on along the main Messotopos road towards Eressos and then done a left at the T junction by the football pitch, you would have come, after 1.5 kms to the same bridge over the Chalandra river that these tracks have led you to. Here you can follow the riverside tracks on both sides for a further 1 km to the sea and beyond to Skala Eressos. This is usually the most productive stretch (often alive with shrikes on passage) and the concrete ford to Skala Eressos can be excellent in spring for close views of waders, wagtails, mud-gathering hirundines, Little Egret, Squacco Heron and Little Bittern especially. There are often birds coming down to drink here, and the whole area is good for shrikes, buntings, Cetti's, Nightingale, Bee-eater etc (though marsh terns are not encountered in quite the same numbers as the Kalloni area). Between the ford and the sea is usually the best area for Purple Heron, (and in autumn, being the only stretch that is wet, it is excellent for Kingfisher and Water Rail). There is a pleasant beach here, though be warned that a section of it is nudist - so be wary where binoculars and long lenses are concerned!

The ford obviously suffers some disturbance from locals using it as a short-cut to the beach; and this is worse now that a new 300 room hotel has recently been completed at the end of the right-hand river bank, and this, together with the construction of additional holiday acccomodation alongside the river has also degraded some of the bankside vegetation, (especially the channel and small bridge nearest the main Skala Eressos road). For this reason, and because of increasing amounts of rubbish in the river, I no longer find this area quite a pleasant or productive as it once was; but it will undoubtedly continue to turn up some good birds - like the Penduline Tit discovered here in April '98, regular Wryneck, occasional Red-breasted Flycatcher and continued sightings of Citrine Wagtail. Moreover, a couple who stayed in Skala Eressos in autumn and who did all their birding on foot rated this area very highly, and recorded good visible migration of birds like Night Heron, swifts, hirundines etc - not to mention regular movements of raptors along the ridge just behind their apartment!

To sum up then, if you follow the right bank (which usually gives the closest views), in order to be able to view or photograph with the light behind you it is best to visit from late afternoon. The advantage of this area is that it can be worked quite quickly, and easily fitted in on a trip to Eressos or Sigri from the Kalloni area - in which case, of course, you may have to visit a little earlier and not get the light exactly in your favour, or end up returning by this route instead (such are the dilemmas of the bird photographer!).

The nearby fields, too, are always worth checking out - especially those en route to the new hotel opposite the 'Primitive Club', and also those over the ford on your left, just before the village. At passage times, various chats, wagtails and pipits are usually attracted to feed around the irrigators (especially in autumn), whilst in winter mixed flocks of Skylark and Woodlark are often to be found. If you continue to the new hotel complex you can then turn left through tamarisks onto another beach with low spiky scrub and a wonderful display of wildflowers in early spring. You can actually drive for 0.4 km to view a small cliff face beyond a longish pool with occasional Kentish and Little Ringed Plover before it presumably dries out in late spring. The cliffs may hold Crag Martin and Red-rumped Swallow, and the beach itself regular Northern Wheatear and Tawny Pipit, Skylark up to early spring, and occasional Hoopoe and Wryneck. No doubt many other migrants are possible, and some seawatching should produce various gulls and shearwaters at the appropriate times.

Those visiting for longer, or staying around Skala Eressos, will no doubt be tempted to explore the hillside behind the village, which usually enjoys a good selection of migrants in season, and also holds several of the usual upland species, including breeding Ruppell's Warbler, Blue Rock Thrush, Masked Shrike and a good chance of Cinereous Bunting. The fields and fig groves to the east of Skala Eressos have also been described as very productive, as has the path leading inland from the eastern end of the beach, and then between the area known as 'Sappho's Hill' and the escarpment further east and thence back into the resort. This has been passed on to me as a recommended early morning route (especially in autumn) by someone who once spent his honeymoon here - beats me where he found the energy!

Anyway, leaving Skala Eressos behind, and pushing on the short distance to Eressos (where several garages will give you the opportunity to top up with petrol) you may wish to explore the upland area behind the town by way of a change. This location (the so-called 'twin peaks' near the farm just above Eressos town) was originally associated in previous literature with Cinereous Bunting, before it was realized how comparatively easy they were to locate further east.

To find the particular spot (not always easy) you take the very last track you come to off Eressos Square, after driving up the hill from Skala Eressos direction. There will be a cafe immediately to your right, and though very narrow initially this track is driveable for up to 3 kms past a farm on your right and up into the hills. This takes you over a small water course fairly early on, with large rocks at the side, and I once had a pair of Cinereous Bunting bathing here with a number of Cretzschmar's. The track can be very rough in places, and is not for the faint-hearted! - though the views can be impressive, and the rugged terrain is a likely spot for

Peregrine, Long-legged Buzzard, Short-toed Eagle etc, and Black-eared Wheatear, Western Rock Nuthatch and Cretzschmar's Bunting are all abundant, with Rock Sparrow likely.

The list that follows covers the birds that are likely in the areas and on the route so far described; bearing in mind that marshland birds are largely confined to the rivers and river mouths mentioned.

SPRING - (River areas and coast) - Shearwaters, Cormorant, Shag, Little Bittern, , Night and Squacco Heron, Little Egret, Grey and Purple Heron, Black and White Stork, Honey Buzzard, Long-legged Buzzard, Short-toed and other possible eagles, Lesser Kestrel, Hobby, Eleonora's Falcon, Lanner, Peregrine, Chukar, Little Crake, Little Ringed and Kentish Plover, Little and Temminck's Stint, Curlew Sandpiper, Ruff, Spotted Redshank, Greenshank, Green, Wood and Common Sandpiper, gulls, Caspian (rare), Sandwich and occasional marsh terns, Rock Dove, Turtle Dove, Cuckoo, Little Owl, swifts, Bee-eater, Roller, Hoopoe, Wryneck, Middle-Spotted Woodpecker, Short-toed Lark, Woodlark, Skylark (to early spring), Crag Martin, hirundines, Tawny and Tree Pipit, Yellow, Citrine and White Wagtail, Rufous Bush Robin, Nightingale, Redstart, chats, Northern and Black-eared Wheatear, Blue Rock Thrush, Cetti's, Great Reed, Olivaceous, Icterine, Subalpine, Sardinian, Orphean, Ruppell's and Barred Warbler, Blackcap, Common and Lesser Whitethroat, Wood and Willow Warbler, all 5 flycatchers possible, Sombre Tit, Nuthatch and Western Rock Nuthatch, Golden Oriole, all 4 Shrike species, Jackdaw, Rose-coloured Starling (Skala Eressos area from mid-May), Spanish Sparrow, Rock Sparrow, finches and Linnet, all 6 bunting species.

AUTUMN - (mainly coast and river areas) - Cormorant, Night Heron, Little Egret, Grey Heron, raptors as above, Water Rail, sandpipers, gulls, Turtle Dove, swifts, Kingfisher, Bee-eater, Hoopoe, Wryneck, Tawny and Meadow Pipit, Yellow, Grey and White Wagtail, Redstart, chats, wheatears, Blue Rock Thrush, Cetti's and Sardinian Warbler, Blackcap, Wood and Willow Warbler, Spotted Flycatcher, Nuthatch, Western Rock Nuthatch, Red-backed and Woodchat Shrike.

70

20) ERESSOS TO SIGRI VIA IPSILOU MONASTERY *(See Map 13, P238)*

This is probably one of the wildest areas of the island, and is arguably one of the best for falls of migrants in spring - exactly why the west coast often seems to attract more than its fair share of migrants is not altogether clear; but in my experience, it certainly seems to be the case. Once again, there are two possible routes - through the middle of the island or along the coast. As is often the case, the former is tarmacked but full of hairpins; the latter probably more interesting (especially where it crosses a river valley and skirts the coast just before Sigri), but it is very rough in places (especially the last 10 kms before Sigri). Ideally, I would approach Sigri on the main road and return on the semi-coastal route in the late afternoon, when migrants seem to be most in evidence, and the light is mainly behind you.

Because the last 10 kms of this route are so rough (though I have it on good authority that it is now a good deal better, and I certainly managed it OK at least once in spring '98!), some people prefer merely to approach from Eressos and then double back when the ford is reached (see map) and the going becomes too difficult for them. That is a pity, as this can be the most productive stretch, and if taken really carefully, the jarring and bone-shaking one often received was frequently outweighed by the birds and the scenery! At all events, I think it worth experiencing once: (though I did feel rather guilty recommending it - in all innocence - to a couple in a four wheel drive vehicle; when I later learnt that one of them was just convalescing from a haemorrhoid operation!). Since the condition of this road could go either way over the next year or so (some reporting that it was nowhere near as bad as they thought, or had actually been improved from the Sigri end - whilst others vowed they'd never attempt it again!), I'll just have to leave it to the individual to check it out and return the same way if they're not happy!

Anyway, proceeding out of Eressos on the main road to the Sigri junction (a winding road of just under 10 kms with some stunning upland scenery and several plus points en route; one being that this is an excellent road for Rock Sparrow, which some seem to experience trouble locating elsewhere - several pairs breed in the vertical roadside rock-face about 4.5 kms outside Eressos (5.2 kms from the Sigri junction if coming the other way), and can often be seen perched on posts or wires bordering the road. There are several opportunities for viewing Cinereous Bunting (especially where the road crosses some steep gulleys), and Red-rumped Swallow also breed under most of these culverts. Other buntings, shrikes and Western Rock Nuthatch are all quite easy, and even the odd pair of breeding Ruppell's Warbler occurs - actually along a narrow steep-sided gulley located by the first noticeable concrete culvert with a weight limit or '30 T ' sign. This is 5.2 kms from Eressos (or 4.3 kms coming from Sigri - in which case it is the third large culvert). A short walk of about 100 metres should locate them in the breeding season. Woodlark and various buntings are also regular here. Finally, 1.4 kms before you reach the main Sigri road junction, a river runs parallel to the road for a short distance on your left, and you look down at this point on an obvious ford approached by a track leading to a farm beyond. This seems to have a reasonable flow up to early or mid-May at least, and proves attractive to drinking and bathing Rock Sparrow, finches, buntings, etc. It may be worth a short stop, especially at a time when water is scarce elsewhere.

At the Sigri junction do a left, and anywhere in this immediate area (for the next km or so until you pass the stone farm building on the right) you are likely to connect with the very localized Isabelline Wheatear. At least 2 or 3 pairs normally breed here, and can often be seen singing from roadside posts and rocks, or hovering by the road. Northern Wheatear may also be present in the area., whilst Red-footed Falcons also sometimes appear on this stretch on passage for a few days (as in spring '95, when they could be observed on roadside rocks and wires for several days in early May). Continuing on as far as the Ipsilou monastery, this is another excellent spot with great migration potential and some sought-after breeding birds, and it is well worth the short drive up to it (steep though it is, and not for those who suffer from vertigo!). The monastery itself can be seen, nestling high on top of a sheer rock-face, from some distance away, and the track of about 1km to its summit is clearly marked.

On the way up (apart from watching the sheer drop to your right!) look out for Cinereous Bunting and Woodlark singing from roadside rocks or trees, and especially for close views of Blue Rock Thrush and also Rock Thrush which has now been proven breeding in the area of the monastery (often actually singing from the roof!) since about '96. Of course, there is no shortage of Black-eared Wheatear, and a good colony of both Rock Sparrow (which appear to have taken over an old Western Rock Nuthatch nest plastered to the north side of the Monastery wall) and Crag Martin (the latter fairly localized on the island) can usually be located, whilst Alpine Swift and Red-rumped Swallow often fly over. Pride of place, however, must go to the nesting pair of Long-legged Buzzard which frequent the rock-face in spring. They may get up when you leave the car, and can often be seen soaring over the valley to your right, where the light is usually more favourable. Some superb views can be had of them directly overhead, and displaying and passing prey at the appropriate times. Those who wish can continue right up past the army-post and visit the monastery for the chance of some more raptor sightings (including fairly regular Lanner and the odd Lesser Kestrel), and you also have the opportunity to look down on some of the birds at reasonably close range. Sometimes time precludes this if wishing to press on to Sigri and Faneromeni, but it can be very worthwhile in good 'fall' conditions.

If you have limited time, then just park and walk up the steps into the monastery courtyard (checking the few stunted trees and crevices in the wall for roosting Little and just possibly Scops Owl) and do an immediate left up the very old stone steps to the stone terrace, which has commanding views across the hillside and valley to the coastline - not to mention the army camp just below! This is usually an excellent spot to look down on breeding Rock Sparrow, Western Rock Nuthatch, Blue Rock Thrush, Rock Thrush if you're lucky, passing raptors, Crag Martin and Alpine Swift - the latter more likely overhead. If, however, time is not at a premium you might also wish to walk right through the courtyard and out of the double steel gates at the back (usually secured from inside but never locked) and down to the flat area below surrounded by large rocks. This may also provide excellent views of Long-legged Buzzard and Rock Thrush below, and at least it doesn't look down on the army camp - so you tend to feel more at ease! Although this is arguably one of the best views on the island it can be extremely windy and bitterly cold here if a north wind is blowing.

However, you can normally escape this by following the path to the right below the monastery walls on the more sheltered side, and it is here in such conditions that you might encounter a spectacular fall of migrants feeding out of the wind amongst the trees and bushes that project from the rocky slopes below. This is most likely in April and May (as in late April '98 especially), when these trees and bushes were literally 'dripping' with Collared, Semi-collared, Pied and Spotted Flycatchers, with smaller numbers of Blackcaps, Wood Warblers etc. This was truly a magical sight for those who witnessed it, and you simply never know what awaits you till you get up there. You can actually follow the path all the way round to the front of the monastery for the complete circuit.

Anyway, as you rejoin the main road to Sigri the roadside posts regularly produce Stonechat (which obviously breeds in the area, as family parties have also been seen), together with more Woodlark, Cinereous Bunting (often showing well just beyond the monastery past the sharp bend - ie near the crash barrier 3.5 kms before the Petrified Forest) numerous Cretzschmar's and a good number of Red-backed and the odd Woodchat Shrike - in spring at least. Summer and autumn is obviously much less productive, as in most upland areas. The last 10 kms or so into Sigri usually produce more of the same, whilst if you have time you can even follow the 'tourist trail' and visit the Petrified Forest 4.8 kms down a track off to your left, which again is clearly marked, but may not always be open. The ridge here always looks promising for raptors, and both Eleonora's Falcon and Lesser Kestrel, (which surely breed on the offshore islands) are regular, together with Long-legged Buzzard, occasional Peregrine and Lanner, migrating Marsh Harrier etc and occasional claims of Golden Eagle. Both Chukar and the odd Roller can sometimes be spotted on roadside rocks. Just beyond the Petrified Forest turn-off there is the first of 2 small stone shepherd's huts with a drystone wall beneath on your left. This usually produces Little Owl (sometimes very prominent, at other times crouching low against the wall, and sometimes pushed out altogether when the sheep are herded into the adjoining pen or the shepherd is ministering to them - often looking like he's about to disappear up the back-end of one!). A sunny, calm late afternoon is usually the best time to see it, and it may just be worth remembering that if returning from Sigri it is located exactly 2.7 kms beyond the obvious army post on the hillside - incidentally a good area for Chukar!

As you drop down here towards Sigri there are more stunning views to your right as you look down to the coast and the green, fertile strip of land leading to Faneromeni ford (see next section). You are also likely by now to have had good views of Lesser Kestrel (often hovering together in some numbers over the nearby ridge or hillside). Although Kestrel does occur here, most of your sightings will be of Lesser. On reaching Sigri itself, the old castle sometimes holds a small colony of Jackdaws, and the harbour always looks promising, but has rarely produced anything of note for me, (though two lucky observers had a juvenile Sea Eagle plunging in the sea here on 7th May '94!). Audouin's Gull should also be possible, and the odd one has been seen on an inlet a litttle further up towards Faneromeni Beach, the next port of call. To simplify things, I will first list the birds so far likely before proceeding with this next section and the eventual return to Eressos on the semi-coastal route.

SPRING - Honey Buzzard, Black Kite, Short-toed Eagle, Goshawk, Levant Sparrowhawk, Common and Long-legged Buzzard, several eagle species possible, Lesser Kestrel, Kestrel, Red-footed and Eleonora's Falcon, Hobby, Lanner, Peregrine, Chukar, Rock Dove, Little and occasional Scops Owl, Alpine Swift, Woodlark, Crag Martin, Red-rumped Swallow, Redstart, Whinchat, Stonechat, Isabelline, Northern and Black-eared Wheatear, Rock Thrush, Blue Rock Thrush, Icterine, Ruppell's, Orphean and Barred Warbler, Lesser Whitethroat, Whitethroat, Garden Warbler, Blackcap, Wood Warbler, Willow Warbler, Spotted, Red-breasted, Collared, Semi-collared and Pied Flycatcher, Sombre Tit, Western Rock Nuthatch, Golden Oriole, Red-backed and Woodchat Shrike, Jackdaw, Rock Sparrow, Cirl, Cinereous, Cretzschmar's and Black-headed Bunting.

AUTUMN - Raptors largely as above (except for Red-footed Falcon), Rock Dove, Black Redstart, chats, a few Black-eared and Northern Wheatear lingering, Blackcap, Icterine, Wood and Willow Warbler, Spotted Flycatcher, Blue Rock Thrush, Rock Nuthatch, Red-backed Shrike, Rock Sparrow, Cirl Bunting.

21) SIGRI TO FANEROMENI BEACH *(See Map 13, P238)*

No trip to the west of the island would be complete without a look at this small fertile coastal strip reached by forking right from the above route (or left if coming from the harbour), and then skirting the shoreline and checking the obvious inlet to your left for any interesting gulls and waders before turning slightly inland through cultivated fields and olive and fig-groves en route to the beach turn-off (reached after about 2 kms), and the the lower ford after another 1 km. The fertile appearance of this area is very obvious when approaching Sigri on the mountain route and looking down to your right, and contrasting it with the rugged and barren looking hillsides surrounding it (especially in autumn). It is hardly surprising, therefore, that both in spring and autumn (when irrigators are more often in use here), it should prove particularly attractive to migrants. The fields can hold all four possible shrike species, pipits, wagtails, chats, flycatchers, Bee-Eaters, wheatears and warblers (Willow

Warbler can be particularly numerous in autumn, feeding on a late hatch of caterpillars, and Yellow Wagtails can be present in considerable numbers around the irrigators both in spring and autumn). With all this potential prey, of course, both Marsh and Montagu's Harriers are likely, and I once located 3 male Montagu's sitting together in the same field! Lesser Kestrel often feed in good numbers over these hay fields when recently cut in spring (usually about early to mid-May), when they are often joined by small parties of Red-footed Falcons.

The turning to Faneromeni beach is not unsurprisingly marked by an old sign saying 'Beach' to the left, and you merely carry on (ignoring the first track to the right for the moment) until you pass a reedy area on your left (good for harriers, the occasional Black Kite and displaying Fan-tailed Warbler) and what is currently a half-finished building to the right, surrounded by chain-link fencing (ideal for chats, warblers, pipits, shrikes and buntings plus occasional Little Owl.) You can usually drive the track across the beach with care as far as the river mouth - but if in doubt it's usually safer to keep going than go through hesitantly and risk getting bogged down!

Faneromeni beach itself, though producing a party of both Collared and Black-winged Pratincoles in May '93, (and looking promising for gulls and terns), should really be viewed more for its scenic potential, and for the reed-fringed river mouth that enters it. This is obviously likely to turn up good numbers of herons, egrets, warblers etc, but access and viewing is not easy; so I prefer to leave it to the more dedicated, and to visit the two nearby fords instead. Nevertheless, there is a reasonable sized reedy pool here under a large rock at the end of the beach and situated just before the river mouth. As this is as far as you can drive it may be worth getting out and checking what you can see of the river through a gap in the reeds. You can certainly make out a steep section of riverbank to the right which is full of what are presumably Bee-eater holes, and they can often be heard here if not seen in the dead trees opposite. Undoubtedly this area must produce Crakes, and I have sometimes flushed Purple Heron from the reeds. Returning back along the beach there is often a pool just to the left after an obvious dip which may well attract both Red-rumped Swallow and Crag Martin to collect mud (see picture 35).

The first (or upper ford) is less well-known than Faneromeni ford proper and is reached by continuing back towards the main track but taking the track left just before it. This has an olive grove to your left and takes you past some new apartment buildings on the right and after 0.3 km over a newly improved concrete crossing over a rocky, scrubby watercourse - usually dry by late spring. This can be good for warblers, Hoopoe and possible Rufous Bush Robin amongst others. From here you pass a few more fields and then down to the concrete ford. You can drive over this easily enough to two diverging tracks on the other side, but both peter out fairly soon (the left one wending its way back towards the river mouth). Apart from a small farm (and other birders of course!) there is not much in this area to cause disturbance, so I often tend to park up here and wait to see what happens. Depending on the time of year and the water levels this can be quite a lot, and it often turns up much the same birds as the lower ford. In spring this includes regular Collared Flycatcher in April, followed by Little and Spotted Crake, Citrine Wagtail, various warblers (including regular River Warbler in early May), sandpipers and the inevitable Little Bittern, Squacco, Night and Purple Heron - numbers peaking in relation to tadpole populations from early to mid-May. Autumn is likely to find this site dry, but it should still produce some good warblers and other migrants.

Returning from here to the main track and doing a left turn takes you after 0.2 km to a crossing over a small dryish river gulley largely bordered by scrub. This may well produce displaying Rufous Bush Robin if you haven't had them already further back up the main track - in May '98 a pair were nest building in bushes just opposite the gate on the right into the olive grove (where they regularly perched). This immediate area must have just about the highest density of these birds anywhere on the island - see later! It is also an excellent area for virtually all the warbler species (especially Barred and Icterine) on spring migration, and the olive and fig groves can often host large numbers of Golden Oriole as well as a host of other migrants. Another 100 metres on takes you past a large pool on the right, largely flanked by quite high rocks and from early May this area often holds a large flock of Black-headed Bunting (often mainly females which arrive later), and Red-rumped Swallow sometimes come to drink or collect mud, whilst Ortolan and other buntings can be regular on migration. It is also worth checking the wires en route for shrikes, Bee-eaters, Red-footed Falcon and Roller in season.

There are a couple of tracks off to the right leading a short distance into the hillside before the main (or lower) Faneromeni ford is reached, but by this stage I usually prefer to press on and check out this wonderful area - which I usually find most productive from late afternoon onwards, when most migrants seem to be present and feeding actively. Also I find it difficult to get there much earlier after all the potentially good stopping places *en route*! Once you arrive at the ford, flanked by a tall tree on your right, several more to the left and a dense growth of high reeds and bamboo on the opposite bank (which can conceal numerous Little Bittern, occasional common Bittern, freqent Night Heron, crakes, Nightingale and a wealth of warblers) you have several choices.

One is to get out of your car, slam your doors in the process and flush everything in the immediate area in the process of walking along the riverbank! Apart from being fairly non-productive this is also likely to spoil it for any later arrivals (who may have travelled some distance to get here and may not be greatly amused!). A second and more logical alternative is to sit quietly in your car (preferably with a drink and a piece of cake to sustain you!) and simply view the area at your leisure - remembering that the best views will be downriver with the light behind you. You really never know what's likely to pop out here, and apart from regular Little Bittern (sometimes up to double figures when the tadpole population peaks sometime in the first half of May), Night and Purple Heron, I have on two occasions (in late March '97 and mid-April '98) been amazed to see a Bittern emerge from this dense cover and stand sentinel-like at the water's edge - totally in the open. This can also happen with normally secretive species like Little and Spotted Crake, and it is the possibility of experiencing such moments that makes me happy to sit here sometimes for hours on end, because, apart from all this cover to your left, the riverside tamarisks and dead trees often host a large number of migrant warblers (Blackcap, Common and Lesser Whitethroat, Great Reed and Olivaceous Warbler especially), not to mention Flycatchers flitting from bush to bush. Whilst in mid-April these will be mainly Collared, all the island species are likely here (sometimes all at once!) and Red-breasted are usually regular from late April into May. For a fairly enclosed site, it can also produce a fair selection of waders, and Citrine often turn up amongst the other wagtails.

Having driven apparently as far as you can go up the gravelly track with isolated boulders bordering the river (rather altered for the worse by some bulldozing activity since the riverbed's original pristine state up to about '94) you then have another choice - whether to attempt the seemingly impossible and carry on up the river or turn round and head back. This may be a difficult decision, though it may well be dictated by time. Another thing that is likely to influence you is the depth and flow of the water at a given time, since this riverbed is gravelly and usually fairly solid and is already traversed on occasions by tractors or the odd pickup truck. Obviously your prospects improve as the spring advances and the level drops, though there is always the posibility of exceptional rainfall and early spring flooding scouring out the bottom and dislodging a few rocks further upstream.

This manoeuvre is clearly not for the faint-hearted, but for those like myself with a certain spirit of adventure it can pay dividends! Once the initial crossing is made the going usually becomes much easier and you should be able to drive on for some distance (surveying the numerous pools especially favoured by wagtails, waders and flocks of bathing and drinking Bee-eaters and Black-headed Buntings on occasions) until you once again cross the river and find yourself driving on a track skirting the left bank. This brings you to an excellent rocky, scrubby area which you can drive for about 0.1 km before parking and exploring on foot or turning round and returning. You can either look down on a further very stony section of the river to your right (with one or two banks where Bee-eaters nest and are normally present in good numbers), or you can check out the whole area for warblers, shrikes and likely displaying Rufous Bush Robin in spring. Even in autumn I think this area would have a lot of potential for turning up something unusual in the pipit or bunting line - Rock Bunting has been recorded nearby for example. Finally, before you return you might like to investigate the tracks heading off left in the direction of the farm, which should link up with the track accessed by crossing Faneromeni ford itself - now described below.

This is actually your third option on arriving at the lower ford. If you decide to walk it then please remember to try and park tidily before the ford in the limited space available without blocking the riverside access for other people. However, although the track beyond the ford rapidly narrows and deteriorates into a rocky, scrub-flanked gulley it is, nonetheless, driveable with care for 1 km. The beginning of this track appears, in early spring, to have a small river running down it (so may be somewhat wet to walk); and this often attracts a number of birds to drink and bathe - I had Wryneck here in April '95, and Redstart are also likely at that time. It is excellent for chats (Stonechat usually breed in the area), flycatchers and shrikes; and Woodlark also occur, along with various warblers, including Orphean. This is best found in the fig grove on your right after passing another track which veers off to your right (presumably linking up with the area mentioned above). Anywhere from here is also good for Rufous Bush Robin, with at least 3-4 singing males regular along this dry boulder-strewn track leading to a small farm with a gate (and numbers actually peaking at 10 by early May '98!). Levant Sparrowhawk may also be seen overhead from late April to mid-May especially.

Moreover, several daytime sightings of Nightjar have been obtained here in early May - on one occasion churring from the top of a drystone wall! However, I can't leave this area without mention of a potential 'mega-tick' here in early May. Several times over the last few years either a female or a male White-throated Robin has turned up (but rarely both). This event usually occurs around 5th May for some reason - so most package holidaymakers tend to miss it! Certainly in '97 the male was showing well in company with a Rufous Bush Robin, and in '98 a female was seen briefly well up the track; but there is still no proof of breeding. On this high point I intend to list possible species so far and then leave the area to concentrate on the alternative coastal return route from Sigri to Eressos - though you may decide for convenience to return along the main road up the centre of the island, which is covered in the final section.

SPRING - Shearwaters offshore, Cormorant, Shag, Bittern (to early spring), Little Bittern, Night, Squacco and Purple Heron, Little Egret, Garganey (possible on pools to early spring), Black Kite, Short-toed Eagle, Marsh, Hen, Pallid and and Montagu's Harrier, Levant Sparrowhawk, Long-legged Buzzard, Lesser Kestrel, Red-footed Falcon, Hobby, Eleonora's Falcon, Quail, Little and Spotted Crake, Collared and Black-winged Pratincole (scarce), Little Ringed and Kentish Plover, Little and Temminck's Stint, Curlew Sandpiper, Ruff, Snipe, Redshank, Green, Wood and Common Sandpiper, gulls (including possible Audouin's offshore), Caspian, Sandwich and Common Tern, (marsh terns rare), Turtle Dove, Cuckoo, Little Owl (scarce), Nightjar, swifts, Bee-eater, Roller, Hoopoe, Wryneck, Middle-spotted Woodpecker, Woodlark, Skylark, Crag Martin, Red-rumped Swallow, Tawny, Tree, Meadow and occasionally Red-throated Pipit; Yellow, Citrine and White Wagtail, Rufous Bush Robin, Thrush Nightingale (irregular), Nightingale, Redstart, Whinchat, Stonechat, wheatears, warblers include Cetti's, Fan-tailed, River, Savi's, Sedge, Reed, Great Reed, Olivaceous, possible migrant Olive-tree and Ruppell's, Orphean and Barred, Garden, Eastern Bonelli's, Wood and Willow Warbler, Common and Lesser Whitethroat, Spotted, Red-breasted, Collared, occasional Semi-collared and Pied Flycatcher, Golden Oriole, Red-backed, Lesser Grey, Woodchat and Masked Shrike, Jackdaw, Rose-coloured Starling (late spring), Spanish Sparrow, Cirl, Ortolan, Black-headed and Corn Bunting.

AUTUMN - Marsh Harrier, Sparrowhawk, gulls, Turtle Dove, Hoopoe, Wryneck Bee-eater, Crag Martin, Red-rumped Swallow, Tawny, Tree, Meadow and possible Red-throated Pipit, Yellow and White Wagtail, Redstart, Black Redstart, chats, warblers (predominantly Willow Warbler), Spotted Flycatcher, Golden Oriole (scarce), shrikes as above (though predominantly Red-backed by September), Jackdaw, buntings as above (rarely after August).

WINTER - Bittern possible, Hen Harrier, Sparrowhawk, Buzzard, Kestrel, Water Rail, Snipe, gulls, Kingfisher, Woodlark, Skylark, Meadow and possible Water Pipit, Grey and White Wagtail, Dunnock, Robin, Black Redstart, Song Thrush, Cetti's, Fan-tailed and Sardinian Warbler, Blackcap, Chiffchaff, Jackdaw, Starling, Serin, finches, Yellowhammer (scarce), Cirl, Reed and Corn Bunting.

22) RETURN FROM SIGRI TO ERESSOS VIA COAST *(See Map 13, P238)*

Drive uphill into Sigri from the castle and simply bear right down a very narrow street with the bank on your left. This brings you out past a very small beach with a parking-space for a few cars bordered by tamarisks and a few other trees round a small fenced-off area to the left, (which has held Red-breasted Flycatcher and other migrants in past years around early May). There is a small water course here flowing under the road and out to the beach - which obviously has potential at the right time, assuming it's still wet. This route can be absolutely superb during the spring migration, and it has the advantage that it crosses a small ford and river valley about 10 kms from Sigri, at about the point the track starts to improve as it heads more inland. Prior to this, though rough, the birding can be good, with flocks of migrating Red-footed Falcons sharing the roadside rocks with the odd Roller, and Eleonora's Falcon and Lesser Kestrel often commuting to the offshore islands.

Ruddy Shelduck sometimes overfly, and shrikes, flycatchers and chats can be quite widespread, though attaining a higher density once the river valley is reached (Red-backed Shrike especially - which can be seemingly on almost every bush or even stalk in a good 'fall'), when Purple and Squacco Heron, Little Egret, Little Bittern, Marsh and Montagu's Harrier, Yellow Wagtails and various warblers are also likely, especially if you take a track to the right to a small stone building before the ford is reached (which may no longer be driveable - so check first). This leads to the river mouth, where it becomes quite deep and wide, and always remains wet (even in autumn). Talking of stone buildings, any of those en route which border the road are worth checking for Little Owl, which often perch prominently on the roof! Rock Sparrows also breed in the walls of some - especially nearer to Eressos.

Once past the ford (which can be good for Little Bittern, the odd Little Egret, Squacco and various warblers including Great Reed) check the nearby rock-face immediately to your right by a gate for Western Rock Nuthatch (several nests are usually visible). After the remains of the old stone bridge beyond it (leading to nowhere, but a good place to stop for a drink and survey the river valley) the road starts to improve and also to climb as it heads away from the coast. The steep gulleys encountered, especially where the ground falls away sharply to your right, are excellent spots for singing Cretzschmar's and Cinereous Bunting, as is almost anywhere between here and Eressos. (The same applies to Rock Sparrow, Western Rock Nuthatch and Black-eared Wheatear). About 3 kms before Eressos, you can sometimes obtain close views of singing Cinereous sitting on roadside posts to your right just before a small stone building on the left with chickens and a tethered dog which always barks when you stop! Between there and the rubbish tip, which is usually smoking, is another building to the right, below the road level, with a small rock-face and posts in front of it; and this is another good spot for close views of Little Owl.

Finally, on the approach to Eressos, look down to the church on your left, where excellent views can be obtained of the White Stork's nest and its occupants, assuming it to be in use - which it certainly was in spring '95, when I photographed a pair mating on top of it! The road brings you out almost opposite the main Sigri turn-off that you went on. Should you wish to do this journey the other way round, just remember to turn left in Eressos 0.2 km past the BP garage at a large blue Greek sign just left of a single obvious eucalyptus tree. This is totally inaccurate, as it clearly says 'Sigri 8.5 kms' when it's actually 14 kms! Then after about 0.3 km just bear left (ignoring a rougher right hand track to the farm) on what is clearly signposted 'Eressos Trekking Trail', and carry straight on past the rubbish tip and eventually the ford to Sigri (or turn back at the ford if you find the going is too rough). Again, this whole area is likely to be far more productive in the spring, as the following list shows.

SPRING - Little Bittern, Squacco, Grey and Purple Heron, Little Egret, Black and White Stork, Ruddy Shelduck (irregular), Short-toed Eagle, Marsh and Montagu's Harrier, Common and Long-legged Buzzard, Lesser Kestrel, Kestrel, Eleonora's Falcon, Little Stint, Wood and Common Sandpiper, Whiskered and White-winged Black Tern (occasional at ford), Little Owl, Alpine Swift, Roller, Woodlark, Crag Martin, Red-rumped Swallow, Tawny Pipit, Yellow Wagtails, Redstart, Whinchat, Stonechat, Northern and Black-eared Wheatear, Blue Rock Thrush, Olivaceous and Great Reed Warbler, Blackcap, flycatchers, Western Rock Nuthatch, Red-backed, Woodchat and Lesser Grey Shrike, Spanish and Rock Sparrow, Jackdaw, Raven, finches, Linnet, Cinereous, Cretzschmar's and Corn Bunting.

AUTUMN - Marsh Harrier, Sparrowhawk, Lesser Kestrel (in much reduced numbers), Kestrel, Hobby, Eleonora's Falcon, swifts, Tawny Pipit, Whinchat, Stonechat, wheatears (including a few late Black-eared), Red-backed and occasional Woodchat Shrike, Jackdaw, Raven, Rock Sparrow, Corn Bunting.

23) ERESSOS TO KALLONI VIA PERIVOLI MONASTERY AND CENTRE OF ISLAND *(See Maps 11 & 13, P236 & 238)*

This section is the last area of the island that remains to be covered. It is certainly very pleasing scenically, and, (like most places on Lesvos) productive for birds. It is, however, a large area, and birds can turn up almost anywhere; so I don't propose to do more than to briefly mention a few sites that may merit further investigation if time permits.

The road from Eressos to the junction with the main Sigri to Kalloni road has been covered well enough, but once you turn right towards Andissa, you are on new ground, and between here and The Perivoli monastery (especially the area where Spanish broom borders the road on a series of sharp bends) is one of the most reliable spots on the island for regular Stonechat (tough stopping to view or photograph them on a series of hairpin bends is another matter!). The even scarcer Red-fronted Serin (largely a rare winter visitor to the island) has also been recorded here in May '94 (by me!). You will shortly pass a turning to the left through olive groves towards the coastal village of Gavathas and ancient Andissa (mentioned at the end of site guide 15), so I won't elaborate further at this stage. Either way (whether or not you decide to take this diversion and search for Olive-tree Warbler reputed to sing from the olives just behind a taverna at Gavathas beach!) you carry on towards Vatoussa until you cross a steep gorge and river valley about 6 kms beyond Andissa, and just beyond it to the left you turn down a small winding road clearly marked 'Moni Perivoli' - this also appears on most island maps. The monastery is only a short distance below, and the view of the valley *en route* to it (especially in spring when many of the trees are in blossom) can in itself be extremely worthwhile. The far rocks seem to be a favourite site of Rock Dove (regularly in double figures here), and I have also had good viws of displaying Goshawk in early spring.

Anyway, as you pull into the monastery courtyard you will be aware of several wonderful old walnut trees, mixed in with a good number of planes flanking the river beyond, several cypress and an extensive area of olive groves. To make it even more attractive to birds there is a good growth of ivy on some of the older trees, with plenty of berries on offer by early spring. As if this wasn't enough there is a small stream which flows from just outside the monastery entrance under a culvert and then out to the river. The shade provided by the trees, the relaxing sound of running water and the almost constant song of the Nightingale (in early spring at least) make this a perfect place to stop for lunch or tea. Although several picnic tables (and even litter bins!) have been thoughtfully provided, I prefer to stay within the confines of the car alongside the small stream in the hopes of obtaining some good shots of drinking and bathing birds.

Of course, you need a certain amount of luck - ie good 'fall' conditions, the right light and no disturbance (especially from the monastery gardener who has the annoying habit of occasionally trundling through with his wheelbarrow to dump rubbish on the riverbank!). Generally though, the area is fairly quiet (apart from the Nightingales of course - which can often be seen really well singing in the open just after their return in early April). For this reason, an early spring visit (just before the trees leaf up) is recommended, and I was particularly fortunate in early and mid-April '97 to connect with confiding Redstart, Pied and Collared Flycatcher and a heavy passage of Whitethroat, Blackcap and Wood Warbler especially - which were literally queuing up with the regular Goldfinches and Greenfinches to drink and bathe immediately below my lens!

A winter visit here also produced both Serin and Siskin, (whilst Red-fronted Serin was also strongly suspected in April '97), and I think there must be the strong posibility of Hawfinch being present at this time - especially in view of all the walnuts and a few cherry trees. Moreover, these old walnut trees are riddled with Middle-Spotted Woodpecker holes, and the olive groves beyond are also an excellent habitat, not to mention the scrub-covered riverbanks. All in all an excellent and underrated spot on a productive migration route, often neglected because those who visit tend to be on the way to Ipsilou and Sigri or are returning back towards evening time and simply can't find the time to fit it in. That's the only problem with Lesvos - simply too many good sites!

Leaving the monastery behind, a further 2 kms along the main road towards Vatoussa, there is an area which I call 'The Grand Canyon', where a high, craggy rock-face borders the road. Apart from its aesthetic appeal it is also a good area for Crag Martin and Blue Rock Thrush, and I have also recorded Black Stork here on top of a large roadside rock - it seems quite likely that they nest somewhere close-by. Keep your eyes open on this stretch also for the odd raptor (Long-legged Buzzard, Peregrine, Lanner and Eleonora's for example), and then keep your ears open along the river that borders the road at Vatoussa for the song of the Nightingales which are all around you! The next stretch of road betwen here and Skalochori is full of hairpins, and can produce almost anything; usually at a time you are least able to stop!. The roadside wires here sometimes produce Masked Shrike, and both Nightingale and Hoopoe are regularly heard.

Beyond Skalochori, and just before the turn-off to Anemotia, there is a BP Garage on your left, where a dirt-track opposite runs parallel to the main road. This used to be known in Marjorie Williams and other literature as the 'Fina Garage Stop', but it has now changed its agency. It makes as good a raptor watchpoint as any (having panoramic views over the surrounding hills) and almost any of the island's raptors are possible here, including Lanner, Peregrine and Eleonora's Falcon, Common and Long-legged Buzzard, Hobby, Common and Levant Sparrowhawk and Short-toed Eagle. Obviously other wandering eagles are always possible at passage times, as they are almost anywhere on the island. Between Filia and Dafia is another series of hairpins, with some excellent views possible of Kalloni Plain just beyond Dafia (especially in late afternoon); and this final rather rocky stretch is good for the usual wheatears, buntings and shrikes. You may remember from section 5) that you can take a short-cut here to Kalloni Inland Lake by following the sign to the right at Dafia for Metoxi and Ag Anargyron. Either way you find yourself back in the Kalloni area where the site guide originally started.

CONCLUSION TO SITE GUIDE

Those who bought the original *Birding In Lesbos* will notice the addition of several new sites in this current guide, and some changes in the description of others. This is hardly surprising after an interval of three years, and on an island like Lesvos it would be quite possible to go on mentioning sites *ad infinitum* (all of which have the potential to produce good birds); but I feel I have to draw the line somewhere! Besides, some may wish to find their own sites, and I have no doubt that the island still has many quiet spots still waiting to be discovered; and it is my hope that this approach may take some of the pressure off the better known ones. Do note, by the way, that most of the place-names seem to have several alternative spellings, which can be rather confusing; and even the best map available (the blue *Toubi's*) is often inaccurate where spelling is concerned!

This site guide, because it is based largely on my own experiences over 10 visits, tends to use the Kalloni area as a starting-point on many of the trips; and it also, of course, tends to be biased in favour of the (early) spring period. The reasons for this are fairly obvious and are really interlinked. I go then because it is the best time for birds, and have to assume that most people will do the same. By all means visit at other times, when the island can still be extremely rewarding, but please don't expect to find all the birds listed present at these sites (especially bearing in mind that with low winter rainfall some of the wetlands may already have ceased to exist by late April or early May - though they may obviously survive longer after an exceptionally wet winter). However, having said that, many who have visited in July and August with fairly low expectations have returned more than happy with what they have seen.

Finally, please remember that things can change from year to year. Though I have tried to make this guide as up to date as possible, there is always the possibility of sites being degraded by human interference or disturbance (even the pressure of large numbers of visitors). Conversely, other areas, like new reservoirs etc could (and indeed some like Petra reservoir already have) come to the fore and prove more attractive to birds in the future; and weather (winter rainfall, prevailing winds etc) can all play their part in ensuring that no two years are quite the same. To me, at least, this is part of the island's attraction , and the fact that there always seems to be something more waiting to be discovered only seems to heighten it!

STATUS AND DISTRIBUTION OF CINEREOUS BUNTING ON LESVOS

Until quite recently, little was known about the breeding numbers and wintering distribution of Cinereous Bunting *Emberiza cineracea*, and even now, to quote from *Birds in Europe : their conservation status* (Tucker and Heath 1994), it remains 'one of Europe's rarest and least known breeding species', with a breeding population estimated at approx. 5000 pairs or less, and a status described a 'vulnerable'. In fact, to quote from Peter de Knijff's paper on Cinereous Bunting, which appeared in *Birding World* (Volume 4 No.11):
'It is, in many ways, an enigmatic bird, with a very restricted breeding distribution, poorly-known migration routes and an alleged winter distribution based on only 11 records of 21 birds during the entire 155 years since the first discovery of the species in western Turkey (by Strickland in 1836)'.

I can really do no better than quote at greater length from de Knijff (whom I was lucky enough to meet on the island in May '95 and several subsequent years).

Distribution and migration

'Two subspecies of Cinereous Bunting are recognized: the western, white- or grey-bellied race, *cineracea*, and the eastern, yellowish-bellied race, *semenowi*. The race *cineracea* breeds from the Greek island of Mytilene in the Aegean sea eastwards and southwards to Develi and Kilis in Turkey. The race *semenowi* is reported to breed from the Gaziantep area in southeast Turkey eastwards to the Turkish borders with Iran and Iraq. In 1904 and 1937, *semenowi* was also found breeding in the Zagros mountains in western Iran. There is no proven connection between the two breeding areas, and contrary to some of the literature, no proof of breeding in Iraq or Syria'.

In fact, birds are now known to breed on at least two of the Aegean islands other than Lesvos. Chios has been a regular breeding site for some time (with breeding first confirmed in 1971 and again from 1991-3) and a small breeding population was also confirmed further west on the island of Skyros in 1995, when a pair were observed feeding young on the north of the island, with at least two singing males at a site in the south. These records are fully documented in *The Birds of Greece*. Moreover, from 7th-9th June 1991 the late David Jackson of the BTO discovered three singing males near the north coast of Corfu 'with others heard along the north of the island' (see letter 'Bunting find' in *Birdwatch* Issue 43); and these records were accepted by de Knijff. Whether they were overshoots or regular breeders is not known (since little additional information has yet come to light); but the other interesting thing is that they were not seen up on the rocky hillsides, but singing at sea level from the tops of small pines. On Chios too, Calabrian pines *Pinus brutia* may be utilized in this way - see *The Birds of Greece*.

As far as migration is concerned, de Knijff identifies two contrasting migration routes - a western route through southern Turkey via Lebanon, Jordan, Syria, Egypt and Israel to Sudan and Eritrea (used predominantly, but not exclusively, by the western race): and an eastern route along the coast of the Arabian Gulf (used, logically enough, by the eastern race only; but with a gap between here and a supposed wintering area at the south-west tip of the Arabian peninsula). On both these routes, birds can be seen any time between February and May, or August and November, when they have occasionally occurred as vagrants to NW Europe.

In practice, however, the birds breeding on Lesvos usually arrive by early April or even late March, and begin to leave in late July through to mid or late August, with perhaps just a few juveniles remaining into September. At such times, they are likely to be distributed more generally throughout the island, and to have a more easterly or northerly bias before dispersing towards Egypt. With plenty of suitable breeding habitat on the island (some of it quite inacessible) the exact numbers of breeding pairs are difficult to calculate accurately; but being a bird of open terrain, with a fairly distinctive song, the task is certainly not as difficult as with Kruper's Nuthatch for example.

Field characteristics

It is not really the task of this book to go into field identification, besides which, on Lesvos, the only confusion possible is with female and immature Black-headed Bunting, which lack yellow on the throat or chin, white in the tail and the streaked underparts of female Cinereous. Juvenile Cinereous Bunting also lack the greenish-yellow tones of Ortolan, or the reddish-brown tinges of Cretzschmar's. As for the call, it is not that dissimilar to Ortolan and Cretzschmar's, but is perhaps not as 'sweet', and is made up of 4-6 notes, rising in pitch, followed by a longer, descending, double note. Whereas the Cretzschmar's call is often likened to the opening bars of Beethoven's 5th *(do-do do- dooo)* Cinereous is more like *dir-dir-dir-dir-dli-dlu*. If this doesn't seem to make much sense at the moment, I can assure you that you will understand what I mean when you hear it - especially when the two are calling side by side, as they frequently are. Finally, the normal contact note is the usual bunting-like *tsik* uttered quite softly and very much on a par with that of Ortolan.

Preferred breeding habitat

De Knijff considered Cinereous Bunting to be quite approachable and reasonably easy to photograph on migration, but (in both his and my experience) birds on their breeding grounds tend to be shyer and less likely to allow a close approach. Although originally described as a breeding bird of rocky, sparsely vegetated slopes at high altitude, birds of both the eastern and western race have also been discovered breeding on slopes at a lower altitude and with lusher vegetation, where they share some sheltered valleys and orchards in Turkey with both Cretzschmar's and Black-headed. (This also ties in with the Corfu breeding season records). *The Birds of Greece*, however, suggests that in Lesvos Cinereous Buntings attain their highest numbers where Cretzschmar's are either scarce or absent 'whereas the latter are very common in similar habitat in nearby areas, implying a high degree of active or passive interspecific competition'. These, however, are not De Knijff's findings (nor are they borne out especially by my own experiences).

Prime habitat on Lesvos can best be described as rocky slopes with very short vegetation, well above sea-level (again, habitat shared with Cretzschmar's), where they have easy access to their preferred diet of seeds and small invertebrates such as beetles and spiders. This is reiterated in *The Birds of Greece*, which mentions a preference for ' dry, open hilly country with low phrygana and scattered boulders' - where they are not always easy to see if not located first by song. It also mentions their reliance on the often abundant bush-crickets that occur in such habitat in late spring and suggests that Quite often, a narrow gulley of less than 50 metres, or the flow-bed of a narrow stream, with some high vegetation and the odd tree, is favoured. Males choose higher points for singing, such as high isolated rocky outcrops, but also telephone wires, and occasionally trees (eg at 'Devil's Bridge' - see site guide18, and also smaller trees on approach to Ipsilou Monastery - see site guide 20).

I have often seen males regularly perched on roadside posts and rocks, although females are much harder to observe, presumably because they are largely occupied with nesting activities from quite an early stage (with eggs being laid in the second half of April). Recently fledged young have occasionally been observed as late as mid-August, suggesting the possibility of double brooding on occasions, though is is by no means certain that this is a common occurrence, and may just have been a replacement clutch. As mentioned birds generally begin to leave their breeding grounds from late July or early August, and are rarely seen much much beyond the middle or third week of that month, except perhaps for a few late lingerers (usually juveniles).

Although there has been the odd breeding season record around Mt. Lepetimnos, and the late David Jackson had at least one singing male just east of Stipsi in mid-May '95, (whilst two singing males recorded on the Bogat headland just west of Nifida on 5th May '97 may simply have been overshoots from the breeding colony just the other side of the gulf in the Apothikes area) it used to be thought that the main breeding stronghold was concentrated west and north of Eressos, but it has become clear in recent years that they are actually much more widespread than previously imagined, with territories starting as far east as Parakila, and even Kalloni Upper East River. De Knijff carried out some rough censussing in May '95, '96 and '98 (based largely on birds he could hear calling from the road - with many in more inaccessible areas obviously overlooked). Based on this, he calculated that the average density in prime habitat ranged between 0.12 pairs per hectare (or 100 sq metres) in '98 and 0.21 pairs in '96. This works out at 3.6 - 6.3 pairs per 30 hectares, compared with 12 pairs of the eastern race per 30 hectares breeding in prime habitat in eastern Turkey. Though likely still to be an underestimate, these estimates were, in part, made up of the following records reproduced in the table on the following page :-

Summary of territories of Cinereous Bunting

Year of census (always between April 25 and May 15)			
Road between	1995	1996	1998
Parakilla - Agra	33	45	15
Agra - Messotopos	20	38	18
Messotopos - Eressos	19	31	11
Andissa - Sigri	38	30	28
Andissa - Eressos	21	17	18
Eressos - Sigri	6	6	5
Total	137	162	95

De Knijff points out that differences between the counts could be caused by obvious differences in the timing of breeding seasons. Whilst in '96 everything was late, in '98 much was very early - though he still felt that this didn't fully explain what appeared to be a much poorer breeding season for this species in '98 (especially between Parakila and Agra, where he found virtually no territories close to the road, and had to work hard to obtain good audible records and sightings).

Conclusion

Whereas it used to be thought that the breeding population of the Cinereous Bunting on Lesvos was not much more than 100 pairs, (see BirdLife International 1994 report), and that these were largely restricted to the west of the island around Eressos, it is now clear, in the light of increased observer coverage, that the numbers are actually likely to be far higher, and to begin anywhere west and north of Parakila, (with perhaps even a few pairs to the east). This could put their true numbers at anything up to 250 pairs (see *The Birds of Greece*). Certainly there seem to be no obvious threats to its future at present, since it breeds mainly on slopes which are too steep for agricultural development. However, the '98 survey results appear to give some cause for concern, and breeding records (especially in the Parakila to Agra area) were well down on previous years, for reasons unknown. Certainly increasing grazing by sheep and goats might adversely affect its breeding habitat in time, and long dry spells in its wintering stronghold could ultimately affect its long-term future; (though there are no figures at present to support these theories). Obviously much more data needs to be collected before we can piece together the full picture on this enigmatic bird.

STATUS AND DISTRIBUTION OF KRUPER'S NUTHATCH ON LESVOS

One would hope that the situation with Kruper's Nuthatch *Sitta krueperi*, which is actually resident on the island, might be easier to ascertain; but in practice this doesn't really prove to be the case. The main problem is, that with little local fieldwork being done, it is really down to visiting birders to make an estimate of its numbers, and this is not as easy as it might seem. Firstly, most birders usually only have one or two weeks at their disposal, and tend to visit the site where they know they are most likely to locate it; which used to be the area around Agiassos, but has now been superseded by the site near the army camp at Achladeri. Secondly, since upland pinewoods are hardly the most productive habitat on the island, people with limited time are unlikely to spend too much time scouring such habitat (of which there is a considerable amount on Lesvos - a lot of it looking remarkably uniform, and, in consequence, not easy to work).

Distribution and breeding

Much of the following information has been gleaned from Simon Harrap's article on Corsican and Kruper's Nuthatches in *Birding World* (Volume 6 No.3); from which, I quote :

' The range of Kruper's Nuthatch is centred upon Turkey, where it is widespread in west and along the south coast, and occurs more locally in the hinterland of the Black Sea coast. It extends into parts of the former USSR, into Georgia, and with another population in the Russian Republic, on the northern watershed of the northwest Caucasus. Perhaps strangely, the species also occurs in Greece, where it is resident on the island of Mytilene in the Aegean Sea (also known as Lesvos, this island clearly has close biogeographical links with Asia Minor, as it is similarly the only European outpost of Cinereous Bunting).'

Breeding pairs in Turkey are thought to number between 400-600, and its favoured habitats are pinewoods at lower altitudes, and fir, juniper and cedar forests at higher altitudes. Although it can occur in Turkey as high as 2500 metres, it is more likely to be found at 1200-1700 metres. Harrap, moreover, makes a connection with the occurrence of Turkish Pine *Pinus brutia*, for which its strong, longish 'tweezer-like' bill would seem ideally suited to extracting seeds from the pine cones. It is known to be largely resident, with pairs maintaining territories throughout the year, possibly, Harrap argues, ' in defence of their hoards of stored food'. Some limited movements to lower elevations can, however, occur in autumn and winter, and are not unusual, (with records then of birds at sea-level in southern Turkey and the eastern Black Sea coast; and even one vagrant on the Greek mainland, at Thessalonika, in October 1955!). *The Birds of Greece* also mentions birds on Lesvos freqently observed in pines at sea level during late summer and winter. They may then join up with roving tit flocks, which is where I observed them feeding in pines around the borders of Megali Limni in January '98, when I failed to locate them at the now regular Achladeri breeding site.

On Lesvos, breeding (with the exception of the Achladeri army camp area - where at least 3 pairs were known to breed in '97; 2 within a few hundred metres of each other and a third about a km further up the hillside) usually tends to take place above 400 metres (often at 600-700 metres - with the highest peaks on the island being 968 metres). These birds are thought to begin laying 2-3 weeks after valley populations at 220-330 metres (although fledglings have been recorded as early as the 3rd May, and Bob Husband recorded a family party above Agiassos on 15th May '91). When I left the island on 25th May '95, however, there was little indication that the breeding pair being observed at Agiassos had even hatched young yet - so some variation is obviously likely, with some birds even laying when others have fledged! Certainly eggs have been found in mid-April, and since the discovery in spring '96 of the breeding birds at Achladeri at a considerably lower elevation not much above sea-level, their fledging dates appear to have been fairly constant (6th May in '97, with another pair nearby feeding fledged young on 9th, when young were also seen fledging from a third nest site a few hundred meters beyond. The regular picnic area site was once again watched being vacated on 7th May '98). Working back from these dates egg laying in early April would seem likely, and ties in well with the pair-bonding behaviour observed at this time.

Of course, there is reason to think that temperature can play an important part in this, with a cold or wet spell delaying egg-laying. Some constants, nevertheless, remain - egg clutch size is usually 5-6, with a period of 14-17 days for incubation and 16-19 days for fledging (the young usually staying in the immediate vicinity for about 8 days).

Factors influencing choice of nest site

With so much apparently suitable habitat available, and yet so few sightings of Kruper's Nuthatch on the island away from the Agiassos and Achladeri areas, it follows that there must be some factors limiting its occurrence apart from the scarcity of the bird. As already mentioned, and reiterated in *The Birds of Greece*, the species is largely found in the vicinity of Calabrian pines *Pinus brutia*, whose seeds almost exclusively sustain it - though sweet chestnuts *Castanea sativa* may occasionaly be used as a nest site above Agiassos. One obvious limiting factor would therefore appear to be a shortage of mature or dead pines containing suitable holes for nesting (especially in large areas of rather uniform and fairly young woodland). This is the main reason that a nest-box scheme has been initited in the fairly relatively young pinewood area around Mikri Limni, where birds are known to occur but nest sites are scarce. Filios Akriotis, who is responsible for the scheme, tells me that in the first year of operation ('98) most boxes were used by tits, but he remains hopeful for the future. If successful, this scheme could also be extended to other deserving areas, but whether it could help expand the breeding area is uncertain. Although some birds excavate their own nest-hole, or occasionally use one vacated by Middle-spotted Woodpeckers, this is not necessarily a common practice, and most sites I have observed have been natural cavities, caused by decay or a broken limb, which the birds have utilized. Indeed, one at Achladeri used in spring '97 was in a pine stump less than two metres tall!

Another limiting factor may be the absence of a regular drinking site, so important to any seed-eating bird. Those in the Agiassos area are fortunate in having at least 2 permanent drinking sites (the water tank and the nearby drinking fountain with a dripping tap - see map 7), whilst the Achladeri site has a small flowing river (at least up to and probably beyond the fledging period) and also a largish and quite deep pool close to the road which could also be utilized. The existence of many permanent puddles in woodland is unlikely, and drinking troughs, which are primarily for cattle, are often some distance away. It is probably no coincidence that one of the few breeding-season records away from the regular areas was of a bird carrying food close to a water trough, (with a 2nd bird calling nearby), about 0.4 kms down the currently unmade road to Achladeri, off the Polichnitos to Agiassos road on 25th May '95. Up to 3-4 birds have been seen on occasions a few hundred metres opposite this drinking trough and small chapel close to the main road junction - with birds seen regularly drinking from the trough as recently as mid-August '98 (when water would have presumably ben very scarce in this area).

Another breeding record comes from the road to Vatera and Ambelikon (again about 0.5 km off that same Polichnitos to Agiassos road: and this was of a bird foraging on the ground for seeds and insects and regularly flying off with beakfuls of food in mid-May '93. Birds have also been seen and heard around the picnic sites on the main road just before and after this turning - though they have probably only come to light here because of the time people might spend here having a leisurely lunch or break, rather than because they are necessarily any more regular here.

All these records, though obviously different territories to those occupied immediately above Agiassos (which in themselves presumably hold several breeding pairs), are nevertheless still in the general area of Mount Olympus. There are only two other sites I know of where birds have been known to occur (though not necessarily every year). One is in some pine woodland a little north-east of Kalloni, around the area of Napeos Apollonas on the blue *Toubi's* map. This was apparently a record of a family party, in about '92, but they do not appear to have been recorded there regularly since (though it is not clear if the area has really been thoroughly searched in the meantime). The other concerns a family party seen recently in May to the right of the main Kalloni-Mytilini road near the old burnt out area before Lambou Mili, about 15 minutes walk from the road along a track opposite a lay-by and very close to the ruins of the old Roman aqueduct marked on the island map. The fact that some of these may have been purely chance encounters brings home the difficulties involved in locating the bird in the first place in such habitat, and leads on logically to a discussion of its call and field characteristics.

Field characteristics

To quote again from Simon Harrap's article :

'Kruper's is characterized by a black forecrown, white supercilium and black eye-stripe and, most notably, a brick red 'breastplate' separating the whitish throat from the remainder of the pale grey underparts......... Compared to the male, the female has the black of the forecrown duller and less well defined at the rear, the eye-stripe paler, and the breastplate slightly more washed-out. The most obvious difference, however, is a buff wash to the lower breast (which is pure grey in the male). Conversely, juveniles .... lack the black forecrown altogether, the eye-stripe and supercilium are poorly marked, and the breastplate is paler and more poorly demarcated from from the drab brown of the remainder of the underparts.'

This is all very well, but assumes you get a good look at a bird which spends a lot of its time high up in the treetops, and is only likely to be seen really well at a drinking or nest site. At the end of the day, then, it is often the call that betrays its presence (though this is less likely to apply once the birds are feeding young). Luckily, however, Kruper's Nuthatch often tends to be quite vocal, and there are, basically, at least 4 differing calls which are likely to identify it. First of all, there is the contact note, which is a soft *wit*, described as resembling a long, soft Great Spotted Woodpecker *kik*. There is also a wheezy Greenfinch-like *dyee,* and when excited a harsh *schra* resembling a Jay's alarm call - these are used by both sexes. Finally, there is the male's song, which is described as a repetition of simple but very variable units, largely unchanged in pitch - either a rapidly repeated *pip-pip-pip* or a more complex, yodelling *wicka-wicka-wicka* which Harrap likens to a displaying Black-tailed Godwit.

If this sounds rather complicated, all is likely to become clear in the field. There are few confusion species likely, since Kruper's and Western Rock Nuthatch *Sitta neumayer* scarcely overlap in territory, and in any case are quite different. The only possible confusion is with the call of Common Nuthatch *Sitta europaea*, which has been occasionally claimed in the Agiassos area, and also proven breeding around Skala Eressos (e.g. May '87 and '98). Generally, however, such overlap is likely to be minimal (with common Nuthatch usually showing a preference for scattered oak woodland to the north and west of the island) - but just keep it in the back of your mind!

Conclusion

Although Kruper's Nuthatch is a widespread breeding bird as close as the south coast of Turkey (from which Lesvos is only some five to eight miles distant), and there is obviously some possibility of immigration from this source, its habits tend to suggest that this would be a rare occurrence, and would, in any case, be difficult to prove. We have to assume, therefore, that the population on Lesvos (the only Greek territory where the species is found) is largely sedentary. In order to be viable and self-sustaining, it is likely to be in the region of 50-100 pairs and possibly higher (see *The Birds of Greece*) centred largely in the south-east of the island, with its stronghold in the upland pine woods around Agiassos and those extending to a lower elevation in the Achladeri area. It remains to be seen just how many more territories there are waiting to be discovered, and locating this bird still remains a great challenge away from its main breeding areas.

In spite of the obvious difficulties of plotting its distribution on the island without more extensive fieldwork, I have endeavoured to show its approximate distribution (together with that of Cinereous Bunting) in the map reproduced below. If anyone obtains any definite breeding records outside these given areas then I would be very interested to know about them!

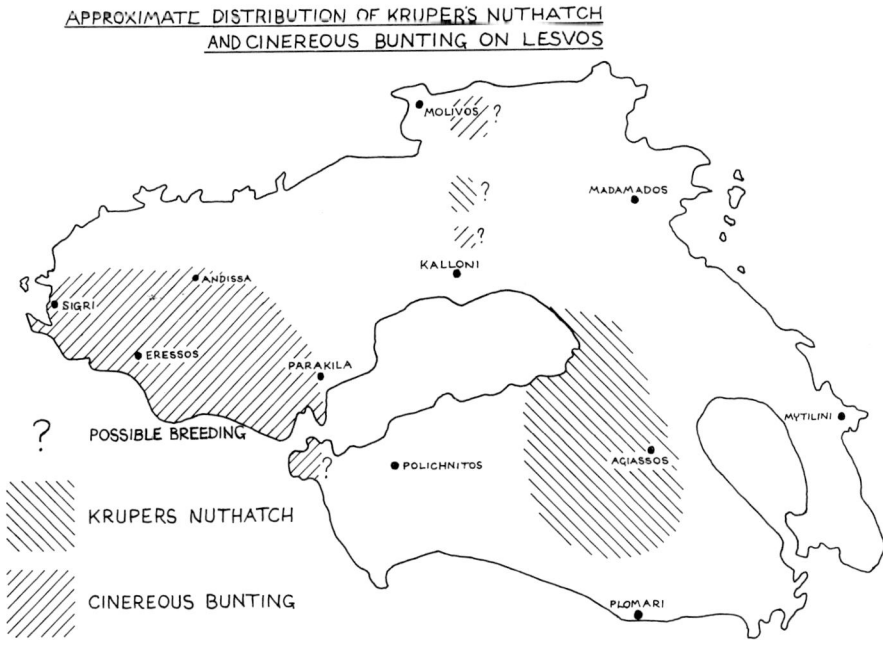

APPROXIMATE DISTRIBUTION OF KRUPER'S NUTHATCH
AND CINEREOUS BUNTING ON LESVOS

LESVOS CHECKLIST

All species known to have occurred on the island are listed in Voous order (as with *The Birds of Greece*) and the key to each abbreviated status is as follows. Small letters rather than capitals signify a scarcer distribution.

CB - casual breeder
MB - migrant breeder
PM - passage migrant
RB - resident breeder

WV - winter visitor
SV - summer visitor (non-breeding)
V - vagrant
E - escaped or recently introduced

☐ **Black-throated Diver** *Gavia arctica*		wv
☐ **Little Grebe** *Tachybaptus ruficollis*		rb
☐ **Great Crested Grebe** *Podiceps cristatus*		WV
☐ **Red-necked Grebe** *Podiceps grisegena*		wv
☐ **Black-necked Grebe** *Podiceps nigricollis*		WV
☐ **Cory's Shearwater** *Calonectris diomedea*		sv
☐ **Mediterranean Shearwater** *Puffinus yelkouan*		SV PM
☐ **Cormorant** *Phalacrocorax carbo*		WV
☐ **Shag** *Phalacrocorax aristotelis*		rb
☐ **Pygmy Cormorant** *Phalacrocorax pygmeus*		wv
☐ **White Pelican** *Pelecanus onocrotalus*		pm
☐ **Dalmatian Pelican** *Pelecanus crispus*		V
☐ **Bittern** *Botaurus stellaris*		wv pm
☐ **Little Bittern** *Ixobrychus minutus*		PM cb
☐ **Night Heron** *Nycticorax nycticorax*		PM
☐ **Squacco Heron** *Ardeola ralloides*		PM
☐ **Cattle Egret** *Bubulcus ibis*		V
☐ **Little Egret** *Egretta garzetta*		PM sv
☐ **Great White Egret** *Egretta alba*		WV
☐ **Grey Heron** *Ardea cinerea*		WV PM
☐ **Purple Heron** *Ardea purpurea*		PM
☐ **Black Stork** *Ciconia nigra*		mb PM
☐ **White Stork** *Ciconia ciconia*		MB PM
☐ **Glossy Ibis** *Plegadis falcinellus*		PM
☐ **Spoonbill** *Platalea leucorodia*		pm
☐ **Greater Flamingo** *Phoenicopterus ruber*		WV
☐ **Mute Swan** *Cygnus olor*		wv
☐ **Whooper Swan** *Cygnus cygnus*		V
☐ **White-fronted Goose** *Anser albifrons*		wv
☐ **Ruddy Shelduck** *Tadorna ferruginea*		RB
☐ **Shelduck** *Tadorna tadorna*		WV pm
☐ **Wigeon** *Anas penelope*		wv
☐ **Gadwall** *Anas strepera*		wv
☐ **Teal** *Anas crecca*		wv
☐ **Mallard** *Anas platyrhynchos*		wv cb?
☐ **Pintail** *Anas acuta*		WV pm
☐ **Garganey** *Anas querquedula*		PM
☐ **Shoveler** *Anas clypeata*		WV pm
☐ **Pochard** *Aythya ferina*		wv

☐	**Ferruginous Duck** *Aythya nyroca*	pm
☐	**Tufted Duck** *Aytha fuligula*	V
☐	**Velvet Scoter** *Melanitta fusca*	V
☐	**Goldeneye** *Bucephala clangula*	V
☐	**Red-breasted Merganser** *Mergus serrator*	wv
☐	**White-headed Duck** *Oxyura leucocephala*	V
☐	**Honey Buzzard** *Pernis apivorus*	PM mb
☐	**Black Kite** *Milvus migrans*	pm
☐	**Red Kite** *Milvus milvus*	V
☐	**White-tailed Eagle** *Haliaeetus albicilla*	V
☐	**Egyptian Vulture** *Neophron percnopterus*	pm
☐	**Griffon Vulture** *Gyps fulvus*	V
☐	**Short-toed Eagle** *Circaetus gallicus*	MB
☐	**Marsh Harrier** *Circus aeruginosus*	PM wv
☐	**Hen Harrier** *Circus cyaneus*	WV pm
☐	**Pallid Harrier** *Circus macrourus*	pm
☐	**Montagu's Harrier** *Circus pygargus*	PM
☐	**Goshawk** *Accipiter gentilis*	rb
☐	**Sparrowhawk** *Accipiter nisus*	WV cb
☐	**Levant Sparrowhawk** *Accipiter brevipes*	pm cb
☐	**Buzzard** *Buteo buteo*	RB WV
☐	**Long-legged Buzzard** *Buteo rufinus*	RB
☐	**Lesser Spotted Eagle** *Aquila pomarina*	pm
☐	**Spotted Eagle** *Aquila clanga*	wv
☐	**Steppe Eagle** *Aquila nipalensis*	V
☐	**Imperial Eagle** *Aquila heliaca*	V
☐	**Golden Eagle** *Aquila chrysaetos*	V
☐	**Booted Eagle** *Hieraaetus pennatus*	pm
☐	**Bonelli's Eagle** *Hieraaetus fasciatus*	rb
☐	**Osprey** *Pandion haliaetus*	PM
☐	**Lesser Kestrel** *Falco naumanni*	MB
☐	**Kestrel** *Falco tinnunculus*	rb
☐	**Red-footed Falcon** *Falco vespertinus*	PM
☐	**Merlin** *Falco columbarius*	wv
☐	**Hobby** *Falco subbuteo*	PM mb
☐	**Eleonora's Falcon** *Falco eleonorae*	MB
☐	**Lanner** *Falco biarmicus*	rb
☐	**Saker** *Falco cherrug*	V
☐	**Peregrine** *Falco peregrinus*	RB wv
☐	**Chukar** *Alectoris chukar*	RB
☐	**Quail** *Coturnix coturnix*	PM mb
☐	**Pheasant** *Phasianus colchicus*	E
☐	**Water Rail** *Rallus aquaticus*	rb wv
☐	**Spotted Crake** *Porzana porzana*	pm
☐	**Little Crake** *Porzana parva*	PM
☐	**Baillon's Crake** *Porzana pusilla*	pm
☐	**Corncrake** *Crex crex*	pm

☐	**Moorhen** *Gallinula chloropus*	RB WV
☐	**Coot** *Fulica atra*	WV cb
☐	**Crane** *Grus grus*	V
☐	**Oystercatcher** *Haematopus ostralegus*	wv pm
☐	**Black-winged Stilt** *Himantopus himantopus*	PM MB
☐	**Avocet** *Recurvirostra avosetta*	CB PM WV
☐	**Stone Curlew** *Burhinus oedicnemus*	MB
☐	**Collared Pratincole** *Glareola pratincola*	PM
☐	**Black-winged Pratincole** *Glareola nordmanni*	pm
☐	**Little Ringed Plover** *Charadrius dubius*	MB
☐	**Ringed Plover** *Charadrius hiaticula*	pm
☐	**Kentish Plover** *Charadrius alexandrinus*	MB PM wv
☐	**Lesser Sandplover** *Charadrius mongolus*	V
☐	**Greater Sandplover** *Charadrius leschenaultii*	V
☐	**Caspian Plover** *Charadrius asiaticus*	V
☐	**Dotterel** *Charadrius morinellus*	V
☐	**Golden Plover** *Pluvialis apricaria*	wv
☐	**Grey Plover** *Pluvialis squatarola*	PM wv
☐	**Spur-winged Plover** *Hoplopterus spinosus*	pm
☐	**Sociable Plover** *Chettusia gregaria*	V
☐	**Lapwing** *Vanellus vanellus*	wv
☐	**Knot** *Calidris canutus*	pm
☐	**Sanderling** *Calidris alba*	pm
☐	**Little Stint** *Calidris minuta*	PM wv
☐	**Temminck's Stint** *Calidris temminckii*	pm
☐	**Curlew Sandpiper** *Calidris ferruginea*	PM
☐	**Dunlin** *Calidris alpina*	pm WV
☐	**Broad-billed Sandpiper** *Limicola falcinellus*	pm
☐	**Ruff** *Philomachus pugnax*	PM
☐	**Jack Snipe** *Lymnocryptes minimus*	wv pm
☐	**Snipe** *Gallinago gallinago*	WV PM
☐	**Great Snipe** *Gallinago media*	pm
☐	**Woodcock** *Scolopax rusticola*	wv
☐	**Black-tailed Godwit** *Limosa limosa*	PM
☐	**Bar-tailed Godwit** *Limosa lapponica*	V
☐	**Whimbrel** *Numenius phaeopus*	pm
☐	**Curlew** *Numenius arquata*	WV pm
☐	**Spotted Redshank** *Tringa erythropus*	pm
☐	**Redshank** *Tringa totanus*	PM WV
☐	**Marsh Sandpiper** *Tringa stagnatilis*	pm
☐	**Greenshank** *Tringa nebularia*	PM wv
☐	**Green Sandpiper** *Tringa ochropus*	wv PM
☐	**Wood Sandpiper** *Tringa glareola*	PM
☐	**Terek Sandpiper** *Xenus cinereus*	V
☐	**Common Sandpiper** *Actitis hypoleucos*	PM
☐	**Turnstone** *Arenaria interpres*	pm
☐	**Red-necked Phalarope** *Phalaropus lobatus*	V

☐	**Pomarine Skua**	*Stercorarius pomarinus*	V
☐	**Long-tailed Skua**	*Stercorarius longicaudus*	V
☐	**Mediterranean Gull**	*Larus melanocephalus*	PM WV
☐	**Little Gull**	*Larus minutus*	pm wv
☐	**Black-headed Gull**	*Larus ridibundus*	WV
☐	**Slender-billed Gull**	*Larus genei*	pm wv
☐	**Audouin's Gull**	*Larus audouinii*	SV wv
☐	**Common Gull**	*Larus canus*	wv
☐	**Lesser Black-backed Gull**	*Larus fuscus*	pm
☐	**Yellow-legged Gull**	*Larus cachinnans*	RB
☐	**Great Black-backed Gull**	*Larus marinus*	V
☐	**Gull-billed Tern**	*Gelochelidon nilotica*	PM
☐	**Caspian Tern**	*Sterna caspia*	pm
☐	**Sandwich Tern**	*Sterna sandvicensis*	wv pm
☐	**Common Tern**	*Sterna hirundo*	MB pm
☐	**Arctic Tern**	*Sterna paradisaea*	V
☐	**Little Tern**	*Sterna albifrons*	PM MB
☐	**Whiskered Tern**	*Chlidonias hybridus*	PM
☐	**Black Tern**	*Chlidonias niger*	pm
☐	**White-winged Black Tern**	*Chlidonias leucopterus*	PM
☐	**Rock Dove**	*Columba livia*	rb
☐	**Stock Dove**	*Columba oenas*	V
☐	**Woodpigeon**	*Columba palumbus*	wv rb
☐	**Collared Dove**	*Streptopelia decaocto*	RB
☐	**Turtle Dove**	*Streptopelia turtur*	PM mb
☐	**Laughing Dove**	*Streptopelia senegalensis*	V
☐	**Great Spotted Cuckoo**	*Clamator glandarius*	pm cb?
☐	**Cuckoo**	*Cuculus canorus*	PM mb
☐	**Barn Owl**	*Tyto alba*	RB
☐	**Scops Owl**	*Otus scops*	RB
☐	**Eagle Owl**	*Bubo bubo*	rb
☐	**Little Owl**	*Athene noctua*	RB
☐	**Tawny Owl**	*Strix aluco*	rb
☐	**Long-eared Owl**	*Asio otis*	rb
☐	**Short-eared Owl**	*Asio flammeus*	wv
☐	**Nightjar**	*Caprimulgus europaeus*	PM MB
☐	**Swift**	*Apus apus*	MB
☐	**Pallid Swift**	*Apus pallidus*	pm sv
☐	**Alpine Swift**	*Apus melba*	PM mb
☐	**Kingfisher**	*Alcedo atthis*	WV cb
☐	**Blue-cheeked Bee-eater**	*Merops superciliosus*	V
☐	**Bee-eater**	*Merops apiaster*	MB PM
☐	**Roller**	*Coracias garrulus*	PM
☐	**Hoopoe**	*Upupa epops*	MB
☐	**Wryneck**	*Jynx torquilla*	PM wv
☐	**Great Spotted Woodpecker**	*Dendrocopos major*	cb
☐	**Syrian Woodpecker**	*Dendrocopos syriacus*	cb or V

☐	**Middle Spotted Woodpecker**	*Dendrocopos medius*	RB
☐	**White-backed Woodpecker**	*Dendrocopos leucotos*	cb or V
☐	**Calandra Lark**	*Melanocorypha calandra*	pm
☐	**Black Lark**	*Melanocorypha yeltoniensis*	V
☐	**Short-toed Lark**	*Calandrella brachydactyla*	mb PM
☐	**Crested Lark**	*Galerida cristata*	RB
☐	**Woodlark**	*Lullula arborea*	RB
☐	**Skylark**	*Alauda arvensis*	WV
☐	**Sand Martin**	*Riparia riparia*	PM
☐	**Crag Martin**	*Ptyonoprogne rupestris*	mb pm wv?
☐	**Swallow**	*Hirundo rustica*	PM MB
☐	**Red-rumped Swallow**	*Hirundo daurica*	MB PM
☐	**House Martin**	*Delichon urbica*	MB PM
☐	**Richard's Pipit**	*Anthus novaeseelandiae*	V
☐	**Tawny Pipit**	*Anthus campestris*	MB pm
☐	**Tree Pipit**	*Anthus trivialis*	PM
☐	**Meadow Pipit**	*Anthus pratensis*	WV
☐	**Red-throated Pipit**	*Anthus cervinus*	PM
☐	**Water Pipit**	*Anthus spinoletta*	WV
☐	**Yellow Wagtail**	*Motacilla flava*	PM mb
☐	**Citrine Wagtail**	*Motacilla citreola*	pm
☐	**Grey Wagtail**	*Motacilla cinerea*	rb WV
☐	**White Wagtail**	*Motacilla alba*	WV cb
☐	**Waxwing**	*Bombycilla garrulus*	V
☐	**Wren**	*Troglodytes troglodytes*	rb WV
☐	**Dunnock**	*Prunella modularis*	wv
☐	**Rufous Bush Robin**	*Cercotrichas galactotes*	MB
☐	**Robin**	*Erithacus rubecula*	WV cb
☐	**Thrush Nightingale**	*Luscinia luscinia*	pm
☐	**Nightingale**	*Luscinia megarhynchos*	MB pm
☐	**White-throated Robin**	*Irania gutturalis*	pm cb
☐	**Black Redstart**	*Phoenicurus ochruros*	WV
☐	**Redstart**	*Phoenicurus phoenicurus*	PM
☐	**Whinchat**	*Saxicola rubetra*	PM
☐	**Stonechat**	*Saxicola torquata*	rb
☐	**Isabelline Wheatear**	*Oenanthe isabellina*	mb
☐	**Northern Wheatear**	*Oenanthe oenanthe*	PM MB
☐	**Pied Wheatear**	*Oenanthe pleschanka*	pm cb
☐	**Black-eared Wheatear**	*Oenanthe hispanica*	MB pm
☐	**Desert Wheatear**	*Oenanthe deserti*	V
☐	**Finsch's Wheatear**	*Oenanthe finschii*	V
☐	**Rock Thrush**	*Monticola saxatilis*	pm cb
☐	**Blue Rock Thrush**	*Monticola solitarius*	RB
☐	**Ring Ouzel**	*Turdus torquatus*	V
☐	**Blackbird**	*Turdus merula*	RB WV
☐	**Fieldfare**	*Turdus pilaris*	wv
☐	**Song Thrush**	*Turdus philomelos*	WV cb

☐	**Redwing** *Turdus iliacus*	WV
☐	**Mistle Thrush** *Turdus viscivorus*	rb
☐	**Cetti's Warbler** *Cettia cetti*	RB
☐	**Fan-tailed Warbler** *Cisticola juncidis*	rb
☐	**Grasshopper Warbler** *Locustella naevia*	pm
☐	**River Warbler** *Locustella fluviatilis*	pm
☐	**Savi's Warbler** *Locustella luscinioides*	PM
☐	**Moustached Warbler** *Acrocephalus melanopogon*	pm wv
☐	**Sedge Warbler** *Acrocephalus schoenobaenus*	PM
☐	**Marsh Warbler** *Acrocephalus palustris*	PM
☐	**Reed Warbler** *Acrocephalus scirpaceus*	mb pm
☐	**Great Reed Warbler** *Acrocephalus arundinaceus*	MB PM
☐	**Olivaceous Warbler** *Hippolais pallida*	MB
☐	**Upcher's Warbler** *Hippolais languida*	V
☐	**Olive-tree Warbler** *Hippolais olivetorum*	mb
☐	**Icterine Warbler** *Hippolais icterina*	PM
☐	**Spectacled Warbler** *Sylvia conspicillata*	V
☐	**Subalpine Warbler** *Sylvia cantillans*	MB PM
☐	**Sardinian Warbler** *Sylvia melanocephala*	rb
☐	**Ruppell's Warbler** *Sylvia rueppelli*	mb pm
☐	**Orphean Warbler** *Sylvia hortensis*	MB pm
☐	**Barred Warbler** *Sylvia nisoria*	pm
☐	**Lesser Whitethroat** *Sylvia curruca*	PM
☐	**Whitethroat** *Sylvia communis*	PM mb
☐	**Garden Warbler** *Sylvia borin*	pm
☐	**Blackcap** *Sylvia atricapilla*	PM WV
☐	**Eastern Bonelli's Warbler** *Phylloscopus orientalis*	PM mb
☐	**Wood Warbler** *Phylloscopus sibilatrix*	PM
☐	**Chiffchaff** *Phylloscopus collybita*	WV mb?
☐	**Willow Warbler** *Phylloscopus trochilus*	PM
☐	**Goldcrest** *Regulus regulus*	WV cb?
☐	**Firecrest** *Regulus ignicapillus*	wv cb?
☐	**Spotted Flycatcher** *Muscicapa striata*	PM mb
☐	**Red-breasted Flycatcher** *Ficedula parva*	pm
☐	**Semi-collared Flycatcher** *Ficedula semitorquata*	pm
☐	**Collared Flycatcher** *Ficedula albicollis*	PM
☐	**Pied Flycatcher** *Ficedula hypoleuca*	PM
☐	**Long-tailed Tit** *Aegithalos caudatus*	rb
☐	**Sombre Tit** *Parus lugubris*	rb
☐	**Coal Tit** *Parus ater*	rb
☐	**Blue Tit** *Parus caeruleus*	RB
☐	**Great Tit** *Parus major*	RB
☐	**Kruper's Nuthatch** *Sitta krueperi*	rb
☐	**Nuthatch** *Sitta europaea*	rb
☐	**Western Rock Nuthatch** *Sitta neumayer*	RB
☐	**Wallcreeper** *Tichodroma muraria*	V
☐	**Short-toed Treecreeper** *Certhia brachydactyla*	RB

☐	**Penduline Tit** *Remiz pendulinus*	V
☐	**Golden Oriole** *Oriolus oriolus*	PM
☐	**Black-headed Bush Shrike** *Tchagra senegala*	V
☐	**Isabelline Shrike** *Lanius isabellinus*	V
☐	**Red-backed Shrike** *Lanius collurio*	PM mb
☐	**Lesser Grey Shrike** *Lanius minor*	PM mb
☐	**Great Grey Shrike** *Lanius excubitor*	V
☐	**Woodchat Shrike** *Lanius senator*	MB PM
☐	**Masked Shrike** *Lanius nubicus*	MB
☐	**Jay** *Garrulus glandarius*	RB
☐	**Magpie** *Pica pica*	V
☐	**Nutcracker** *Nucifraga caryocatactes*	V
☐	**Chough** *Pyrrhocorax pyrrhocorax*	V
☐	**Jackdaw** *Corvus monedula*	rb
☐	**Rook** *Corvus frugilegus*	V
☐	**Hooded Crow** *Corvus corone*	RB
☐	**Raven** *Corvus corax*	rb
☐	**Starling** *Sturnus vulgaris*	WV
☐	**Rose-coloured Starling** *Sturnus roseus*	PM
☐	**House Sparrow** *Passer domesticus*	RB
☐	**Spanish Sparrow** *Passer hispaniolensis*	RB PM
☐	**Tree Sparrow** *Passer montanus*	cb
☐	**Rock Sparrow** *Petronia petronia*	RB
☐	**Chaffinch** *Fringilla coelebs*	RB
☐	**Brambling** *Fringilla montifringilla*	wv
☐	**Red-fronted Serin** *Serinus pusillus*	wv
☐	**Serin** *Serinus serinus*	RB
☐	**Greenfinch** *Carduelis chloris*	RB
☐	**Goldfinch** *Carduelis carduelis*	RB
☐	**Siskin** *Carduelis spinus*	wv cb?
☐	**Linnet** *Carduelis cannabina*	rb
☐	**Twite** *Carduelis flavirostris*	V
☐	**Crossbill** *Loxia curvirostra*	V cb?
☐	**Scarlet Rosefinch** *Carpodacus erythrinus*	pm
☐	**Bullfinch** *Pyrrhula pyrrhula*	wv
☐	**Hawfinch** *Coccothraustes coccothraustes*	WV cb
☐	**Yellowhammer** *Emberiza citrinella*	wv
☐	**Cirl Bunting** *Emberiza cirlus*	RB
☐	**Rock Bunting** *Emberiza cia*	wv cb?
☐	**Cinereous Bunting** *Emberiza cineracea*	MB
☐	**Ortolan Bunting** *Emberiza hortulana*	PM cb?
☐	**Cretzschmar's Bunting** *Emberiza caesia*	MB
☐	**Little Bunting** *Emberiza pusilla*	V
☐	**Reed Bunting** *Emberiza schoeniclus*	wv
☐	**Black-headed Bunting** *Emberiza melanocephala*	MB
☐	**Corn Bunting** *Miliaria calandra*	RB

(TOTAL - 320 SPECIES)

1) **Black-necked Grebe** - Regular winter visitor offshore
2) ♂**Little Bittern** - Confiding spring migrant
3) **Bittern** - Early spring passage

4) **Squacco Heron -**
Widespread on wetlands in spring

5) **Black Stork -** Localized breeder present from late March

6) **White Stork** - Familiar sight in the Kalloni area
7) **Great White Egret** - Locally common winter visitor to salt pans and surrounds
8) **Greater Flamingo** - Winters at both sets of salt pans in good numbers

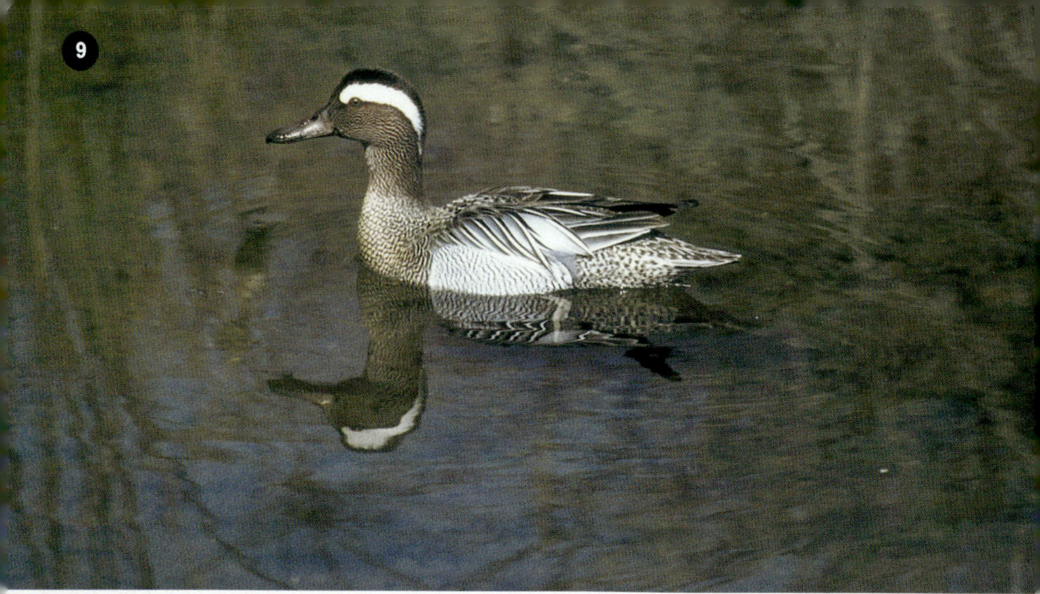

9

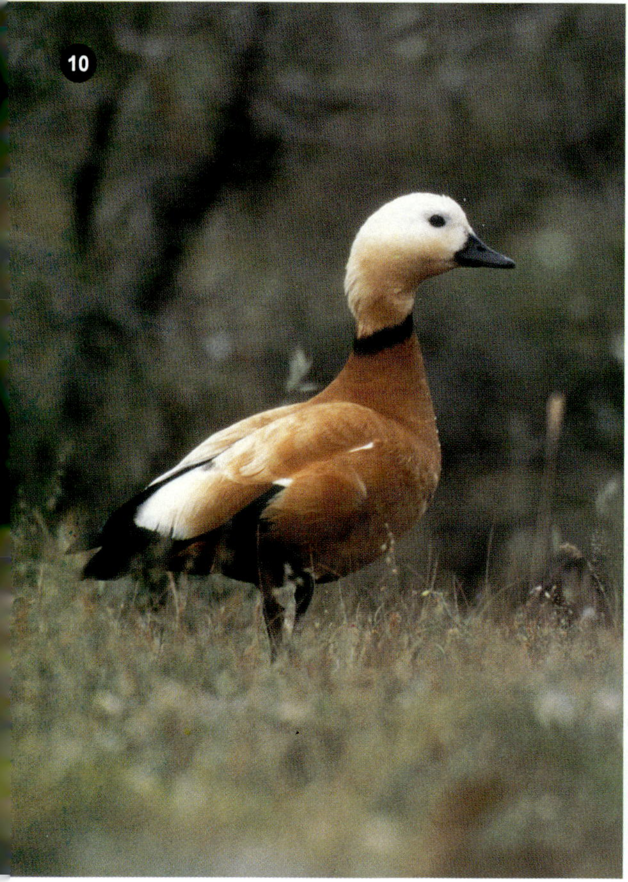

10

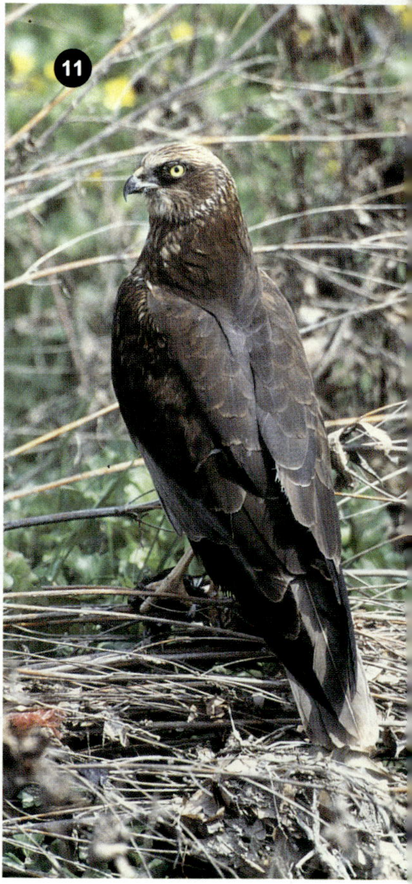

11

9) ♂ **Garganey** - Spring passage peaks late March
10) **Ruddy Shelduck** - Surprisingly wary resident

11) ♂ **Marsh Harrier** - Common in early spring and also winters at Dipi Larssos

12) ♀ **Montagu's Harrier-**
    Good spring passage at Kalloni Salt Pans

13) **Long-legged Buzzard** - Regularly seen in upland areas

14) ♂ **Lesser Kestrel** - Sigri area favoured

15) **Hobby-** Regular passage in April
16) ♂ **Red-footed Falcon -**
     Often spectacular spring movements   17)   **Eleonora's Falcon -** Likely offshore breeder

18) **Spotted Crake -**
Scarce but regular spring migrant around Kalloni Inland
Lake

19) **Little Crake -**
Common and often quite confiding
in early spring

20) **Stone Curlew** - Regular breeder in Kalloni area   21)   **Collared Pratincole** - Kalloni Salt Pans favoured

SYSTEMATIC LIST

Black-throated Diver *Gavia arctica*
Regular winter visitor offshore in small numbers from November to mid-April (occasionally
into May). Biggest recorded gathering 25 offshore from Skala Polichnitos Salt Pans in
February '95. Apart from an unconfirmed report of a bird in Kalloni Bay on the rather early
date of 21st October '96 there are only 3 other records - of a summer plumage bird off
Alikoudi on 5th April '86, another late summer plumage bird lingering in Achladeri Bay on
21st April '97 and one seen in company with Red-breasted Mergansers in Nifida Bay on 23rd
January '98.

Little Grebe *Tachybaptus ruficollis*
Locally common resident, breeding in small numbers (perhaps 10 pairs or so). Potamia River a
regular breeding site (pair with young seen 8th June '97), and also seen Kalloni East and West
Rivers (adult with 4 young seen spring '95), Parakila Marsh (adult with 1 young spring '95 and
adult with 4 young mid-May '96 and adult with 4 young 30th May '98) and even Kalloni Pool
(May '95). Also proven breeding at Dipi Larssos, where an adult was seen with 4 young in
early May '98 and almost certainly on the well vegetated pool known as Mikri Limni, where at
least 1 pair still present late April '98. A gathering of 9 on Petra reservoir 26th July '96 had
risen to 26 by 4th September and 38 by 20th October; whilst 35 there on 9th September '97
had risen to between 60 and 70 by the month's end. A winter peak of 50+ birds there in
January '98 had declined to 15 by mid-April, but 42 were again present by 11th August, rising
to 53 on 19th and 92 by 18th September! Elsewhere gatherings of between 5-10 birds were
observed on Potamia River, Kalloni Pool and Kalloni Inland Lake from mid-October '96 and in
January and up to mid-April '98. Owing to continued high water levels on Kalloni Pool up to 3
birds were still present there in early August '98 and may well have bred, whilst an adult with 2
juveniles was also seen along Kalloni Salt Pans channel in mid-September '98.

Great Crested Grebe *Podiceps cristatus*
Regular winter visitor offshore in small numbers October to May. Favoured areas are Mytilini
harbour and Geras and Kalloni Bays. Usually seen in ones and twos, but up to 10 counted in
Kalloni bay in calm conditions 4th April '85 and 19th March '87, 20 there 25th March '86
(declining to 6 by 11th April), 15 at East River mouth 26th March that year and 2 recorded on
15th May '98 (the latest date). Also noteworthy was a gathering of 20+ there on 20th March
'97 and 15 sheltering from gale-force winds in Skala Kalloni harbour on the same date (in
company with a single Black-necked Grebe). There were still 7 at West River mouth on 25th
March and 19 at the Vouvaris river 'Derbyshire' next day (with 20+ offshore from Achladeri at
the same time), reducing to 9 by 3rd April. A record 21 were seen there on 11th April '98 in
calm settled conditions - suggesting a build-up prior to departure. One was still present off
Achladeri on 25th, and odd stragglers sometimes linger into May - eg 3 seen in Kalloni Bay on
10th May '91 and one exceptionally late record of a bird off Skala Kalloni beach on 30th May
'98. Interesting summer records of a single on Petra reservoir 4th August '96, with a juvenile
present there between 4th-11th at least. Otherwise recorded in Kalloni Bay from 4th
September '98 and 26th September '97 - both single birds.

Red-necked Grebe *Podiceps grisegena*
Scarce winter visitor November to April. Very few records, except for one unusual
(unconfirmed) report of a bird at Kalloni Salt Pans mid-July '94, still in full summer plumage.
However, *The Birds of Greece* lists 5 August records for the country, so perhaps this record is
not quite as unusual as it seems.

Black-necked Grebe *Podiceps nigricollis*
Regular winter visitor in reasonable numbers late September to late April (sometimes lingering into May) mainly offshore, but also on reservoirs and river mouths - occasionally salt pans. First record of a single bird on Kalloni Inland Lake 28th September '98. Six were regular on Skala Polichnitos Salt Pans from 30th September '94, with 7 offshore from Kalloni Salt Pans on 5th October '94 and 5 together in Achladeri Bay on 18th January '98. Six were also seen together at East River mouth on 18th April '92, whilst a larger concentration concerned 12 at Petra reservoir on 27th January '98. Earliest record was of one there on 9th September '97, followed by a bird regular at mouth of Kalloni West River from 15th to 29th September '94. Latest record of 3 in Kalloni Bay 20th May '95, and a maximum of 4 together there (by the Salt Pan headland) on 10th May '95, and 5 on 19th April '97 (reducing to 2 by the month's end). Calm conditions in Kalloni Bay on 28th March '86 enabled an accurate maximum count to be carried out, producing 30 birds in total! There were also 2 birds on the Potamia reservoir in mid-April '97 - but this site was dry in '98!

Cory's Shearwater *Calonectris diomedea*
Mainly a summer visitor from mid-March to late October in small numbers, though 40+ from Molivos cliffs 28th May and 1st June '93 and *c*60 seen resting on sea off Petra on 1st October '94, with 50 fishing offshore at nearby Anaxos (in company with a few Yelkouan) on 30th August '96, 150+ in a mixed feeding party off Eftalou on 15th May that year. Exceptional records of 400+ seen on a boat trip from Sigri to Eressos on 9th June '96, 300+ east of Molivos on 16th September '97 and *c*800 flying east past Eftalou on 27th September '94. Rare in winter.

Mediterranean Shearwater *Puffinus yelkouan*
Resident, seen offshore in small numbers in all months. Also a spring migrant from March-May (peaking early to late April, when regular westerly passage noted). Most favoured area seems to be north coast around Molivos (where big offshore movement noted 15th April '95), but also seen to the west off Sigri, to the south off Plomari and to the east off Mytilini, where *c*40 near airport on 21st May '95. A gathering of 100+ in Nifida Bay on 28th March '98 (following a period of strong north-easterly winds), 150+ past Skala Eressos on 16th May '87, and several hundred next day, with 300+ offshore on 22nd May '95. Finally, 20+ at Skala Sikimmia on 1st June '93, 50+ off Molivos on 29th May '95 and *c*80 off Tavari 31st May '96. Also in May '96 high counts from Vatera included 164 on 3rd, 347 on 10th and 363 on 12th (with 90% heading west). The biggest concentration that year, however, occurrred off Eftalou on 15th, when 700+ birds were feeding quite close offshore! (Up to 1000 birds had also been seen nearby off Skala Sikimmia from 15th-16th April '92). A heavy and continuous southerly passage off Faneromeni beach on 15th May '96 involved 500+ in under half an hour, and on 29th April '97 was estimated at 1800 birds per hour - whilst 'good numbers' were also passing offshore in strong westerly winds from 11th-12th May that year. Equally impressive was a record of *c*500 off Kalloni West River mouth on 17th April '98 heading up the gulf (following 120+ at East River mouth 2 days earlier). However, none of these compare with an incredible 2000 off Skala Kalloni sitting in rafts and exploiting an obviously abundant food source during flat calm conditions on 4th April '86 - rising to a stunning 3000 on 6th-7th but reducing to 1000 by 10th. Birds may breed on offshore islands, but not proven. Certainly the figure of *c*1000 seen offshore between Sigri and Eressos in mid-June '98 is rather late for passage.

Cormorant *Phalacrocorax carbo*
Regular and widespread winter visitor in small numbers offshore and around river mouths, from September to late April (with some lingering in the summer months). These birds belong to the continental race, *P. c. sinensis* - see *The Birds of Greece*. Less frequently seen than

Shag, but favours similar areas - ie offshore from Eftalou and Skala Eressos. Also regularly seen in Geras and Kalloni Bays (with birds frequently seen resting on the old wooden jetty by Kalloni Salt Pans headland). Two were still in Kalloni Bay on 15th May '95 and 1 was at West River mouth as early as 4th August '98, whilst 3 were seen between Skala Eressos and Sigri on 10th August '97, with 14 offshore from Mytilini on 28th, 3 birds seen from Potamia River Bridge on 8th September '98 and 8 birds between Eressos and Sigri on 25th September '94. Largest recorded gatherings were of c30 at East River mouth on 29th March '98, 70+ fishing off Skala Eressos on 14th April '95 and c200 indulging in a frantic feeding frenzy amongst a large shoal of fish just offshore from Skala Polichnitos on 23rd January '98! Twelve plus birds were still to be seen in that area on 5th May '97 and a juvenile was present at East River mouth in mid-June '98.

Shag *Phalacrocorax aristotelis*
Resident around coast in small numbers (at least 15 pairs according to *The Birds of Greece*-which belong to the Mediterranean race *P. a. desmaresti*). Both adults and immatures seen - especially around the north and west coast, where maximum of 11 on islands offshore from Klio beach on 30th May '98, 11 beyond Eftalou on 1st October '94, 20 there on 14th August '96; with 27 in Eressos Bay mid-May '87 and mid-January '98 and 30+ there on 28th May '94 being dwarfed by a total of 50 seen between Molivos and Eftalou in August '91.

Pygmy Cormorant *Phalacrocorax pygmeus*
Irregular migrant and scarce but regular winter visitor usually between early November and mid-April (occasionally early May) - see *The Birds of Greece*. Only records of singles on 29th October '95 at Dipi Larssos Reedbed (a potential wintering site) and on Kalloni East River (inland from the lower ford) between at least 9th-20th August '96 and again on 11th April '97. An unconfirmed report of 3 on rocks near Sigri on 6th August '96 would be unusual, since reedy pools are usually preferred. More typical away from the favoured area was a bird seen on Anaxos beach pool on 25th August '97 (later seen heading out to sea) and one from the Eftalou road also heading north towards Turkey on the late date of 11th May '98.

White Pelican *Pelecanus onocrotalus*
Irregular migrant March to May, more usually in autumn. Passing spring birds most likely *en route* to the Danube Delta are often caught and tamed by local fishermen - hence some of the records below! Apart from the 2 birds which were resident at Skala Eressos for several years from October '93 (which, though free-flying, were regularly fed and of suspect origin) most records are of the odd injured bird, like the one on Kalloni West River on 11th May '93 or the bird residing from at least '97-'98 in Skala Kalloni harbour. But genuine migrant May 15th '87 flying high and circling West River mouth, and also over Skala Kalloni beach on 19th September '95, with 10 soaring north-west of Petra on 20th October that year, a bird sporting a yellow ring at Polichnitos Salt Pans 21st October '96 and a further 2 over Kalloni Salt Pans on 3rd September '97 (with possibly the same birds - 2 juveniles - seen there 2 days later). An adult and a juvenile were also seen coming in off the sea between Molivos and Petra on 6th September '97 and 2 adults were also seen at Skala Polichnitos Salt Pans on 10th and 14th September that year, with the sighting of a single bird (not the tame one!) around Kalloni Salt Pans from at least 5th-7th October. Bearing in mind the closeness of the dates there seems likely to be some duplication amongst these records.

Dalmatian Pelican *Pelecanus crispus*
Scarce migrant or vagrant. Only confirmed records of 2 adults at Skala Kalloni on 1st April '85, an immature from 3rd-10th April the same year, an adult again at the Salt Pans on 6th April '86 and one at the mouth of West River on 3rd September '97 (see above). However, 15

birds (including one juvenile) were seen resting at Kalloni Salt Pans on 7th August '98, and a distant flock of c15 seen flying distantly in a V formation on 8th September '95 over Haramida were also thought likely to be this species.

Bittern *Botaurus stellaris*

Scarce winter visitor and passage migrant from October to early May - but perhaps more regular than originally thought (especially between late March-late April). One seen flying from the reeds alongside Kalloni East River ford on 11th April '95, and observed several times upriver from the ford up to 25th April '96 (after which one was seen well along Kalloni Inland Lake ditches for a few days). There were also records that year (probably involving 2 or 3 birds) from West River and Parakila Marsh, with a bird roosting at Kalloni Inland Lake to mid-May and possibly beyond. Another good scattering of records through to early April '97 saw one flying in to Potamia River (just downriver from the road-bridge) on 19th March; from where it was observed feeding on several dates over the next few days. Another was located at Faneromeni ford on 24th March that year, and there were further sightings at Inland Lake ditches again from 30th March-2nd April. The last '97 sightings were at Parakila Marsh and Mikri Limni Marsh on 8th April. No wintering birds were found in January '98 (though weather conditions were exceptionally mild at the time). However, a marked passage involving at least 3 birds led to sightings on 31st March '98 at both Kalloni Salt Pans and Parakila Marsh. The next sighting was not till 11th April at Faneromeni ford (sadly found dead shortly afterwards - presumed hit by car). Thereafter there were no records until 2 long-stayers were located (on Kalloni Pool from at least 17th-29th April) and at the small marsh near Derbyshire (at least 27th April-3rd May '98). A bird was also seen again at Faneromeni ford on 25th April (with what was probably another bird on the Chalandra River Skala Eressos the same day). One was also seen briefly round the Inland Lake ditches on 11th April and again on 1st May '98, but earlier scrub and reed clearance rendered this previously favoured habitat largely unsuitable. All these recent records suggest the incidence of true wintering birds to be low (especially bearing in mind the lack of any substantial stands of reeds away from Dipi Larssos). A bird recovered shot near Madamados on 2nd February '97 and released 3 weeks later provides the only evidence of wintering; but clearly the severity of the weather on the mainland is an important factor here. However, an early spring passage peaking between late March and mid-April would appear quite pronounced. Much of the food taken appears to be frogs and tadpoles, which may explain the absence of autumn records, when this food source would be in much shorter supply and many of the favoured wetlands simply wouldn't exist. However, 1 bird was seen at Anaxos in the second half of September '97, and at Haramida marsh in 'late autumn' that year.

Little Bittern *Ixobrychus minutus*

Mainly a locally common spring migrant from early April to late May or early June (peaking late April to mid-May), when can be found in most suitable wetlands (even small ditches) in large numbers. Rarer from mid-August to late September. First recorded along the Potamia River on 4th April '97, and around Kalloni Inland Lake on 9th April that year, but mid-month is more usual. It almost certainly breeds in Dipi Larssos Reedbed, with occasional localized breeding suspected elsewhere. Otherwise, favoured areas are Kalloni East River, Potamia River, Skala Eressos River (especially by the ford), Faneromeni ford (where 5+ on 6th May '95 and 7 on 11th May '98 - peaking at 10 on 14th!) and the ditches bordering Kalloni Inland Lake, where some of the highest densities are encountered. Numbers there tend to peak early to mid-May, with double figure numbers on a hundred yard stretch of ditch on 8th May '93! For a normally secretive bird, the migrants in Lesvos can be amazingly confiding and approachable in their quest for tadpoles! A male was seen away from the usual areas on a small ford near Petra reservoir on 18th May '96, with regular sightings of single birds around the river mouth at Vatera mid-month (with up to 7 there on 15th May '98) and 2 regular in drainage ditches near Anaxos beach in mid-May '98. Late spring records concern 2 females at Kalloni Inland Lake on 23rd May '98, a bird flushed from Parakila Marsh on 29th May the same year, and one present on East River up to 5th June '88. More significant was a single bird and a pair seen on East River ford from late May into early June evrry year from '96-8 (with at least 1 bird still present from 5th-17th June '97 and reports of up to 3 there the first week of June that year - 3 being seen again on 17th August) and finally a male seen in the same area on 6th and 8th July '98 and a female / immature there on 12th and 19th August '98. At least 1 bird was also present around Kalloni Inland Lake from the third week of August to early September '97. In the light of all these records, a recent summering and probable breeding pair would seem likely in the Kalloni area. The only other autumn records are of a female along Kalloni Salt Pan channel 10th August '95, a bird calling at dusk over Haramida Marsh on 10th September '96 and a female / immature again by the East River ford from mid to late September '94 (the latest recorded).

Night Heron *Nycticorax nycticorax*
Mainly a spring migrant from late March to mid-May (peaking mid-April to early May), and more rarely from early September to mid-October, when easily overlooked. Earliest record of 10 over Malemi Hotel on 22nd March '97, with a single bird on Kalloni East River 3 days later and again on 29th March '98. Regular at Faneromeni ford (where 4 birds in mid-May '96), on Chalandra River Skala Eressos, and Kalloni Inland Lake and East River, where a roost in overhanging willows peaked at 6 birds on 11th April '95, with the last 2 seen on 22nd, but a further 9 overhead on 21st May. Also seen on Potamia River, where 1 on 11th April '95. Six birds were roosting at Parakila Marsh on 7th May '96, with 3 still there mid-month, and 1 on 25th. A roost of 5 adults was observed at Kalloni Inland Lake on 22nd April and again on 9th May '97 (with 7 seen in flight near East River on 23rd April), and there were also 2 adults on 6th May at Faneromeni ford, with 1 juvenile a week later and up to 5 birds feeding there on 11th May '98 (attracted no doubt by the glut of tadpoles!) Up to 4 were feeding in Kalloni Salt Pan channel on the evening of 18th May '95, and 1-2 roosting in pines alongside the Vouvaris River near Achladeri from at least 17th-18th. The largest gatherings include a flock of 8 seen there on 13th April '95, 10 there on 4th April '97, 10 flying over the river-mouth at Makara on 3rd May '98, a party of 13 at Parakila Marsh and Kalloni Inland Lake on 16th May '97 (probably the same birds), and the incredible number of 54 at Skala Kalloni coming in from the south on 18th April '92! Apart from singles seen on Kalloni Pool in May '98 most days up to 29th, the latest spring records are of an immature at Vatera river mouth 1st June '98 and on Kalloni East River 6th June '88 - though more unusual was a party of 3 by the East River ford on 4th June '98. In autumn a total of 21 flew south over Skala Eressos and out to sea on 10th September '89, whilst a flock of 5 adults and 9 immatures landed briefly at the Chalandra River mouth Skala Eressos on 7th September '94, before heading due south out to sea. Between 15th-22nd September that year several flocks of between 15 and 20 birds were also seen heading out to sea (with 3 flocks totalling 52 birds on 20th - probably disturbed by shooting). An adult and 5 immatures were still roosting in tamarisks close to Skala Eressos 22nd September '94, whilst between 1 and 2 birds were regularly heard calling at dusk over Haramida Marsh most evenings between 31st August-6th September '96. Finally, single immatures were seen at East River ford 11th August '96 and around Kalloni Inland Lake a week later, whilst 2 birds were present on Kalloni Pool 19th September '98 during exceptional autumn water levels there. It seems likely from these records that autumn passage is heavier than was originally thought - with much of it not being documented at this time of year, owing to a lack of visiting birders.

Squacco Heron *Ardeola ralloides*
Common spring migrant from early April to late May (peaking late April-early May) and occasional from late August to early October. Widespread in all suitable wetland areas, where birds often very obvious and confiding. Kalloni East River a favourite site, where up to 17 counted in one short stretch on 18th April '95. Also around Kalloni Salt Pans channel, where a late bird observed on 24th May the same year, with another still on Kalloni Pool. Potamia River, Parakila Marsh and Faneromeni ford are also favoured sites, and migrants can sometimes be seen resting on Skala Kalloni beach eg 10 on 18th April '92 and 25 1st May '98 (see below) - following 18 seen flying over 'Derbyshire' the previous day. Earliest record of 1 bird at Kalloni Salt Pans on 31st March '97, with the next at East River on 6th April that year (where there was still a late bird up to 31st May at least), but mid-April is a more typical arrival date. Spring '98 saw Kalloni Pool especially favoured, where 3 birds in mid-April had grown to 12 by the month's end - peaking briefly at 34 on 1st May when they were joined by a flock disturbed from the beach! Two were still present on 29th May, with 1 on the late date of 10th June and 6 claimed the next day. Apart from singles at Faneromeni beach on 7th August '96, Anaxos on 20th August and on the Chalandra River Skala Eressos on 1st September that year, the only autumn records are of 5 birds (a mixture of adults and immatures) flying into Chalandra River Skala Eressos in September '89, and 7 flying over olive groves near the sea at Gavathas on 15th September '89; together with 2-3 calling over Haramida Marsh on 8th September '96. More noteworthy, however, was a flock of 20+ seen flying from the East River mouth across Kalloni bay on 22nd August the same year!

Cattle Egret *Bubulcus ibis*
Scarce vagrant or irregular passage migrant. Only 2 recent records - of a bird first seen at Sigri on 16th May '95, and probably the same bird over Kalloni East River later that day, and associating with cattle at the back of the Salt Pans on 20th. Another was seen at Vassilika on 7th May '96.

Little Egret *Egretta garzetta*
Common migrant in all wetland areas from late March to late May (peaking mid-April to early May). Also a small autumn passage from late August to early October, with the odd wintering and a few summering birds possible (the latter mainly immatures). For this reason, can be encountered in virtually any month; but peak concentrations usually around Kalloni Salt Pan channels and surrounding pools, where flocks of 40+ not unusual from mid-April to mid-May, and 50+ on flooded fields there 17th April '95 and up to 120 birds present at the pans from 20th-21st, with a flock of 80+ in the channel between 26th April-2nd May '97. Still 30 on pools east of the Salt Pans on 18th May and 9 were still present at 'Derbyshire' after overnight storms on 1st June '94; whilst a pair was seen at Parakila Marsh on the late date of 10th June '97 (with a single near East River on 13th). A party of 12 migrants was seen heading south over Kalloni Inland Lake on 31st May '98 and 9 were still present at Kalloni Salt Pans in mid-June '98. Otherwise the biggest recorded gathering was of *c*200 birds at Kalloni Salt Pans on 22nd April '84 (falling to 100 by 25th). Much scarcer in autumn, when only records of a bird on Petra reservoir 4th August '96, up to 2 on Kalloni East River, at Dipi Larssos pools and Kalloni Salt Pans from 3rd-7th August that year (with 3 at the latter site on 14th, 4 there from 11th-17th August '97 and up to 12 on 12th August '98), 2 on rocks near Tavari and 1 on the Chalandra River Skala Eressos on 23rd September '94, with 1 briefly on Kalloni East River the next day. Six were seen at 'Derbyshire' from 18th to 23rd September '94, and 2 also at Kalloni Salt Pans on the latter date, with 2 present on 12th August '89, 3 on 22nd August '96 and 9 on 19th August '97 - reducing to 3 in the first half of September. Nine seen at Kalloni West River on 9th September '97 may have been the same birds. The biggest autumn numbers concern a party of 13 flushed from Anaxos beach on 27th August '96, following a sighting of 26 seen

flighting from nearby offshore islands a week earlier. There were also 15 seen at Kalloni Salt Pans on 4th September '96, 10 there in the first week of August '98 (reducing to 4 by 2nd September) and 20+ present at Skala Polichnitos on 31st August '97 and 9th September '98. Only one winter record - of a single bird feeding with Great White Egret in Kalloni Salt Pan channels on 21st January '98. Otherwise the earliest spring records concern 1 on West River 20th March '97 and 3 birds on Kalloni Pool 23rd March '98.

Great White Egret *Egretta alba*
Locally common winter visitor from October to May, mainly confined to the 2 sets of salt pans and surrounding pools, 'Derbyshire' and Kalloni East and West Rivers. Apart from 3 seen offshore between Anaxos and Petra on 28th August '96, 2 at Skala Polichnitos on 31st August '97 and 2 at Kalloni West River mouth on 6th September that year, and 1 at Kalloni Salt Pans from 9th September '98 groups of 11 and 10 seen there on 27th September '97 and '98 respectively are the earliest records, with 12 on Kalloni East River on 28th September '98 possibly relating to the same birds, 1 at Skala Polichnitos Salt Pans from 30th September '94, up to 9 wintering on Kalloni Salt Pans the same year, and a maximum of 6 on West River by 23rd October '96. Between 25-30 were observed roosting at the Kalloni Salt Pans in mid-January '98, with birds spreading out to feed in nearby wet areas and field margins during the day. This would suggest up to 50 or so potential wintering birds, if both salt pans are taken into account. Certainly a gathering of 30 birds there was confirmed there on 7th April '98. Odd birds (usually immatures) can linger up to late May (eg 3 in non-breeding plumage seen at 'Derbyshire' 11th May '96) but a party of 11 seen on Kalloni Salt Pans up to 11th June '98 was far more unusual, as were 2 sightings of a single bird at 'Derbyshire' on 9th and 22nd July '97 and another (immature) bird around Kalloni Salt Pans between at least 3rd-14th August '96. It is difficult to say whether all such sightings relate to immatures that may never have left or some to early returning birds; but *The Birds of Greece* suggest that this species may be on the increase throughout Greece - so more frequent sightings are likely!

Grey Heron *Ardea cinerea*
Winter visitor and passage migrant from August to May, with passage evident early March-late May (peaking around mid-April) and mid-August to mid-October - well distributed in all suitable wetlands. A few may summer. For this reason can be seen in most months, but favoured areas mouth of Kalloni West River, both sets of salt pans and 'Derbyshire' (where 10+ on 24th March '98). Five were on Kalloni Salt Pans by 6th September '94, with maximum counts of 10 there on 14th September '98, 10 at West River on 10th September '98, 12 flying over there on 3rd September '97 and 17 present on 24th April '95, 12 at Skala Polichnitos Salt Pans on 21st August '97, 13 present on 5th October '94, 25 there 21st October '96, 23 again at Kalloni Salt Pans on 7th April '98 and 25 there on 11th April '95, with 28 recorded on 1st April '97 and 17 on East River 3 days later. Four were still present there on 19th May and 5 late birds were still to be seen at 'Derbyshire' after storms on 1st June '94. An early record of 15 birds from Kalloni Salt Pans on 5th August '96 and 7 there in the first week of August '98.

Purple Heron *Ardea purpurea*
Passage migrant, occurring mainly in spring (from late March to mid-May, but peaking mid-April) in any suitable wetland areas, especially those with plenty of cover - even quite small ditches where not always easy to spot. Much rarer in autumn (from September to early October - when many of the wetlands are dry). First records of a single on Kalloni East River 22nd March '98, 4 together on Kalloni Pool 30th March '98, and 2 together on Kalloni East River 31st March '97. Passage usually peaks mid-April, when birds are regular at both the above sites, together with Kalloni Inland Lake and ditches, Parakila Marsh, Haramida Marsh, Dipi Larssos, Chalandra River Skala Eressos, Faneromeni ford (where 6 birds on 8th April

'86) and both sets of salt pans. Kalloni East River, however, remains a favoured site (eg 6 together there 11th April '95, with 6 around the Salt Pans on 24th). One is often greeted with the rather incongruous sight of birds flushed from East River perched precariously on the tops of nearby olive trees - they are also often seen in the surrounding flooded or damp fields or thr tracks *en route* to the Salt Pans (presumably stalking frogs). Maximum count 7 flying over Skala Eressos on 18th May '87 (with 5 there on 28th April '98), 8 over Kalloni Salt Pans on 7th April '98, 16 flying in off the sea at Skala Kalloni on the late date of 24th May '96, and 14 over Kalloni East River on 28th April '97 (presumably part of a flock of 19 flushed from a small pool just east of the river earlier in the day). A melanistic bird frequented the East River for a few days in early May '95. Otherwise occasionally recorded up to end of May (when mainly immatures lingering) - eg 1 on Kalloni Pool during the last week of May '98 (up to 30th) and another bird still present on Parakila Marsh 29th May '94 and 1st June '98 (along with a bird at Kalloni Inland Lake on the same date in '96 constituting the latest spring record). The only autumn sightings are of 1 near Achladeri on 8th August '94, 1 at Skala Kalloni on 29th September '94, 4 at Kalloni Salt Pans on 10th September '95 and 1 there on 24th September '96 and 5th September '97 (following a spate of sightings in the Kalloni area involving at least 2 birds between 24th August-5th September at least), with one at West River 3rd August '96 (the earliest autumn date) and a juvenile there with Grey Herons on 10th September '98, and at the nearby Potamia River on 19th September that year. Other single juveniles were recorded at East River ford on 20th August '96 and at the Chalandra River mouth Skala Eressos on 5th August '98 (the earliest autumn date). The latest autumn record by far is of a bird on East River 19th October '95.

Black Stork *Ciconia nigra*
Summer visitor in small numbers from late March to October, and also a passage migrant. Somewhere between 3 and 5 pairs usually breed in remote areas - according to *The Birds of Greece* usually in Calabrian Pine *Pinus brutia*. Most likely breeding areas are around Achladeri (where 4 seen together on 4th August '94) and close to the Perivolis Monastery beyond Vatoussa, where a bird often perched on high rocks in May '95. It may be birds from here that are regularly seen feeding on the Chalandra River (often well inland from Skala Eressos), or this could involve a further breeding pair. Another likely sight is the area inland from Kalloni East River, where 5 were seen in flight on 24th April '98 and a bird was showing well on top of rocks on 28th June that year. Birds regularly observed feeding on Kalloni East and West Rivers, Potamia River, and anywhere between Kalloni Salt Pans and 'Derbyshire', where 6 were feeding together on 18th May '95 (and 7 on 20th). Though usually flighty, occasionally (as in mid-May '98) an ultra-tame individual can be observed feeding at close range on Kalloni Salt Pans channel. Seven also flew over the pans on 6th May '93, 5 were feeding there on 7th June '98, an impressive gathering of 14 was flushed from a small pool just east of East River on 11th June '97 - there were still 8 feeding at East River on 17th June that year. Birds regularly seen on small coastal pool beyond 'Derbyshire' towards Achladeri. First recorded 23rd March from Potamia Valley, and autumn records of 1 on Kalloni Salt Pans 19th September '89, 1 on the East River 24th September '94, with 1 or 2 feeding on the West River between the 15th and 29th. One seen at 'Derbyshire' on 20th September '95 and around Kalloni Salt Pans for several days up to at least 22nd October that year - the latest recorded date. Highest counts likely in autumn, when 9 birds (including 1 juvenile) were at Kalloni West River on 6th August '96, with 7 birds there (including 5 immatures) a week later. Fourteen birds were seen over Kalloni Inland Lake on 27th August '97, with the same number again on 31st, seen over Skala Kalloni on 30th and in Potamia Valley on 4th September, with 9 over the Salt Pans 2 days later. Five birds were also present at Skala Polichnitos Salt Pans on 16th September '98, with 2 seen at Kalloni Salt Pans up to 20th. All these counts were eclipsed by one of 20 over West River on 20th August '97 and the same number again over Kalloni Inland

Lake on 28th. Unusually, 2 wintering birds were seen throughout January '98 commuting between the 2 sets of salt pans.

White Stork *Ciconia ciconia*
Localized summer visitor and breeder from early or mid-March to late August or early September. Also a passage migrant (eg up to 35 together in field at Kalloni Salt Pans 2nd May '95 and at least 34 in the same area for several days from 7th May '98 - when around 30 circling East River and a flock of 60+ wheeling over Petra on 8th and a similar number - possibly the same birds - seen over Kalloni Salt Pans; with 28 at Megali Limni on 18th May that year). Somewhere between 5 and 7 pairs usually breed, with their main stronghold in the Kalloni area (2 chimney tower nests in Kalloni, 1 on Papiana Church, 1 in Kerami). Also sporadic nesting on Skala Eressos Church, Agiassos and a chimney tower at Polichnitos (to which a bird had already returned by February '95). Apparently there were 2 nests in this vicinity in '98, both still tenanted on 9th September! Presumably the same bird was seen there in mid-January '98, and it is reported that this particular bird never leaves. Birds regularly observed feeding on Kalloni East River and Kalloni Pool. Numbers build up in August, with 6 birds on Kalloni East River on 6th August '94 increasing to 16 by 10th. An unusual record concerns a migratory gathering of no less than 147 birds at Vatera river mouth on 23rd August '97 - counted by a birder who'd been dozing on the beach and woke up thinking he must be dreaming! All had left within half an hour. Equally if not more impressive was a flock of c300 birds watched overflying the Kalloni area in mid-August '85! Up to 3 birds were seen at Kalloni East and West Rivers and both sets of salt pans between 9th and 12th September '98, with 5 seen riding thermals at Haramida Marsh on 9th and 1 still present at Skala Polichnitos on 16th. A late bird seen circling there on 21st October '96 could have referred to the local resident.

Glossy Ibis *Plegadis falcinellus*
Common spring migrant from late March to mid-May (peaking early to mid-April) - rare in autumn. Earliest record of 4 birds at Parakila Marsh 19th March '97. Fairly regular around Kalloni Salt Pans, where 30 seen overflying on 24th March '98, up to 100 in mid-April '87, flock of 30 seen soaring on 8th May '94, and numbers peaked at between 80 and 90 on 17th April '95, with 77 on 18th, reducing to 32 by 24th, and last seen 4th May. In addition, 3 were also seen on Skala Polichnitos Salt Pans on 19th April that year, and in a flooded field between Molivos and Eftalou a week earlier. Also regular on Kalloni East River, where up to 65 from early to mid-April '97 (peaking at 130 in the area on 18th April, falling to 70 on 21st, but still 14 on 14th May), small marsh opposite 'Derbyshire', where 22 on 9th May '92, and Kalloni Pool, with birds also feeding in flooded fields around the Inland Lake tracks from 10th-11th April '97. A flock of 75 had been seen on both West River and Kalloni Pool on 6th April. By contrast birds in spring '98 were less widespread and more sporadic in occurrence, with none at all on East River (possibly because of heavy flooding there in March reducing the food supply), and main sightings from the Salt Pans area and the large flooded field, with 22 on 1st April rising to 70 on 12th and falling to 30 by 15th, 18 by 21st, still 21 on 28th, with the last 6 seen there on 4th May, but with 5 still on nearby Kalloni Pool from 11th-14th and just odd singles thereafter. Latest spring records concern 2 birds at the river mouth near Vatera on 23rd May '97 and 3 birds commuting between Kalloni Pool and Parakila Marsh from at least 5th-16th June '97. The highest numbers ever recorded involve c240 birds feeding in fields around Skala Kalloni on 15th April '84 and no less than 400 birds departing in groups north and east from Kalloni Salt Pans on the evening of 27th April the same year! The only autumn records are of 60 flying high over Gavathas region heading south-west towards Sigri on 15th September '89, a single bird commuting between East and West River mouths on 20th August

'96 and 1 present on Kalloni Pool in the first week of August '98 during record summer water levels there. A single bird was also seen at Skala Polichnitos Salt Pans on 9th September '98.

Spoonbill *Platalea leucorodia*
Rare migrant from March to May, occasional from September-October. Usually seen around the Kalloni Salt Pans, where 2 birds seen on 18th and 22nd April '84 (with 2 also at Skala Kalloni on the latter date and 1 there from 24th-27th), another 2 there on 6th April '86, 2 from 14th-16th and 1 on 18th April '87 and 1 bird observed on 20th May '91, with 1 briefly in the channel on 14th May '92. Also up to 2 glimpsed from a distance feeding in a pool between the Salt Pans and 'Derbyshire' in early May '95 (with 1 seen up to 16th). Five at Kalloni Salt Pans on 11th May '92 was unusual, but 2 (1 immature) were seen feeding together at Skala Polichnitos Salt Pans on 9th April '97, and a flock of up to 20 birds seen to land between Kalloni East River and Salt Pans on 20th April that year was truly exceptional. Spring '98 produced only 1 overflying bird at Kalloni Salt Pans on 14th April, but a group of 7 flew over Sigri harbour on 27th April. Three late records - of 5 birds in the 'Derbyshire' area from 1st-2nd June '94 after heavy overnight rain and strong north-easterly winds, and a bird at Skala Polichnitos Salt Pans on 17th May and 3rd June '97 - presumably the same individual. Reported only 5 times in autumn - a flock of 13 circling the Kalloni Salt Pans on 21st October '96 (which eventually headed off north), a single there on 8th September '98, increasing to 3 birds on 16th, with 11 flying over on 29th September '98 and 2 at Kalloni West River mouth on 3rd September '97 - 1 remaining the next day.

Greater Flamingo *Phoenicopterus ruber*
Winter visitor from late September to May (and occasional non breeding visitor at other times -see *The Birds of Greece*), largely confined to the 2 sets of salt pans - though also seen feeding sporadically at 'Derbyshire' and East and West River mouths (eg 150+ at East River mouth on 28th September '98 and 160+ feeding at West River mouth on 22nd January '98 following heavy flooding). The wintering population may be increasing, with as many as 500 birds divided between the 2 salt pans in January '98 (almost double the number previously thought to winter). On 22nd January '98 at least 460 were counted on Kalloni Salt Pans alone! The earliest record for Skala Polichnitos Salt Pans consisted of 8 birds on 21st August '96, 52 birds on 31st August '97 and 34 on 13th September '95, whilst 27 on 10th September '97 had grown to 140+ on 14th. Kalloni Salt Pans, however, held only 2 early individuals at the beginning of September '95, 1 on 8th September '97 (rising to 24 by 17th), whilst *c*120 (including 18 juveniles) were present there at the end of September '96 (rising by 21st October to 159 - of

which about 30 were juveniles). A count of 150+ was made there in mid-April '85, 182 birds were present on 22nd April '97 (down to just 12 by 2nd May), and an all-time record of 600 was reached on 26th September that year (falling to 350 in the first week of October - presumably as birds moved on or shifted their allegiance to Polichnitos Salt Pans). In autumn '98 40+ birds in mid-September had grown to 200+ by the month's end and c300 by 2nd October. Elsewhere a flock of 25 flew over Petra Bay on 4th May '95 (with 18 flying north-east offshore from Molivos the next day). A party of 12 (including several juveniles) was resting on the sea off Molivos on 5th September '94, but most spectacular was a fly-past of 350 heading northeast over Molivos at sunset on 27th April '98! That year also up to 36 birds were still being seen at Kalloni Salt Pans on 22nd May, falling to 26 by 3rd June, but with 16 still present up to the exceptionally late date of 11th June. These lingerers are likely to be non-breeders, since the bulk of the wintering population has usually departed by late April.

Mute Swan *Cygnus olor*
Occasional hard weather winter visitor from mid-October to mid-March. *The Birds of Greece* points out that this species normally winters further north, but mentions notable southerly influxes caused by severe weather in the '85 and '93-4 winters especially. In line with this a small family party remained on Kalloni Pool during the '93-4 winter, but only 1 bird returned the next year. An immature wintering there up to late March '97 was subsequently found dead. Amazingly, 1 recorded on Kalloni Salt Pans between mid and late May '88, and also on a small pool near Mytilini on 2nd May '96! The most obvious evidence of a hard weather movement concerned 15 on Kalloni Salt Pans on 10th February '95 and the same number offshore from Skala Kalloni on 7th February '96.

Whooper Swan *Cygnus cygnus*
Irregular and scarce hard weather winter visitor from December to February, as in the '93-4 winter when one joined the Mute Swans on Kalloni Pool (coinciding with a very severe spell of weather in northern Greece, and a big southerly influx of this species). No other records known.

White-fronted Goose *Anser albifrons*
Sporadic winter visitor from November to late February or early March, with numbers fluctuating according to severity of weather. Reported in *The Birds of Greece* as reaching as far south as the northern Aegean islands (including Lesvos) in periods of severe weather - eg the '81 winter. Otherwise little else known. Intriguingly, the silhouette of a goose seen in flight in late April '98 could well have been this species by a simple process of elimination!

Ruddy Shelduck *Tadorna ferruginea*
Resident, but also a partial migrant and winter visitor in small numbers. Numbers present are obviously strongly influenced by the seasonal drying up or flooding of their favoured habitats (see *The Birds of Greece*). Peak sightings can occur anytime between late March and the second half of May around the back of the Kalloni Salt Pans and at 'Derbyshire', where 40+ were seen on 19th March '97, 36 on 23rd March '98, 25 birds were present on 15th April '85 and a flock of up to 50 had built up by 22nd May '95, with 31 on 30th May '96 (with 29 still present 5th June that year, 30 on 1st June '94 after overnight storms, with just a single pair by 13th June '97 and 7 on 1st June '98). Also recorded in the area of Kalloni West River, and the odd pair seen over the river valley near Sigri (with a pair at Faneromeni on 19th April '95 and 20 at sea off Skala Eressos on 23rd May that year). Otherwise reputed to breed in good numbers around the bay below Palios on the north-east coast, and several birds seen on small pools in that area 21st April the same year and in each spring following. Also a pair with young reported from Kalloni Inland Lake in late May '94, and a pair thought to be nesting in a

rock-face near Agra mid-May '95 and a pair with recently hatched young seen on the river near Kalloni Salt Pans 13th May '97. Generally a wary bird, however, and difficult to get anywhere near. Scarce in autumn, though this may be more to do with lack of water at this time. Nonetheless, an impressive total of 46 birds was counted on Kalloni Salt Pans 11th August '96, falling to 18 by 14th, with just 2 seen there on 9th July '97 and 2 at 'Derbyshire' on 1st August '98 and 1 on 18th. A new site that year was Petra reservoir, where 5 birds were seen on 19th August. Up to 6 birds were present in the flooded field behind Kalloni Salt Pans in January '98, rising to flocks of 35+ during March and the first half of April, after which the area was rapidly drying up and many had dispersed - much earlier than previous years. However, 22 were seen in the area on 1st May that year.

Shelduck *Tadorna tadorna*
Mainly a locally common winter visitor from November to March, (probably not more than a couple of dozen or so), though a small spring passage, and perhaps again in autumn. Mainly occurs on the two salt pans and at 'Derbyshire', but usually only seen in ones and twos, though several on Kalloni Salt Pans 7th May '93, 4 there 25th April '95 (rising to 10 by 20th), 4 again 19th March and 23rd April '97, with 2 on 23rd March '98. Six were also seen on Skala Polichnitos Salt Pans 28th March '98, but the biggest gatherings by far are of 15 at Kalloni Salt Pans on 22nd April '84 and 3rd April '85 and 18 from 29th-31st March '86 (decreasing to 4 by 6th April but up to 10 again on 9th - suggesting passage). Latest record of 1 at Kalloni Salt Pans on 11th May '98, 4 there on 18th May '97 and 2 still present there on the very late date of 25th May '87. First recorded there on the early date of 4th September '96 (a single).

Wigeon *Anas penelope*
Irregular winter visitor in small numbers from late October to late March. Few sightings outside this period, but 4 birds seen at Skala Kalloni in the first week of April '85, whilst 2 were present at 'Derbyshire' on 3rd April that year, and a late bird was seen between the Salt Pans and 'Derbyshire' on 13th. One autumn record - of a bird on Kalloni West River 11th and 13th October '94.

Gadwall *Anas strepera*
Irregular winter visitor in small numbers from November to February. No records outside this period and none seen on a January '98 visit - probably because of unseasonably mild weather.

Teal *Anas crecca*
Winter visitor in small numbers and scarce passage migrant from late August to mid or late March. Earliest records of 3 birds at Kalloni Salt Pans on 5th August '96, with 2 there on 12th and 6 at Kalloni West River mouth on 14th. Two were seen there on 12th September and 11th October '94, with small single figure numbers recorded on Skala Polichnitos Salt Pans from 28th September that year, a maximum count of 30 overflying the pans on 22nd, and a single bird there again on 21st October '96. A single drake was seen at Kalloni Pool on 15th April '84 (with a female there on 31st March '85 and at 'Derbyshire' on 3rd April that year). Up to 3 were present at Skala Kalloni on 25th March '86, with 5 at the Salt Pans on 29th March and 1 up to 2nd April. There were 10 on Kalloni Pool 19th March '97 (with the last record of a single bird on 21st), and 11 around Kalloni Salt Pans on 7th October that year. In January '98 6 birds on Kalloni Pool had grown to an impressive 40 by 22nd, and 6 were seen at Kalloni West River on the latest recorded date of 17th April.

Mallard *Anas platyrhynchos*
Irregular winter visitor in small numbers from November to March, with irregular nesting possible (see *The Birds of Greece*). Apart from late records along Kalloni East River on 16th

April '84 (a pair), 18th April '92, 19th May '93, Mikri Limni 25th April '98, a pair on Kalloni Pool 22nd April '84 and 1st-3rd April '85, a female on 10th April '87, an unseasonal (and possible cross-bred) drake there on 22nd May '95, a male at 'Derbyshire' on 7th March '86 and a female at Dipi Larssos on 9th August '96, at Petra reservoir exactly a month later (and again from 5th-6th August '97), and at Kalloni Inland Lake 24th October, a pair was also seen at the latter site in the middle 2 weeks of August '96, on 22nd March, 4th April, 8th June '97, and again during late September and the first week of October that year. Finally another unseasonal female was present at this favoured site on 12th July '98.

Pintail *Anas acuta*
Winter visitor from late September to late March, and small passage from April to early May and again in autumn. Confined largely to 2 salt pans (cg 6 regular on Skala Polichnitos Salt Pans from 28th September '94). A single bird was also present on Petra reservoir 29th September '97. Evidence of a small spring passage comes with records of $c15$ at Kalloni Salt Pans on 18th April '84, reducing to 4 offshore by 22nd, 15 again on 3rd April '85 and 20 at 'Derbyshire' on the same date (reducing to 3-4 birds by mid-month), and 4 flying out to sea on 7th May '94, later relocated on Kalloni East River. This site also held a drake on 19th March '97, with one (or the same bird) on West River mouth the next day. An exceptional gathering in Kalloni Bay peaked at $c500$ birds on 22nd March '97 (after heavy storms on 20th). Four birds were frequenting the rapidly drying pools in the large field behind Kalloni Salt Pans for a few days from 27th March - 8th April '98 (along with large numbers of Garganey) and 3 drakes were also seen on Polichnitos Salt Pans on 3rd April that year, with 2 still present on 10th.

Garganey *Anas quercedula*
Spring migrant from early March to mid-May in good numbers (peaking late March to mid-April). Occasional offshore or on new reservoirs from early August to late September. Counts of 7 on Kalloni East River 12th May '95 (with 4 on West River on 14th) with 14 on Kalloni Pool (a regular site) on 27th March '97 and 50+ there on 22nd March '98. Also seen on Kalloni Salt Pans, where late record of 1 drake on 16th May '94 (dropping from a maximum of 3 on 8th), and more recently on the new Potamia reservoir (where 5 birds on 28th March '97). Elsewhere a maximum count of 20+ at Parakila Marsh (another favoured site) on 22nd April '96, and 16 on the Chalandra River Skala Eressos at about the same time. More dramatic were counts of 180 at Skala Kalloni on 31st March '85 (reducing to 100+ by 4th May and 15 by mid-month), and a movement of 100+ seen in Kalloni Bay on 22nd March '97, in company with large numbers of Pintail - see below. Numbers then peaked at 150+ on Kalloni Salt Pans 3 days later. On 23rd March '98, however, at least 200 were present in the flooded field behind the pans, reducing to $c130$ by 28th - with several seen displaying on 31st on the main road 'garage' pool. Elsewhere 80 were seen flying in off the sea at Achladeri on 9th April that year, with a peak of 300+ offshore there on 11th! First recorded from Kalloni Pool on 21st March '97, and last recorded there 19th and 25th May '97 (3 drakes), with a single male lingering up to the very late date of 8th June that year and again up to mid-June May '98 - with a pair earlier present both there and on Kalloni East River on 18th May. Unusual records of 2 birds at Kalloni Salt Pans on 4th September '96 and 7 there on 26th September '98, and 6 birds at Petra reservoir on 28th July '96 (reducing to 1 by 7th August) with an eclipse-plumage bird there on 4th, 7th and 9th August '97, rising to 3 on 12th. Autumn records may now be more regular in occurrence since this reservoir has come to maturity, and the importance of wet sites in autumn is borne out by the report of 5 birds (2 females and 3 immatures) on Kalloni Pool in the first week of August '98, rising to 13 on 16th - when the site was unusually wet.

Shoveler *Anas clypeata*
Scarce but regular winter visitor from late September to mid or late April, and passage migrant (mainly in spring) - though there is also a small autumn passage from mid-August to October. However, it is often difficult to separate the two - see *The Birds of Greece*. A drake was on Kalloni East River on 24th September '94 and another on Parakila Marsh for a few days in mid-April '95. Also a pair on Kalloni Salt Pans on 15th April the same year (following a flock of 20 seen on 10th). Maximum count of 23 on Kalloni Pool 20th March '97 (reducing to 3 by 27th and none thereafter). In January '98 numbers peaked at 30+ there on 22nd after heavy overnight flooding; but the unprecedented number of at least 46 was recorded there on 27th March that year after gale-force winds and further severe flooding the day before! Four birds were still present on 25th April, but none thereafter. Elsewhere yet another record gathering occurred in the flooded field at the back of Kalloni Salt Pans, where 50+ birds were counted in association with several hundred Garganey and *c*20 Ruddy Shelduck on 31st March '98. Presumably this was a pre-migratory peak, as only about 8 remained remained by 7th April. A duck and 5 drakes also frequented the Salt Pan channel for several days from 1st-3rd May '96 - the latest spring date. Two autumn records, of a female at West River mouth on 12th August '95 and a male in the recently flooded field behind Kalloni Salt Pans from 23rd September '98.

Pochard *Aythya ferina*
Irregular winter visitor from October to March. Prefers deeper water than other ducks, so fairly scarce; but may benefit from recently constructed reservoirs. This fact was borne out by the sighting of 5 birds on Petra reservoir on 27th January '98 - following on from a party of 3 on Kalloni Pool on 12th. More unusual was the record of a single bird at the Chalandra River mouth Skala Eressos on 5th August '98.

Ferruginous Duck *Aythya nyroca*
Regular but scarce passage migrant from mid-March to late April and September-October. (when large flocks may be encountered on the sea). Otherwise seems to prefer well vegetated freshwater wetlands - see *The Birds of Greece*. There were 7 (an island record) present at 'Derbyshire' during the first 3 days of April '85 - reducing to 4 birds by 10th. Elsewhere a male was on Kalloni Pool 11th April '87 and a pair were seen at Mickri Limni on 28th March '98, with a single bird at Petra reservoir on 5th April and a fine drake joining the Garganey on Kalloni Pool for a couple of days from 16th April that year. It may well be that these sightings merely reflect an increase in observer coverage at this time.

Tufted Duck *Aythya fuligula*
Scarce winter visitor from November to February. Because of its liking for deep water this duck has only been recorded since Petra reservoir has come to maturity. It was here that a party of 4 was observed during a cold snap on 27th January '98.

Velvet Scoter *Melanitta fusca*
Irregular and scarce winter visitor in small numbers offshore from late September to March - though *The Birds of Greece* alludes to mainly inshore records elsewhere. Only record an unconfirmed report of 15 at sea off Sigri on 25th September '94.

Goldeneye *Bucephala clangula*
Very scarce winter visitor - usually only to mid-March, though birds may linger into late April (see *The Birds of Greece*). In practice, this species has vagrant status on the island, with just one record - of 3 birds (including one male) seen off Achladeri on 5th April '86.

Red-breasted Merganser *Mergus serrator*
Winter visitor offshore in small numbers from October to April. One female seen resting at outlet of Vouvaris River near Achladeri 2nd October '94 and in early May '95, with a party of 6 seen in Kalloni Bay on 19th March '97, 7 at West River mouth on 23rd January and 9 there on 14th January '98 (with 4 fishing in Nifida bay on 23rd). One was also present offshore opposite Parakila Marsh on 24th March '98, with a female seen at Kalloni Salt Pans on 9th April. Unusually, a male was also showing well downriver close to the East River ford on 30th March that year. Latest spring record a male at East River mouth from 6th-7th May '95.

White-headed Duck *Oxyura leucocephala*
Vagrant, most likely in winter - with only about 30 records from the whole of Greece since 1960. Sadly the only record is of a female shot in December '91 (see *The Birds of Greece*).

Honey Buzzard *Pernis apivorus*
Passage migrant from mid-April to late May (peaking mid-May) and mid-August to mid-October (peaking mid-September). Also breeds in small numbers (perhaps as many as 10-15 pairs) mainly in pinewoods to the east of the island (eg above Agiassos - where regularly seen, and 2 observed circling with a Common Buzzard on 6th May '98). Earliest record 17th April '98 between Andissa and Sigri, with 1 the next day between Petra and Molivos and also above Messotopos - where being mobbed by 3 Common Buzzards). Other typical counts 3 at Argennos in late May '95, and 12 (with a further 3 later) over Skala Eressos on 23rd September '94. Peak sightings usually occur in mid-May and September (eg 2 above Agiassos mid-month '90, and 2 near Stipsi 14th May '91, 3 flying south along Kalloni Upper East River 15th May '96 and 4 over the 'Derbyshire' area during a general raptor passage on 10th May '98). Also 2 over Gulf of Geras 24th May '90. Two different birds seen heading south in the Eressos area on 7th and 8th September '94, with 2 groups of 12 and 3 doing likewise on 22nd, and 6 south of Mytilini on 20th. Five seen over Haramida Marsh on 8th September '95, with an impressive record of circa 25 above Agiassos on 13th. At least 2 were seen near Molivos in the first week of September '96, with a single nearby in the Ampelia valley on 3rd. An observer in September '97, however, saw no less than 50+ circling the hills above Petra on 6th - this must rank as an island record! Four birds were seen from Molivos castle on 28th July '98 (following two over Petra reservoir the previous day), and several close sightings were obtained of a perched bird along Kalloni East River in August that year, with one seen on 19th identified as an adult female. Latest dates concern 1 at the same site on 28th September '94, (with 2 probables flying south over Kalloni Salt Pans on 6th October '94).

Black Kite *Milvus migrans*
Passage migrant in small numbers between late March and late May, and again from September to October. One or possibly 2 birds seen near Sigri 21st April '84, 1 moving north through the Potamia Valley on 10th April '87, 1 over Skala Eressos in late May '92, with another near Filia 16th May '94, and singles near Sigri and Kalloni Salt Pans in same period. Also seen heading north near Anaxos on 12th May '95, at Vatera river mouth on 3rd May '96 and between Filia and Andissa on the late date of 15th June '96, flying low south-east of Agra on 2nd May '97 between Eftalou and Molivos the next day, in off the sea at Skala Kalloni on 8th May, roosting in a tree near Kalloni Inland Lake two days later and over Ipsilou monastery on 14th May that year. Earliest record was of a bird at Faneromeni on 29th March '98, with another at Vatera on 14th April, near Petra on 22nd (with possibly the same bird over Kalloni Inland Lake next day), and over Eftalou on 28th, with a fourth sighting at Derbyshire on 10th May. The increase in spring records could well be down to a higher birding presence earlier on. Seemingly scarcer in autumn (though possibly just because of a lack of observers at this time). Singles noted at Skala Eressos on 17th and 20th September '94, over the rubbish tip on

the back road between Eressos and Sigri 13th August '96, and 2 birds were seen well coming in off the sea between Petra and Molivos on 6th September '97. There is also an unconfirmed report of 4 circling together over Skala Kalloni on 22nd August that year. Finally singles were seen circling above Agiassos on the early dates of 30th-31st July '98 and at Haramida on 9th September that year.

Red Kite *Milvus milvus*
Rare vagrant (as throughout the Greek islands), with April perhaps being the most likely month - see *The Birds of Greece*. One record only - of a single bird at Sigri on 20th April '84. Always the danger of confusion with the very similar form of Black Kite, which is far more regular in occurrence.

White-tailed Eagle *Haliaeetus albicilla*
Rare vagrant, though winters in mainland Greece and parts of Turkey. Most likely to be encountered when migrating along the Turkish coast. Only four records, of an immature plunging into the sea off Sigri on 9th May '94, an adult seen offshore on 19th, another near Vatoussa on 16th May '95, and a fourth offshore from Molivos on 25th April '98. The timing of these records is consistent with spring passage.

Egyptian Vulture *Neophron percnopterus*
Scarce passage migrant from mid-March to mid-April and also from August-September. *The Birds of Greece* suggests that all Greek birds leave Europe via the Bosphorus. Once again, most records probably refer to wandering or immature birds, since the island has only recently been better covered in March and April. Immatures reported from Skala Eressos Valley on 14th May '87 and 19th May '91, with sightings of a wandering adult in late May '95 at Ipsilou monastery and above Agiassos. A single adult bird was seen again from Ipsilou monastery on 24th April '98 heading north. Presumably the same bird had been seen earlier at Agra.

Griffon Vulture *Gyps fulvus*
Vagrant. Only 4 records, consisting of 1 seen near Eressos on 11th May '89, 3 birds soaring near Filia on 7th May '96 (seen earlier in the day over the Potamia valley), 3 seen again between Skoutaros and Filia on 11th May '97, and an exhausted individual picked up and taken into care near Vatera on 13th September '97. This bird had been seen earlier in the day at Skala Sikimmia, and even more significantly was bearing a Croation ring. It was thought to have taken poison, but was successfully released on Crete (where the species is quite common) a fortnight later.

Short-toed Eagle *Circaetus gallicus*
Summer visitor from mid or late March to early October in reasonable numbers (both the normal and the rarer white-headed form being observed). May occasionally winter and pass through on migration (eg 3 migrating high above road west of Vatoussa 17th May '87, and 5 over Haramida Marsh 8th September '95). However, 4 in the air together at Nifida on 12th April '95, near Filia on 14th April '98 and also over Kalloni Inland Lake on 29th April and the Potamia Valley on 3rd May '98 (with up to 6 a week later) may simply have been a gathering of local birds. Otherwise frequently seen hovering over rocky hillsides (and regularly emerging carrying a snake!), especially to the north and west of the island. Up to 3 regular between Eftalou and Skala Sikimmia mid-April '95 and 6 seen along the track from Petra to Molivos on 10th May '98. A pair was also observed displaying and calling above Agiassos on 20th April '95. Birds regular in hills around Eressos, Potamia Valley, and often around Kalloni Salt Pans. The earliest records concern a bird over Kalloni Inland Lake on 23rd March '97, with 1 over Kalloni Salt Pans on the same date in '98, and 3 together between Keramia and Dipi Larssos 2

days later. The latest records are of 1 around Kalloni Salt Pans on 23rd September '98, 1 over Kalloni East River and 2 at Skala Eressos 23rd-24th September '94, with 1 at Parakila on 25th, 1 in the Potamia Valley on 30th September '98, the Vatoussa region in early October '86 and a single near Skalochori on 3rd October '97.

Marsh Harrier *Circus aeruginosus*
Regular passage migrant from late March to late May (peaking late March to mid-April) and in smaller numbers from late August to mid-October. A few may winter (eg up to 4 females and 1 male at Dipi Larssos in mid-January '98). Otherwise first recorded at Skala Polichnitos Salt Pans on 20th March '97 (a female) and Kalloni Pool 22nd March '98 (a male). Often seen quartering rough fields around Kalloni Salt Pans, Kalloni East and West Rivers and river valley near Sigri and Faneromeni (usually singly, but sometimes several together - eg 5 females over Kalloni West River on 20th September '94, 4 at Kalloni Salt Pans on 20th April '97 and 12th May '98, and 4 females and a male together at Dipi Larssos Reedbed on 30th March '98). A female at the Salt Pans was seen to kill and eat a Gull-billed Tern on 19th April '92, and the same fate befell a Yellow-legged Gull there in mid-April '98! Females were also flushed from the carcasses of this species on 2 occasions - in early April '97 and late March '98; whilst another female in the area at the same time was seen flying off with a snake (still alive!), and yet another along West River on 26th April that year was carrying a rat. Passage of males probably peaks in late March/early April - eg 3 males together with 2 females which passed through Parakila Marsh within 20 minutes on 29th March '98. Later individuals include 1 at Kalloni Salt Pans on 11th April '95, 1 at Skala Eressos on 14th, 1 near Perama on 16th, 3 at Faneromeni from 16th-19th, 2 moving north at Parakila Marsh and 2 at Kalloni Salt Pans (both on 20th) - also 1 immature male present in the Kalloni area on 21st May '91, and one full adult there in mid-May '93, with one over Dipi Larssos Reedbed on 12th May '94 and near Faneromeni ford 3rd May '98. Latest spring records include a female at the Salt Pans on 24th May '94, behind Anaxos 25th May '96, over Kalloni East River on 27th May '97 and 1st June '94, and over West River on 26th May '96, with another seen sporadically there between 22nd May-1st June '98 (which, together with the above, constitutes the latest spring record). More likely to be seen in autumn along the north coast *en route* from the Turkish mainland (eg 12 over Anaxos on 20th September '94 and 1 male in off the sea at Molivos castle on 10th September '97). However, following a female seen at Skala Eressos on 20th September '94, loosely associating with a movement of falcons, at least 12 were counted in 20 minutes on 23rd - all heading south-east. Unusual autumn record of a male around Kalloni Pool from 14th-16th September '98, and one summer record of a female/immature over Kalloni West River on 31st July '97. Late dates 1 female near Molivos 1st October '94, and a pair and 1 single female near Sigri 3rd October that year. Most impressive record was of 22 flying high over Haramida Marsh on 18th September '95!

Hen Harrier *Circus cyaneus*
Scarce winter visitor in small numbers from November to early or mid-April, with a small spring passage possible to early May (eg 1 'ringtail' in the river valley near Sigri 8th May '94, and another in the Skala Kalloni area briefly on 14th May '95 and behind the Salt Pans on 5th and 10th May '98). Also a small autumn passage possible from early September to mid-October - though often taking place at a higher elevation than spring. Although wintering birds may be seen in a variety of habitats they prefer open flat areas, especially around wetlands. For this reason Kalloni plain is especially favoured, but sightings are also regular around the Faneromeni area. At least 3 females and 2 males were wintering around Kalloni Salt Pans in January '98 - though interestingly no birds were recorded over the potentially attractive reedbed habitat at Dipi Larssos at this time. Two 'ringtails' were often seen hunting together up to early April, and a male was still present in the Kalloni area up to 15th April '85, up to at

least 8th April '97 and 17th April '98, with a female carrying prey seen to land in the road between the West River and Potamia River on 20th April '98! Always some danger of distant birds being confused with female Montagu's, which is much more likely in late April to mid-May. However, single 'ringtails' and 1 male were recorded around the Kalloni area on several dates from 18th-23rd April '84 (most heading north), a 'ringtail' around Skala Polichnitos from 2nd-3rd April '86, 7th-11th April '95 and 18th April '98, with a late pair seen together above Petra on 2nd May '97 and a female flying over Kalloni West River next day. Only one autumn record - of a 'ringtail' migrating down Skala Eressos valley with a general movement of falcons on 20th September '94.

Pallid Harrier *Circus macrourus*
Scarce passage migrant between late March and mid-April, with Kalloni Salt Pans a favoured area. Also possible, but less likely, from mid to late September, and 2 'ringtails' over Haramida Marsh on 12th September '95 may have been this species. Definite record though of a second year male seen well coming in off the sea at Molivos castle on 10th September '97, and a female seen well at the back of Kalloni Salt Pans on the late date of 9th May '98. More regular earlier in the spring, however - with records of a 'ringtail' observed perched along West River on 13th April '98, an adult and immature male heading north from Skala Kalloni on 16th April '84, a male at Skala Kalloni from 8th-10th April '85, another at Sigri on 8th April '86, 16th April '87 and 19th April '98, 2 'ringtails' near Achladeri on 18th April '87, 1 at Skala Kalloni next day, 1 near Aspropotamus on 15th April '92, 2 at Kalloni Salt Pans 2 days later, (with 2 males there on 22nd April '98), an immature male at Achladeri on 12th April '95, another 'ringtail' at 'Derbyshire' on 9th April '97 and immatures over East River on 25th April '98 and beyond Faneromeni ford on 29th (where seen perched). The latest record is of a 'ringtail' at Kalloni Salt Pans on 10th and 12th-14th May '98, but a juvenile was seen well for five minutes flushing waders from Kalloni Pool on the early autumn date of 18th August that year.

Montagu's Harrier *Circus pygargus*
Regular passage migrant between early April and mid-May (peaking mid to late April), with smaller numbers possible from September to October. Singles seen regularly around Kalloni Salt Pans and East River area - eg 4 (including 2 males) together at Kalloni Salt Pans on 20th April '97 and 3 males and a female together there on 27th April '98. Following a storm on 19th April '92 no less than 12 birds (including 2 males) were in the area - reducing to just 2 by the next day. Also seen around Sigri and Faneromeni Beach area, where 2-3 males were present on 17th April '95, and 3 males were sitting together in a field mid-May '93, eclipsed by 6 (1 male) seen in the area on 20th April '84 and no less than 8 birds (including 6 males) there the next day! A female was seen to take a Little Bittern from the reeds around Kalloni Inland Lake on 23rd April '98, whilst lizards and snakes seem to figure fairly regularly as prey items at the back of Kalloni Salt Pans, where flocks of feeding Short-toed Larks on the beach are also frequently harassed! Earliest records of a female at Skala Kalloni on 9th April '98 and at Kalloni Salt Pans on 10th April '97 and 11th April '98 (when 2 males and a female were present), with a male over Kalloni East River on 11th April '95. An adult male was still present at Kalloni Salt Pans on 17th May '98, but generally rare after 3rd week of May, and only autumn records of a pair around the Salt Pans on 8th and 9th September '95, a female or juvenile near the Potamia road bridge in the middle 2 weeks of August '96, a pair just west of Anaxos heading south on 3rd September that year, with a single nearby 2 days earlier and a 'ringtail' between Kalloni East River and Salt Pans on 14th September '98. Latest record of a female at Skala Eressos on 17th and 19th October '95.

Goshawk *Accipiter gentilis*
Localized resident in small numbers, breeding mainly in upland coniferous and mixed woodland - though seen in a variety of locations when hunting. Regular in the woodland above Agiassos, where singles seen 20th May '92, 4th October '94, with a pair soaring there 18th May '94, and a bird carrying food on 16th May '95. Also 1 seen above Petri on 11th May '94, the oak woods west of Skalochori on 13th May '91 (where a pair was watched on several occasions in spring '85), on the Sigri road on 19th May '92, with birds regular up the Potamia Valley, the woodlands around Achladeri and even close to Mytilini - where seen on 6th October '94. A juvenile female was observed east of Molivos on 3rd August that same year, and singles were seen between Petra and Skala Sikimmia on 19th and 20th May '98 and were regular around Petra reservoir in mid-August that year. One was also over Haramida Marsh on 8th September '95, with a male seen on 15th. Interesting record of a bird along the track to Kalloni Inland Lake on 4th September '97 (earlier seen chasing but failing to catch a Collared Dove) dining on a chicken! Sadly one picked up dead on the Vatera-Ambeliko road on 4th May '98 appeared to have been shot. Also seen on several occasions in April '98 both perched and hunting in low-level flight over the marshy area between Kalloni Salt Pans and 'Derbyshire', with a pair seen together over East River mid-month. Generally easier to see in winter and early spring, when either displaying or mobbing other raptors - eg one mobbing a Booted Eagle over Kalloni Inland Lake on 14th April '97, another circling with 2 Hen Harriers over Kalloni Salt Pans on 26th January '98, displaying over Perivoli monastery on 29th March '98 and mobbing a Raven below Ipsilou on 23rd September '98.

Sparrowhawk *Accipiter nisus*
Mainly a winter visitor in large numbers from late September to mid or late March. According to *The Birds of Greece* a few pairs almost certainly breed (eg 1 seen over Agiassos late July '94). Otherwise, earliest records 1 near Mytilini on 9th September '95, above Agiassos on 13th, and over Skala Kalloni fields on 21st September. One near Sigri on 24th September '94 was being mobbed by Ravens. Also regularly seen above Agiassos and around Skala Eressos from late September that same year and reported as already quite widespread on the island in the first half of September '97. (In addition, 3 different birds were observed heading south-east over Skala Eressos on 26th and 27th October '92). Small *accipiters* seen between late April and September, or on migration (like the 3 seen migrating over Skala Eressos 14th May '87) more likely to be Levants, though at least 10 definite records, of a bird at Molivos on 7th April '95, 1 near Skala Kalloni 21st May '92, of 2 at Eressos on 15th May '87, 2 above Vafios on 7th May '95, 1 near Agiassos on 8th and 14th May that year, between Petra and Kalloni on 3rd May '97 and 19th May '98, near Achladeri (a likely nesting area) on 13th May '97, calling there on 28th May '98, between Eftalou and Skala Sikimmia on 20th May '98 and near Stipsi on 3rd August '94. Very common in the Kalloni area in winter, where seen regularly in a variety of habitats up to late March or early April. Following sightings of a female soaring over Petra Valley on 30th July and 7th August '98 a bird was also positively identified near Mytilini airport on 20th August that year.

Levant Sparrowhawk *Accipiter brevipes*
Passage migrant between April and May (peaking late April to early May), and possibly late August to September. The odd pair may breed. Faneromeni seems to be a favoured area, with a bird first recorded there on 24th April '98 and further sightings on 25th, 27th and 29th (with one observer reporting up to 6 on 27th). Singles also seen in that area on 6th May '97 and 19th May '92, with a pair soaring over deciduous woodland north-east of Petri on 8th May '94, singles near Eftalou 11th May '95, above Vafios 6th May '97 (an adult male), over Potamia Valley on 26th April '98, flushed from Ipsilou monastery courtyard 2 days later, and migrating along the north coast between Petra and Molivos on 8th and 16th May that year.

Unusual record of a female over Petra reservoir on 12th August '96 trying to take Little Grebes! A juvenile seen near Haramida (south of Mytilini) on 19th September '94 was described as slightly larger than a Sparrowhawk. An adult was also seen over Kapi (north-east of the island) on 24th. In September '95, 1 seen over Haramida Marsh on 12th, with a juvenile there on 10th and 15th. A juvenile was also seen well at Skala Kalloni on 19th August '97 and a further 2 juveniles were also at the Chalandra River Skala Eressos on 8th September that year - with a juvenile hunting the hills above Eressos on 6th August '98. In the light of all these records breeding must surely take place. The biggest recorded migratory gathering was of 18-22 over a ridge at Dipi Larssos on 10th September '96.

Buzzard *Buteo buteo*
Resident in small numbers, though perhaps more widespread in the east of the island. Also a fairly common winter visitor (especially to the Skala Kalloni and Salt Pans area), with a small passage likely in early spring and autumn. Seen regularly over wooded hillsides (eg above Eftalou, Agiassos and Skala Polichnitos, but also quite regular between Kalloni and Eressos). Maximum numbers 4 south of Mytilini on 16th September '94 and 5 on 18th, with 7 coming in off the sea at Molivos on 6th September '97 - possibly indicating the beginning of a minor winter influx.

Long-legged Buzzard *Buteo rufinus*
Resident and partial migrant in reasonable numbers, commoner in the west of the island. Regularly seen around the Potamia Valley and east of Molivos, but real stronghold in the mountains between Eressos and Sigri. A pair regularly breed on the rock-face below Ipsilou Monastery, often giving superb views. Maximum of 4 seen together near Andissa on 16th May '87, 4+ between Kalloni and Sigri on the same date in '95, 3 between Stipsi and Pelopi on 4th August '94, and 5 together over the Potamia Valley on 28th March '97 (another regular breeding site). Generally less obvious in autumn and winter, though birds often regular around Kalloni Salt Pans and Dipi Larssos in early spring - with late March being a particularly good time to see displaying birds. Two seen well over Kalloni West River 26th September '94 (with 1 on 28th), and 1 over hills near Eressos also on 28th October '92. Interesting record of a bird coming in off the sea at Mytilini on 22nd September '94.

Lesser Spotted Eagle *Aquila pomarina*
Scarce passage migrant from late March to May and also possible in September (though breeding in the north of the country - see *The Birds of Greece*). Immature birds may migrate later, which probably explains records of 1 on 19th May '91 between Eressos and Andissa, 2 over Kalloni Salt Pans on 17th May '93 (heading north-east), 1 between Stipsi and Klio on 28th May that year, 1 near Petri on 17th May '94, but a definite adult bird seen above Eftalou commuting from Turkey on 15th May '96, with an immature over Agra the next day and another or the same bird over Skala Kalloni 2 days later and then heading south over Molivos on 20th. Thereafter a single west of Eressos on 4th May '97, with a further 3 together between Petra and Molivos on 1st May '98 and a sub-adult just north of Kalloni mid-month. Autumn records involve a sighting over Haramida Marsh on 12th September '95 and 31st August '96, 1 seen heading south over Skala Kalloni on 20th September '94, and no less than 3 in off the sea at Mytilini on 22nd (the latest date recorded).

Spotted Eagle *Aquila clanga*
Scarce and irregular winter visitor between October and March - vagrant status outside this period. Only 6 records - of a bird over Kalloni Salt Pans on 2nd April '86 and 11th May '97, an early bird flying south along the coast at Sigri on 13th September '89, even more unusual of a low-flying bird on the coastal track near Skala Sikimmia (seen well as it hung in the wind) on

the surprising date of 9th August '96 (with a single seen near the Petrified Forest at Sigri in the third week of October possibly being the same bird), and one over Kalloni Salt Pans on the late date of 11th May. Clearly not enough records for any real pattern to emerge.

Steppe Eagle *Aquila nipalensis*
Vagrant - three records only, which The Birds of Greece suggest are likely to refer to birds straying from the main migration route via the Bosphorus and Turkey. An adult moving east over Limonas monastery on 11th May '97 (with 2 birds seen together near the Petrified Forest later that day), and a bird between Agiassos and Mytilini on 15th May '98. Both were seen by a *Limosa* group and a full field description was obtained. There are also several other reports from the first half of May '98 which the observers didn't wish to pass on to me!

Imperial Eagle *Aquila heliaca*
Very rare vagrant or winter visitor from Eastern Europe - now almost extinct in Greece. *The Birds of Greece* records one sighting from the island on 17th September '89. Otherwise a pair seen migrating over the south of the island on 5th May '94, a report of a single bird in mid-May that year in the Kalloni area and 1 over the Potamia Valley on 30th September '98 are the only records. The latter obligingly confirmed its identity by its goose or Raven-like call!

Golden Eagle *Aquila chrysaetos*
Vagrant or irregular visitor, with the possibility of the odd bird wandering from its wintering quarters in Turkey - eg a juvenile and a sub-adult over Kalloni Salt Pans (seen off by a Buzzard!) on 2nd April '86. Though occasionally claimed from the area of Mount Lepetimnos (eg an adult and an immature frequenting the hills above Petra for the second half of August '92) the only other confirmed records are of a 2nd year immature over the Petrified Forest near Sigri on 1st October '94, with another nearby on 7th May '96 and a sub-adult near Madamados on 10th August that year. Other claimed sightings of 2 adults from the Sigri area in the third week of April '97 may be worth following up.

Booted Eagle *Hieraaetus pennatus*
Regular passage migrant in small numbers between mid-April and mid to late May, and occasionaly from mid-August to mid-October. In line with the rest of Greece, light phase birds predominate (see *The Birds of Greece*). Two were seen near Eftalou 8th May '94, 1 over Anaxos the same date in '95 and another (or the same bird) east of Molivos the same day. Also a light phase bird seen south-east of Skalochori on 11th May that year, and another from the Stipsi to Klio road on 28th May '93. Interesting record of 5 together over the Petra to Molivos track on 20th May '94. Autumn records concern a dark phase seen between Skalochori and Skoutaros on 20th September '86, and another dark phase over Skala Eressos and Kalloni East River on the same date in '94! A rash of sightings over Haramida Marsh in September '95 consisted of 3 together on 12th, and 1 on 16th, 17th, and 19th (with 1 there on 9th September '98); whilst the only '96 records concerned a pale phase at Faneromeni on 18th May, a bird seen at 'Devil's Bridge' on 4th August and 1 over Haramida on 31st August. A light phase was recorded over Kalloni Inland Lake (mobbed by a Goshawk) on 14th April '97, with a dark phase three days later at Haramida, over hills north-west of Kalloni Salt Pans and along East River on 27th, yet another west of Eressos on 4th May '97, a pale phase over East River on 11th-12th April '98, and above Sikimmia next day, with another dark phase seen at Faneromeni on 24th April. There were 3 together north of Kalloni on 10th May that year, (following 1 just north of Mytilini the previous day), with 2 (dark phase) birds seen the next day between Eressos and Andissa and a single over Kalloni Salt Pans. A pair moving east over the hills behind Anaxos on 15th May may have been the same birds. Finally, a very unseasonal pale phase bird flew over the track to the Petrified Forest on 7th July '98.

Bonelli's Eagle *Hieraaetus fasciatus*

Scarce resident, with the probability of a breeding pair (or even 2) most likely somewhere around Mount Lepetimnos, though perhaps also in the mountains near Eressos. A pair (one very dark individual) was sighted between Eressos and Messotopos on 19th, 21st and 26th May '87, and again above Skala Eressos in mid-May '88. A further pair was seen high over the mountains behind Kalloni on 10th May '91, another pair between Molivos and Skala Sikimmia on 10th April '95, an immature at Sigri on 11th May, and a further pair and an immature over the Eressos road west of Andissa on 16th. (The time period between sightings, and the plumage variation described suggests different birds were involved). A bird was also seen over the Potamia Valley on 15th May '90, at Achladeri on 17th May '91, over Kalloni East River on 18th May '92, and over nearby fields on several dates in late September '94. A very pale immature was also soaring near Skala Eressos on 18th and 24th September '94, and an adult bird was above Agiassos on 4th October that year. Another immature was located just west of Andissa on 16th May '95, with a pair seen near Ipsilou monastery on 10th August and a further sighting of a juvenile over Haramida Marsh on 9th September that year and an adult on 11th. A sub-adult was noted over Apothikes on 16th May '96, but more interesting was an adult displaying high over the mountain-side south-east of Petri on 26th May that year, with an immature in the hills behind Anaxos on 31st, a near-adult (possibly the same bird) seen over Skala Kalloni on 2nd June and above Agiassos the next day. Up to 3 birds were around the back of Kalloni Salt Pans and the Potamia Valley on 5th May '97 (with an immature seen at Faneromeni ford the day before), no less than 2 pairs over the mountains between Kalloni and Molivos from 11th-12th May, an adult near Petri on 26th, reported several times from the area above Agiassos (with a further sighting of a near-adult bird there on 3rd June; seen at Skala Kalloni the day before, near Anaxos on 31st May and at Apothikes on 16th). Also that year a bird was seen above Agiassos on 12th September, following the spectacle of no less than 3 together coming in off the sea at Molivos on 6th September (seen later that day over Anaxos) - suggesting the possibility of occasional wanderers from Turkey. Later still one was recorded between Kalloni East River and Salt Pans on 8th October, following 2 together there on 5th. On 15th April '98 one was seen above Kalloni Inland Lake, and on 28th another or the same bird circled the Potamia Valley, with a later sighting near Molivos on 8th May and north of Kalloni on 10th May that year and a 'possible' near Petra on 19th. Clearly with all these records some duplication must exist, but breeding must surely occur in the light of this bird's largely sedentary status, which is often governed by the occurrence of its favoured prey species like Chukar and Brown Hare (see *The Birds of Greece*).

124

Osprey *Pandion haliaetus*
Passage migrant from late March to early May (peaking mid-April) and September to October
in small numbers, usually near the coast and rarely seen far inland. In autumn singles were seen
at 'Derbyshire', Achladeri, Polichnitos Salt Pans and Kalloni Bay between 25th September and
4th October '94, a bird was seen over Haramida on 30th August '96 and a juvenile was over
Kalloni West River on 7th September '97, with a bird also seen around Kalloni Salt Pans from
5th-6th October that year and singles over Kalloni Bay and Salt Pans, 'Derbyshire' and East
and West River on several dates between 4th-30th September '98 possibly all relating to the
same bird. Spring records include 2 birds together at 'Derbyshire' on 10th April '95 and singles
at Kalloni Salt Pans on 15th April '87, at West River mouth on 27th April '96, near Parakila 2
days later and frequenting the same area in early May '97 (with possibly the same bird seen
perched in a tree between the Salt Pans and 'Derbyshire' on 2nd May '97). But in '98 a spate of
records ensued - 31st March (East River), 7th April (Dipi Larssos), 8th April (Kalloni Inland
Lake - a different bird), 17th April (West River and Skala Kalloni area), 28th April (Kalloni
Salt Pans), 3rd-4th May (Kalloni Bay and West River - where up to 2 birds seen) and the
latest ever date of 19th May between 'Derbyshire' and Kalloni Salt Pans (again involving 2
birds). This would suggest that spring passage is heavier and more protracted than was
generally thought and no doubt reflects increased observer coverage at this time.

Lesser Kestrel *Falco naumanni*
Summer visitor from late March to October, breeding offshore from Sigri. Mainly confined to
the west of the island, where outnumbers Kestrel, and small flocks regularly seen on the
approaches to Sigri from Andissa, often hovering and planing over the ridge a few miles
before the village. Usually seen in 3's and 4's, but count of 17 there mid-May '91, 18 on 4th
May '95 and 17th April '98, and 20 (all males) hunting over recently cut fields at Faneromeni
on 21st May '91, with at up to 32 doing the same thing on 16th May '96! At least 11 birds had
already returned to the Faneromeni area by 29th March '97, and 23 were logged there on 24th
April '98. Odd birds occasionally seen elsewhere both north and south (eg 2 at Moria aqueduct
on 15th April '92, a male feeding with Red-footed Falcons around Kalloni Salt Pans on 26th
April '98, 3 birds near Petri on 26th May '96, a pair around Molivos castle on 17th May '98,
and 2 around Mytilini on 5th September '96 and 19th September '95) and recent reports of up
to 2 pairs regularly hunting around Anaxos and commuting to offshore islands in late May and
early June and August '96 suggest a small breeding nucleus in the north of the island also. In
fact, birds were still being seen around Molivos and Skala Sikimmia in mid-September '97. In
July '98 a bird was also seen flying to an offshore island near Makara (in company with several
Eleonora's Falcons) on 8th July '98. Up to 17 were feeding over irrigated fields at Faneromeni
on 3rd August that year, with 3 at Kalloni Salt Pans next day and several sightings north and
west of Kalloni in that period. Latest records of 2 birds just outside Sigri on 22nd October '96
and a single bird near Eressos 25th October '92.

Kestrel *Falco tinnunculus*
Scarce resident, surprisingly uncommon compared to the rest of Greece. Persecution may be a
contributory factor, though difficult to prove, and may simply be under-recorded. Mainly
single birds are seen in a variety of locations, but a pair on Garmias Island on 31st May '94
were most likely breeding. A pair also seen on wires at Kalloni Salt Pans on 29th April '95,
and probably commoner there in autumn and early spring. A pair also recorded around Skala
Eressos in late May '95, with 2 pairs east of Molivos on 10th May '94 and another pair at
Anaxos on 26th May '96 and between Petra and Molivos on 20th October that year. One or
two birds fairly regular around Kalloni Salt Pans and Skala Eressos in both January and March
'98, and continued sightings along the north coast between Molivos and Anaxos suggest likely
breeding on coastal cliffs or offshore islands.

Red-footed Falcon *Falco vespertinus*

Passage migrant in large numbers from mid April to late May (peaking late April and the first half of May), with much smaller numbers possible from September to early October. Parties can occur almost anywhere, along the coast or inland up in the hills. However, the area between Kalloni East River and Salt Pans seems particularly favoured, and at least 50 were over the rough hillside near the pans on 8th May '93, with 60+ there on 14th, reducing to 30 on 17th and none by 19th. Thirteen on wires by the pans on 8th May '94 had risen to 20 by the 11th, but these numbers were dwarfed by the 250+ that passed through on the evening of 30th April '95, with only 6 left by 2nd May. The Sigri area is also a regular spot, with up to 200 on hillside rocks on 9th May '93, and a smaller flock near the Sigri-Eressos road junction in early May '95 - with 30+ birds seen near Andissa on 29th April '97. All these records pale into insignificance compared to an estimated flock of up to 400 around Molivos Castle at this time (with 260 on 4th dropping to 170 the next day). By contrast, only 11 autumn records - 2 over Kalloni East River on 17th September '97, a male on wires by the East River ford on 19th September '95, a flock of at least 30 migrating down Skala Eressos valley (heading south-east) on 20th September '94, a single near Anemotia 3 days later, 2 birds - a juvenile and a male - in the Skala Kalloni area in late September that year, a male near Sigri on 1st October, a female at Ipsilou monastery and Kalloni West River on 2nd October '97, with a male at Kalloni Salt Pans on 5th October and a female on wires by Kalloni East River on 6th October '94 - the latest date recorded. Spring passage during '98, however, was especially protracted (possibly because of unsettled weather in May). A first year male was seen around Kalloni Pool on the exceptionally early date of 10th April '98, with numbers peaking at around 35 on the beach at the back of the Salt Pans from 26th-27th April that year - when ultra-tame birds congregating on low bushes waiting for a break in the weather presented a wonderful photographic opportunity - see cover! There was also an interesting record of circa 50 birds roosting on wires at Faneromeni with a few Lesser Kestrels on the evening of 11th May. Moreover, birds were still being seen in reasonable numbers on the wires opposite Kalloni Salt Pan channel up to mid-May, with 27 there on 15th and 50+ hawking insects over East River the next day (in company with several Eleonora's Falcon). One or two birds were then seen at 'Derbyshire', above Petra and at Faneromeni (up to 19th May - the latest spring record), and that autumn several small groups were seen feeding over fields between Kalloni East River and Salt Pans between mid and late September (up to 27th).

Merlin *Falco columbarius*

Scarce winter visitor from November to early April. The only definite records are of a male seen on rocks at 'Derbyshire' on 4th April '97 and in the same area on 12th-13th. The small falcon seen chasing larks and pipits around Kalloni East River in the third week of April that year may also have been the same bird.

Hobby *Falco subbuteo*

Passage migrant from early April to mid-May (peaking the second half of April) and September to October. A few birds may breed in the pinewoods to the east - perhaps 3 or 4 pairs. Singles seen almost anywhere, but regularly in the Skala Kalloni area and the north coast east of Molivos. Earliest date 9th April '95 at Skala Polichnitos and 11th April '98 over Malemi hotel. The Faneromeni area, Kalloni Inland Lake, 'Derbyshire' and Kalloni East River and Salt Pans seem favoured, and sightings there in spring '98 peaked between 25th and 27th April, following a short spell of unsettled and wet weather - when the odd dejected and bedraggled bird was seen sitting on fence-posts around East River! On 26th, moreover, 3 birds were seen together at Faneromeni ford. Possibly commoner in autumn, especially around Kalloni Salt Pans, where 1 seen in late September and on 5th and 10th October '94 and no less than 5 were observed catching insects between the pans and the sea during a spell of unsettled, stormy weather on 27th September '96. Also seen around Skala Eressos on 16th September '94 and 7th September '96, with 2 at Haramida Marsh on 19th and 21st (terrorizing a swallow roost!) 1 at Skala Kalloni on 9th September '95, and latest records of 1 at 'Derbyshire' heading south on 12th October '94 and a juvenile perched on a rock inland from East River on 21st October '96. A bird seen over East River on the unusual date of 14th July '96 would also suggest local breeding, as may a late bird over the Grand Canyon near Vatoussa on 31th May that year, another hawking for insects over 'Derbyshire' on 1st and 2nd June, and a bird mobbed by hirundines over Skala Kalloni on 10th August '96.

Eleonora's Falcon *Falco eleonorae*
Summer visitor from mid-April to mid or late October. Somewhere between 10 and 20 pairs could breed on offshore islands, especially around Sigri and Anaxos - although this is not 100% confirmed in *The Birds of Greece*, which only suggests breeding on nearby Chios and Limnos. Also, since wandering birds range widely, occur in a variety of habitats and elevations and don't breed until mid or late July when few birders are present, definite breeding (though almost certain) is harder to prove. Earliest records 14th April '98 (a dark phase bird over Molivos) and 16th April '95, when 1 near Madamados, and one between Skala Sikimmia and Molivos. The first group seen was of 4 birds feeding on insects over a hilltop near 'Derbyshire' on 23rd April '98. Reputed to breed on or offshore from the north-east coast, and birds regularly seen over Petra and Anaxos, especially in late summer (with 1 seen near Molivos castle on 29th July '96) - certainly reported to be present in good numbers around Anaxos in late May-early June '96, with a group flying over offshore islands on 20th August that year. Also often seen in Kalloni area (Potamia Valley, East River etc) and may breed on Garmias island, where 5+ on 31st May '94 and a pair seen soaring on 25th September that year. A juvenile seen at Haramida on 1st September '96 may have fledged locally. Maximum counts 6 between Agra and Messotopos 14th May '91, 6 over the Potamia Valley 9th May '94, 6 above Skala Sikimmia 10th May '95, 7 between Molivos and Petra 16th May '93, 7 over Eftalou Valley on 4th June '97, 8 over Kalloni Upper East River (with a high proportion of dark-phase birds present) mid-May '96, 10+ between Kalloni and Sigri on 16th May '95 and double figure numbers feeding over the valley beyond Filia on 15th May '94. These were dwarfed by a count of 15 at Eressos and 17 at Andissa (including an all dark bird) in mid-May '87, with the same number on 8th May '96, 14 over East River on 10th May '97, with a record 22 over Anemotia the same day and circa 30 there on 16th May '98! Several were also hawking for insects with Red-footed Falcons over Kalloni East River and Salt Pans on 3rd May '98 and numbers peaked at the Salt Pans on 16th May that year - when at least 8-9 birds were present with a much larger number of Red-foots after a spell of unsettled weather. A pair was also seen to fly to an island offshore from Makara on 8th July '98, suggesting another possible breeding area. There were daily sightings over the islands offshore from Petra in early August '98 (up to 3 birds together), and up to five were hunting dragonflies over Petra reservoir from 8th-9th, with 4 still present on 7th September. Birds were regularly seen at Skala Eressos up to 26th September '94, and the latest records concern 1 scattering a flock of finches near Kalloni Inland Lake on 11th October '94, and 3 hawking over pine woods near Kalloni on 29th October '92.

Lanner *Falco biarmicus*
Scarce resident - likely to breed in rocky terrain at moderate altitudes of approx 500-1000 metres (see *The Birds of Greece*) - especially to the west of the island. Ipsilou monastery seems a favoured area. One seen soaring over the hillside at Petra on 27th May '94, another on 30th May '96 near the Petrified Forest, 1 between Messotopos and Skala Eressos on 1st July '96 and 1 watched flying into a dead tree in the Potamia Valley on 6th June that year. Also seen taking a Crested Lark in the the hills above Eressos on 30th September '86, with 1 in the

same area 17th May '87, 1 dashing up Kalloni East River 12th May '93, and near Filia on 1st and 6th August '94. Other birds were observed north of Petra on 19th May '93 and 15th and 18th May '95 (near Vafios), from Anaxos Hotel 2nd May '96, near Argennos on 17th May '96, near Ipsilou monastery 6th May '97, 13th April and 5th May '98 (when both a male and a female seen), north of Kalloni on 13th April '98 and near Sigri on 14th May that year. Although the sighting of 3 birds near Sigri on 19th May '92 was impressive, the most spectacular remains that of a bird scything through a flock of Ruff at Kalloni Salt Pans on 8th April '98 - with 2 birds being seen nearby on 21st and another single on 10th May. (A first-summer bird had also terrorized the waders there on 2nd and 12th May '97). More autumn records concern an immature seen on an island offshore from Sigri on 11th August '95, a bird over Skala Kalloni 4 days later, another seen from the road to Agia Paraskevi on 23rd September '94, over Haramida Marsh on 12th September '95 and over Kalloni Inland Lake on 30th August '97. Another was seen near Eressos on 9th September that year being mobbed by circa 100 Alpine Swifts!, and again between Sigri and Eressos on 4th October, between Sigri and Faneromeni on 7th September '98 and feeding on a rock by the roadside at Skala Polichnitos Salt Pans on 12th September that year.

Saker *Falco cherrug*
Extremely rare winter visitor and scarce passage migrant from March-April and September-October, recorded fewer than 50 times in Greece (see *The Birds of Greece*). Only records for the island 23rd October '92 and 18th April '98 (the latter at Kalloni Salt Pans). A probable Saker was also glimpsed briefly chasing a Sparrowhawk up Kalloni East River the next day.

Peregrine *Falco peregrinus*
Resident in small numbers - certainly commoner than Lanner. Possibly a few more in winter. Well distributed throughout mountain ranges and suitable cliffs (eg pair regular around cliffs between Petra and Molivos, and pair seeen feeding young on hill above Petra 5th May '95, and with fledged young over the nearby cliffside Ruppell's Warbler site on 10th May '97 - a known breeding site). A pair were regular over nearby Petra reservoir in mid August '98 (presumably now a reliable food source). Also often seen in spring over Kalloni Pool, Salt Pans and East and West Rivers, particularly coinciding with a large passage of waders or marsh terns. Kalloni Pool is regularly visited in the evening as an easy food source, and several kills were observed between late April and mid-May '97-8 - mainly of unfortunate Whiskered Terns! Just such an attack took place at the Upper East River ford on 24th April '96, and the bird (a slightly inexperienced immature) attempted to pluck its prey within 10 feet of my car before quickly realising its mistake and abandoning its victim (again a Whiskered Tern) - which then promptly flew off apparently none the worse for its ordeal! Also fairly regular in the Eressos and Sigri area and western approaches and often seen too around the steep rock face overlooking Dipi Larssos Reedbed - where birds regularly predated the large Starling roost in January '98.

Chukar *Alectoris chukar*
Scarce and localized resident. Main stronghold in the rocky hillsides to the west of the island, (where group of 4 flushed from sand dunes between Sigri and Faneromeni 29th September '86), but the area between Kalloni and Molivos is also favoured, as is the headland beyond Mytilini airport; and birds also seen inland from Kalloni East River in mid-May '95. Birds may be more often heard than seen, however - as a main quarry species with local hunters in autumn and winter, individuals are usually fairly wary. It is even rumoured that captive bred birds released for 'sport' near the Limonas monastery are actually drugged with ouzo first - which may explain why birds are sometimes easy to see here! Interesting record of a bird with 20 chicks on the Stipsi to Klio road on 28th May '93, and also with a smaller number near Petra on 31st May '94. Coincidentally a group of 7 adults was also seen at the former site on

6th August '96 (with 6 between Petra and Molivos on 9th August '98), whilst 14 were seen between Andissa and Eressos on 5th August '98, and 4+ adults with 14 chicks were alongside the road to the Petrified Forest (another favoured area) two days earlier.

Quail *Coturnix coturnix*
Localized summer visitor (from mid or late March to early October) and common passage migrant up to early May and especially from late August (peaking the first half of September) - though easily overlooked. First recorded at Kalloni Salt Pans on 31st March '86. One flushed from track between Kalloni East River and Salt Pans 11th and 26th April '95, and regularly heard calling in that area from early to late April especially. A female was on the track between Kalloni and the Inland Lake on 24th April '97, and 2 birds were seen to fly across the the East River-Salt Pan tracks 4 days later. Also heard at Skala Polichnitos on 5th April '86, nearby Skamioudi on 9th April '98, and Eressos on 14th May '87 and seen in an olive grove at Faneromeni on 17th April '95. In autumn a bird was still calling near Kalloni East River on 8th August '96 and from fields near Molivos castle on the late date of 10th September that year, with singles recorded at Haramida Marsh on 17th and 20th September '94 and 10th September '95 by the ringing party. Like Chukar this is a favourite quarry species in autumn, when mortality is likely to be high.

Pheasant *Phasianus colchicus*
Small feral population in existence of birds released by hunters and escapes from captivity. Birds kept on small farm near East River mouth can often be heard calling, and this may explain the origin of 1 seen and heard on the Upper East River 29th May '96. Circa 30 birds were actually seen in 2 carrying baskets on the back of a pick-up truck near Kalloni Inland Lake in late October '96! Elsewhere just 2 records, of a bird seen from the Agiassos-Polichnitos road (close to the picnic site) on 13th May '97 and another heard nearby at Megali Limni on 12th September that year.

Water Rail *Rallus aquaticus*
Localized resident, breeding in small numbers (mainly around Dipi Larssos Reedbed, where regularly heard and seen April-May '98 - eg 3 birds+ on 4th April), but commoner and more obvious in winter and early spring - when numbers may be swelled from immigrants further north or cold weather movements. Spring records of a single bird on Kalloni West River on 11th May '91, another (with a damaged wing) on the Potamia River mid-May '93, a bird at Haramida from 14th-16th April '97 and Parakila Marsh from 20th-22nd April and 14th May. Also regular in winter and early spring around Kalloni Inland Lake, where a bird was present on 19th March '97 and throughout January '98. Birds were often to be seen on Kalloni Pool during April and May '98 - with a minimum of 2-3 seen up to late April (4 on 16th) and one still present up to at least 23rd May and again in mid-August. Because of high water levels there that year it seems likely that one or two birds may have been resident, and the presence of a adult and 2 juveniles there throughout September would suggest breeding. One was also on the East River between early and mid-August '89, and in autumn '94 a confiding individual was seen well by the ford just before dusk on 25th and 26th September. (A bird was present at the same site in September '95 and also from at least 2nd September '97). Another was seen sporadically at the head of the Chalandra River Skala Eressos from 7th September to 3rd October '94 (probably a regular site at this time - one also seen there 16th September '89 and mid-January '98). Also recorded at the reedy pool at the back of Faneromeni Beach on 24th September '94 and at 'Derbyshire' on 5th October '97.

Spotted Crake *Porzana porzana*
Passage migrant in small numbers from late March to early May. A few may winter from October to March and breeding is also suspected. Very skulking and likely to be easily overlooked. First recorded on the early date of 21st March '97 round Kalloni Inland Lake ditches (where a bird present until 28th - after which it or another bird was seen on 14th April carrying nesting material, and again on 19th). Singles were also seen there 19th April '95 and 11th-14th April '98 (in company with up to 8 Little Crakes!). Two were present there together with 2 Little Crakes on 24th April '96. Elsewhere 1 around Kalloni Pool on 3rd May '95 and a very confiding long-staying bird at Faneromeni ford feeding in the open on tadpoles between 22nd April and at least 3rd May '97 (with possibly the same bird still present on 13th and a second bird at the river mouth on at least 29th April). A bird was also ringed at Haramida Marsh on 15th April '97. Other singles were seen briefly at Skala Eressos and Faneromeni ford on 27th April '98 and again on 7th May that year - whilst the latest spring record is of a bird near East River bridge on 18th May '96. Just one autumn record - of a single present on Kalloni Pool between at least 11th-17th September '98.

Little Crake *Porzana parva*
Locally common passage migrant from late March to mid-May (peaking mid-April), rarely from mid-August to mid-October. A few may winter from October to March (though not confirmed) and may possibly breed. More often seen than Spotted Crake, especially along Kalloni East River, Kalloni Pool, Parakila Marsh, Faneromeni ford and Kalloni Inland Lake ditches. Earliest dates 23rd March '97 on Chalandra River Skala Eressos and Parakila Marsh (where 2 males seen on 20th April '95 and 3 birds seen on 28th March '97, and again on 20th April - rising to 4 on 22nd) and 25th March '98 round Kalloni Pool. Also an immature bird noted around the ditches from 15th to 19th April '95, with an adult there on 2nd May that year, and 2 birds on 22nd April '96 (see above). Elsewhere, single birds seen at Ntipi (near Dipi Larssos) in late April '96 and at Vatera river mouth on 21st April '97, with at least 4 different birds seen between East River ford and river mouth 2 days earlier, and a single still present on 2nd May. In addition, an adult and an immature were feeding together at Faneromeni ford from at least the 12th to 15th May '94. Other late dates 1 on Chalandra River Skala Eressos on 18th May '87 and 27th April '98, and 1 on Kalloni East River from 21st to 22nd May '95 and 13th May '96 (where a long-staying pair still being seen round the ford on 21st May '96 raised the possibility of nesting) - especially since a bird was seen there again at least from 12th-18th August that year. Up to 8 birds were present in the favoured area of Kalloni Inland Lake ditches on 12th April '98 (possibly being more concentrated than usual because of remedial work there making much of the habitat unsuitable for them.) Numbers had reduced to 6 the next day and only 2 by 14th - suggesting peak passage was over. However, a pair was present on 27th April and 3 were again reported on 7th May, 2 on 9th and 1 on 10th, with a male seen on East River on 8th May. Unusually one was also present around Kalloni Pool from at least 13th-17th September '98.

Baillons Crake *Porzana pusilla*
Very scarce passage migrant from late March to mid-May (peaking the second half of April). Even rarer in autumn - from late August to early October. Only records of a male at the mouth of the Chalandra River Skala Eressos on 23rd April '84 and one long-dead specimen found by Kalloni East River on 27th April '98. This 14 year gap shows the scarcity of occurrence of this species compared the other crakes - although some must surely have been overlooked.

Corncrake *Crex crex*
Regular passage migrant in small numbers from mid-April to early May and occasional mid-September to mid-October (also listed as a rare passage migrant on the nearby island of Chios

- see *The Birds of Greece*). Rarely seen unless flushed - as on mid-May '96 from a hillside near Andissa, and the first half of May '97 from a meadow just behind Petra (with another recorded in the Skala Kalloni area a day or so earlier). More recently an unusually confiding individual was present at Kalloni Salt Pans from 13th April '98 (where it was encountered at very close range walking along the track in front of the car!). It was also heard calling (unusual on migration) and was present for at least 5 days - probably longer. It or another bird was seen there again on 23rd and 28th April. An injured bird found near Thermi on 17th April and taken to the nearby Wildlife Hospital sadly died the next day. In the light of these recent records it would seem likely that several birds pass through the island in spring - with many undoubtedly overlooked. Autumn movements are less certain, but one caught and ringed at Haramida Marsh on 13th September '98 (see ringing report) was the first ever to be ringed in Greece.

Moorhen *Gallinula chloropus*
Resident, and winter visitor from October to April; with numbers and distribution largely governed by water levels. Regular on Kalloni East River, Chalandra River, Kalloni Inland Lake and ditches, and (until early summer at least) Parakila Marsh. Evidence of breeding includes a pair nest-building at the river mouth near Thermi in mid-April '95, 2 juveniles on Kalloni East River 6th August '94, 2 adults with 2 juveniles there between mid-July and early August '96, and single juveniles also seen at Kalloni Inland Lake and Dipi Larssos at the same time, whilst a bird with 2 young was present on Kalloni Inland Lake 7th July '97. Between early and mid-June that year birds were also seen by East River ford with anything between 2 and 9 chicks! Moreover, following high water levels in May '98 at least 2 pairs were present there (with 3 and 5 young respectively) in mid-July, whilst additional pairs with 2 small young each were present on both Kalloni Pool and Inland Lake.

Coot *Fulica atra*
Winter visitor in variable numbers from October to mid-April and occasional breeder (see *The Birds of Greece*). Used to be considered surprisingly scarce, with the main stronghold being Dipi Larssos Reedbed, where at least 7 still on 16th April '95. Otherwise, the only other records were of 1 on the Potamia River on 10th May '93, and 2 even later individuals in the area of 'Derbyshire' on 12th May that year. However, up to 15 birds were still present on Kalloni Pool on 7th April '97, with up to 10 there as late as 15th May and a juvenile seen on Kalloni Inland Lake 7th July. This trend continued into '98, when at least 150 birds were still present on Kalloni Pool 22nd March, falling to *c*15 on 3rd April, but rising again to 26 on 12th and *c*50 in mid-May, with up to 23 in early June - and still described as 'numerous' there up to 11th June at least, with 32 present the previous day including one with young. Two birds were also still to be seen on Parakila Marsh on the normally late date of 18th May. A January '98 visit produced peak counts of 400+ at the nearby West River mouth on 16th - birds were obviously commuting between here and Kalloni Pool via Kalloni bay, where many were often to be seen on the sea. The importance of the 'new' reservoir at Petra for this bird was made apparent when a record count of circa 500 birds was made there on 13th January '98, with 20+ again in mid-September that year. Apart from winter hard weather movements, it seems likely that high water levels in late spring (as with Kalloni Pool in April-May '98) may encourage birds to linger in larger numbers than usual. further proof of breeding comes with the report of an adult and 2 juveniles at Dipi Larssos on 5th August '96, and another adult on Kalloni East River a week later. Seven birds still present on Kalloni Pool on the very late date of 18th June '97 were, however, showing no signs of breeding; but record water levels there in spring '98 (see under Moorhen above) resulted in a pair with 5 young being seen there in mid-July, with up to 10 birds in early August and at least 5 adults still on East River pools.

Crane *Grus grus*
An irregular passage migrant - Occasional from early April to early May but more likely in autumn, or as a vagrant in winter. However, a small party was heard calling after dark and moving north across Kalloni bay on 7th April '95. Otherwise, just 1 recorded calling and circling Kalloni Salt Pans on 8th May '96 and another frequenting the large flooded field behind the Salt Pans intermittently between at least 16th and 25th April '97 - on 20th it was seen circling Kalloni Pool.

Oystercatcher *Haematopus ostralegus*
Scarce winter visitor and passage migrant from September to May. One seen at East River mouth on 1st April '85, a pair commuting between Kalloni East and West Rivers and Vouvaris river 'Derbyshire' from late March to at least 22nd April '97 (after the storms of 20th March) - with a single bird around Kalloni West River mouth and Salt Pans on 23rd and 28th April, and also on 12th May - when last seen. The only sizeable gathering so far recorded concerned 12 on Skala Kalloni beach on 23rd March '98 (again after heavy overnight storms). Thereafter a maximum of 3 was recorded at Kalloni Salt Pans on 9th-10th April, with just 1 by 14th - still seen sporadically there and at West and East River mouths until at least 29th. A bird was also seen at Dipi Larssos beach on 6th April, at Sigri next day and Skala Eressos on 28th. Two late spring records of singles at Alikoudi pool on 13th May '98 and on the Kalloni Salt Pan headland 14th-16th May '96 were eclipsed by the sighting of a pair at Kalloni East River mouth on the exceptional date of 15th June '98.

Black-winged Stilt *Himantopus himantopus*
Locally common summer visitor (especially to Kalloni Salt Pans, Kalloni Pool and Parakila Marsh) and passage migrant from late March to May and September to early October - with earlier dispersals from mid-July onwards as favoured wetlands dry up. First record of 7 birds at Kalloni Pool on 22nd March '98 and 5 birds at Parakila Marsh on 25th March '97. Breeds in variable numbers on Kalloni Salt Pans (sometimes just the odd pair or two in the channel - as in '91 - but several pairs in '87 and '93, and 5+ in '94 (after up to 20 birds on 27th May), 6 in '97, and 2 pairs still apparently on nests there on the late date of 3rd August '96). A flock of 60 seen there on 20th April '95 was probably composed mainly of migrants, as was a party of 16 resting on Alikoudi beach 19th April '98. Water levels are obviously crucial to breeding success, as with Kalloni Pool, where double figure numbers usual in spring (with 14 there on 12th April and 2nd May '95, 20+ on 22nd May '96, *c*26 in the first half of May '97 and 25 on 24th April '98) - with 5 pairs attempting to breed in late May '93 and 8-10 pairs in '98 - though regrettably some clutches were destroyed by local dogs! By 6th June '96 there were already at least 16 chicks visible there (with more apparently on the way!) and in mid-July '98 record spring water levels resulted in up to 30 birds (including at least 10 young) still being present - several having hatched by the end of May. Also breeds on Parakila Marsh, where 20 in mid-May '93, circa 25 on 29th May '94, with where 5-6 breeding pairs present on 20th April '95 and a maximum of 18 on 6th May '95 - with 4 nests in mid-May '98) and Kalloni West River. However, breeding numbers here on the pool behind the rubbish tip have shrunk from up to 8 pairs to just 3 in '98 because of encroaching rubbish dumping! Elsewhere one bird preyed on tadpoles at Faneromeni ford in mid-May '94, and a pair was also present on the Chalandra River 17th May '87. A pair with 2 juveniles frequented Kalloni East River in late June '94, when there were still 6 on Kalloni Salt Pans, with 7 still in the area late July and 36 still there on 5th August '96 (reducing to 31 by 12th). A pair also appeared to be defending territory around Kalloni Inland Lake on 7th July '97. Maximum count at the pans of 50 birds on 6th April '86, 47 birds on 13th April '95, with 20 there on 30th July '96 and mid-June to early August '97 (rising to 35 mid-month), 38 in early August '98 and up to 20 (adults and juveniles) around Petra reservoir from 3rd-14th August '96, with 4 around Kalloni Inland Lake on 7th

and 8 still at Skala Polichnitos Salt Pans up to mid-September '97 (following a peak of 50+ at the end of August). Just 9 were present at Kalloni Salt Pans by 8th September '98. The latest record is of 1 at 'Derbyshire' on 11th October '94.

Avocet *Recurvirostra avosetta*

Passage migrant from March to May and September to October. Breeds in variable numbers, and may also winter, but peak numbers are bolstered by migrants - especially from mid to late April - eg *c*50 at Kalloni Salt Pans on 3rd April '85 rising to 200+ by 13th, and 80 there on 29th March '86 rising to 200 2 days later, 250 by 2nd April, but down to 60 next day. Most sightings around Skala Polichnitos and Kalloni Salt Pans or 'Derbyshire', with 6 at the latter on 21st. May '92 and 7 on 31st May '93. Also occasional at Parakila Marsh and Kalloni West River. Maximum counts at the pans of a breeding colony of 117+ on 25th May '87, with 146 counted there on 12th May '91 and 100+ on the same date in '93 (with chicks recorded from the 13th). In '95, birds had returned there by February, and at least 13 nests were counted on 25th April, though these appeared to all fail due to draining of the pans. However, 40-50 birds were seen there on 2nd May, with 2 still up to the 18th. In spring '97 105+ were recorded on 19th March, and in late April up to 100 birds were still present, but usually in an area of the pans that was largely hidden from view. However, entry to the pans was obtained on 18th May, and this showed at least 8 pairs to be nesting - 1 already with chicks. Only 20 birds (including just 4 young) were still present at the end of July - after a peak of 33 on 7th. On 3rd June '98 *c*60 birds and just 4 young were recorded, reducing to a maximum of 6 birds mid-month. Breeding success therefore largely dependent on stable water levels, and can vary dramatically from year to year. Hopefully this may improve now that the pans are again being worked commercially and some sort of management plan to take account of the needs of breeding birds is being drawn up. Certainly at least 20-30 (with at least 8 young) were again present there on 8th July '98, with a peak of 145 from 4th-12th August (at which time 43 were on Kalloni Pool during record summer water levels there!). Evidence of wintering is shown by a record of 90+ birds seen around the pans in mid-January '98. The only other late summer or autumn sightings are of 3 birds at Petra reservoir on 30th July '96 and 60+ birds at Kalloni Salt Pans on 5th August '96, reducing to 39 by 12th, but with *c*150 birds present again up to 23rd October. There were also 29 birds present there on 29th September '97, 150 there on 8th September '98 (increasing to 200+ by the month's end) and 50+ birds at Skala Polichnitos Salt Pans on 31st August '97.

Stone Curlew *Burhinus oedicnemus*

Summer visitor from early April to October, with perhaps 20-30 breeding pairs (with their stronghold in the Kalloni area - where 7 breeding pairs located in mid-April '87). Also a migrant from April-May and mid-August to early October. Seen regularly around Kalloni Salt Pans (at least 2 breeding pairs and up to 5 together on 10th April '98 - nests found close to road alongside channel '93 and '94, and by headland in '95, with pair displaying by roadside 2nd May '95). A maximum of 7 birds were seen in the dunes on 20th April '97 - suggesting that breeding was not yet underway. Also a pair regularly breeding on shingle spit East River, with a pair usually each side of West River bridge (first recorded there 4th April '85, 5th April '98 and 11th April '97, with at least 7 present in mid-July '96 and a pair with young in late May '98). Also seen on dry river beds (eg Potamia River and around Molivos and Eressos - heard Chalandra River 27th April '95). Skala Polichnitos Salt Pans are another regular site, with 1-2 breeding pairs along the beach most years and 5 together there 21st April '97. By 18th May '98 a pair there already had 2 young. Unusual record of a single bird (presumably a newly arrived migrant) on Mytilini beach between the town and airport on 14th April '95, and occasional sightings from olive groves - with a regular pair (presumed nesting) in such habitat just west of Skala Vassilikon in the first half of May '98. An autumn gathering just inland from the West

River bridge peaked at 18 birds on 1st October '94, but none were seen after the 8th. There was a minimum of 8 birds (seen from the main Mytilini road) around Kalloni Salt Pans between 6th-8th August '96 and *c*15 there on 6th October '97 - falling to 11 two days later. These counts, however, were eclipsed by the incredible sight of 70+ birds (again in the rocky area between the Kalloni Salt Pans and the main Mytilini road) in mid-September '95; whilst the first week of August '98 saw a maximum of 57 in the same area, reducing to circa 20 by 19th September and just small numbers by 1st October. A good number of these may have been migrants rather than local breeders.

Collared Pratincole *Glareola pratincola*
Widespread passage migrant from mid-April to mid-May (peaking late April). First reported from Kalloni Salt Pans on 17th April '92 and 19th April '98. Apart from 2 recorded on Faneromeni beach 11th May '93, 2 seen at Skala Eressos on 16th May '87 and 6 at Sigri on 18th, with 1 on 11th May '95 and a single bird at Skala Polichnitos Salt Pans on 15th May '91; most records relate to the Kalloni area. Seven were on Kalloni Salt Pans on 17th May '87, with 4 there on 25th and 20 on 17th April '92 - rising to 30 by 24th , but with only 7 remaining by 25th. In May '91, 14 were on the East River on 11th, with 4 on the Salt Pans the next day, and 10 on the same date in '93! Six were on the East River on 6th May '94, and 4 near the West River the next day. Meanwhile, a flock of 35-40 birds seen briefly over the Salt Pans on 8th had shrunk to 2 by 14th. Finally, a single bird on the marshy field behind the pans on 4th May '95 was in company with at least 10 others by 7th; and the next day 1 appeared on the West River and 3 on Kalloni Pool. In spring '96 numbers were lower, with a maximum of 9 over Kalloni East River on 18th May and 12 over West River on 20th. In spring '97, however, a flock of *c*25 was watched hawking insects over East River (in company with at least 20 Red-footed Falcons) on 26th April, when 19 birds were in the large field at the back of the Salt Pans - rising to 50+ on 30th and falling to 30 on 4th May, 20 next day, 2 up to 8th and 1 lingering until 19th. Twenty birds were also seen there on 1st May '98, and *c*15 were over East River on 28th April. Latest date 5 at the Salt Pans on 24th May '98 (following up to 25 on 18th), with a single still on 4th June.

Black-winged Pratincole *Glareola nordmanni*
Scarce passage migrant from mid-April to May and occasional in August-September. Not always easy to differentiate from Collared Pratincole. Six were present briefly on Kalloni Pool the evening of 15th April '87 before departing west, and 1 was seen well and photographed (by me!) with 2 Collared on Faneromeni beach on 11th May '93; with a further 2 amongst a flock of Collared on Kalloni East River 8th May '93 and 6th May '94. Six birds overhead there on 9th (with 2 Collared), to quote Bob Husband : 'showed clearly the black underwing coverts and auxiliaries plus lack of trailing white edge to the secondaries. Even the shorter tail streamers could be detected.' There were also several sightings around Kalloni Salt Pans from April/May '98. These usually concerned one or two birds in company with much larger numbers of Collared (eg 2 on 21st April, 3 on 27th and 2 on 30th), but a party of 7 was seen on 10th May - the largest recorded gathering. One was still present on 12th - the latest spring date. The earliest record is of 5 birds at Kalloni Salt Pans on 11th April '86. One autumn record - of a juvenile on Kalloni West River 15th September '98 following a storm, which settled within 4 metres of the observer's car!

Little Ringed Plover *Charadrius dubius*
Localized summer visitor and passage migrant from March to October, breeding around both sets of salt pans, Dipi Larssos, Kalloni West and East Rivers and various beaches (eg pair on eggs Vatera beach late May '95). First record of 4 at Marmaro on 23rd March '97, with at least 14 present at Skala Polichnitos Salt Pans by 26th and 7+ at Kalloni Salt Pans on 28th

March '98. Also regular on Chalandra River Skala Eressos and Kalloni Pool, where up to 2 in early May '95, and 3 on 21st. Kalloni Salt Pans channel held 4-5 in early June '91, and the East River a maximum of 4 in early May '95, with 3 there on 6th August '94. A gathering of 20+ at Skala Polichnitos from 7th-9th April '95 probably consisted mainly of newly arrived migrants. Latest record of up to 6 regularly seen at 'Derbyshire', Kalloni Salt Pans and East River in late September '94.

Ringed Plover *Charadrius hiaticula*
Passage migrant from early March to early May (rare), but commoner from early August to late October. Mainly seen around the two sets of salt pans, but between 1 and 4 on Kalloni Pool from 2nd-7th May '95 and 4 there 3rd May '97. Counts of 3-4 around Kalloni Salt Pans on 10th and 16th May '93, 2 on 17th May '95, 2 on 19th May '96, 26th April and 2nd May '97 and 4 on 17th May '98 were eclipsed by 12 seen there on 12th May '91. Also recorded from Chalandra River Skala Eressos, and 'Derbyshire' (where 1 bird seen on 28th April '98), Kalloni Pool (which held 2 birds on 3rd May '97), Kalloni East and West Rivers (where up to 6 birds present 20th April '97 and 3 on 31st May '98). The latest spring record was a bird at East River mouth on 6th June '97. First autumn record concerned 4 birds on Kalloni Pool from 8th-9th August '97 and 1 at Kalloni Salt Pans on 12th August '98, but autumn numbers peaked at 30 on Kalloni Salt Pans Channel on 18th September '89, with 2 on Kalloni East River on 20th September '94, singles at Skala Eressos beach pool from 17th-22nd and several around Kalloni Inland Lake on 28th. A bird was on Potamia River 6th September '97 (with 3 there on 4th September '98), and 2 juveniles were also seen on Petra beach on 31st August '96, with 2 again on Kalloni East River 16th September '97 and 2 at Kalloni Salt Pans on 28th, with 3 at Skala Polichnitos Salt Pans on 12th September '98. Last recorded 17th October '95 on the East River and 21st October '96 at Skala Polichnitos (a single bird).

Kentish Plover *Charadrius alexandrinus*
Widespread resident in all suitable coastal wetlands, but numbers probably augmented by passage birds between early March to early May and late August to mid-October (see *The Birds of Greece*). Nests in similar locations to Little Ringed Plover, but Skala Polichnitos and Kalloni West River particularly favoured, with 5-6 at the latter on 23rd March '98 - a bird had already hatched 2 chicks there by 12th April that year. Also 8 on Kalloni Salt Pans on 5th May '95 and up to 20 by the month's end, with 10 (including juveniles) on 29th July '95 and 8th September '98. The West River held up to 30 birds on 16th September '98 and 50+ between 3rd-4th September '97, and numbers peaked at 30+ on Skala Polichnitos Salt Pans on the 29th September '94. Fifteen were still on Kalloni Salt Pans on 12th October and 24 on West River pools 21st October '96 (reducing to 2 by 24th), but with up to 3 figure numbers recorded at Skala Polichnitos Salt Pans on 21st. Birds more scattered and less obvious in winter, and very few seen in January '98.

Lesser Sand Plover *Charadrius mongolus*
Scarce vagrant. Never before recorded in Greece, and only a few times in Europe, there is a report of a bird thought to be this species at Kalloni West River mouth on 13th September '98, with 2 present next day seen well alongside Little Ringed, Ringed and Kentish for size comparison.

Greater Sand Plover *Charadrius leschenaultii*
Scarce migrant from March to May and August to September. A late record of 2 birds (both seen and photographed) at Kalloni Salt Pans from the end of May to 3rd June '98.

Caspian Plover *Charadrius asiaticus*
Rare vagrant with just 2 records - as many as for the whole of Greece! (see *The Birds of Greece*). One flattened corpse in winter plumage found by the floodlights at Molivos castle on 17th April '84 seems likely to have flown into the lights whilst migrating. This was followed by the sighting of an adult in breeding plumage feeding in fields with a flock of Ruff at Skala Polichnitos on 18th April '87.

Dotterel *Charadrius morinellus*
Very scarce passage migrant between mid March to late April and late August to late October. Only one record - of a bird seen around the 'Derbyshire' end of Kalloni Salt Pans on 3rd September '97.

Golden Plover *Pluvialis apricaria*
Winter visitor in small numbers from late October to March (but with a spring passage possible from late March to late April and more rarely in autumn (see *The Birds of Greece*). Numbers likely to be variable and related to hard weather, but lack of observer coverage at this time makes it difficult to back this up. However, 5 were seen in flight over Kalloni East River on 14th January '98 (in company with *c*70 Lapwing), with 10 over West River mouth on 23rd after extensive flooding. By far the most impressive gathering, though, was of 60+ birds feeding in the fields between Kalloni East River and Salt Pans on 23rd March '98 (in company with 4 Fieldfares and after heavy snow and hail showers overnight!). Numbers had halved the next day and reduced to 12 by 27th, after which no more were seen there apart from 1 on 10th April. In addition to a party of 9 seen at Skala Polichnitos Salt Pans on 26th March '97, and 1 seen at Skala Kalloni on 15th and 19th April '87 there are late records of a single bird with 8 Grey Plover at Kalloni East River mouth on 8th May '96, and 3 birds (1 in full summer plumage) in the large field at the back of Kalloni Salt Pans on 10th May '98 (the last spring record). Two early winter sightings (on the headland behind Kalloni Salt Pans on 18th September '89, and at West River on 13th September '95) may relate to autumn passage.

Grey Plover *Pluvialis squatarola*
Winter visitor in small numbers and locally common passage migrant from March to May, in lesser numbers from September to October. Mainly seen at head of Kalloni East and West Rivers and both sets of salt pans, but Skala Polichnitos beach also favoured (where 2 summer-plumaged birds on 8th May '96 and 1 on 7th May '97). Earliest records of 3+ at Kalloni Salt Pans on 2nd April '86, 9 there on 4th April '98, 4 at Skala Kalloni on 10th April '86, and 1 there on 22nd April '84 (followed by 4 at the Vouvaris river mouth near Pirra on 27th and no less than 10 (an island record) at 'Derbyshire' on 27th. A single was present at Kalloni Salt Pans on 28th April '98 (rising to 4 two days later and at least 6 on 14th May) - with 2 there on 17th May '87, 3 on 1st May '97, 4 on 11th May '96 and 5 on 11th May '91, with 1 remaining to early June. (Along with 1 seen at Kroussos river mouth near Tavari on 27th May '98 this constitutes the latest spring date). A male in breeding plumage was present in the Salt Pan area on 12th and 13th May '93, and again between 16th and 19th May on the nearby shoreline. One was seen there on 7th May '94, with a group of 5 on the beach 9th May '95. The most recent maximum count, however, was of 8 on the West River mouth on 11th May '94 (with 6 there on 4th May '97), equalled by a similar number at East River mouth on 8th May '96, 7 on 10th May '98, with a late bird there on 24th May '98, and 5+ at Alikoudi pool on 15th. Autumn records concern 1 on the shore at Sigri on 1st October '86, a juvenile at West River mouth on 19th and 20th September '94 and 1st October '97, 1-2 regular on Skala Polichnitos Salt Pans from 28th September '94 onwards, 1 on Kalloni East River bank on 20th and 21st September '95 and 1 on West River 6th September '97. Two summer plumaged adults were also present at Kalloni Salt Pans on 6th August '98 and again from 2nd-8th September.

Spur-winged Plover *Hoplopterus spinosus*
Scarce passage migrant from late March to May - rarely in autumn. Thought to be declining in numbers (see *The Birds of Greece*), hence few records, mainly of single birds. Earliest record of a single near Kalloni East River mouth on 26th March '86, followed by a pair at Skala Kalloni on 8th April the same year, and 2 on Skala Kalloni Pool 15th April '87 (reducing to one the next day). One was also seen at Skala Polichnitos Salt Pans on 15th May '91, at Kalloni Salt Pans on 17th April '92, at West River mouth in late May '92, 17th May '94 and 19th April '97, 1 briefly in Kalloni Salt Pans channel on 15th May '94 and another feeding alongside the tracks between Kalloni East River and Salt Pans from 21st-22nd April '96. However, in spring '98 a stronger birding presence was responsible for several records. These included a bird around Kalloni Salt Pans on 9th-10th April, with it or another bird on Kalloni Pool from 10th-11th and 2 together there from 14th-16th. There were then no further sightings until 29th-30th April, when a bird was seen on the Chalandra River Skala Eressos. The final spring records involved singles on Kalloni East River, where 1 was observed at the river mouth on 6th May and it or another was seen well from the main road bridge between 12th-14th. Just two autumn records - of a bird, again on East River, in late August '97 and one standing by the roadside at Kalloni Salt Pans on 5th September '98.

Sociable Plover *Vanellus gregaria*
Vagrant, occurring anytime in spring or autumn. One definite record of a bird at Kalloni West River mouth on 14th May '94, and a flock of *c*12 seen distantly on Kalloni Salt Pans at the same time were considered likely to be this species.

Lapwing *Vanellus vanellus*
Winter visitor in small numbers from October to late March - most regular in the Kalloni area. One was seen at Skala Kalloni on 4th April '85, 1 at Kalloni Salt Pans on 20th April '87, whilst 2 exceptionally late birds were seen around Kalloni West River in mid-May '96, and a single bird between Kalloni East River and Salt Pans on several occasions in late March '97 was reputedly still present on 27th April. Earliest records of single birds on Kalloni West River 16th September '97 (regular also on East River in early October). Otherwise not recorded till 19th October '95. In January '98 no less than 70 were in flight over Kalloni Salt Pans on 14th, and *c*80 were seen over East River on 21st following torrential rain and flooding overnight. A flock of 26 over West River mouth 2 days later may have involved the same birds. By late March, however, just a single bird was feeding between Kalloni East River and Salt Pans - it was regular up to 29th. It or another bird re-appeared in the flooded field at the back of the salt pans almost a month later - on 27th-28th April.

Knot *Calidris canutus*
Surprisingly scarce passage migrant, mainly in spring (April to May), and occasional winter visitor. Described in *The Birds of Greece* as 'very rare on the islands' - with only three records, and fewer than 40 for the whole of Greece. Only recorded at Kalloni Salt Pans, where 2 on 16th May '91, 1 on 14th May '93, and 2 from 26th to 27th May '95. In spite of an increased birding presence on the island in early spring (especially over the last two years) no new confirmed records have come to light - at least that I know of!

Sanderling *Calidris alba*
Scarce passage migrant, mainly in spring from late March - late May (peaking mid-May) and in smaller numbers from mid-August to late September. Apart from 1 on Skala Eressos beach from 15th to 16th May '87 and 4 there on 11th May '93, mainly recorded from Kalloni Salt Pans, where 7 were present on 16th May '93, 8 on 12th and 15th May '94, with a maximum of 10 on 11th May '91, and several on the nearby headland. Four were feeding there from 3rd

May '95, rising to at least 5 on 8th and 8 on 18th - with up to 11 in the area between 1st-2nd May '97 and 6 on 30th April '98. A further 10 were also along Kalloni West River 3rd May '97, with a single at Dipi Larssos beach on 6th May that year. Largest numbers, however, concern a flock of circa 25 offshore from Kalloni Salt Pans on 28th April '97. The only autumn records are of a single bird which was regular along West River in the first week of August '96, 2 birds seen at Skala Polichnitos Salt Pans on 12th September '98 and 2 at Kalloni Salt Pans 3 days later on 15th.

Little Stint *Calidris minuta*

Passage migrant in large numbers from early April to late May (peaking the first half of May), and in smaller numbers from late July to mid-October (peaking late August and early September). A few may winter. Occurs on virtually any wetland, even small pools, but Skala Polichnitos Salt Pans, 'Derbyshire', Kalloni Pool, East and West Rivers and Kalloni Salt Pans channel most favoured (where circa 40 first recorded on the early date of 1st April '85). Around 100 were recorded there on 11th April '86, 50 on 12th May '91, with 200+ on 10th May '93, rising to nearly 500 from 11th to 14th! At least 200 were there on 8th May '95 (with 270 counted on 18th), with 10 still present on 24th May '94, circa 200 on 17th May '95 and 120+ in the first half of May '96, with numbers peaking at *c*320 birds on 23rd April '97, rising to an amazing 550 on 1st May!, 100+ birds 30th April-7th May '98 (on which date *c*60 were on West River), 200+ from 9th-12th May and small numbers still up to 9th June (with 8 still present 1st June '94, 9 on 3rd and 2 on 7th June '98) and a maximum of 7 there from mid to late July '97. Twenty-two birds were also still present on East River 31st May '94. It was described as 'by far the commonest wader around Kalloni Salt Pans' in mid-August '96 (where 100+ were watched feeding on 21st and 50+ recorded between 31st July and 5th September '97, with 40+ on 7th August '98 and 35 on 11th September), and other autumn records include up to 6 on Kalloni Pool 18th August '98 (when the site would normally be dry), 3 feeding in the Chalandra River Skala Eressos on 8th August '89 and 6 on 10th September that year, up to 4 there from early to late September '94, a maximum of 15 at 'Derbyshire' on 23rd September, and 7 at Skala Polichnitos Salt Pans on 9th October (with 8 there on 10th September '97 and up to 60 from 16th-20th September '98). The latest record concerns at least 10 on Skala Polichnitos Salt Pans 21st October '96.

Temminck's Stint *Calidris temminckii*

Passage migrant from mid-April to late May (peaking late April to early May) and less frequent from mid-August to mid-September. Mostly seen in small numbers on Kalloni East and West Rivers and Kalloni Pool and Salt Pans channel, with at least 3 on West River 28th April '84, 5 there on 7th May '93 and 6-8 on the pans the same day. Four birds were present at the pans on 25th April '98 (rising to 4 on 30th, 6 on 5th May, 8 on 8th and 9 on 9th), with 6 on 1st May '97, up to 8 from 2nd to 4th May '95, and 12 on Parakila Marsh on 16th May '87. Three birds were also seen at Dipi Larssos pools on 3rd May '98, while 6 were also present at Skala Polichnitos Salt Pans on 12th-13th. Nine autumn records - of a single bird frequenting the Kalloni Salt Pans in the first half of August '89, 2 there on 4th September '98, one on the Potamia River (near the road bridge) in mid-August '96 and a juvenile at Kalloni Inland Lake on 16th and 27th August '97 (with 2 there on 30th), another 2 juveniles on Kalloni Pool 21st August '97, a single adult from 6th-7th September and 2 there on 17th August '98, with 2 at East River on 6th September reducing to 1 next day.

Curlew Sandpiper *Calidris ferruginea*

Passage migrant in good numbers mid-April to early June (peaking late April to mid-May - by which time many are in resplendant brick-red breeding plumage) and in much smaller numbers from late July to late September. First recorded at Kalloni Salt Pans on 6th April '98 (4 birds) -

but more typically from Skala Polichnitos on 21st April '97 (10 birds) and 24th April '98 (a flock of 32), but Kalloni Salt Pan channels usually the favoured area (with 34 there on 17th May '87, 30+ on 12th May '91, 40+ on 13th May '93, and 55 on 15th May '94). In '95, 18 on 8th May had grown to 54 by 10th and 115 by 18th, and May '96 saw a peak of c45 birds on 16th; whilst up to 120 were present there on 3rd May '97, 81 on 1st May '98 - rising to c300 on 14th and still 180 on 18th May. Also regularly recorded in smaller numbers on the Chalandra River Skala Eressos, 'Derbyshire', Kalloni Pool and East and West Rivers (the latter held 42 on 15th May '95 and c25 on 16th May '96). On the same date in '92, a flock of 25 was feeding on the Skala Polichnitos Salt Pans. Latest records of 1 at Dipi Larsos on 28th May '98, 1 at Kalloni Salt Pans on 30th May-1st June '94 and 1 still present there 8th June '97. Scarcer in autumn, and the only records are of 12 at Kalloni Salt Pans on 5th August '96 (reducing to 2 by 12th - with 5 there on 30th September '97 and just 1 by 5th October - following a single in mid-August), 4 there on 18th August-4th September '98 (increasing to 50+ by 16th September and reducing to 26 by 19th, with 1 still present on 1st October), 1 on the Chalandra River Skala Eressos 19th September '89, 1 at 'Derbyshire' on 23rd September '94, 1 at Skala Eressos on 16th-17th September and 3rd October'94, with 2 at Skala Polichnitos Salt Pans on the latest recorded date of 5th October that year; (though a creditable flock of 30 was logged there on 13th September '95 and 50 on 12th September '98).

Dunlin *Calidris alpina*
Scarce passage migrant and winter visitor from August to May. One on the Chalandra River 15th May '87, 4 on Kalloni Pool on 21st May '95, 1 on Kalloni East River September 22nd '94 (with 1-2 at 'Derbyshire' about the same time and up to 2 on Skala Eressos beach pool from 16th-27th September), 2 on Skala Polichnitos Salt Pans 10th September '97, 3 there on October 9th '94, 3 at Kalloni East River on 12th and 2-6 at Kalloni Salt Pans 30th April-2nd May '97 and 29th April and 14th May '98 being typical records. Groups of 9 at 'Derbyshire' on 3rd April '85, up to 10 on the headland behind Kalloni Salt Pans on 5th May '95 and 12 in the area on 19th April '98 were slightly more unusual, as was a similar number on Kalloni Pool on 8th and 9th May '92, and a small flock at the Chalandra River Skala Eressos on 9th May '93. There were counts of 20+ at Skala Polichnitos Salt Pans 21st October '96, 40 at Kalloni Salt Pans 5th August '95 (all gone by mid-month) and 33 there in flooded fields on 20th January '98. However, the best gathering to date concerned no less than 250 birds seen amongst a large gathering of waders at Kalloni Pans on 6th April '97! A bird still in full summer plumage was on Kalloni Pool 16th August that year, and 6 were at the Salt Pans on 12th August '98 - reducing to 2 in the first half of September, with 3 present on East River 30th September.

Broad-billed Sandpiper *Limicola falcinellus*
Scarce passage migrant from late April to late May and (more commonly) from early August to late September. One confiding individual located on Kalloni West River 24th August '94, 2 there mid-August '89, with possibly two different birds seen on Kalloni Salt Pans from 2nd-12th August (see *The Birds of Greece*), 1 or possibly 2 birds feeding there with a large flock of 100+ Little Stint on 21st August '96, a juvenile seen there from 13th-14th August '97, 1 from at least 4th-8th September '98 and 1 seen at Polichnitos Salt Pans on 21st August '93 and 31st August '97. One was reported feeding from the pools near East River ford on 12th August '98, and it or another bird was present on Kalloni Pool 16th-17th, with 2 birds seen at this site next day. All were showing well and proved quite approachable. These records all fall in line with the peak passage period of mid to late August as detailed in *The Birds of Greece*.

Ruff *Philomachus pugnax*
Common and widespread passage migrant from late February to May and August to September at usual wetland sites and also flooded fields and temporary pools wherever these

occur. Males probably pass through earlier, as largely females have been recorded from late March to May. First recorded 20th March '97 from Kalloni Salt Pans, with 250 present on 26th including the occasional male. Counts there in spring '85 produced a peak of 350 birds in mid-April, whilst April '87 saw a maximum of 250 mid-month and spring '97 produced a total of 500-600+ between 18th-23rd April (with 100+ still present in mid-May) - whilst in spring '98 the pans hosted *c*300 on 27th March, 350 on 8th April and *c*500 on 21st. Twelve were on the East River in mid-May '91, and Kalloni Pool held up to 6 on 3rd May '95, with the last sightings of 2 on the Salt Pans on 30th (though up to 30 still on Kalloni Pool on the same date in '94, with 12 remaining on 1st June). The last birds had also left the pans by 30th May in '96, though a single was still present on the late date of 7th June '97. The only autumn records consist of 4 birds at Kalloni Salt Pans on 5th August '96, 3 there 6th August '97, 4 on 29th and 31st July '98, and 1 at the West River mouth on 20th September '94 and 15th September '98, with several on the East River and Skala Polichnitos Salt Pans from 22nd September '94. However, Kalloni Pool held 49 birds on 5th August '98 (reducing to 1 from 17th-18th August and 16th-17th September) when the site was unusually wet.

Jack Snipe *Lymnocryptes minimus*
Widespread but scarce and secretive winter visitor from late October to mid-March, and passage migrant up to late April and early May. No recent records, and unsurprisingly described in *The Birds of Greece* as 'more often seen bagged by hunters than alive!' - especially knowing its preference for well vegetated fresh or brackish marshland habitats.

Snipe *Gallinago gallinago*
Winter visitor and passage migrant in reasonable numbers around most suitable wetlands from mid-August to early May (peaking late March to mid-April). Spring records mainly of singles (eg 1 around Kalloni Inland Lake on 8th May '93, 1 on Kalloni West River on 10th May '94, 1 on fields bordering the Salt Pans on 12th, 1 on the Potamia River on 6th May '95, 2 on Kalloni Pool 2nd May and 1 there from 13th-16th May that year, 3 on 26th April '98 and 3 on East River at the same time). Good numbers were present at Parakila Marsh on 19th March '97, but the amount of available cover there makes counting very difficult; and this applies to many of the favoured sites - Kalloni Pool and Dipi Larssos especially. Birds becoming more widespread in autumn, and 1 on the East River on 6th August '94 (with another single record there on 26th September) was followed by 1 at Skala Eressos river mouth in early September and 1 over the West River on 7th October, 3 on 12th; but an unprecedented 24 there on 11th, presumably heralding the start of the autumn influx. It would be interesting to speculate how many of these might survive the winter shooting season! A memorable spectacle involved the sighting of no less than 55 together on West River 22nd January '98, when extensive flooding had forced them all on to a small strip of salt marsh between Aegean hotel and the road bridge! Clearly water levels and the severity of the weather in this period can have a substantial effect on numbers - as of course can disturbance from shooting! Five birds were present around Kalloni Pool on 18th August '98, when the site was unusually wet for autumn.

Great Snipe *Gallinago media*
Scarce passage migrant from mid-March to early May (peaking by mid-April), rarer from late August to early October (when wetlands are generally less productive). According to *The Birds of Greece*, less inclined to fly than Common Snipe - so more easily overlooked. Most regularly seen on Kalloni East River, except for 1 record from the Salt Pans in the first week of May '94. This bird was later relocated above the East River bridge. Two on Kalloni Pool on 5th May '95 were probably the same 2 seen over the West River that day, and from 21st to 22nd a bird was again found on the lower reaches of the East River. The only other confirmed record is of a single seen on a stream near Petra 2nd May '97.

Woodcock *Scolopax rusticola*
Fairly widespread winter visitor in variable numbers from late October to early March. This is a popular quarry bird for local hunters, who often only succeed in flushing it with the use of dogs! It favours hillsides with mixed deciduous and evergreen scrub close to streams and damp areas. In January '98 the hills around Achladeri seemed particularly favoured (judging by the strong hunting presence there!). Elsewhere just 1 bird was seen alive - flying across the road at dusk near Madamados mid-month.

Black-tailed Godwit *Limosa limosa*
Locally common passage migrant from early March to early May (peaking late March to early April) and in smaller numbers from early August to September (peaking late August to early September). Thirty birds were feeding by the roadside at Skala Kalloni on 4th April '85, whilst double figure numbers were recorded on Kalloni Salt Pans 15th April '95 (with 3-4 again on 5th May, 1 there on 17th May '87, and 1 on Kalloni West River 19th September '94, with a bird frequenting 'Derbyshire' later in the month and 1 on the Salt Pans headland from 4th to 5th October that year. A bird was also present on Skala Polichnitos Salt Pans 31st August '97, with 2 there on 3rd September '98 and 1 at 'Derbyshire' on 23rd September '94 (the latest autumn record) - whilst 2 birds on Kalloni Pool 30th April '97 were a first for that site. A large count of 70 at Kalloni Salt Pans on 19th March '97 (the earliest recorded date) had risen to an impressive 350 by 25th (down to just 17 by 13th April - with 2 late birds feeding on Kalloni Pool and West River from 1st-2nd May that year, and a confiding individual last seen at the Salt Pans on 4th. In '98 160+ feeding in flooded fields there on 23rd March had grown to 250 by 7th April and declined to just 6 by 27th. These records are very much in line with the normal spring peak, but more unusual was a report of 8 birds present on Kalloni Pool in the first week of August '98 during record summer water levels for that site - with 1 bird remaining on 16th.

Bar-tailed Godwit *Limosa lapponica*
Rare and localized passage migrant and winter visitor in very small numbers, with virtually vagrant status on the island. Passage birds can occur anytime in May, but the peak period is early to mid-month. Wintering birds may occur from November, but their preference for tidal mud- and sand-flats severely limits their occurrence and distribution. Just 2 records, of 14

birds resting on the shingle bar at the mouth of Kalloni West River on 15th April '84; and a single at Kalloni Salt Pans on 11th-13th May '98. This 14 year gap shows the scarcity of this bird, though it is possible that most godwits seen have always been assumed to be Black-tailed. Clearly closer scrutiny may need to be paid in future! Interestingly, the party of 14 is only 6 short of the Greek record (see *The Birds of Greece*).

Whimbrel *Numenius phaeopus*

Scarce passage migrant from mid-March to mid-May (peaking mid-April) and occasional from mid-July to early September (see *The Birds of Greece*). Surprisingly, nothing was known of the occurrence of this species on passage until a fairly distant party of 20+ was seen at Kalloni Salt Pans from 3rd-6th April '97, followed by a bird heard and then seen at close range near Kalloni East River mouth on 14th April that year. Thereafter several records followed for spring '98, including 2 at Kalloni Salt Pans on 3rd April (with 5 feeding in a nearby field the next day), 1 at Faneromeni on 6th April, 2 at Skala Eressos the next day, 2 at Alikoudi pool on 19th, 1 at Kalloni Salt Pans on 26th April and 1st May, and a long-staying ultra-tame individual on Skala Polichnitos beach which delighted photographers (myself included!) from 27th April-1st May. The last birds of the spring was seen at Kalloni Salt Pans on 7th and 14th May. There are only 2 autumn records - of singles at Haramida on 12th September '98 and Kalloni Salt Pans on 17th September that year. More unusual still was a record of a bird flushed from rocks on the coastal track near Sigri on 28th January '98 (by me!). Both good sight and sound records were obtained, and it seems likely this may have involved a wintering bird (a very rare occurrence - see *The Birds of Greece)*. Since then a few retrospective records have been received showing the occurrence of single birds around the Skala Kalloni area on 22nd April '84 and 1st and 8th April '85.

Curlew *Numenius arquata*

Winter visitor and passage migrant in small numbers from mid-March to early May and mid-July to late October (peaking early to mid-September). Usually only small numbers are recorded - eg 1 on the headland behind Kalloni Salt Pans on 24th April '95, 18th September '89 and 5th October '94. Other sightings on East River 11th May '91, 6th August and 12th October '94, (with 4 birds there on 4th September '97), around Kalloni Salt Pans on 5th August '96 and 11th August '97, (with 2 there on 2nd September, 5 on 28th, and 2 more 13th April '97 and 13th August '98, and at mouth of West River 10th May '91, 11th May '98, 21st and 28th September and 11th October '94, and 26th March '98 (4 birds). Also 1 lingering around Skala Polichnitos Salt Pans from late September '94. In addition 2 birds were seen on Skala Kalloni beach 24th October '96 and 9th September '98 . More unusual records concern single birds reported at Kalloni Salt Pans on 7th July '97, at Sigri on the same date in '98 and Kalloni West River 3 days later. Biggest concentrations, however, concern 5 at Skala Kalloni on 9th April '87, 9 there on 1st April '85, 9 at Kalloni Salt Pans on 26th September '98, 21 flying past the Salt Pan headland on 25th March '97, 15 in the same area on 20th January '98, rising to 21 on 26th, and up to 26 feeding in fields between Kalloni East River and Salt Pans on 30th March '98, with smaller numbers present for several days in that area - eg just 5 remaining by 2nd April, but 21 recorded briefly on 27th April. Even these numbers are eclipsed by a peak of 40 birds present at the Salt Pans on 31st March '86 (reducing to 27 by 3rd April, with the last 6 seen on 6th) - whilst 42 were seen there on 22nd March '97- an all-time record. Last spring record of a single at the Salt Pans on 22nd May '98. Two birds seen rather distantly there the week before and originally claimed by some as possible Slender-billed Curlew *Numenius tenuirostris* were ultimately considered on better viewing to be Eurasian Curlew - both *N. a. Arquata* and *N. a. orientalis* and intermediates being referred to in *The Birds of Greece*.

Spotted Redshank *Tringa erythropus*

Passage migrant from mid-March to mid-May (peaking mid-April), with smaller numbers possible from early September (or occasionally even July) to mid-October. Again, not common and mainly recorded from Polichnitos Salt Pans (where 6 birds present on 7th April '95) and Kalloni Salt Pans, where first reported 11th April that year. Two were feeding in the channel on 15th May '91, with singles seen there from 11th to 16th May '93, and between 7th and 16th May '94, with 3 reported on 6th, 2 from 7th-8th and 10 on 20th April '98, Two were also on Kalloni Pool on 7th May '94 (with 1 remaining to 15th) - with 2 again present on 28th April '97, and a further 2 on the Salt Pans 4th May '95, with 1 at the headland on 7th. The earliest spring record, however, comes from Kalloni West River - where a single bird was present from 26th March '98, with 6 feeding in flooded fields between Kalloni East River and Salt Pans next day. Three birds were also feeding on the main road 'garage pool' opposite Kalloni Salt Pans on 6th April that year, up to 8 were again at the Salt Pans on 20th and a superb summer-plumage individual was along the Chalandra River Skala Eressos on 28th April '98. The biggest spring gathering, however, goes back to a party of circa 40 seen on Kalloni Pool 14th April '84. The only autumn records are of 1 at Skala Polichnitos Salt Pans 10th and 14th September '97, 1 at 'Derbyshire' on 23rd September '94, 1 at Kalloni Salt Pans on 5th August '98, 6 on 5th August '96 (rising to 12 on 12th), and 2 present 5th October '97, with 1 there on 6th October '94 being the latest autumn record.

Redshank *Tringa totanus*

Winter visitor and passage migrant from early March to mid-May (peaking late March to early April) and from mid-August to late October (peaking late Sepember to early October). A few pairs may also breed (most likely around Kalloni West River mouth and the 2 sets of salt pans) - see *The Birds of Greece*. Surprisingly, one of the scarcer waders on the island, and originally the only spring records were of several on Kalloni Salt Pans on 15th April '95, 2 on Kalloni Pool on 2nd May '95 and 1 on the pans on 8th and 12th May '94. Otherwise latest spring records concern singles at Kalloni West River on 11th May '98 and Kalloni Salt Pans up to 13th. Seen from mid-July both at the Salt Pans and Skala Eressos, and also 2 seen on Kalloni West River on 21st August that year, rising to 3 on 31st, when 1 also on Kalloni East River. The earliest return date concerns a single bird at the Salt Pans on 7th July '97. There were several on the West River in September '95, with 1 on the nearby beach on 17th and 21st and 1 at the river mouth on 11th October, with up to 8 there on 19th October '95. Apart from a flock of 14 seen at Skala Kalloni on 14th April '85 and 20+ at West River mouth on 25th March '97 one of the the largest concentrations occurred on Skala Polichnitos Salt Pans, where numbers peaked at *c*25 on 28th March '98, 30+ on 10th September '97, 50+ on 1st October '94, 60+ in mid-September '95, 80+ on 14th September '98 and 100+ on 21st October '96, 31st August '97 and 20th September '98! 'Derbyshire' held 15+ on 21st April '98 and Kalloni Salt Pans hosted 13 on 14th August '97, 20 on 5th August '96, and an impressive 60+ on 12th, with 50 on 30th September '97 and 56 during the first week of August '98, reducing to *c*25 mid-month, but up to 30 on 11th September. There is clearly some overlap between wintering and migrating birds, but Skala Polichnitos would appear to be the best autumn-early spring location.

Marsh Sandpiper *Tringa stagnatilis*

Passage migrant in small numbers from mid-March to mid-May (peaking the first half of April) and late July to mid-October (peaking the first half of September). Usually seen in small numbers (eg 1 Kalloni Salt Pans channel 12th May '91 and '92, and 16th and 19th May '93, with 1 on Kalloni Pool from 2nd to 4th May '95). However, 2 birds were regular at the latter site from 12th to 22nd April '95, with 3 seen on East River 3rd May '97 and 24th-25th April '98, and up to 7+ on the Salt Pan channel 21st April '97 (down to 1 by 25th), with up to 3 birds in the main road 'garage pool' opposite the Salt Pans up to at least 28th. A flock of between 25 and 30 seen on Kalloni Pool 11th April '95 is indicative of peak passage, as was a group of 20 at Skala Polichnitos on 7th April that year, 16 on 20th, 13 on 9th April '97, 20 at Kalloni Salt Pans on 13th April '85 (rising to 30 next day) 12 there on 23rd April '98, 12 at Skala Kalloni on 6th April '86, 12 there on 12th April '87 - rising to 30 by 15th, 15 at 'Derbyshire' on 13th April '97 and 19 at Kalloni West River on 20th. First reported from the 'garage pool' opposite Kalloni Salt Pans, where 2 birds present on 24th March '98 (with 2 there again on 26th and 27th April and up to 12 round the pans on 23rd), and Skala Polichnitos Salt Pans, where 10 birds were seen on 26th March '97 and 4 on 10th April '98 - with a similar number at Mickri Limni Marsh around the same time and 3 on Kalloni Pool mid-month. Three were also seen on East River 28th April. The latest spring record is of a single bird on Kalloni Pool 29th May '98. Only autumn records 1 at Kalloni Salt Pans on 31st July, 5th and 8th August '96 and 13th-14th August '97, 3 there from 1st-2nd August '98 (falling to 1 on 3rd but up to 4 by 17th - with just 1 present there and on Kalloni Pool next day), up to 4 there on 8th and 26th September '98 and 2 at Skala Polichnitos Salt Pans on 5th October '94 (with 10+ there 31st August '97, falling to 2 on 14th September, and up to 8 on 12th September '98) and 1 (unfortunately with a damaged wing) on the latest recorded date of 21st October '96.

Greenshank *Tringa nebularia*
Passage migrant from mid-March to mid-May (peaking the second half of April) and in slightly smaller numbers from mid-July to late October (peaking the first half of September). A few may winter. First record of 6 birds at Kalloni Salt Pans on 30th March '97 (rising to 13 by mid-April). Regularly recorded from Skala Polichnitos and Kalloni Salt Pans and East and West Rivers - eg 2 on the Salt Pans from 14th to 17th May '91, 7th May '93, and 3 on the East River on the same date and on 20th April '97 (with a record of 6 at 'Derbyshire' on 24th May '94). Two were on the East River on 2nd May '95, and 4 again on the Salt Pans on 7th. Also recorded in that year at Skala Eressos ford (1 bird on 5th May) and Kalloni Pool (1 on 3rd May), with up to 5 bird at a coastal pool at Nifida on 25th April '98. A late bird was at Kalloni Salt Pans on 9th June '97 - with a party of 15 there on 12th April '87 and up to 30 on 22nd April '95; whilst 15 were seen at Skala Polichnitos on 20th-21st April '95 and c19 birds were present on West River 20th April '97. However, pride of place goes to the gathering of no less than 40 birds at 'Derbyshire' from 24th-27th April '84. Autumn records include 1 on the East River 29th July '94 (the earliest return date) and 2 there on 6th August, 1 on the West River on 21st August, at Skala Eressos pool on 30th, and singles regularly on Kalloni Inland Lake and Salt Pans from 22nd September, with 6 on Polichnitos Salt Pans on 4th October, rising to 8 by 9th. Up to 9 there mid-August '97 had risen to 20+ by 31st - falling to 8 by mid-September. In autumn '98 there were already 4 birds at Kalloni Salt Pans by 31st July, with up to 6 on 8th September. The latest record is of 5 still present at Skala Polichnitos Pans on 21st October '96.

Green Sandpiper *Tringa ochropus*
Winter visitor from October to late April, with a spring passage peaking in late March-mid April (sometimes through to May) and return passage already underway from early or mid-July. Allowing for late or lingering birds, sightings in almost any month are therefore possible (see *The Birds of Greece*). Kalloni East and West Rivers and the Chalandra River Skala Eressos are particularly favoured sites, and numbers on Kalloni East River rose from 12 birds on 21st March '97 to 20 by 31st - thereafter declining to 6 by 12th April, 1 next day and none thereafter. Spring '98 saw a maximum of 10 at East River decline to 2 by 16th April, with 1 seen at Faneromeni ford and Potamia River on 28th. Also regularly recorded at Parakila Marsh (where 2 birds still present on 29th April '98), Kalloni Inland Lake (where 6 birds on 12th

April '97 and 7 on 8th April '98), Kalloni Pool and both sets of salt pans, with the latest spring record of 1 present at Kalloni Salt Pans on 5th May '95, and earliest autumn records a single on Kalloni Inland Lake 12th July '98, 2 at Petra reservoir on 26th July '96 (rising to 7 by 5th August) and 1 on 27th July '98, with 2 at 'Derbyshire' on 1st August '98, singles also on Kalloni East River 3rd August '96 and Dipi Larssos 2 days later, with 3 on the Chalandra River Skala Eressos 15th August '89, 3 on East River 7th September '97 and 4 there on 14th August '98. Up to 10 were present at Skala Polichnitos Salt Pans on 9th September '98, but the maximum recorded gathering was a flock of *c*25 flying over East River mouth on 9th August '97.

Wood Sandpiper *Tringa glareola*
Passage migrant in considerable numbers from early April to late May (peaking mid-late April) and in much smaller numbers from late July-early October (see *The Birds of Greece*). Found in any suitable wetlands, even the smallest pools, and by far the commonest spring passage wader on Lesvos. First recorded on 28th March '97 from the main road 'garage pool' opposite Kalloni Salt Pans (a favoured site) but more typical date 12th April (when 7 birds seen there in spring '95). Between 80 and 100 were in the Salt Pan channels by 22nd April that year, when at least 40 were on the West River pools and the Kalloni Pool held in excess of 100 birds. Numbers throughout the island peaked in the first week of May, and had declined by mid-month, with only 2 remaining on Kalloni Pool on 21st May and the last bird seen on the Salt Pans on 28th - with a straggler reappearing on 8th June. (In May '96 most birds had again left by mid-month, and 20 birds remaining on 24th had all disappeared by 30th). In spring '97 numbers there peaked at 200 in mid-April, whilst in '98 150+ on 24th April were down to 75 on 7th May and 25 2 days later- suggesting a likely departure date. There was also a peak of 60 birds on East River 24th April. Only summer/autumn records concern 8 on Kalloni East River 5th July '98, 10 on 13th-14th July '96 (falling to 1 by 27th), 7 there on 29th July '94, 3 at Kalloni Salt Pans on 5th July '96, 2 there on 15th July-1st August, 20 on 5th August (reducing to 8 on 12th), 5 on 8th September '98, 2 on Kalloni Inland Lake on 7th August '96, 1 on the West River in mid-August '89, 3 at Skala Polichnitos Salt Pans on 10th September '97, 1 frequenting Chalandra River Skala Eressos from 14th to 20th September (with a juvenile there on 2nd and 16th September '94) and 1 at 'Derbyshire' on 18th September that year. Up to 13 birds on Kalloni Pool during the first week of August '98 (rising to 20 mid-month and present in small numbers until 9th September) was unusual for the time of year, but was due to record autumn water levels.

Terek Sandpiper *Xenus cinereus*
Vagrant. Only 2 records (coincidentally both in mid-May) of singles - on Kalloni Salt Pans on 14th May '93, and at 'Derbyshire' from 16th to 17th May '95.

Common Sandpiper *Actitis hypoleucos*
Passage migrant from late March to mid-May (peaking second half of April) and late July - late September. First recorded from Kalloni East River on 19th March '97 (a single bird), with another seen at Dipi Larssos on 1st April '98. Widespread in ones and twos in all suitable wetlands, particularly favouring Dipi Larssos, Kalloni East River and Skala Eressos fords and any small coastal inlets, such as the headland at Kalloni Salt Pans. Also seen on the ditch around Kalloni Inland Lake in mid-April '95. Maximum of 3 seen on Chalandra River Skala Eressos from 15th to 20th May '87 (with 5 there on 23rd April '95), 4 on Kalloni Salt Pans on 2nd June '93, 3 around Kalloni East River ford on 20th April '95, 7 around Skala Kalloni on 20th April '97, 12 at East River mouth on 11th April '86 and an impressive total of 20 birds along East River on 3rd May '97 (with none seen after 6th), and 5 seen together by an inlet at Haramida Marsh on 13th April '98. More coastal bias in autumn reflects lack of water in rivers

and around fords (eg 4 together on the shore between Anaxos and Petra on 31st August '96), though 2 on the East River on 29th July and 9th August '94, with 3 on 6th August and 7 together at West River mouth on 8th August '96, 5 in Kalloni Salt Pan channel on 8th September '98 and 4 seen from Potamia River Bridge on 17th September that year. Earliest autumn records concern singles around Kalloni East River, Kalloni Pool and Salt Pans between 7th-11th July '98, and latest a single on Eressos beach 3rd October '97. One winter record from Potamia river in mid January '98. Displaying birds have been observed on East River in the past (April '84), but there is no further proof of breeding.

Turnstone *Arenaria interpres*
Regular passage migrant in small numbers from late March to late May (peaking mid-May - by which time usually in full summer plumage). Also in much smaller numbers from early August to mid-October. Apart from 1 on Skala Eressos beach on 15th and 22nd May '87, 4 at the mouth of the East River in mid-May '91 (with 25 there on 17th May '95 being a record count!), 2 on the beach near Achladeri on 9th May '92, 1 on Petra beach on 19th May '93, 1 on Kalloni West River on 18th and 19th May '94, a single at Skala Polichnitos beach on 8th May '96 and 3 at Faneromeni river mouth on 13th May '97, nearly all records come from Kalloni Salt Pans. Seven were on the Salt Pans channel on 17th May '87, with 3 on 5th and 16th May '91. Otherwise mainly reported from the headland at the back of the Salt Pans, where 4 were seen on 19th May '93 and 2 on 7th May '95 had grown to 5 by the 11th and peaked at 14 on the 18th, with 1 still on 25th, and no less than 15 on 16th May '96. Three birds were also seen there intermittently from 5th-17th May '97 (with 5 at East River mouth on 3rd), and 5 were recorded there on 18th May '98. Last spring record of a single flying along Vatera beach on 2nd June '98. Just one autumn record - of a bird at Kalloni Salt Pans in mid-August '96.

Red-necked Phalarope *Phalaropus lobatus*
Vagrant. Two birds 'scoped' at Kalloni Salt Pans on 16th May '98 constitute the island's only record. Although records from Greece are almost annual (usually between early May-late September) August seems the favoured month (see *The Birds of Greece*).

Pomarine Skua *Stercorarius pomarinus*
Vagrant. Just one record - of a bird seen offshore from Vatera (in company with large numbers of Mediterranean Shearwater) on 10th May '96. Good scope views were obtained for about two minutes, and the bird was identified by an experienced seawatcher as an adult with full tail spoons.

Long-tailed Skua *Stercorarius longicaudus*
Vagrant, not recorded elsewhere in Greece. Only one record - of a single bird off Mytilini in October '96.

Mediterranean Gull *Larus melanocephalus*
Fairly common winter visitor and passage migrant from August to early May (with main spring passage late March-mid April and autumn passage being smaller and more protracted). First summer/autumn record a single adult in Achladeri bay on 8th July '96, followed by 1 in Skala Kalloni harbour on 16th, 8 at Skala Polichnitos Pans and 2 at Dipi Larssos on 22nd, 4 adults and a juvenile on 29th July '94 at Skala Kalloni, and 2 adults there on 7th August (as against 13 in the first week of August '98). One or two adults were still regular in the area during the second half of September, and 1 was offshore from Mytilini airport on 29th October '92 - with a flock of circa 30 present on Petra reservoir 20th October '96 and up to 30 at Polichnitos Salt Pans on 17th September '97 and 22 on 19th September '98. In May '91, 2 were around the Salt

Pans on 15th-16th, 1 on the East River on 17th and 2 on Skala Kalloni Pool on 21st. April '92 produced a party of 30 at East River mouth on 19th after a heavy storm, whilst in early May '94 1-3 over Petra beach had grown to 30 by 6th, with 9 over Parakila Marsh on 12th and 25 on 15th. Even this number was dwarfed by 104 over Skala Kalloni (heading west) on 9th, and 130 on 12th! April '95 produced 2 in Plomari harbour on 20th but chiefly immatures around Kalloni Pool and Salt Pans, with a maximum of 4 on the headland (and 3 on the East River) on 9th April. However, an adult and a juvenile were on the West River on 8th, and 6 adults graced the Kalloni Pool on 10th. The last record was of a first summer at the Salt Pans on 15th April. September '95 saw concentrations of $c25$ in Mytilini harbour on 19th, with 50+ at Skala Polichnitos Salt Pans mid-month. In spring '96 5 adults were seen over Vatera on 8th May, but up to 67 (including 2 first-summers and a number of second-summers) had been seen in Petra Bay the day before. The biggest gatherings usually occur in late March and early April - with 200-300 birds seen at Skala Kalloni from 1st-2nd April '85 (and none thereafter), 200 seen there in early April '86, 200+ offshore from Skala Sikimmia on 21st March '97 and close on 1000 birds resting on the sandspit at Dipi Larssos on 25th March '98! There was also a noticeable passage in Mytilini harbour up to 31st, with 20+ birds still at Dipi on 4th April, 8 at Kalloni Salt Pans on 9th and 2 at East River mouth on 30th April, 9 late birds there on 12th May and 3 bathing briefly at Kalloni Pool next day. An exceptionally late bird was seen at the pans on 16th June '98 and September that year saw a gathering of 150+ at Skala Polichnitos Salt Pans on 9th.

Little Gull *Larus minutus*
Scarce winter visitor and passage migrant from August to May. Again, mainly 2nd year birds seen in May, with 2 immatures at Kalloni Salt Pans on 14th April '85 (joined by an adult next day), 1 on 22nd April '87, 2 there on 11th, 12th and 16th May '91, 2 on Kalloni Pool 19th April '87 (with an immature from 21st-22nd), 1 on 5th May '94, and up to 4 immatures regular on the Salt Pan headland between 12th and 28th May '95. Between 4-5 birds were seen at Skala Kalloni from 25th-28th March '86, with 2 up to 29th and an immature at East River on 9th April that year. Two were also present off Mytilini on 14th April '92, whilst 2 adults were seen feeding in Vatera Bay on 13th May '96. The only autumn records are of an immature at Kalloni Salt Pans on 1st August '98, a second winter there on 15th and 17th August that year, a juvenile and 2 adults on 13th September, a juvenile with 3 adults next day and one on Petra beach 2nd October. One immature on Kalloni Pool on 16th January '98 had been joined by up to 3 adults following overnight storms on 22nd. Sadly, most of these birds were oiled.

Black-headed Gull *Larus ridibundus*
Chiefly a winter visitor in reasonable numbers from late July to late April. A few (usually immatures) may summer. Mainly seen around Kalloni Salt Pans and East River, where small numbers were regularly seen between mid-July and early August '94 and mid-July '96. However, a party of 22 was present in Petra Bay on 10th July '96, with 26 birds at Dipi Larssos on 11th August that year and 42 birds at Kalloni Salt Pans the next day (with 50+ there by 6th August '97). Also to be seen in Skala Kalloni harbour in September '94 and 20 were seen nearby on 17th October '95 and at the gull roost on Skala Polichnitos Salt Pans in late September and the first half of October (where $c60$ were recorded 21st October '96 100+ birds were present from mid to late September '97 and $c400$ on 20th September '98!). Up to 80 were seen at Skala Kalloni from 2nd-4th April '85, but few thereafter; and 150 there and 100 at East River mouth at the end of March '86 had dropped to single figures by early April. Two were at the East River mouth on 22nd April '95, but by May mainly first-summer birds remain (eg 2 on the East River 7th May '93, with 9 on 12th, reducing to 6 on 13th. Eight were still at the pans on 14th, and latest records there of 3 on 18th May '95 and 1 on 20th). An early

autumn bird was seen at Kalloni Salt Pans on 9th July '98, and c50 were present there by 12th August.

Slender-billed Gull *Larus genei*
Irregular winter visitor from September to April and scarce passage migrant from mid-March to mid-April. This status is largely borne out by only 11 records - of 2-3 birds around Skala Kalloni on 15th April '84, 2 there with a flock of Black-headed on 2nd April '85, an adult over East River on 19th April '92, a bird present with good numbers of Black-headed and Mediterranean Gulls on Kalloni Pool on 20th March '97 (following gale-force winds overnight), another adult bird seen briefly around Kalloni Salt Pans on 3rd and 6th April '98 and also 1 frequenting Kalloni East River mouth from 28th-29th April that year. There is also a record of a first-winter bird seen with a small flock of Black-headed Gulls at Kalloni Salt Pans on 21st August '96 (the earliest autumn record), an adult there on 8th and 11th September '98 (with a first winter on 14th) and an unconfirmed report of a bird offshore from Mytilini on 28th August '97. The latest spring records concern one at East River mouth on 13th May '97 and an unconfirmed report of 4 seen together over Kalloni Pool on 16th.

Audouin's Gull *Larus audouinii*
Scarce all year round visitor. Initially very few records, but increasingly reported of late (especially from the north-east coast). This may reflect more than just increased observer coverage, as this species is known to be expanding its range - see *The Birds of Greece*. One bird seen at Sigri in mid-May '91 (with an exceptional sighting of 3 together in the harbour on 21st), another on 9th May '94, a single first winter on the Kalloni Salt Pans headland on 5th May '95, an adult on the pans on 9th, with a final record of a single on the inlet between Sigri and Faneromeni beach on 14th. In May '96 one was recorded heading west past Vatera on 8th, offshore from Eftalou on 16th, amongst Yellow-legged at Faneromeni beach on 13th - whilst in '97 just one was seen offshore from Sigri on 5th May. In spring '98 a bird was around East River mouth on 20th April, and single birds were seen quite regularly along the north coast from Molivos to Skala Skimmia between 27th April and 18th May (when a summer-plumaged bird was watched at close quarters in Skala Sikimmia harbour). The biggest gatherings in this period concern 6 seen offshore from Eftalou on 18th April and 4 on 12th May. The only autumn records are of a single frequenting Kalloni West River between early and mid-August '89, a 3rd year bird flying offshore from Molivos on 23rd September '94 (plus 1 offshore from Sigri on 25th), 4 offshore from Mytilini on 28th August '97, 1 at Skala Polichnitos on 31st, 1 at Molivos on 17th September '97, 2 adults west of Skala Sikimmia on 2nd August '98 and a second summer on rocks just south of Sigri next day.

Common Gull *Larus canus*
Rare winter visitor from early November to late March (though with a preference for inland freshwater lakes - see *The Birds of Greece*). Known to winter in small numbers, mainly around Kalloni Salt Pans and Mytilini harbour, and 1 immature seen at the mouth of East River on 26th March '86 falls into this category. Outside of this period there are only 3 records - of a sub-adult at the mouth of Kalloni East River on 26th April '97, perched on the salt pans jetty 23rd August that year, and a bird in the flooded field behind the Salt Pans on 24th April '98.

Lesser Black-backed Gull *Larus fuscus*
Scarce passage migrant from September to October - rarer from April to May. In some cases may be confused with dark-backed Herring Gulls, and only definite records of 1 at Skala Kalloni on 10th April '86, 1 at Kalloni Salt Pans on 12th May '91, 3rd May '96, 20th April '97, 13th May '98 and the late dates of 6th and 15th June '97 (with 2 claimed near Petra on the unusual date of 26th July that year), 1 offshore at Skala Sikimmia on 1st October '94, 6 seen

on a boat trip from Eressos to Sigri on 25th September '94, 1 at Skala Eressos on 29th March '97, 1 with Yellow-legged Gulls near Kalloni Inland Lake on 10th May '97. More unusual was a record of 5 seen together at Kalloni Salt Pans on 11th September '98, followed by a first winter bird in Skala Polichnitos harbour a week later.. Adults seen at Vatera on 2nd and 5th May '96 were identified as belonging to the race *intermedius*, which would usually apply to the majority of wintering records. Most migrants, however, are normally of the race *L. f. fuscus* (see *The Birds of Greece*). Nevertheless, an adult of the north Russian race *L. f. heuglini* was positively identified at Kalloni Salt Pans in the first week of August '98 by an observer familair with this species. It may be only the third record for Greece.

Yellow-legged Gull *Larus cachinnans*
Widespread resident. Breeds on islands offshore from Sigri, and common almost everywhere, especially both sets of salt pans, Dipi Larssos, north and west coast, rubbish tips and Kalloni East River (where 3 figure numbers often resting inland from bridge, and also on fields between East River and Salt Pans). At least 150 were resting at Skala Polichnitos on 13th September '95, with over double that number in Haramida Bay on 1st September '96 and *c*350 off Eftalou on 3rd May '97.

Great Black-backed Gull *Larus marinus*
Vagrant. One record only - from Mytilini harbour between at least 17th-21st January '98.

Gull-billed Tern *Gelochelidon nilotica*
Passage migrant in small numbers from late March to mid or late May (peaking late April), rarely from August to September. Unlike other terns, may forage more over farmland, so not confined so much to waterways and wetlands - see *The Birds of Greece*. Earliest date 1 at Kalloni Salt Pans on 31st March '98 and at Skala Kalloni on 2nd April '86. Usually seen in ones and twos at East and West River, Kalloni Pool and Salt Pans (eg 1 East River 18th May '92, 13th May '93, 11th May '94, and 3rd May '95, with 1 on Kalloni Pool on 15th and singles at the Salt Pans, 'Derbyshire' and West River from early to mid-month, and an isolated record from Sigri on 9th May '94). Larger gatherings include a record of 60 at Kalloni Salt Pans after heavy storms on 19th April '92, 35 at 'Derbyshire' on 24th April that year, up to 23 at Kalloni Salt Pans pans on 13th May '94, with *c*45 flying over Parakila Marsh the day before, 30 at the pans on 20th April '95 (with 19 still on 18th May), 45 on 16th April '97 and 20+ on 10th May '98. Last record of 2 at Kalloni Salt Pans on 30th May '94 and still up to 9 present on 3rd June '98 (with 1 still at East River mouth on 8th). Just one autumn record - of a bird at Kalloni Salt Pans on 1st August '98.

Caspian Tern *Sterna caspia*
Scarce and irregular migrant from early April to late May and mid-August to early October (when theoretically more likely - see *The Birds of Greece*). The only confirmed records are of a bird seen at Skala Kalloni on 22nd April '87, 3 birds feeding in Molivos bay on 7th May '94, 2 at Kalloni East River mouth on 27th May '95, 1 around Kalloni Salt Pan channels on 18th May '96 (and at East River mouth 2 days later), 3 seen at 'Derbyshire' from 3rd-9th April '97, a single seen resting at Kalloni East River mouth with other terns on 26th April, (following 2 around West River mouth at dawn), with another or the same bird around the Salt Pans and East River mouth from 10th-12th May that year and 3 over Faneromeni ford on 11th May '98. Rather surprisingly, only one autumn record - of 5-6 birds feeding offshore near Mytilini airport on 25th August '93.

Sandwich Tern *Sterna sandvicensis*
Widespread winter visitor in small numbers from October to April, with a small passage up to mid-May and between early August and mid-October. Circa 30 seen at Skala Kalloni on 15th April '84 is the maximum gathering, though 20 were present there on 1st April '85, with 13 at East River mouth on 28th March '86 (last seen 1st April), and up to 25 were roosting on the pier at Mytilini during the '94-5 winter. Three-four birds were seen offshore from Madamados on 21st April '95, with 1 on Kalloni Salt Pans 17th May '87, 1 found dead alongside Kalloni West River in mid-May '94, and 3 at the East River mouth on 24th April '95, with 5 there on 18th April '98 and 1 still on 12th May '97. A very late bird was seen along Kalloni Salt Pan channel on 26th May '96, a migrant was seen offshore from Plomari on 14th August '89, 3 were around Molivos harbour on 23rd August '93 and 6 migrants or early returning birds were seen in Mytilini harbour on 11th September '97, with a further 2 east of Molivos on 17th.

Common Tern *Sterna hirundo*
Widespread summer visitor from late March or early April to late August or early September, with numbers supplemented by passage migrants in April and early May. First seen 29th March '86 at Skala Kalloni (a single), with 2 there on 1st April and 20 briefly at the Salt Pans the next day. Five were also seen at Skala Eressos on 5th April '97. A more typical date, however, was 11th April '95 on East River. Breeds in variable numbers around Kalloni and Skala Polichnitos Salt Pans (where 15-20 birds present on 20th May '96), East and West Rivers, 'Derbyshire' etc (eg good-sized colony at the pans in '87, at least 5 pairs in Skala Kalloni area May '91, 3+ in '94, but 10+ pairs breeding at the West River pools on 30th May '93). Also likely to breed on isolated beaches (eg beaches by Pirra, Parakila Marsh and Skala Polichnitos Salt Pans). Six on Kalloni Pool on 2nd May '95, and up to 10 regular at Kalloni Salt Pans in late May, but widespread from at least 24th April. Maximum numbers involve 100+ seen at Skala Kalloni in a northerly movement on both 15th and 22nd April '84, 60 at East River mouth on 18th and 25th April '92, 15+ on 30th April '98 and 100+ at the Salt Pans on 3rd May that year. Also seen from mid to late May (and therefore likely to be breeding) around Mytilini harbour, Sigri and Skala Sikimmia, with 10 in Molivos harbour on 2nd August '94 and 25+ over the sea near Skala Sikimmia in the first week of August '98. Up to 10 were still present at Kalloni Salt Pans during the first week of August '98, reducing to 4 on 12th. Latest autumn record of 4 birds at Skala Polichnitos Salt Pans and another 4 near Achladeri - both on 31st August '97.

Arctic Tern *Sterna paradisaea*
Vagrant. Three records only, of 2 birds at Kalloni East River mouth on 14th June '96 and 10th May '98 and 2 over Kalloni Salt Pans on 21st April '98.

Little Tern *Sterna albifrons*
Locally common summer visitor and passage migrant from mid-April to late August or early September (with a migratory peak in late April/early May). Breeding distribution very similar to Common, though probably in smaller numbers. First seen at 'Derbyshire' on 19th April '97 (6 birds) and 21st April '98 (when no less than 27 were recorded from East River mouth). Usually at least 1 pair nesting there, with another 2 on the West River and 2-3 around the Salt Pans, but 5+ pairs breeding at the West River pools on 30th May '93. Otherwise, maximum numbers 6 on the West River on 3rd May '95, 6+ on the East River on 9th, 11 at the pans on 2nd May '97 and 40 there on 21st May '91, with 30 at East River mouth on 25th April '92, and 16 on the West River 19th May '94 (suggesting higher breeding numbers that year, when birds also seen on Kalloni Pool and 'Derbyshire' in mid-May). Maximum count, however, was of 70 birds at Kalloni Salt Pans on 3rd May '98, whilst 12 were still present on 12th August that year. Last record of 3 birds over Kalloni Inland Lake on 31st August '97.

22) **Spur-winged Plover** - Scarce but regular spring migrant
23) **Curlew Sandpiper** - Numbers peak early May, when many in pristine plumage

24) **Marsh Sandpiper** - Early spring migrant

25) **Wood Sandpiper** - Commonest wader by
mid-late April

26) **Whiskered Tern** - Good spring passage

27) **Little Owl** - A familiar sight

28) **Scops Owl** - Perseverance can pay off!
29) **Middle Spotted Woodpecker** -
    Widespread in both woodland and olive groves

30) **Kingfisher** - Common in autumn and winter
31) **Bee-eater** - Regular breeder around Kalloni
    East River and Salt Pans

32) **Great Spotted Cuckoo** - Scarce but regular
      migrant - may have bred

33) **Calandra Lark** - A good spring find!

34) **Woodlark** - Commoner to west and north

35) **Crag Martin** - Localized breeder in upland areas

36) **Red-rumped Swallow** -Widespread summer visitor
37) **Red-throated Pipit** -Kalloni Salt Pans a favoured
      spring site

38) **Tawny Pipit** - Localized summer visitor

39) ♂ **Black-headed Wagtail -**
Often a spectacular spring passage

40) ♂ **Citrine Wagtail -**
Regular and much admired spring migrant!

41) **Rufous Bush Robin** - Impressive display from late April

42) ♂ **Black Redstart** - Common winter visitor

43) **Nightingale** - Widespread and much appreciated spring songster!

44) ♂ **Black-eared Wheatear** - Numerous in upland areas
45) **Isabelline Wheatear** - Localized breeder to west of island

46) ♂ **Blue Rock Thrush** - Wary upland resident

Whiskered Tern *Chlidonias hybridus*
Passage migrant from mid-April to late May (peaking early May - though generally in slightly smaller numbers than White-winged Black). A small autumn passage is possible from mid-August to mid-September. Earliest record of 3 at Kalloni Salt Pans on 6th April '86, followed by 4 there on 12th April '87 and 4 at East River on 16th April '98, with several resting on Chalandra River Skala Eressos on 5th May '95, and a maximum of 15 over Kalloni Pool on 9th May that year (with 21 over East River the same day) reducing to 4 by 10th. Also regular on Kalloni Salt Pans, with 7 there mid-May '87, 14 on 12th May '91 (rising to 23 on 15th), c270 with other marsh terns on 19th April '92 after a heavy storm, with 30+ on 14th May '93, down to 10 on 17th and not seen after 19th. In spring '94, 30 on 9th May had reduced to 13 on 12th and 11 on 18th, with birds regularly commuting between there and the East River (so exact numbers always difficult to estimate). Up to 40 were present on Kalloni Pool in mid-May '97, when East River also held an influx of at least 40 birds resting on stalks by the road bridge. Latest spring records 2 commuting between the East River and the Salt Pans from 28th-30th May '94, and 2 on the West River pools on 30th May '93, a few still present on Kalloni Pool, Kalloni East River and Salt Pans up to 3rd June '96 (with 3 at the former till 10th) and from 8th-12th June '97, with 12 still present at Kalloni Pool on 11th June '98 and 1 up to 15th - the latest spring date (following a peak of 50+ there on 10th May, falling to 25 by the month's end and 9 on 3rd-4th June). However, there is an unconfirmed report of a bird being seen in the Skala Kalloni area in early July '90. Also unusual were records of 3 birds at Kalloni Salt Pans on 3rd August '96, 1 adult on the East River 6th August '94 and 2 on 9th (with 1 present since at least mid-July), 10+ at Skala Polichnitos on 31st August '97 and a late juvenile there on 30th September '94. Two birds were also seen in the '97 autumn near Achladeri and over Kalloni West River mouth on 31st August and 3rd September respectively. Finally, 3 juveniles were seen over Kalloni Salt Pans on 1st August '98 - with an adult over Kalloni Pool a few days later, an adult and 2 juveniles over the pans throughout the first week of August and 2 summer plumaged adults present on 12th, 1 remaining on 14th and small numbers seen on 1st October (the last recorded date).

Black Tern *Chlidonias niger*
Scarce passage migrant from mid-April to May (peaking late April to early May) and late July to early October (peaking the first half of September). Nowhere very plentiful, and probably the rarest of the terns in spring, but arrival can be earlier than and separate from other marsh tern passage - see *The Birds of Greece*. First record of 2 around Kalloni Pool on the early date of 8th April '86, after which a maximum of 3 seen there in mid-May '84, 4 on the East River in mid-May '91, with a few on 2nd May '94, 2 there on 7th May '95, and a small group on 9th. Apart from 10 birds present amongst 300 odd marsh terns at Kalloni Salt Pans on 19th April '92 after heavy storms, usually only small numbers on Kalloni Pool in company with other marsh terns early May '94 and '95 - though 2 there from 8th to 11th May '94, with 4 on 12th, and up to 10 on 4th May '95, but just 1 on 30th April and 8th May '97. Spring '98 saw one bird present there on 27th-28th April, with a maximum of 3 on 15th May, falling to 2 on 20th (when one also over East River). Also recorded from Kalloni Salt Pans (eg 1 on 22nd April '87, 4 on 20th May '91, 1 on 5th May '94, 1 on 3rd May '97, 1 on 20th April '98, 3 on 12th May and up to 12 on 14th May that year) - with 1 record from Skala Eressos River on 11th May '94. However, a record number of 20 were seen at Skala Kalloni during an obvious northerly passage on 22nd April '84. The latest spring record concerns 4 over Kalloni East River on 26th May '94. Though in theory the most likely tern to be encountered in autumn, the only definite records are of one at Petra reservoir on 6th August '97, a juvenile at Kalloni Salt Pans on 13th August, and another over Potamia reservoir on 27th-28th August the same year, with an adult present at the Salt Pans on 13th August '98, 5 there on 13th September, 10 on

14th-15th, 4 on 17th-18th and 1 till 29th September. These records followed a spell of unsettled stormy weather.

White-winged Black Tern *Chlidonias leucopterus*
Passage migrant in large numbers from mid-April to late May (peaking early May, but occasional from early August to mid-September) in all suitable wetlands. First recorded 18th April '98 (4 birds at Kalloni Salt Pans), and 20th April '97 (3 birds on Kalloni Pool), with numbers often building up spectacularly in the area of the Salt Pans, East River and Kalloni Pool. A flock of up to 60 was on the East River in mid-May '90, 31 on 10th May '91 (with 15 at the pans on 14th). At least 30 were on Polichnitos Salt Pans on 9th May '92, with 3 figure numbers on Kalloni Salt Pans from 6th to 8th May '93, and similar numbers there and on the East River from 5th to 8th May, tailing off by 13th. Eleven still on Kalloni Pool on 21st May '94. Passage in spring '95 was earlier, with numbers on Kalloni Pool peaking at an impressive 250 on 2nd May, halving every day over the next 2 days, with 16 remaining on East River by 9th. Spring '97 saw an even earlier passage, with a peak of 160 birds over Kalloni Pool on 29th April and at least 50 feeding near the East River inner ford on 4th May, whereas numbers in '98 were somewhat lower and saw a maximum of 50 around the Salt Pans and 80+ over Kalloni Pool on 10th May. Latest records are of 2 birds at the pans on 1st June '94, a single bird there on 2nd June '95 and 2 still present at Kalloni Pool on the late date of 10th June '96. Just 3 autumn records - of a single over Skala Kalloni beach on 20th September '95, a moulting adult and 2 juveniles at Petra reservoir on 14th August '96 and a single there on the late dates of 26th-28th September '98.

Rock Dove *Columba livia*
Resident around the coast in small numbers. Largest number at one site 7 near Eressos on 17th May '87, but one seen over Andissa beach on 22nd May '91, and 3 birds (presumed nesting) on island off Skala Eressos on the same date and again in mid-May '94 and mid-July '98, with 5 at Sigri on 25th and 2 at Garmias Island on 31st May '94. Also seen around Molivos Castle 28th May that year, with 2 seen north-east of Petra on 16th May '93, and 3-4 in the gorge west of Klio the day before. Five were seen in the hills just east of Petra on 7th May '94, with 4 west of Anaxos 2 days later. Seven flew over Anaxos on 24th May '96 and 16 flew to 'Rabbit Island' from Anaxos on 3rd June that year (including a flock of 11). Breeding on these northern offshore islands would therefore seem highly likely. Otherwise nowhere that regular,

and not always easy to distinguish from feral pigeon. Elsewhere the largest gatherings involved 2 flocks totalling up to 35 birds on the cliffs around Faneromeni beach on 19th April '95, 6 over Kalloni East River 23rd October '96, 6-7 west of Eressos on 9th August '89 and 12th May '97, 11 over Kalloni Salt Pans 7th October that year, and 13 seen feeding together on fallen seeds under a large plane tree near Perivoli monastery on 12th January '98 - with 10 observed on roadside rocks in the same area on 6th April that year and 7 at nearby Ipsilou monastery on 13th May.

Stock Dove *Columba oenas*
Very scarce passage migrant or vagrant. Also winters in northern Greece and a few may sometimes spread south, but no records to back this up. The species has a very uncertain status in much of Greece, but the likelihood of some passage between April-May and September-October is alluded to in *The Birds of Greece*. In spite of several unconfirmed reports of small flocks flying offshore, there is only one definite record - of a bird seen at close range in a garden at Klio on 30th May '98. Clearly more sightings would be welcome!

Woodpigeon *Columba palumbus*
Rare winter visitor from October to March and localised breeder in the more remote wooded areas. Not quite so rare in occurrence nowadays as originally thought. Recorded most often from the wooded hills between Vafios and Sikimmia, but also between Petra and Kalloni and the Achladeri and Agiassos areas. Seen in hills east of Molivos in mid-May '90. Two were reported in pinewoods above Agiassos on 20th May '91, 1 in olive groves near Achladeri on 15th May '92, and 1 in pinewoods north of Kalloni on 14th May '93 (with 1 near Lafionas on 19th). A pair was seen over deciduous woodland above Petri on 11th May '94, with singles south of Mount Lepetimnos in mid-May, in woodland between Mytilini and Kalloni from mid-late September, and at Skala Eressos on 23rd September. On 9th May '95, 2 were seen over woods above Skala Sikimmia, and on 13th an extraordinary record of 15 seen between Petra and Kalloni! More recently, single birds were seen between Plomari and Vatera on 3rd May '97, between Petra and Kalloni in early May '97, 3 near Achladeri on 16th April '97, 1 on 8th May and 2 nearby on 27th September that year; with singles at Mikri Limni on 1st June '98, between Vafios and Sikimmia on 3rd August '97, late April '98 and again calling near the Kruper's site at Achladeri mid-month and again in early June. This area must surely be a breeding site, and it seems likely that more birds have been recorded there since the popularity of the site as a known Kruper's twitch! The strangest record concerns a juvenile on top of a lamp post next to Skala Kalloni football pitch on 12th August '97!

Collared Dove *Streptopelia decaocto*
Abundant resident in virtually all locations, especially near human habitation.

Turtle Dove *Streptopelia turtur*
Widespread passage migrant from April to May and late August to late September, with several pairs staying to breed. First recorded 13th April '98 east of Vafios, and widespread by 3rd week, with 10+ seen at Faneromeni on 22nd and 15+ near Messotopos on 30th. Up to 40 were seen between Petra and Molivos on 10th May '94, whilst other double figure numbers reported in spring occurred near Sigri (peaking at *c*30 birds on 26th April '84 and 20 on 17th April '95), *c*20 on the track beyond Faneromeni ford (a favoured site) on 6th and 15th May '95, and 30 seen heading north from Molivos on 5th. Kalloni East River, Potamia Valley and Skala Eressos are also favoured areas. In autumn flocks of up to 40 regularly seen in early August '94 and impressive total of 70+ at Petra reservoir on 4th September '96! Numbers thinning out after mid-September, but 5 still at Kalloni East River on 11th September '98 and 2

around Kalloni Pool on 15th. Last recorded 23rd September '94 (perhaps a lucky survivor from the shooting season for this bird, which starts on 20th August in earnest!)

Laughing Dove *Streptopelia senegalensis*
Vagrant. One record only, documented in *The Birds of Greece*, of a bird seen at Achladeri on 24th May '94.

Great Spotted Cuckoo *Clamator glandarius*
Scarce passage migrant from late March to mid-May. Only a few records exist - of a bird briefly around Kalloni Pool on 26th April '84, 2 at Kalloni Salt Pans from 15th-16th April '87, one heard at the back of the pans on 4th May '95 (with 2 birds present there on 8th), and another (or possibly one of the pair) seen inland from the East River bridge on 16th and 20th. Thereafter one was watched between Agra and Messotopos on 9th May '96, with a further record from the Molivos area on 14th May that year. Spring '97 saw a temporary change in status, when a pair first seen along the tracks between Kalloni Salt Pans and East River on 4th April seemed to take up permanent residence around the Salt Pans, where they were regularly seen calling and indulging in courtship behaviour (with the male frequently observed feeding and mating with the female on the perimeter fence) right up to early May. A further sighting at 'Derbyshire' on 5th May probably refers to one of these birds, though a pair seen south-west of Agra on 4th may have been different birds. Although the normal host bird for this species is the Magpie (see *the Birds of Greece*), which is absent from the island as a breeding species, it may not be beyond the realms of possibility that the nests of Hooded Crow could be used in such a situation. Whilst breeding could not be 100% proven on this occasion, it seems more than likely - especially in the context of a juvenile seen near Molivos on 18th May '95. Spring '98, however, saw a return to its earlier status of a scarce migrant, with only 1 report of a bird 1 km south of Agiassos on 28th April (in spite of good numbers of birders being present throughout April and May).

Cuckoo *Cuculus canorus*
Passage migrant from April to May and late August to early or mid-October. More often heard than seen in a variety of habitats, but especially areas of pinewood and scattered trees. A few pairs almost certainly breed. Earliest records 2nd April '97 from Kalloni Salt Pans and 4th April '86 near Agia Pareskevi, with noticeable falls observed on 18th April '87 (when no less than 14 birds counted between Achladeri and Skala Polichnitos), 19th-20th April '95, when 12 were on wires at Skala Polichnitos Salt Pans (with a further 28 seen between there and Achladeri next day!). April '96 again saw good concentrations at Skala Polichnitos (where 6 birds were counted on 26th). The following day saw the rare occurrence of a 'hepatic' (or all-brown) bird in company with other Cuckoos at Kalloni Salt Pans (also seen near Sigri on 13th May '93), with others not being recorded till 2nd May '97 (at 'Derbyshire') and 15th April '98 (again near Achladeri). However, recent retrospective records suggest that the occurrence of this form may have been slightly commoner in the past - eg 1 near Agiassos on 24th April '84, 2 at East River mouth next day, and 3 (out of 12 birds) present at Achladeri during a 'fall' on 12th April '95. Less numerous in autumn (when not so obvious in any case) and only records of a bird over the clifftop Ruppell's site near Petra on 2nd August '98, another perched on a fence at Faneromeni next day, 3 west of Eressos (including at least 1 juvenile) on 13th August '89, an adult still vocal at Molivos on 8th and 9th September '97, a juvenile at Sigri on 21st September '86, an adult at Skala Eressos on 20th September '89, and another juvenile near Kalloni West River in late September '94. Some of these early or mid-August records may relate to local breeders. Otherwise the latest record is of up to 3 birds near Molivos harbour on 27th September '97 and 1 lingering between Kalloni East River and Salt Pans until 28th September '98.

Barn Owl *Tyto alba*
Resident and widespread (though with so much food available birds strictly nocturnal - so more often heard than seen). Regular around Skala Kalloni and Papiana, where quite often seen or heard around water tower - sometimes in company with Scops. A pair was seen flying around an old building there on 10th May '93 (now demolished). In late May '98 they were definitely sharing the water tower with the Scops (being watched emerging from holes in the opposite side!). Also heard regularly from area of boarded-up building near Skala Kalloni school in May '94, with several sightings in street lights from the Orange Taverna and behind Villa Yannis. More surprisingly, even reported calling from the centre of Mytilini, obviously helped by the glut of derelict buildings in the vicinity! Also seen roosting on a water tank at Arisvi on 16th May '95, with 2 birds roosting for several evenings on the Vrissa Travel building adjoining Skala Kalloni square in mid-September '95 often to be seen hunting the fields either side of the main road! Birds were regularly seen entering the boarded-up top storey of this building via the chimney during April and May '97 - almost certainly feeding young. Though still to be seen in spring '98 the building in question was often being worked on at night, so their future tenancy remains uncertain. A bird seen around Kalloni Pool on 6th and 11th September '98 was also seen in the grounds of the Pasifai hotel. Apart from a bird occasionally seen emerging from the 'minarette' between Parakila and Devils Bridge at dusk, Molivos Castle remains a regular roost and nesting site, with several observations between at least '95 and '98 - in late June '97 2 adults and 3 juveniles were watched there illuminated by the glow of the floodlights! A bird was also seen around 'Michelle's Studios' on the hillside above Anaxos on 19th May '98. Sadly, injured birds are frequently dealt with at the Lesbian Wildlife Hospital at Thermi (both *T.a. alba* and *T.a. guttata*), and a road casualty was noticed on the main road alongside Kalloni Salt Pans in early May '98.

Scops Owl *Otus scops*
Resident - by no means uncommon, but easily overlooked if not heard. Widespread both in olive groves and pine trees, even close to habitation (e.g. heard in centre of Mytilini April '95, and also around Molivos and grounds of Malemi Hotel Skala Kalloni in May). A pair have frequented the area of the water tower in Papiana most years since at least '91, and in May '95 one regularly emerged just before dusk from one of the small holes near the top of the structure. Later in the month the pair were located roosting together in the avenue of eucalyptus opposite the tower; and mating was regularly observed almost every evening in the light of the street-lamp! The same pattern has emerged every year since, though with birds often most visible at their daytime roost up to late April before nesting is fully underway. However, on 1st May '98 there were reliable reports of an adult already feeding a juvenile at one of the holes on the water tower - perhaps this can be explained by an exceptionally warm and settled April that year encouraging earlier nesting. It may also explain why the birds were not seen roosting regularly in the eucalyptus up to late April as per usual (in fact not after 17th). This association with eucalyptus extends to other sites - eg the taverna surrounded by trees just outside Kalloni on the Molivos road (where 2 birds seen 30th April '98), along with the apartments just beyond the West River heading towards Skala Kalloni. Birds are regularly recorded at Molivos (especially round the castle), and 5-6 calling males were reported around Petra on 9th May '94 (with 1 seen entering a hole in the eaves of a nearby house). In the last week of April '98 2 birds were also occasionally seen roosting around Ipsilou Monastery. Undoubtedly many more sites await discovery - this bird is a true master of disguise!

Eagle Owl *Bubo bubo*
Scarce resident. Presence confirmed by existence of a few (albeit fairly old) stuffed specimens in shops and tavernas. Though several likely (north-facing) breeding crags exist, these tend to be fairly remote, and need to be visited regularly in early spring (ideally March) just before

sunset to listen for the call. In such circumstances, the lack of records is hardly surprising! According to locals, used to be regularly heard between Dafia and Filia (though not recently). One local claims to have seen one perched on a rock at dusk not far from Kalloni school 'within the last couple of years'. A birder staying at Vasso Studios Skala Kalloni, however, reports seeing a very large owl which he felt certain must be this species flying past his balcony on 6th August '95. Though seen late (after 11pm) the bird was illuminated by street lamps as it flew into view - it was described as 'huge, broad winged and large bodied, with a wingspan similar to the armspan of a man'. This would seem to offer the most conclusive proof yet of this bird's continued existence as a breeding bird on the island, albeit in much reduced numbers. Clearly more precise records would be welcome!

Little Owl *Athene noctua*
Widespread resident, equally at home in upland areas and lowland plains, and often around human habitation, where frequently roosts and nests in old stone huts, cattle sheds etc (especially between Kalloni East River and Salt Pans). Regularly seen on wires around Skala Kalloni, and even nests on Kalloni Two Hotel and Arisvi water tower! Also particularly widespread between Eressos and Sigri (on the rough coastal track, Ipsilou monastery and the small shepherd's hut on the approach to Sigri near the Petrified Forest - where up to 7 territories recorded in mid-May '94). April to mid-May is usually the peak time for daytime sightings. Scarcer in the north and east of the island (though regular around stone hut next to Petra reservoir and also Molivos castle), and much harder to locate in autumn and winter.

Tawny Owl *Strix aluco*
Scarce resident, easily overlooked - only records of birds heard around Petra on 9th May '94 (and also in July that year), near Molivos in the first week of August '96, calling around the Scops Owl site at Papiana between mid-April and early May '98 and flushed by a Barn Owl from the roof of 'Michelle's Studios' just above Anaxos on 18th May '98! Conclusive proof of breeding comes from the record of 2 young calling near Agios Stefanos in June '97.

Long-eared Owl *Asio otis*
Scarce resident. Once again, the logistics of locating such a retiring species (which breeds in pinewoods and has such a large area of suitable habitat to choose from) account for the paucacity of records - just two in fact - of a bird flushed from pines in the picnic area alongside the Vouvaris River just before Achladeri on 17th May '95, and another flushed from exactly the same area on 24th April '98!. What is needed is more birders on the island in June or thereabouts to listen for the hunger-calls of the young!

Short-eared Owl *Asio flammeus*
Rare and irregular winter visitor from October to March. An unusually late record of a bird mobbed by waders and Hooded crows over Kalloni Salt Pans on 27th April '96.

Nightjar *Caprimulgus europaeus*
Summer visitor in good numbers from mid-April to early October. First records of a daytime churring bird near Skalochori on 11th April '98 and one flushed from an olive grove near Kalloni West River on 13th April '97. Birds often seem attracted to roads, with 1 found dead on the Sigri road on 11th May '95, 1 seen between Petra and Anaxos (sitting in road!) on 14th May '95, and a further road casualty just outside Molivos the next day. Three males were churring between Filia and Skoutaros on 30th May '96 and 2 near Petri the next night, with at least 5 churring along the track between Anaxos and Skoutaros on 19th May '98 and 4 hawking around Tamarisks at Anaxos sea-front on 16th May that year and at least 3 churring from a nearby hillside on 19th - whilst one was even catching insects over the swimming pool

of the Lassia Apartments Petra in the same period! Elsewhere, several churring birds were around the entrance to the Potamia Valley on 18th May '95. Also regularly heard churring around Molivos, the back of Skala Eressos, the hills around Andissa and the area both before and beyond Faneromeni ford, where daytime churring birds were sometimes located on drystone walls in early May '97 and '98 (with the extraordinary record of 12 birds sitting on the track on the evening of 12th May '98). A daytime calling bird was also located sitting in a pine tree at the Kruper's site at Achladeri on 17th May '97 and several birds were observed hawking for insects (with at least 4 churring) just after sunrise over the track leading into the hills just adjacent to 'Derbyshire' in late May '98 (which had produced a good number of evening flight views and churring birds in early June '96). Another unusual occurrence of 1 flushed by a Long-legged Buzzard near Kalloni East River on 14th May '93! Also autumn records of 1 there 25th September '94 and at Haramida Marsh on 16th, with 2 regularly seen hawking insects around a street lamp opposite Vasso Studios and even round the village square during August and early September '95! Three birds were seen around Kalloni Inland Lake on 2nd September '97, 1 at Haramida Marsh on 10th September '98 and the latest by Kalloni Pool 2nd October '94 and on the track between East River and Skala Kalloni on 4th.

Swift *Apus apus*
Summer visitor from mid or late March to September in good numbers - with migrants sometimes passing through into October. First record of 6 birds over Kalloni Salt Pans on 22nd March '97, a single bird at Dipi Larssos on 25th March '98 and circa 20 at Mytilini on 31st March '85. Quite common in most towns and villages, and also likely to nest on cliffs, rocky crags etc - eg large numbers seen at dawn and dusk around small island in Petra Bay mid-May '93. Elsewhere, maximum of 100+ over Kalloni East River 9th May '95, and 200+ over the Salt Pans on 15th (following a vast movement on 14th estimated at 1000 birds per hour moving north-east!), 100+ over West River on 18th May '98, but several thousand seen over the Potamia Valley and Kalloni East River on 25th April '92. At least 50 were seen over Agiassos on 6th July '97 - a likely breeding area. Seen in much smaller numbers in autumn, and scarce after mid-September, though 2 at Skala Kalloni on 14th September '98 and 15 over East River with large numbers of Alpine Swifts on 19th September. Latest record of 15 at Petra on 25th September '97 and 'several' over Skala Eressos on 28th September '89.

Pallid Swift *Apus pallidus*
Regular passage migrant and scarce summer visitor from early April to mid-October - though breeding not definitely proven (see *The Birds of Greece*). Several feeding with Common Swifts at the back of Skala Eressos from mid-late May '87 and 1 over Molivos Castle on 28th May '93 and 22nd May '96. Certainly regular in that area, and 1 observer in mid-May that year claimed 'hundreds each day' in the Petra-Molivos area, where also seen well on 19th July '97 and 2nd June '98 (2 birds). Also seen between Parakila and Agra on 24th July and 8th September '96, and regularly observed over Kalloni East River from 13th-25th July that year (where at least 1 identified amongst common Swifts on 24th April '98), with a single bird reported at Vatera on 4th May '97 and a gathering of at least 6 birds over Kalloni Inland Lake on 28th May '98. The best record, however, concerns 25 watched wheeling around Mytilini castle 2 days later! Probably commoner than sightings suggest, since by no means easy to separate from Common Swift unless good views are obtained (as they were when 3 birds were watched feeding low over crops at Faneromeni on 3rd August '98). Last recorded 7th September '94 at Eressos and 12th September '95 over Haramida Marsh, though (being a late breeder) this species can linger well into October.

Alpine Swift *Apus melba*

Summer visitor and passage migrant (peaking the second half of April) in reasonable numbers from late March to late September or early October. First records of *c*20 at Gavathas on 29th March '86, with several at Molivos 2 days later and 50+ over Dipi Larssos Reedbed on 1st April '98, with 2 at Skala Polichnitos Salt Pans on 19th April '95, and a large party over the quarry just outside Eressos on 28th. Regularly seen in that area (and also over Ipsilou monastery), and may breed on the island in Skala Eressos bay (where 10+ birds regularly seen mid-late July '94), and also the island offshore from Makara - where 4 birds were seen on 8th July '98. Elsewhere, maximum counts of 30+ at Anaxos in late May '93, *c*100 around Garmias Island on 31st May '94 (again suggesting breeding), and 50+ over Potamia Valley on 30th July '94. Circa 50 hawking round 'Rabbit Island' on 31st May '94 and 80+ on 4th and 5th June '96 are also indicative of breeding, and regular evening concentrations of 50+ were recorded there in the first week of August '98. The biggest recorded gatherings, however, concern 150 at Sigri on 8th April '87, 200 at Pigi on 7th April '95 and 300 over Skala Eressos on 14th April that year! Unlike Common Swift, still recorded in good numbers in autumn; being seen around Skala Eressos, Andissa and Kalloni Plain until at least late September most years, with 40 over Eressos on 7th September '94, at least 12 on 22nd and 30+ over Kalloni Inland Lake on 24th (with 100+ there on 3rd September '97, 30+ on 15th September '98 and 70+ on 2nd October that year). Seventy+ passed over Haramida Marsh on 10th September '95, at least 85 were hawking above East River bridge on 22nd September '98 and no less than 180 were seen over Panagias monastery just north of Kalloni on 29th September that year! Last record of 70+ over Anaxos on 4th October '98.

Kingfisher *Alcedo atthis*

Autumn and winter visitor from late July to April and occasional breeder. Extremely numerous in autumn and early winter around the coast and virtually all wetlands, with numbers gradually declining from February onwards. This influx is thought to originate largely from eastern Europe, and favoured sites in autumn include Kalloni Inland Lake, East and West Rivers, 'Derbyshire' and Chalandra River Skala Eressos, with birds also seen regularly all along the coast (especially in autumn). First recorded at 'Derbyshire' 22nd July '96 and then on East River 29th July '94 with at least 4 birds around the area of the ford by mid-late September, 2-3 at 'Derbyshire' and 2-3 at Kalloni Inland Lake from 22nd, and 4 on West River 11th October. Also at least 2 regular on Chalandra River between early September and early October, and scattered birds seen around the coast throughout - at Skala Polichnitos Salt Pans, Mytilini, Sigri and Skala Sikimmia harbours for example, with 4 together on the shoreline between Anaxos and Petra on 30th August '96. Startling numbers were seen at Sigri from 3rd to 4th October '86, when up to 10 birds at a time were fishing from rocks in the harbour! On 11th April '95, there were still at least 2 birds around Mytilini harbour, and 1 or 2 around East River ford until mid-month, when a bird was also at the river mouth near Thermi, with another on Kalloni Salt Pans channel on 18th. Finally, 2 frequented the ditches around Kalloni Inland Lake until 19th, with a single bird seen up to 24th. Breeding was strongly suspected there in spring '97, when a pair was lingering and indulging in courtship behaviour up to at least late April - with one seen apparently flying from a bankside hole. Also in that year retrospective breeding records were obtained for both Messotopos and the Eressos area for the '96 season (via the Hellenic Ornithological Society), and in June '98 a bird was seen feeding recently fledged juveniles near Petra - on the stream where a bird was still prsent on the late date of 3rd May the previous year. Clearly water levels at this time are critical, and high water levels around Kalloni Pool in spring '98 led to several late April records there, with a bird still round Kalloni Inland Lake on 30th April.

Blue-cheeked Bee-eater *Merops superciliosus*

A scarce and irregular passage migrant from April to May. The only records concern 2 birds seen at the back of Kalloni Salt Pans on 10th May '98 by 2 independent observers. Four unspecified bee-eaters seen there on the early date of 11th April that year may also have been this species. Surprisingly, the other record relates to a bird seen well for 45 minutes (and photographed) at Kalloni Salt Pans in the first week of August '98 - a very unusual date.

Bee-eater *Merops apiaster*

Widespread and locally common summer visitor and passage migrant from late April to late September/early October (peaking late April to early May). Spring migrants may appear irregularly - often not staying long in one place and freqently flying so high they can only be located by sound (see *The Birds of Greece*). First recorded at Faneromeni (a favoured area on migration) on 13th April '98 (6 birds), then 18th April (10 birds), with further records from the Potamia Valley next day and at Achladeri from 20th April '97 (with 'good numbers' over Kalloni Inland Lake on 21st and 50+ on 27th April '98) and at Faneromeni Beach from 27th April '95 - with a marked influx on 29th, when also widespread at Kalloni Salt Pans, with the first few nesting pairs returning to East River (where up to 13 pairs attempted to breed). This colony received a temporary set-back in June '97 when the west bank near to the sea was bulldozed and lorryloads of rubble were then dumped on top (ostensibly to alleviate the risk of flooding!). Thankfully breeding birds prove fairly resilient and opportunist (being very willing to colonise new areas and newly deposited spoil-heaps) and several pairs are usually found nesting also around the Salt Pans, Inland Lake ditches, Potamia River, 'Derbyshire', Faneromeni and Skala Eressos river area, with breeding activity also noted between Eftalou and Skala Sikimmia and Molivos-Vafios area. Flocks of 50 and 100+ were still seen heading north up to 21st May '95. Twenty-five seen over East River on 10th August '94, and several migrating flocks seen and heard up to the 2nd or 3rd week of September, with 60 or more over Eressos at a great height on 7th September, 20 there on 20th and just 2 by 23rd, $c120$ over Haramida Marsh south of Mytilini on 15th, 50 on 19th and $c60$ on 21st. A few small groups also seen over East River between 17th and 25th, but none thereafter. A heavy passage was noted throughout the island in mid-August '97 and early to mid-August '98 (when 30 were usually present at Kalloni Salt Pans and $c50$ over Petra reservoir most days). A flock of at least 150 passed over Haramida Marsh on 9th September '95 and 200+ over Molivos on 5th September '97! Otherwise $c40$ were seen in the Kalloni area on 22nd September '98, with several groups still heading south up to 30th. The latest record is of 3 still in the Skala Kalloni area on 1st October '97.

Roller *Coracias garrulus*
Scarce passage migrant from early April to mid-May (peaking late April) and in smaller numbers from mid-August to late September (peaking early September). A few pairs could also breed - see *The Birds of Greece*. Recorded in ones and twos (rarely more) from a variety of locations, occasionally lingering for a day or so. Most favoured areas around both sets of salt pans, Kalloni Inland Lake, 'Derbyshire' and Sigri-Faneromeni area, but birds can turn up anywhere and wires are always worth scanning! First recorded 12th April '98 near Messotopos, with 2 near Kalloni Inland Lake from 20th-21st April '97 and 14th April '98. Also seen 3rd May '97 between Eftalou and Molivos, 4th and 5th May '95 on roadside wires south of Kalloni, around the Salt Pans, nearby at Achladeri and near Sigri, (and south of Agia Paraskevi on 9th); on 6th May '93 on wires south-east of Kalloni (with 1 at Petra on 7th, near Filia on 11th and at Skala Kalloni again on 12th), near Skala Polichnitos Salt Pans on 9th May '92 (with 2 there on 21st April '97), below Andissa on 10th May '94, in the Potamia Valley on 10th May '98, near Sigri on 13th May that year and again near Sigri and between Molivos and Sikimmia on 14th May '91, on wires behind Villa Yannis Skala Kalloni on 16th, at 'Derbyshire' on 15th May '94, and an immature on wires at the entrance to Potamia Valley on 17th May '95. Two birds were seen together at Faneromeni on 25th April '97 and 28th April '98. The 2 latest records, however, were of singles at Skala Eressos on 20th May '88, and around Kalloni Salt Pans on 28th May '92. Finally, just 6 autumn records - of 1 at Petra reservoir on 7th-8th August '98, a juvenile at Skala Eressos on 8th August '89 and on wires between Kalloni East River and Salt Pans in mid-August '96, 2 adults in Skala Kalloni fields on 10th September '95, a bird in trees behind Skala Eressos beach on 16th September '89 and 1 around Kalloni Inland Lake on 17th September '98 (the latest record).

Hoopoe *Upupa epops*
Summer visitor from mid-March to October, and passage migrant (peaking early April and mid-August to early October. Fairly thinly scattered, but by no means uncommon, and birds heard calling (more often than seen) in a variety of locations, though olive groves especially favoured. Less noticeable by May when nesting. Sporadic sightings of singles along Kalloni East River, but more regular there in autumn, when also up to 3 on West River from early to mid-August '93 and 7 west of Eressos on 13th August '89, with 5 in a field at Eressos on 14th September '95. Also favours areas of semi-open oak woodland and steep-sided valleys (eg at least 5 calling between Skoutaros and Skalochori in mid-May '98), and quite regular on approaches to Skala Eressos from Messotopos, the woodland above Agiassos, and the oakwoods above Eftalou, where at least 3 birds were calling on 17th May '93, with 6 between Kalloni and Andissa on 8th May '95. Four birds were seen together at 'Derbyshire' on 1st August '97. First recorded on 20th March that year at Kalloni Salt Pans, with 4 seen together at Faneromeni 2 days later and 4 present along East River on 1st April. The last records come

from the Potamia River Bridge on 19th September '98, between Petra and Molivos on 26th, Skala Eressos on 24th September '94 and Kalloni East River on 28th September that year.

Wryneck *Jynx torquilla*
Passage migrant in reasonable numbers from late March to late April and late August to mid-October - a few may winter (as suggested by ringing recoveries). An easy bird to overlook, and likely to be under-recorded. First reported on 21st March '97 along Kalloni East River (where seen feeding on 12th-13th April '97 and 25th-26th April '98) and also at Gavathas on 30th March '86, Skala Eressos on 17th April '87 and below Ipsilou monastery three days later. Elsewhere seen at Parakila Marsh on 28th March '97, in oak woodland near Skalochori on 5th April '85, heard calling at Pigi on 7th April '95 (with 2-3 at Lisvori 2 days later), along the Chalandra river Skala Eressos on 15th April '97, 'several' reported around Skala Sikimmia on 17th April '92, singles between Achladeri and Vassilika on 18th April '98 and 21st April '97 (2 birds), calling at Kalloni Salt Pans on 20th April '97, above Agiassos on 20th April '95 (where heard calling on 24th April '84), with another at Sigri on 20th April '84, near Faneromeni ford 23rd April '95, Skala Eressos beach on 28th April '98, 1 or possibly 2 birds near Messotopos on 30th April that year and a late bird calling near Agiassos on 14th May '95. In autumn, the ringing party recorded singles at Haramida Marsh on 16th and 21st September '94 and 9th and 17th September '95 and no less than 3 on 15th September '98. A bird was also seen at Skala Polichnitos Salt Pans on 12th September '98, at Kalloni on 15th September and above Agiassos on 18th September that year, near Kalloni East River on 28th September '94, with sightings from Kalloni Inland Lake area on 25th September and 5th October that year and 15th September '98. Last recorded in that area on 8th October '97.

Great Spotted Woodpecker *Dendrocopos major*
Scarce and localized resident (uncommon in the country as a whole) and according to *The Birds of Greece* favouring both coniferous and deciduous woodland above 700 metres. A cursory glance at the distribution map would indicate the occurrence of this species to be extremely unlikely. However, it was reported from Parakila on 19th April '84, the Potamia Valley on 21st April '87, the Agia Paraskevi area in mid-May '91, near Gavathas on 24th April '92, and Bob Husband and his group (on the last of his Sunmed *Go Greek* birdwatching holidays in May '94) recorded it as 'heard or seen on both visits to the pinewoods above Agiassos 11th and 18th' - where one was definitely reported on 24th April '84. This (especially the call) would seem to offer fairly conclusive proof of its occurrence. A pair was also seen near Papiana on 10th April '87, with a single bird seen in the woods above Petra on 1st October '97.

Syrian Woodpecker *Dendrocopos syriacus*
Scarce resident or vagrant - generally occurring from sea level to medium altitudes (see *The Birds of Greece*). Status of this bird is somewhat open to doubt, and logistics of separating it from Middle Spotted are likely to require close and quite prolonged views. Nevertheless, this species is listed in Marjorie Williams' *Birdwatching in Lesbos*, and 1 was reported from the Sikimmia area on 1st June '93, 1 was seen well in the garden of an apartment at Skala Eressos on 23rd August '93, a 'probable' from above Agiassos on 30th September '94, and a fairly detailed sighting (including some prolonged 'scope views) of a bird in the thickly wooded area between Lambou Mili and Arisvi on 20th May '91. A further two were identified both by sight and call in an olive grove near Petra on 21st October '95 by someone familiar with the species in mainland Greece. He obtained particularly good views of one of the birds, and described its 'all black crown and solid white patch between eye and lower neck - ie no black line between nape and moustachial stripe, as in Great Spotted'. The call was described as a 'chuk - less powerful and less metallic than Great Spotted's, more reminiscent of a Redshank in tone'. Such

a detailed description would seem to clinch it - though some still remain sceptical of this bird's occurrence on the island. More records would, of course, be much appreciated!

Middle Spotted Woodpecker *Dendrocopos medius*
Widespread resident, especially in olive groves and orchards. This bird occurs just about anywhere on the island, and nest-holes are often quite easy to locate in old olive and pine trees, and especially in the area of sweet chestnuts above Agiassos, the Kruper's site at Achladeri (where regular) and also along Kalloni East River. At least one youngster had already fledged from a site near Papiana water tower on 24th May '98. Sometimes nests quite close to human habitation, and a pair even found nesting in an old fence post at Vatoussa in April '98! Harder to locate outside the breeding season, when frustratingly fleeting views often obtained.

White-backed Woodpecker *Dendrocopos leucotos*
Vagrant. Little is known of the distribution of this bird, which is described in *The Birds of Greece* as a montane species, occurring at 800 metres and upward. Although by rights this bird should not occur on the island, there are one or two unconfirmed reports - one rather surprisingly from the olives bordering Kalloni East River in mid-May '96. However, there is at least 1 reliable record - of a bird seen well in the oakwoods above Skalochori on 12th April '87 at an elevation of approx 600 metres. In view of the fact that this is a very under-watched area it remains to be seen whether this chance sighting merely involved a vagrant, or whether there may be a small breeding enclave in this area. Only extensive fieldwork in this region is likely to produce an answer - but any further sightings would be very welcome!

Calandra Lark *Melanocorypha calandra*
Scarce and irregular passage migrant - mainly in spring (April-early May) - favouring sand dunes and saltmarsh edges especially. Though *The Birds of Greece* alludes to breeding on nearby Limnos and Kos, and the species is listed in Marjorie Williams' *Birdwatching in Lesbos*, there were no definite records until 2 birds were observed in the flooded field behind Kalloni Salt Pans on 2nd and 3rd May '96, where, coincidentally, a bird was also present 1st-3rd May '97! One was also seen at 'Derbyshire' that year on 23rd April and on Skala Eressos beach in early May, whilst another single was seen at Dipi Larssos beach on the early date of 9th April '98.

Black Lark *Melanocorypha yeltoniensis*
Hard-weather vagrant. Just one record for this species, which was seen on the island during extensive snow cover in the winter of '86-7. Regrettably the exact dates are not available.

Short-toed Lark *Calandrella brachydactyla*
Localized summer visitor from mid to late March up to early or mid-September to open, flat, sandy areas and pastureland with sparse vegatation (eg the large sheep field at the back of Kalloni Salt Pans). Also a noticeable passage in early April and late August. First recorded 20th March '97 at Kalloni East River mouth (a flock of 40), and 25th March '86 at Skala Kalloni, with 20 birds present by the end of the month and movements of 200+ birds arriving from the south on 3rd April and another 250 seen at the Salt Pans by the evening, with a further 200+ present at Kalloni Pool with vast numbers of wagtails on 6th and large numbers still coming in off the sea up to 9th April - when at least 300 birds were recorded. Thereafter numbers declined somewhat, and passage had obviously peaked. In April '92 60 migrants were at Kalloni Salt Pans on 17th - rising to 200 by 19th (with 120 at 'Derbyshire' the previous day); and in April '95 circa 200 migrants at Faneromeni on 17th had shrunk to 80 2 days later. Otherwise regularly recorded in small groups around some of the drier areas e.g. 2 near

Molivos mid-May '91, regular around 'Derbyshire', Kalloni Salt Pans, West and East Rivers, Skala Eressos beach area, and between Sigri and Faneromeni beach. Party of 6 seen on headland near Agios Stefanos on 21st April '95, and 5-6 were regularly seen feeding alongside the East River later in the month. Peak numbers, however, seem to occur at the back of Kalloni Salt Pans, where several pairs were found breeding close to the perimeter fence in the large sheep field by the headland, and 10+ birds were observed feeding between the pans and the sea on 9th May '95, with circa 100 counted on 4th April '85 and 40+ there in mid-late April '98 before breeding commenced in earnest. An autumn gathering of 20+ around the pans on 31st August '94 and 25 on 17th September, with 16+ seen along the road to the Petrified Forest on 3rd August '98 and just 2 at Kalloni Salt Pans by 10th September. Last recorded on 22nd September '94 at Mytilini beach.

Crested Lark *Galerida cristata*
Abundant and widespread resident seen in just about every type of terrain - especially open, flat areas with sparse ground cover. Flocking noticed in autumn and winter around stubble fields etc.

Woodlark *Lullula arborea*
Fairly common but localized resident, more noticeable to the west and north of the island, and often in quite open, rocky terrain. Often seen on main approach to Sigri, a few kilometres beyond Ipsilou Monastery - where watched in display flight on 29th March '98 and a pair feeding recently fledged young on 23rd April '95, with 3 seen between Sigri and Faneromeni in late May. Also seen and heard on main road between Eressos and Sigri at that time, with up to 10 along the Skoutaros road on 10th May; and a further 3+ heard singing near Skalochori in mid-May '91 with c12 birds together at a small puddle between Dafia and Eressos on 28th May '94. It was also described as 'common in open wooded areas east of Skalochori' in mid-May '93, with 2 singing south-east of Molivos at the same time. In addition, several were recorded between Kalloni and Molivos in early May '94, with 3 west of Vatera in late May '95. Three were seen in the Potamia Valley on 31st July '94, and 2 were near Filia on 6th August - with 4 singing males near 'Derbyshire' on 21st April '97 and a bird still in song near Ariana on 5th July '98. Finally, several concentrations were noticed between Sigri and Faneromeni, with up to 10 birds seen in the dunes on 2nd October '86, 7 in the same area on 13th September '89, and a small party seen around Skala Eressos on 28th October '92. As a largely non-migratory bird in this part of the world, these gatherings were more likely to represent autumn flocking than anything, and this is confirmed by records of 6 feeding with Corn Buntings near Ampelia on 4th September '96 and the presence of a feeding flock of at least 30 along the Chalandra River Skala Eressos on 28th January '98, with smaller flocks also to be seen along Kalloni East River at that time.

Skylark *Alauda arvensis*
Winter visitor from October to late March in small numbers. Up to 20 birds were present on Skala Polichnitos beach 26th March '97; whilst 6 were still on Skala Eressos beach 29th March '98 and 50+ were feeding in fields by Kalloni East River in January the same year, with a peak of 180+ seen on 23rd March. Outside this period, 1 reported at Petra on 2nd May '97, 2 flushed from Skala Polichnitos beach on 5th, 1 claimed over the beach behind Kalloni Salt Pans on the unusual date of 9th May, and another on the roadside at 'Derbyshire' on 13th May '97 - with 1 in display flight around Skala Kalloni fields on the very late date of 23rd May '96 suggesting possible breeding. There was also a record from Kalloni Pool on 10th June that year, and from the Anaxos area in mid-June - which tie in with the above. Two very early birds were around Kalloni Salt Pans on 5th August '96, with a single bird at Haramida Marsh on

19th September '94, 1 at Kalloni West River on 30th September '98, 5 birds at Sigri on 3rd October '97 and 10 along East River on the more normal date of 19th October '95.

Sand Martin *Riparia riparia*
Passage migrant from mid or late March to late May (peaking mid-April to early May) with smaller numbers from late August to early October. Breeding is possible, as (like the Bee-eater) this species can be quick to exploit man-made nest sites resulting from excavation, road building etc - see *The Birds of Greece*. First recorded on 29th March '97 (a large passage over East River) 31st March '98 (a passage ovwer Kalloni Pool) and 3rd April '86 at Kalloni Salt Pans. Migration usually peaks earlier than other hirundines, with huge numbers (perhaps even running into four figures) on the Potamia River from 11th-12th and 18th April '95, but very few thereafter; with the last small groups reported at Faneromeni ford on 14th May and between Kalloni East River and Salt Pans, where 50 birds were present on 21st. Spring '92 saw quite good numbers near Mytilini on 7th May, but spring '93 (as with Swallow) was quite exceptional, with hundreds over virtually any stretch of water (and especially Kalloni Salt Pans) until mid-May, when adverse winds abated. None were seen after 18th. On the late date of 30th May '96, however, heavy storms produced an astounding total of 500-1000 birds over East River - there are no spring migratory records after that date. In spring '97 peak passage was around 23rd April and again from 2nd-3rd May (with none noted after 6th), but again in May '98 more unsettled weather resulted in a large concentration of several hundred birds on wires along Kalloni East River on both 3rd May and the comparatively late date of 18th (with circa 50 over Petra reservoir next day). Usually scarcer in autumn, though a particularly heavy movement of 200 or more took place over Kalloni East River (in company with other hirundines) on 17th September '94, and several thousand were involved in a similar movement at Skala Eressos on the same date. Last recorded over Kalloni Inland Lake on 6th October, with 3 over East River on 12th. One bird trapped at Haramida on 18th April '97 was bearing a Budapest ring.

Crag Martin *Ptyonoprogne rupestris*
Localized summer visitor and partial migrant from March to October in suitable upland areas - especially gorges, cliff faces, rocky outcrops etc, chiefly to the west of the island. A colony of about 20 seen around the 'Grand Canyon' between Andissa and Vatoussa on 18th May '87 still in existence May '95, and another small colony of 6+ found at the same time between Andissa and Eressos. Also seen regularly (and likely to be breeding) around Ipsilou Monastery. A pair was also found nesting beyond Eftalou on 20th May '98 and below the Potamia Valley road bridge on 13th July '98. Elsewhere, seen over Skala Eressos peaks in mid-May '88 and collecting mud from a pool on Faneromeni beach in mid-May '97 and a pool near the river mouth east of Vatera (where breeds on nearby crags) at the same time. In autumn 3 were seen near Agra on 30th August '94, 5 were present around Faneromeni on 7th September '98 and single birds were over Skala Eressos beach on 8th September '89 and 25th September '94, with at least 15 seen over nearby hills on 23rd and 6 there on 10th October. Six were also seen again in the hills above the village on 24th October '92. Although a mainly migratory species on the northern mainland (see *The Birds of Greece*), it seems possible that a proportion of the breeding population on Lesvos may overwinter - though often at a lower elevation, where birds can regularly be seen feeding over wetland areas like Kalloni Inland Lake and Dipi Larssos in late autumn and early spring. Several were feeding low over the river near Dipi Larssos during adverse conditions on 25th March '98, but none were noted in January '98.

Swallow *Hirundo rustica*
Passage migrant and summer visitor in considerable numbers from March to October. Large movements noted at Skala Kalloni in early and mid-April '85 and mid-April '87 - when

between 5-7000 hirundines (mainly swallows) were feeding between Skala Kalloni and 'Derbyshire', and between 11th and 15th April '95 around Kalloni Salt Pans, 'Derbyshire' and river mouth near Thermi - with 100+ still over Kalloni West River on 2nd May. In spring '93, migration peaked later when adverse winds held up passage and left hundreds swarming over Kalloni Salt Pans from 10th-11th May especially, after which winds began to ease, and they were seen in more 'normal' quantities by 16th. Spring '97 saw a huge movement on 2nd and 3rd May, with no discernible passage thereafter. First recorded on 19th March '97 (a single) and 22nd March '98 over Kalloni Pool - with large numbers of grounded migrants particularly noticeable at Kalloni East River after wet weather on 26th April. In autumn, numbers usually declining by mid-September - when c600 were over Dipi Larssos Reedbed (a regular autumn roost) on 16th September '94, 200+ passed over East River on 17th (with 'thousands' heading out to sea from Skala Eressos in a south-easterly direction) and c300 were over Haramida Marsh on 19th. There were still 20+ around East River on 12th October, and several small parties heading south until at least 13th. Last record a single on 24th October '92.

Red-rumped Swallow *Hirundo daurica*
Widespread summer visitor from March to October, frequently breeding under bridges, roadside culverts and even old wells throughout the island - though usually at slightly higher elevations than Swallow and less associated with people and open farmland. First recorded 22nd March '97 at Marmaro and 25th March '98 near Dipi Larssos, and regularly observed between April and May collecting mud from puddles around Skala Polichnitos, above Agiassos, near Skala Sikimmia, Anaxos, Skalochori, Skala Eressos, Faneromeni beach, Potamia Valley etc. Sometimes further influxes are noted later in the spring - eg 'good numbers' over Kalloni Inland Lake on 21st April '98, 100 at Eressos on 22nd April '92 and several hundred around Skala Kalloni and 'Derbyshire' from 12th-13th April '87 and 30th April-2nd May '97 - where concentrations of up to 16 birds were recorded between Petra and Molivos and around the Skala Kalloni area. Five pairs were also found nesting together in a large rock on Faneromeni beach 7th July '98. At least 3-4 were over Kalloni Inland Lake daily in autumn '94, with up to 10 seen feeding over irrigated fields along the Chalandra River Skala Eressos on 16th, 19th and 26th September, and 100+ feeding over irrigated crops at Faneromeni in the first week of August '98. At least 50 were over Haramida Marsh on 14th September '95, with double that number on 31st August '96 and 250+ at Anaxos on several dates in the first week of August '98. Late nesting was confirmed with the sighting on 15th September '98 of several juveniles just out of the nest at Kalloni Inland Lake, where birds last recorded on 5th October '94.

House Martin *Delichon urbica*
Summer visitor from mid-March to October (arrivals peaking early to mid-April), breeding in huge numbers. Nests on hotels in the vicinity of Kalloni Pool can be counted almost in the hundreds, and flocks of birds can always be observed collecting mud from any surviving puddles or small pools (with Skala Eressos ford, West River and Kalloni Pool being particularly favoured). In spring '95, some birds had returned by the unusually early date of late February! Otherwise birds first recorded on 19th March '97 over Kalloni Inland Lake. Early returning birds sometimes suffer very heavy mortality if adverse weather sets in and destroys their food supply (as it sometimes can at this time of year) - eg a brief snowfall on 22nd March '98. Certainly nest building is often well underway by mid-April, and flocks of more than 200 were recorded around Skala Kalloni on 19th April '97 and 7th April '98. Less numerous in autumn, with some birds departing as early as mid-August onwards - but 40+ seen flying south from Skala Eressos on 26th September '94, and last recorded 6th October.

Richard's Pipit *Anthus novaeseelandiae*
Vagrant and scarce passage migrant from April-May September-October. This long-distance wanderer is, as elsewhere, somewhat erratic in occurrence; and only records are of 2 associating with other pipits opposite Villa Vasso Skala Kalloni on 16th September '94, and more recently a bird seen and photographed at the back of Kalloni Salt Pans between 18th and 19th April '98. It or another bird was seen a few days later at 'Devil's Bridge', and again on the track between Apothikes and Makara on 26th April. There is also an unconfirmed report of a bird along Kalloni East River on 3rd September '97.

Tawny Pipit *Anthus campestris*
Localized summer visitor from late March to early October in suitable dry habitat. First record of a single at Kalloni West River on 5th April '98 and 2 birds at Vatera on 9th April '97. Elsewhere a wide scattering of records, but 'Derbyshire' especially favoured (at least until major road work there in spring '95), and a pair present throughout May '94 were almost certainly breeding, as most likely were a pair at Polichnitos Salt Pans on 7th. At least 4 birds were present at Kalloni Salt Pans on 23rd April '98, with 10 at Skala Polichnitos Salt Pans on 27th. An adult carrying food near Kalloni East River mouth on 20th May '96 and a juvenile located inland from East River on 17th July that year, and 2 at the back of Kalloni Salt Pans in early June '98 also suggested local breeding there, as did records around Molivos and between Anaxos and Petra in early June '96. Also 1-2 breeding pairs west of Skala Eressos beach on 16th May '87 and between mid and late May '91, with a single bird seen in a field at Faneromeni on 7th May '95, at Sigri harbour on 7th May '97, with 2 birds nearby on 19th May '98. Autumn records mainly relate to Skala Kalloni, the Salt Pans and 'Derbyshire', where a single was seen on 22nd September '94. In addition, birds were seen most days in stubble fields around Skala Kalloni between 15th and 29th September, with a maximum of 5 near the East River in this period, and 6 at the Salt Pans on 18th, 15 at Kalloni Salt Pans on 4th September '95, 10+ in fields near Molivos castle between 10th-15th September '97, 3 on 22nd September '94, reducing to 2 on 25th and 1 on 27th, and a flock of 8 flushed from dunes between Sigri and Faneromeni beach on 24th. Last records of 2 on Kalloni Salt Pans on 6th October that year, and 2 there on 8th October '97, with an even later bird at Skala Eressos on 20th October '95.

Tree Pipit *Anthus trivialis*
Passage migrant in small numbers from mid or late March to early May (peaking early to mid-April) and in smaller numbers from late August to mid-October (peaking mid-September). First recorded from the Potamia Valley on 23rd March '98 (2 birds - with 4 at East River ford next day, when also 5 seen at Faneromeni), and from Molivos on 26th (4 birds). Also seen at Skala Kalloni 1st April '85 and Molivos on 7th April '95, with a 'fall' at Faneromeni on 16th April '98, 40+ at Skamioudi on 25th, and a peak of 18 birds along East River 20th April '97 and 40+ at Kalloni Salt Pans a week earlier. At least 40 were also seen in the Sigri area on 26th April '84 and 50+ were present there on 17th and 20th April '87. Elsewhere 3 feeding at West River on 4th May '97, 1 nearby on 10th May '94, with another near Vatera harbour on 17th May '96, at Filia on 29th May '93 and a 'probable' near Achladeri in mid-June '98 raising the intriguing possibility of breeding. In autumn a single was seen at Skala Kalloni on 16th September '94, with another between the East River and Salt Pans, and at Skala Eressos (both on 25th) and 6 on wires by the Chalandra River ford on 3rd October. One was also trapped at Haramida Marsh by the ringing group on 20th September (with several flying over calling on 18th), and small numbers were regularly seen around Skala Kalloni between mid and late September that year, with another 2 over Haramida Marsh on 8th September '95, and a peak of 20+ there on the same date in '96. A small autumn passage of birds heading south over Molivos in September '97 peaked at 10 on 17th, but numbers feeding in alfalfa fields between

Kalloni East River and Salt Pans reached 30+ on 19th September '98. Last recorded 21st October '95 at Petra.

Meadow Pipit *Anthus pratensis*

Winter visitor in good numbers from mid-October to late March. First recorded 26th September '97 in the Kalloni area, but more typical date 17th October '95 on Kalloni East River, with a more general arrival at Petra and Skala Eressos between then and 21st. Twenty seen in hills above Eressos on 28th October '92, with a similar number seen at Skala Kalloni on 31st March '85, 7 between the East River and Salt Pans on 25th March '97, 12 at the Salt Pan headland on 31st March and 10 there on 3rd April '98. Birds were seen around Skala Kalloni until 18th April '87, with a maximum of 10, whilst 3 were still present at Skala Polichnitos Salt Pans from 7th-11th April '95. Particularly late birds were reported near East River ford on 2nd and 10th May '97, at Sigri on 13th May that year and near Molivos in mid-May '90.

Red-throated Pipit *Anthus cervinus*

Passage migrant from late March to May and September to October. A few may winter. Most favoured area Kalloni Salt Pans, and first records of 2 there on 8th April '86 (following 2 at Sigri the previous day), then 2 on 16th April '98 at the roadside garage pool opposite Kalloni Salt Pans and 3 on 19th April '95 at a puddle on the track between Kalloni East River and the Salt Pans (coincidentally at the same site where 2 were present on 7th-8th May '94, with up to 7 seen nearby on the former date, and 1 still on 12th). Numbers around the back of the Salt Pans rose to possibly 3 figures by 21st April, but were jittery and difficult to count. Between 10 and 15 birds were still feeding around the large pool opposite the salt workings on 3rd and 4th May '95, but these numbers were dwarfed by a huge concentration (possibly running into 3 figures) in the damp field between the pans and the headland from at least 3rd to 5th, (by which time the whole area was largely dry). This favoured area also hosted a large concentration of birds in late April '97 and '98, which peaked at circa 100 on 25th April '97 (declining to just 6 by 2nd May), and at least 75 on 27th April '98 - rising from 10 on 18th. Numbers here had actually risen to over 200 on 20th April '92! Only other spring locations reported were the West River, which held 2 birds on 10th May '93, Vafios (where 2 birds flew north on 7th May '95), and Sigri, where the latest spring record concerned *c*25 birds on 11th. There was also a reliable report of 45 seen at 'Devil's Bridge' on 21st April '98. One bird was still present at the back of Kalloni Salt Pans on 13th May '96 and 14th May '98 - the latest spring record. In autumn '94 the Salt Pans again played host to a large 'fall' on 12th October, after torrential rain and strong winds on 11th. Further birds were also seen around 'Derbyshire' and Kalloni West River, at least until 13th. No records thereafter, so whether any stayed to winter is not known. In October '95 a single bird was recorded at Petra on 19th with 3 on Kalloni East River up to that date. Two birds were at Haramida on 8th September '96, a single bird was seen near water in the area of Molivos castle on 10th September '97 and 2 were noted around the back of Kalloni Salt Pans 21st-22nd October, when an impressive autumn gathering of *c*40 birds was also present in cultivated fields at Sigri.

Water Pipit *Anthus spinoletta*

Winter visitor in small numbers from October to late March or early April in suitable wetland habitat. Only a handful of records at this time - of 2 birds seen at Skala Eressos on 26th September '94 and more recently wintering birds at Kalloni West River and Salt Pans in January '98, with near summer-plumaged birds seen near Petra Reservoir on 26th March '98, and at Kalloni Salt Pans 2 days later. One was also present at Parakila Marsh on 31st March (the last date recorded). Two very early winter-plumaged birds were feeding along Kalloni Salt Pans channel on 12th August '96.

Yellow Wagtail *Motacilla flava*

Abundant passage migrant from late March to May and late August to early or mid-October. First record of 12+ Black-headed and a Blue-headed at Kalloni East River mouth on 20th March '97 and 6 Black-headed at Kalloni Salt Pans on 23rd March '98. A bewildering array of sub-species occur in spring, and are even harder to separate in autumn, when the peak pasage usually occurs! Basically, both Blue-headed *M. f. flava* and Grey-headed *M. f. thunbergi* occur in passage (with a late record for the latter of 8th June '96 on Kalloni Pool) whilst the Black-headed *M. f. feldegg* is both a widespread migrant and breeder in reasonable numbers around Kalloni Salt Pans, West River, Parakila etc (eg singles seen both at West and East Rivers and Dipi Larssos Reedbed between mid and late July '96, a juvenile at Parakila Marsh early June that year, and a pair feeding young at 'Derbyshire' on 9th July '97, with up to 5 on Kalloni Pool and 2 at East River in the first week of July '98 - following exceptionally high water levels. On 6th April '86 at Kalloni Pool a huge passage involved *c*3000 birds (including 500 White Wagtails) - most of which departed the same day. Similar but smaller movements took place up to 9th April, when *c*500 were involved. The observers broke the ratios down to predominantly Balkan types, but including Blue-headed, Ashy-headed, Sykes and up to 50 *flavissima*. A smaller passage at the Salt Pans peaked at 3-400 birds on 25th April '92, but in April '87 numbers around Skala Kalloni reached a maximum of *c*1000 birds on 13th, whilst at Skala Eressos in May that year it was the Blue-headed that predominated. In May '91 around the Kalloni area, it was the Black-headed form, and in that area in spring '94 and '95, all three were equally represented, especially amongst the huge passage on Potamia River 11th April '95, the river mouth near Thermi between 14th and 17th and Faneromeni ford on 27th April. Several hundred were also seen associating with sheep between Molivos and Skala Sikimmia on 16th. By early and mid-May, however, largely Black-headed were being seen, with a maximum of 8 at the Kalloni Salt Pans between 2nd and 4th, and at least 6 on West River on 8th. In late summer, numbers reached 13 there on 5th August '94 (suggesting successful breeding), and at least 5 were on East River on 9th. In April '97 *c*400 were seen going to roost over West River bridge on the evening of 4th, whilst the damp field at the back of Kalloni Salt Pans attracted up to 500 birds on 25th - of which the bulk were Grey-headed, with smaller numbers of Blue-headed and Black-headed. Mid-April '98 again saw a large passage with much the same composition - good numbers being seen at both Alikoudi beach and Faneromeni (where *c*500 on 16th-17th were drinking and bathing around irrigators and up to 150 at a time were counted feeding in newly-mown hay fields). Numbers peaked again on 27th, when hundreds of exhausted (and several moribund) birds were present around Faneromeni ford in classic 'fall' conditions. In the autumn massive numbers of birds pass through the island, frequently hidden in tall crops around Kalloni and Eressos Plains until flushed. 'Hundreds' of Black-headed were reported west of Eressos on 13th -14th August '89, and in excess of 120 birds were counted in a cut field at nearby Skala Eressos on 25th September '94, with probably 3 times as many in a nearby field, in the company of chats, warblers, shrikes, wheatears etc - all retrieving green caterpillars! At least 400 came in to roost at Skala Eressos beach pool at dusk on 17th, whilst 300 were roosting at Dipi Larssos Reedbed the next day (when 60 were on Kalloni Salt Pans), and Kalloni Inland Lake also held large numbers, with at least 40 there in late September, and birds regularly seen in the area until at least 12th October. With so many birds involved, all in different autumn plumages, picking out sub-species was very difficult, but all 3 were certainly present. A single Blue-headed Wagtail was present along West River on the late date of 17th October '97, whilst up to 38 Black-headed (mostly immatures but including several fine males) were present on Kalloni Pool in the first week of August '98, when the site was unusually wet.

Citrine Wagtail *Motacilla cinerea*
Scarce passage migrant from April to May, rare in autumn. This species seems to be more frequently recorded of late than its original status in *The Birds of Greece* would suggest - though this may just be down to an increased birding presence in April and early May. First record of a male on Kalloni West River 6th April '97, a pair on the Chalandra River Skala Eressos 10th April '98, a female at Skala Polichnitos on 12th April '95 (where a pair was also present on 19th April '98), and a male around East River Upper ford from 13th-15th April '97. The latest spring record is of a female at Eressos on 21st May '86 (see *The Birds of Greece*). A male was seen at Kalloni Pool on 10th May '91 and 1st May '97, with another at Skala Eressos on 14th May '91, 14th April '95 and 27th-29th April '98, (with 2 males next day and a pair also present on 29th April '96), a bird at 'Derbyshire' in mid-May '92, one at Kalloni Salt Pans on 10th May '94, a male present in the large flooded field behind the pans on 24th April '98 and a female on Kalloni Pool on 10th and 15th May '95, with a pair also seen on East River at that time, and another female at Sigri on 11th. In spring '96 single females were seen at a pond by Anaxos Hotel on 3rd May and at Faneromeni ford on 10th (on which date in '98 there was also a male present). Following a female behind Kalloni Salt Pans on 29th April '97 (with a first-summer male at Faneromeni ford on the same date), another male was seen along the Vouvaris river between 'Derbyshire' and Achladeri on 4th May, a first summer male was reported from Faneromeni on 12th May, and a particularly fine male was present in the drainage channel near Skala Kalloni football ground on 14th May that year. Unusual record of 3 birds together (including 1 male) feeding on sandflats in Sigri harbour on 16th-17th April '95 - with the 2 females remaining until 19th. Also between 2-5 birds were reported on Kalloni East River 5th September '97 - the only autumn record.

Grey Wagtail *Motacilla cinerea*
Scarce and localized resident, (especially around fast flowing boulder-strewn streams) - becoming more widespread in winter. Recorded between Molivos and Skala Sikimmia on 10th April '95 and mid-September '97 - but main breeding season records from fast-flowing river on the main Agiassos to Polichnitos road (just before the Vatera turn-off is reached), where a pair has been seen virtually every year from '91-'98 between early and late May, perched alongside the road with food. Few other reliable sites are known at this time, though a bird was seen flying over the car park in Agiassos on 4th and 6th May '98 and 2 singles were seen at the Kruper's site at Achladeri on 10th May that year. Two birds were also seen on the river near Sigri on 17th May '92, 1 was present between Andissa and Sigri on 7th May '95, and on the Voulgaris River east of Andissa on 29th, whilst another was reported from the East River on 14th and 21st May '91. A party of 3 adults with some juveniles was a good find at Kalloni East River on 5th July '96. In autumn '94, 1 was again present at the breeding area on 29th September, with another at Kalloni Inland Lake on 6th October. One bird was also seen on 3rd near Skala Eressos, where up to 4 had regularly been seen in late October '92 and a single bird was present near 'The Primitive Club' on 29th August '97. Another was reported from the area of Mytilini airport on 22nd October '95, with several records from Kalloni East River in the third week of October '96 (peaking at 3 birds on 20th) and early October '97 (peaking at 3 birds on 6th). In January '98 single wintering birds were seen both on and inland from Kalloni East River and also around 'Kalloni ditches' and Kalloni Pool. Following a sighting on the Chalandra River Skala Eressos on 29th March that year a late bird was also seen along East River on 18th April, and a juvenile was reported amongst Yellow Wagtails at Faneromeni on 7th September that year, with a bird seen at Petra reservoir on 26th September.

White Wagtail *Motacilla alba*
Largely a winter visitor from mid-September to late March or early April. A few may breed. Circa 20 on the beach at Skala Kalloni 1st April '85 were probably migrants, as were *c*500

briefly present on Kalloni Pool 6th April '86, in company with huge numbers of Yellow Wagtails (see above). Numbers had declined to 100 next day, with a further 100 at 'Derbyshire' on 8th - mostly gone by 10th. Double-figure numbers still feeding with Yellow Wagtails at the river mouth near Thermi on 14th April '95. These had begun to thin out by 17th, though still 4-5 on 21st and 3 in the area on 9th May. Elsewhere, 50+ present at Kalloni Salt Pans on 23rd March '98 were most likely to be returning migrants, as were a three figure number seen at 'Derbyshire' on 28th. Two birds were seen on Faneromeni ford 23rd April '95, with 3 at Andissa on 10th May, 1 at Kalloni East River on 14th (also 20th May '98 and 31st May '94), with 1 on the coast road just east of Vatera on 27th May '97. One was also seen on the Chalandra River Skala Eressos between mid and late May '87, with 1 on the Krioneri River near 'Derbyshire' and 4 (surprisingly) on the Vouvaris River near Achladeri between mid and late May '91, 2 on the river near Sigri 17th May '92, 1 at Anaxos on 3rd June '93 (with 2 there up to 15th May '98) and a single near Skala Polichnitos Salt Pans in mid-June '98. Proof of breeding came with the discovery of a pair feeding at Anaxos on 8th and 10th May '95, with a juvenile nearby on the latter date. A pair on Kalloni East River 9th June '98 (later seen with 2 young on 6th July) was also conclusive. Two birds on Petra reservoir on the very early date of 28th July '96 are also likely to have been local breeders, along with 1 seen on the Chalandra River Skala Eressos 3rd August '89 and 5 seen along Kalloni East River on 5th August '98. The species becomes increasingly more widespread throughout September, with 7+ around Skala Eressos on 8th September '94, up to 30 around Kalloni Inland Lake from 28th September, and several at a puddle by Kalloni Two Hotel on 2nd October. Twelve were also seen feeding around the West River pools on 7th October '94.

Waxwing *Bombycilla garrulus*
Vagrant, only recorded in exceptional invasion years such as the 1965-6 winter, when good numbers reached the island between December and March. A later invasion in January '73 seemed to pass the island by (see *The Birds of Greece*).

Wren *Troglodytes troglodytes*
Scarce and localized resident (easy to overlook if not heard), becoming more widespread as a winter visitor between October and March. Seen or heard occasionally, but usually in upland habitat, and especially from the woodland above Agiassos, where up to 4 seen in mid-May '95 and between 10 and 15 singing males heard during a circular walk on 6th May '98! Also recorded from the dirt track between Anaxos and Skoutaros in mid-May '98. A pair were watched in the Potamia Valley on 22nd April that year feeding young in a nest composed almost entirely of shredded fragments seemingly of cactus or similar like plant!

Dunnock *Prunella modularis*
Sparsely distributed winter visitor from mid or late October to late March, found especially in overgrown olive trees, bushy areas and field hedgerows. Only 5 records (hardly surprising considering the timing) of 2 early birds around Skala Eressos on 25th September '94 and singles along Kalloni East River 21st October '96, at Dipi Larssos on 29th January '98 and outside Malemi hotel on 22nd March that year. One unusual record of a bird seen in scrub around Molivos castle on the very late date of 14th May '95.

Rufous Bush Robin *Cercotrichas galactotes*
Locally common summer visitor from late April to late August. A very early bird was singing at Gavathas on 30th March '86, but in spring '95 (apart from 1 chance sighting between Parakila and Agra on 13th April) birds not really noticed until singing and displaying in earnest at regular nesting sites from about 23rd onwards. These sites included the track from Sigri to Faneromeni ford just before the beach turn-off and the narrow gulley just beyond Faneromeni

ford (where at least 3-4 displaying males can often be observed; with a grand total of 10 seen in the area in late May '94 and again on 5th May '98!) and the rocky outcrop at 'Derbyshire' where 2 pairs were nest-building in May and further pairs were subsequently present beside the track to the farm on the other side of the main road. A pair was also seen sporadically near Petra reservoir and 2 birds were seen at the same time just inland from the East River bridge on several occasions (with both 'dust bathing' on 18th May). This site (just by the pumphouse) held circa 3 pairs in mid-May '96, and several more displaying pairs were located along the track inland from East River (just past the sheep pen) in late April and early May '98. Three were also frequenting the dried-up, scrubby section of the Chalandra River north of the Messotopos road (where several also holding territory from 19th May onwards in the spring '87 season); and such habitat appears to be much favoured on the island. Away from these areas, a bird was reported on the road to Parakila in mid-May '94, and at nearby 'Devil's Bridge' in early May '98, and up to 5 were seen at Vatera on 11th May '96 - with at least 2 pairs nesting in the area by late May '98 and a pair around Tavari ford in May '97 and at nearby Kroussos in late May '98. The back of Kalloni Salt Pans is now also known to be a regular site, and in spring '97 the first bird was seen on 27th April (26th in '98), with up to 2 pairs later present. Just 6 autumn records, of 2 birds at the Salt Pans on 5th August '96, 2 adults and an adult with 2 juveniles at Faneromeni on 3rd August '98, and a single at Kalloni East River on 5th August '98 and near Kalloni Inland Lake on 30th August '97 and 30th September '94 - an exceptionally late date.

Robin   *Erithacus rubecula*
Abundant winter visitor from October to mid-March and sporadic localized breeder. At other times very scarce and largely confined to upland areas (eg 1 seen in Sweet Chestnut Woodland above Agiassos on 12th April '95, and 2 there in early May - with 2 singing males on 1st June '96). Several also regular there by late September '94, (with 1 being seen as early as 25th August suggesting likely breeding - confirmed by the presence there of 3 singing males on 6th May '98, followed by 3-4 adults and 3 juveniles in the first week of August that year). Otherwise singles seen away from that area at Faneromeni on 7th September '98, in the Potamia Valley on 26th September '98, near Messotopos on 3rd October '94, and seen most days in Skala Eressos in the last week of October '92, with a big 'fall' on 26th and a few seen in woods near the airport on 29th. Described as 'quite common' around Petra by mid-October '95, and widespread throughout the island (especially in olive groves and uplands) during a January '98 visit. One bird ringed at Haramida on 15th April '97 had a high fat score.

Thrush Nightingale   *Luscinia luscinia*
Scarce passage migrant from April to May and late August to mid-October, when may be more common (see ringing records below!). Obvious difficulties of distinguishing from Nightingale, and extremely skulking behaviour when not singing clearly make for under-recording. Favours damp coastal habitats, and first recorded on 21st April '97 at Kalloni Inland Lake. Otherwise recorded more regularly from the north of the island - eg a bird in the hills west of Anaxos on 11th May '93 (with it or another near Molivos 4 days later), 1 singing above Petra on 7th May '95, and more recently singing birds behind Anaxos beach on 13th May '96, showing well at Skala Eressos on 4th May '97, and another at Anaxos Garden hotel on 8th May '98 and in scrub by the ford on the Anaxos-Skoutaros track on the late date of 21st May that year. Autumn records consist of 1 west of Eressos on 14th September "89, a bird around Kalloni Inland Lake on 27th August '97, 2 trapped and ringed at Haramida Marsh on 19th and 21st September '94, with a single at the same site on 8th September '95, and 5 different birds ringed there from 30th August-7th September '96 - with no less than 15 ringed in September '98!

Nightingale *Luscinia megarhynchos*

Widespread summer visitor in suitable habitat from early April to October. First heard singing 29th March '86 at Kalloni Salt Pans and 31st March '97 around Kalloni Inland Lake, but 12th April '95 above Agiassos more typical, and thereafter heard (and quite often seen in the open) there and in almost all overgrown valleys and damp thickets, especially just west of Vatoussa (Perivoli monastery in particular), the river feeding Dipi Larssos Reedbed (where at least 4-5 singing birds from 4th April '98), around the Potamia Valley, Kalloni Inland Lake and East River, Chalandra River Skala Eressos and Faneromeni ford. At both the latter two sites birds were observed singing in the open on 12th April '87 (at least 9 at Faneromeni ford) and between mid and late April '95 - suggesting they may well have been recently arrived migrants. Similarly olive groves on the approach to Kalloni Inland Lake produced at least 20 recently arrived migrants feeding in the open on 19th April '97. To give an idea of density, circa 25 were recorded in the pine forest above Agiassos on 1st June '96, so Bob Husband's description of it as 'less common now in the Skala Kalloni area owing to habitat loss' is rather relative. To most people birds still seem to be everywhere! Clearly less obvious in autumn, though a few birds were still reported singing occasionally in Petra valley during the last few days of July '98. Otherwise likely to be seen drinking or bathing around puddles and irrigated areas - eg Faneromeni and above Agiassos where seen well in early August '98. Just 4 late records, of a bird around Kalloni Inland Lake on 5th September '98, near Andissa on 22nd September '94, and 1 trapped at Haramida Marsh 19th September that year and on 8th September '95. The latest record by far, however, was of a bird at Skala Eressos on 20th October '95.

White-throated Robin *Irania gutturalis*

Vagrant and possible casual breeder. The first definite record (reported in *Birding World* Vol. 7 No. 6) concerned a singing male near Molivos on 16th May '94. Apparently there is also a report in *Dutch Birding* about this time of a pair (again near Molivos) showing breeding behaviour, but this needs to be substantiated. Following on from this a female was recorded near Eftalou on 5th May '96, with a male seen nearby the next day. Thereafter breeding was claimed from a nearby steep-sided gorge for both this and the preceding year (though precise details and location were witheld at the observer's request). Suffice to say that the male was seen carrying either food or nesting material on 28th May '95 (see *The Birds of Greece*) with similar evidence for '96. This was given extra credence by an unconfirmed report of a pair seen on the hillside between Petra and Molivos on 27th July '96. Since then it appears to have reverted to its original vagrant status (or more accurately extremely scarce spring migrant), with a male first seen on a fence along the Sigri-Eressos road 3rd May '97 and located beyond Faneromeni ford 2 days later possibly lingering a few days, but a female seen at this favoured site on exactly the same date in '98 not being located the next day. There were, however, unconfirmed reports of a male singing in a steep-sided gulley between Eftalou and Skala Sikimmia in late April that year. This may well have been the same site from which breeding was claimed in '95 and '96, but suppression and the sensitive nature of the site has made exact confirmation difficult.

Black Redstart *Phoenicurus ochruros*

Common winter visitor from late October to late March. Described as 'very common' in Skala Eressos from the last week of October '92, with up to 10 birds seen daily. Early returning birds seen at Skala Eressos on 21st September '94 and at Petra on 29th September that year, with 1 returning by 16th October (rising to 2 on 19th and 4 by 21st), and seen daily in a variety of locations from 19th October '96. Regular and widespread around the Kalloni area in January '98, with a large exodus very evident on 22nd March '97 (when at least 5-6 birds were gathered on wires behind Kalloni Inland Lake) and also on 24th March '98, when several birds (including at least 4 or 5 brightly plumaged males) were gathering on wires around Kalloni

Pool. A pair last seen on 31st March that year along Kalloni East River. Apart from a 'sick' female (apparently afflicted with 'bumblefoot') still present at the back of Kalloni Pool up to at least the beginning of May '98, there is one exceptionally late record of a male around Ipsilou monastery on 7th May '96.

Redstart   *Phoenicurus phoenicurus*
Passage migrant from early April to early or mid-May and September to October. Fewer records than expected for a bird we often associate with quite large 'falls' in the migration period, and apparently not as common in autumn as *The Birds of Greece* would suggest - though may be simply due to a shortage of observers then. First records of a male near Skala Polichnitos on 4th April '98, 2 at Sigri on 5th April '85, a male at Perivoli monastery on 10th April '97 and in the Potamia Valley on 11th April '95. Another 2 males were seen near Skala Polichnitos on 18th April '87, and single males were recorded between Parakila and Agra on 13th April '92, and at Sigri from 21st-22nd April '92, with another (a female) at Faneromeni ford on 23rd and a fine male between Sigri and Eressos on 6th May, with none thereafter. A bird was present near Achladeri on 8th May '96 and a female was bathing around Faneromeni ford on the rather late date of 14th May that year. In spring '97 1 was seen near Kalloni East River on 21st April, whilst a pair were seen near Sigri on 24th and a male was present at Ipsilou monastery on 29th April. A male was also seen near the Kruper's site at Achladeri on 27th April '98, with a pair at Faneromeni ford on 17th and another male from 5th-7th May that year. The biggest 'falls' so far recorded took place at Faneromeni, when 4+ on 16th April '92 had grown to 10 next day (reducing to 8 on 19th). Latest spring dates concern a female near Mytilini on 16th May '96, and a male near Skala Kalloni on 18th May '91, with a female the next day. Only autumn records are from above Agiassos (where 1 or 2 were regular between late September and early October '94 and mid-September '97), Molivos (where singles were present on 13th and 15th September '97) and Skala Eressos, where 1 was seen on 13th September '97 and the latest recorded date of 25th October '92. Two birds were also still being seen inland from East River between 2nd and 6th October '97, with 1 near Achladeri on 5th and 2 there on 16th September '98, with 1 near Anaxos on 26th September that year.

Whinchat   *Saxicola rubetra*
Common and widespead passage migrant from early April to mid-May (peaking the second half of April) and mid-August to mid-October (peaking early to mid-September). Numbers in spring can be very variable, as with Spotted Flycatcher, but would appear to be equally widespread in autumn if September and October '94 were anything to go by. First recorded at Skala Kalloni on 3rd April '85 and Apothikes 5th April '97, and on 7th April '86 (when 8 birds were present). Also seen at Dipi Larssos from 7th April '98 (3 birds) and Skala Kalloni from 11th April '95, with a moderate 'fall' noticed on 18th and 'considerable numbers' present at Skala Vassilikon on 25th April '98. The biggest of these tend to occur to the west of the island, as with a large 'fall' on the coastal section between Sigri and Eressos on 9th May '93 (with smaller numbers around Skala Eressos from the later date of 20th May '87, and c30 again in the Sigri area on 22nd April '92 and 11th May '95). Numbers in the Skala Kalloni area in spring '97 peaked at 25+ on the much earlier date of 21st April (with 'good numbers' around the Salt Pans on 26th), following 7 along East River on 13th (with c20 at the Salt Pans on 20th April '92 and 6 along West River on 18th April '98). Three were still present at Sigri on the late date of 16th May '98. However, in autumn '94, birds were widely spread, and appeared equally common around Skala Kalloni and the Potamia Valley, where the last was seen on 12th October. One early autumn record of a bird at Petra reservoir on 6th August '97, and 5 were seen around nearby Molivos on 19th August '98. The latest record is of a single at Skala Eressos on 19th October '95. Several scattered reports of males singing and pairs

holding territory in May raise the possibility of breeding - though this would need to be confirmed by the presence of recently fledged juveniles.

Stonechat *Saxicola torquata*
Scarce but fairly widespread resident, originally only recorded regularly from the area above Andissa (where a pair was seen in mid-May '94 and late April '95 and every spring since) and just below Ipsilou monastery - but now known to breed more widely. Singles seen near Sigri on 19th May '92 (with family parties consisting of 2-3 males, a similar number of females and at least 5 immatures on a 'rocky heath' just south of Sigri in early August '98), by the Molivos-Petra road on 6th and 16th May '95, with a family party there mid-month confirming breeding and a male and 3 immatures seen at the clifftop Ruppell's site in early August '98. Pairs were also seen with juveniles at Vatera on 8th May '96 and beyond Faneromeni ford on 5th May '98. A male frequented 'Derbyshire' between 6th and 7th May '95 - a pair had also been seen there on 8th October '94, with 3 nearby on 9th, and had been described as holding territory there in late May that year, whilst 2 pairs and a single male were present in mid-May '98. Breeding also seems likely at nearby Achladeri plain, where birds and occasional juveniles regularly seen. Autumn records of a party of 3 juveniles at Megali Limni on 12th September '97, a female just outside Agiassos on 4th October '94, and 1 or 2 seen regularly around Skala Eressos in the last week of October '92, with up to 7 there on 20th October '95 (and 6 at Petra the next day). There was also a gathering of some 20+ birds in a field at Faneromeni on 23rd March April '97. This would suggest some sort of migratory movements at this time (if only of a fairly local nature) - with birds clearly being more obvious around lowland areas in winter and early spring. According to *The Birds of Greece* most Greek Stonechats are of the race *S.t. rubicola*. Certainly the males often appear quite striking, and it seems possible that the eastern race (either *S.t. variegata* or *armenica*) may occur as migrants. Although there is currently only one record of the former for Greece, the authors admit it is likely that many records may not have been reported. It may therefore be worthwhile for future observers to pay special attention to the rump and tail pattern - see the article *Identification of Siberian Stonechat* by Andy Stoddart in *Birding World* 1992 Vol 5 No 9 P348-356. The results could be interesting!

Isabelline Wheatear *Oenanthe isabellina*
Localized summer visitor from late March (more usually early April) to late September. Most often recorded from the area west of Andissa by the Sigri-Eressos junction, where a few pairs usually breed (at least 2 in '94 and 3+ in '97-8) and are often visible by the roadside (especially when feeding young in May). First recorded there 6th April '98 and 1 still around the Sigri area on 8th September '97. Elsewhere, 1 seen at Kalloni Salt Pans on 29th July '94 and 17th September '97, with another near Achladeri on 9th August '94, a sighting approx 5 km west of Parakila in mid-May '96, near Skoutaros in mid-June '96, 2 near Molivos castle on 3rd-4th August that year (with 1 near Petra on 11th), and 2 again near Molivos on 13th and 26th September '97 (with 1 seen near the castle on 8th May '98), 2 near Tavari in May and early June '97 and a pair carrying food alongside a track at the 'BP Garage raptor stop' on 7th July '96. Three adults and 7+ immatures were seen along the road to the Petrified Forest in early August '98. Otherwise late autumn records of singles at Kalloni on 22nd September '94, East River 28th September '98 and 1st October '97, and at Skala Eressos from 16th-26th September '94 - with an especially late one there on 26th October '92.

Northern Wheatear *Oenanthe oenanthe*
Localized summer visitor and widespread passage migrant from March to May and August to October. Not uncommon in spring, with the first seen around Kalloni Pool on 23rd March '98. 'Several' at Molivos on 12th April '95 (where seen feeding young from 17th-23rd May '96), and seen especially around Kalloni Salt Pans, where 2-3 recorded from 13th April '95 onwards

until late May and breeding proven in '97 (a pair with fledged young by early June) and '98 - when bred in old pipes just by the new water treatment building! Elsewhere main breeding stronghold appears to be to the north-east of the island, though pair breeding at 'Derbyshire' in late May '94, and 3 pairs present at the Isabelline site (see below) on 22nd May '95. Far more widespread in autumn, when up to 100 birds seen in a field at Sigri with Yellow Wagtails on 18th September '86, and 50+ birds were present along the Chalandra River Skala Eressos on 16th September '94. Birds were also seen regularly around Skala Kalloni in autumn '94 until at least 12th October, with the last bird recorded there on 19th October '95. Single birds were still being reported at Kalloni Salt Pans up to 23rd October '96 (the latest date recorded). Moreover, up to 10 were present in the area on 4th October '97, with 8 still up to at least 8th.

Pied Wheatear   *Oenanthe pleschanka*

Scarce migrant from March to May and August to October and occasional breeder. The difficulties of separating this from the black-throated form of Black-eared have already been mentioned, and may help explain the paucacity of records. Nevertheless, *The Birds of Greece* mentions one definite breeding record - near Akrasi in 1988. Undoubtedly others must have been overlooked amongst the huge numbers of Black-eared. However, 3 definite sightings obtained in spring '95 - a male at Skala Sikimmia on 9th May, with a pair near Ambelikon (which the observer thought might have been nest-prospecting!) on the same date, and a single male north of Petra on 11th. A singing male was again observed in the hills north of Petra on 2nd May '97. Single males were also seen near Sigri on 18th April '98, in the Potamia Valley on 9th May '96, with additional birds reported at 'Derbyshire' (a juvenile in mid-August '96), between Sigri and Eressos on 23rd August '97 and around the Potamia reservoir on 2nd September that year, also seen near Molivos (a male) on 5th, 6th and 10th.

Black-eared Wheatear   *Oenanthe hispanicus*

Summer visitor from late March to mid or late September in huge numbers - with birds belong to the eastern race (*melanoleuca*). Both dark (or buff) and pale (or white) forms occur, though the latter (many with black throats) tend to outnumber the former, and can be found in almost uncountable numbers in any rocky areas, outcrops and gullies (but possibly more vegetated areas than Wheatear - eg the Kruper's site at Achladeri), but especially anywhere west of Parakila. Birds also nest regularly around Molivos and Mytilini castles, Ipsilou monastery etc. At least 50 territories were recorded between Andissa and Sigri, and over 60 between Andissa and Eressos in early May '95! Birds were seen from 5th April that year at Molivos, where several buff males were noted (especially around the Ruppell's site). Otherwise first recorded from 21st March '97 at back of Kalloni Inland Lake. Autumn records tend to become thin on the ground after the middle of September, and many birds have already left by mid-August or dispersed to recently ploughed fields at lower elevations. However, circa 20 birds were still present at Molivos on 15th September '97 (and one on Petra headland up to 26th). Several were around Skala Kalloni in September '94 and still 6 males seen in the Eressos area on 23rd September, with 1 near Ipsilou Monastery and 1 at Molivos Castle next day and the latest records of 14 in the Skala Eressos area on 28th, with 1 seen at Apothikes on the same date in '97 and another along Kalloni East River on the same date in '98!.

Desert Wheatear   *Oenanthe deserti*

Vagrant. Only a handful of records, on a par with the rest of Greece. The most recent concerned a bird seen near Anaxos on 11th May '98 (when an unsettled spell of weather produced several interesting records including an Isabelline Shrike nearby).

Finsch's Wheatear *Oenanthe finschii*
Vagrant. Two records only - of an adult male seen and photographed at Megalochori near Agiassos on 10th June '93 (See *The Birds of Greece)*; and more recently a male singing and holding territory at the top of the Potamia Valley from at least 15th-20th May '98. This bird was seen well by several observers and full written descriptions were received.

Rock Thrush *Monticola saxatilis*
Scarce passage migrant during April and likely breeder. First record of a pair at Ipsilou monastery on 13th April '98, where a male has been seen showing breeding behaviour (regularly singing from the roof of the monastery, indulging in full display flight and carrying food) every May since '96 - when at least 2 males were reputedly present on 11th. Ironically, only the above record of a female exists for this site, though one was seen below Molivos castle on 30th August '97 and also on Mount Olympus on 25th May '98. Also unusual was a male seen opposite the Ruppell's site between Petra and Molivos on 16th May '98. Elsewhere presumed passage males have been seen between Dafia and Filia in late April '97 and '98.

Blue Rock Thrush *Monticola solitarius*
Widespread resident around rocky upland areas and cliffs. Particularly common west of Vatoussa, and nesting birds especially visible around Ipsilou Monastery in April and May. Also seen regularly around the clifftop Ruppell's site between Petra and Molivos, and even breeding on Molivos and Mytilini Castle. In fact, birds have recently even held territory around some ruined buildings in the centre of Mytilini, though no proof of successful breeding! Four seen together near Stipsi on 3rd August '94 is the largest group reported.

Ring Ouzel *Turdus torquatus*
Rare and irregular winter visitor and passage migrant from March-April and October-November. No recent records, but *The Birds of Greece* documents a record from nearby Chios on 29th September '74.

Blackbird *Turdus merula*
Thinly but widely distributed resident, with numbers augmented by wintering birds. Partly because of their habit of feeding on olives at this time, they are not especially popular with the locals, and (like thrushes) tend to be shot in quite large numbers, which may go some way to explaining their comparative shyness! This is another species which has recently been found to be much commoner and more widespread than was thought.

Fieldfare *Turdus pilaris*
Scarce winter visitor from October to February. Only record outside this period was of 4 birds at Kalloni Salt Pans on 23rd March '98 (following a bitterly cold snap with overnight hail and snow showers!).

Song Thrush *Turdus philomelos*
Common and widespread winter visitor from October to April, and occasional localized breeder in upland areas - which regrettably often meets same fate as Blackbird! First record of 2 birds by Kalloni West River on 13th October '94, with large numbers seen in woods close to Mytilini airport by 29th. Certainly very common in the Kalloni area and throughout in both January and March '98, though thinning out by early April. At least 6 together in a flooded field near Molivos on 26th March that year were probably returning migrants, as were 10 at Achladeri on 5th April. A pair also seen in the Sweet Chestnut Forest above Agiassos both in mid-May '94 and early May '95. The presence of a singing male from at least 10th-15th raises the likelihood of a small breeding nucleus in the area. Three birds were again seen there on 7th

May '97, at least 1 singing male on 6th May '98 and 2 in early August '98, with 1 reported near Mikri Limni in early June '98, and from the Kruper's site at Achladeri on 1st June, a recently dead bird found in the garden of Malemi Hotel on 4th May and 1 in a garden at Anaxos on 6th August that year. Future spring records from the Agiassos area would be welcomed!

Redwing *Turdus iliacus*
Winter visitor from October to mid or late March in more regular numbers than Fieldfare - most often seen in open woodland, olive groves and orchards. First recorded 23rd October '96 over Kalloni East River, and last date 2 above Agiassos on 26th March '97.

Mistle Thrush *Turdus viscivorus*
Scarce and localized resident - especially in upland coniferous woodland. Also favours medium and low altitude Calabrian pine *Pinus brutia*, oak and sweet chestnut woodland.
Recorded regularly from the wooded area above Agiassos (where seen several times between mid-April and mid-May '95 in the Sweet Chestnut Forest) and also more recently in the pinewoods near Achladeri (where regularly heard and seen - on several occasions feeding young - around the Kruper's site). One was also present in the oak woods near Skalochori on 8th April '85, and another was reported between Agra and Messotopos on 14th May '95, with 1 by the Perivolis Monastery the same day (apparently the valley west of Vatoussa is also a regular site). Further records of a single 3 kms north-east of Vassilika on 25th May '95 (where 1 or 2 pairs were present in the nearby green valley known as Megali Limni almost opposite the Ambelikon junction), and from spring '93 of singles near Lambou Mili, on the edge of the pine forest north of Kalloni, and just west of Filia between 7th and 9th May. A bird was also seen near Kalloni Inland Lake on 7th August '96, with 2 there in mid-July '98.

Cetti's Warbler *Cetti cetti*
Localized resident, common in suitable damp habitat; though more often heard than seen! Main stronghold the area around Dipi Larssos Reedbed, the ditches around Kalloni Inland Lake, Potamia River, East and West Rivers, Parakila Marsh and the Chalandra River. Bursts of song heard throughout the year.

Fan-tailed Warbler *Cisticola juncidis*
Scarce resident, with numbers fluctuating from year to year. Originally only recorded from Kalloni Salt Pans in May '87, and the West River and area north of Polichnitos during May '91 and '92 (and West River again in mid-July '96). Also recorded from Faneromeni on 21st April '84, with several birds around Kalloni Inland Lake on 19th April that year. More recently, seen at Kalloni Pool from mid-April '85, with singles recorded from Haramida and Dipi Larssos at the beginning of September '96, in coastal reeds near Achladeri on 21st April '97 and at Parakila Marsh on 27th April that year. Thereafter a more complete coverage of the island in April '98 showed it to be far more widespread than was thought, with aerial display flights regularly observed at Kalloni West River (where a pair still present upstream from the roadbridge on 4th July), Kalloni Salt Pans (close to the main road), the coastal strip near Achladeri, Polichnitos Salt Pans (near the beach turn-off), Dipi Larssos Reedbed, the ford on the coastal track between Eressos and Sigri, Faneromeni (the reedy areas near the ford) and even the edge of Mytilini airport! Birds obviously more skulking outside this time, and likely to be overlooked, but 1 was seen at Kalloni Salt Pans on 4th September '98 (with 2 showing there and at Dipi Larssos on 21st) and 2 at Skala Polichnitos on 12th and 16th September '98.

Grasshopper Warbler *Locustella naevia*
Very scarce passage migrant from April to May, and mid-August to early October. Very secretive and inconspicuous and hence easy to overlook unless singing. Only records of singles

heard singing both at Skala Eressos and the Kalloni Salt Pans in the second half of May '87. According to *The Birds of Greece* this paucacity of sightings suggests that a good proportion of migrants may simply overfly the area without landing.

River Warbler *Locustella fluviatilis*
Scarce passage migrant from late April to late May (peaking early to mid-May), and late August-September. First reported from the small stream bordering Mytilini airport perimeter fence on 14th April '95, and from Kalloni Salt Pans on the same date in '98. Elsewhere 1 was heard and glimpsed morning and evening at Petra from 6th-7th and 12th-16th May '93, with another (or the same bird) south-east of Molivos between 15th-17th. Three-four males were again singing in dense stream-side vegetation near Petra on 8th May '94, with 3 still 2 days later. Also heard from 7th-10th and 14th-17th May that year around Kalloni East River, and glimpsed there on 17th. Possibly 3 different birds were involved in all at that site. A bird was heard at Vatera on 6th May '96, singing near Malemi hotel 2nd May '97, along Kalloni East River from 2nd-3rd May '97 (the same dates up to 3 were singing at Faneromeni ford - where still at least 1 on 4th˙and again on 12th) and along the Sigri-Eressos on 5th. A bird was also seen at Skala Eressos on 26th-29th April '98 (also in Potamia Valley on the latter date and again at the nearby Inland Lake on 26th April and 2nd-4th May), heard at Faneromeni lower ford on 3rd May and near Stipsi on 16th May that year. Hardly surprisingly, autumn records are scarce, with just 1 juvenile ringed at Haramida on 31st August '96.

Savi's Warbler *Locustella luscinioides*
Passage migrant in moderate numbers from late March-early May (peaking mid-April), and also in September. First recorded 6th April '97 near Kalloni Inland Lake, along Kalloni East River on the same date in '98, at Dipi Larssos on 11th April '98 and from Kalloni Salt Pans on 19th April that year, whilst a bird was singing at Skala Kalloni on 15th April '85 and up to 3 birds were singing at Haramida in mid-April '97, with 2 in song at Parakila Marsh on 22nd-23rd and one singing at Faneromeni ford on the rather late date of 14th May '96. Quite likely to be heard around East River in late April or May (eg 1 singing 21st April '97), and an intriguing record of a bird there in mid-July '94 and again on 17th July '96 (and also around Kalloni Pool on 5th and 17th July '98) - though no records from elsewhere at this time. Obviously likely to be overlooked in autumn - though the ringing party trapped 1 at Haramida Marsh on 12th, 15th and 18th September '95, on 31st August, 1st (2 birds), 3rd, and 10th September '96, and one was also seen around Kalloni Inland Lake on 24th August '97. Further records from Haramida concerned 2 there on 8th and 11th September '98.

Moustached Warbler *Acrocephalus melanopogon*
Localized winter visitor from early October to mid-April. Most regular around Dipi Larssos Reedbed at this time, but also claimed regularly from the Anaxos area as late as May (with a bird near Molivos on 10th May '95, 3+ in Anaxos reedbed from 9th-11th May '93, 1 there in the first week of May '97 and another at Anaxos Garden hotel on 7th May '98, singing from scrub and rank herbage in Anaxos village on 15th May that year - when another bird was seen by the ford on the dirt track between Anaxos and Skoutaros). Also claimed from Kalloni East River, Kalloni Pool (where 3 birds were present 28th April '98) and Parakila Marsh, where one was in song on 3rd May '97. A calling bird present around Kalloni Pool 5th-9th May '98 was seen well on the 6th and 9th. However, these records need to be qualified by pointing out the risk of confusion with the oddly marked eastern race of Sedge Warler occurring on passage.

Sedge Warbler *Acrocephalus schoenobaenus*
Common passage migrant between mid-March and late May (peaking late March to mid-April), rarer between August and late October (peaking late August to mid-September). First

reported from Skala Eressos on 29th March '97, Kalloni Pool on 6th April '98 and Sigri on 8th April '86. Recorded regularly at Kalloni Inland Lake, Kalloni Pool and East River, Parakila Marsh, Skala Eressos and Dipi Larssos Reedbed, and described by one observer (staying in Petra in May '93) as : 'fairly common from 10th in suitable habitat, including field edges with tall vegetation'. Several birds reported along the East River between 9th and 12th May '94, with 2 singing near Malemi hotel Skala Kalloni on 2nd May '98 and a late bird at West River on 6th June '97. Few autumn records, though 2 birds seen in hedges bordering olive groves around Kalloni in September '94, 1 at East River in the second half of the month, and a late record of 2 near Faneromeni on 1st October '86. Five were trapped between 19th and 20th September '94 at Haramida Marsh by the ringing group, with 7 trapped between 17th and 18th '95, suggesting perhaps, that autumn passage may peak around the middle of the month (though more information is obviously needed to substantiate this).

Marsh Warbler *Acrocephalus palustris*
Passage migrant in reasonable numbers from early April to late May (peaking late April to mid-May) and more commonly from late July-late September. Breeding is possible, as this bird's requirements are not confined to dense reedbeds, but also embrace patches of brambles and tall bankside vegetation - see *The Birds of Greece*. First record of 'several' around Kalloni Inland Lake on 7th April '97, where one or two birds were regular in the ditches from 1st-3rd May '95. Originally, most records were usually somewhat later (eg above Petra lay-bys and near Anaxos on 13th May '96, around Skalochori and behind Skala Eressos 15th May '91, Kalloni area from 21st, and near Eftalou on 22nd). In May '94, first heard singing along the Chalandra River on 10th, along East River from 14th-15th and Kalloni Inland Lake at the same time. The main influx around Skala Eressos in May '87 didn't appear to begin until 24th and 25th; but these records may simply reflect observer bias. In spring '97, for example, at least 5 birds were present along Kalloni East River on the much earlier date of 21st April (with 2 on the same date in '98 and a male singing there on 7th May that year). Rather more unusual was a bird still singing there between 5th-6th June '98 - which suggests possible breeding in the locality. Birds were also singing that year at Faneromeni lower ford on 3rd May, Potamia Valley on 6th, and with 2 singing in scrub near Petra Reservoir on 7th, in Petra olive groves on 11th, 1 at Ipsilou monastery on 11th-13th, 2 on 18th and 1 at Parakila Marsh on 25th. Probably more common in autumn, though harder to locate. However, the ringing totals for a six-day period in September '94 give a good indication, with 10 birds trapped on 19th, 2 on 20th and 3 on 21st at Haramida Marsh. Clearly this only represents a fraction of the total number of migrants passing through at this time, especially considering the difficulty of separating Reed and Marsh in autumn (see ringing totals at back of book).

Reed Warbler *Acrocephalus scirpaceus*
Localized summer visitor and passage migrant in small numbers from late March to late September (with spring passage peaking late April to early May and autumn passage August to late September - sometimes well into October). Seen from 29th March '86 at Kalloni Salt Pans and 10th April '85 in the Potamia Valley, but the main breeding stronghold is Dipi Larssos Reedbed, where plentiful by mid-April '98. Elsewhere not so common, with records mainly from Sigri and Faneromeni area, Parakila Marsh in May '94, Potamia River on 10th May '93 and 12th June '97 (possibly breeding), Vatera River in May '96 (where up to 35 recordrd on 6th), near Kalloni East River ford on 21st May '91, 5th and 7th May '94, and virtually throughout May '95 (with 3+ there on 15th April '98), south-east of Molivos on 15th May '93, and from Anaxos on 28th (being described as 'quite common' in that area between 10th and 17th). There was a huge fall in that area in spring '97, with at least 25 singing males counted along a sample 150 metre stretch of stream near Petra on 2nd May. Also a bird present on Kalloni West River 30th May '98 and singing on the Chalandra River Skala Eressos

from 25th-26th May '87 and 11th July '98, and 2 singing from reeds at Faneromeni River mouth on 7th June '97 and 7th July '98. A single bird was also present at the same river mouth on 7th August '96 - which all suggests another likely breeding area. In autumn '94, a total of 4 trapped at Haramida Marsh (2 on 19th and 2 on 21st September) by the ringing group.

Great Reed Warbler *Acrocephalus arundinaceus*

Localized summer visitor from April to September, quite common in suitable damp habitat. First seen along Potamia River on 4th April '97 and at Sigri on 8th April '86, but birds not singing regularly around Faneromeni ford until 23rd April '95, after which a marked arrival noted at Kalloni East River on 28th, when several birds in full song. At least 4 were noted there on 12th May '98. Also heard regularly along Chalandra River (where 2-3 singing regularly from 16th-23rd May '87), the river between Sigri and Eressos on the coastal route, Parakila Marsh and Dipi Larssos Reedbed. In addition, 3 birds were around Kalloni Pool in late May '95, and 2-3 were reported from a somewhat drier location south-east of Molivos in mid-May '93 (with at least 2 singing there on 10th May '94, and 2 around Petra reservoir on 3rd June '96. By the third week of May birds are generally less easy to locate, and harder still in autumn, though 1 was seen well at close quarters on the Chalandra River 14th September '89. Four were trapped at Haramida Marsh between 15th and 21st September '94, and 4 on 17th September '95. An individual of the distinctive eastern race *Zarudnyi* was discovered on Kalloni East River ford by a *Limosa* party on 7th-8th May '97. Breeding no closer than northern Iraq this may well constitute a first for Lesvos.

Olivaceous Warbler *Hippolais pallida*

Widespread summer visitor from mid-April to September in all suitable scrubby damp habitat with tamarisks and willows present. First recorded singing in the Potamia Valley on 12th April '98 and along the Chalandra River on 13th April '95, at the stream by the airport on 14th, and at the river mouth near Thermi on 21st, with good numbers at Faneromeni ford on 23rd. Thereafter becoming more widespread around Skala Eressos River, Sigri, Parakila Marsh, Kalloni Pool, Kalloni Inland Lake and East River (where at least 3 on 13th April '98, several singing 24th April '97 and 'omnipresent' by 5th May that year). A count in the Vatera area on 3rd May '96 produced no less than 45 birds, reducing to 35 on 7th. Three were around the picnic site between Keramia and Vassilika on 5th May '95 and 40+ were seen between Molivos and Sikimmia on 9th, with 6+ on East River on 10th May and circa 50 in the Skala Kalloni area on 14th - whilst 5 were seen again at Faneromeni ford on 16th. By far the commonest warbler after Subalpine at this time, and present in all lowland areas where suitable breeding habitat occurs. Still described as 'common in many suitable tangly riparian places' in early August '98, and last records of a bird near Anaxos on 26th September '98 and of 2 around Kalloni Inland Lake on 28th September and 6th October '95.

Upcher's Warbler *Hippolais languida*

Vagrant. Though regular in nearby Turkey, the occurrence of this bird is poorly documented in Greece - receiving no mention at all in *The Birds of Greece*. However, there is at least one reasonably certain record - of a bird near Tavari on 7th May '96, which was watched feeding for some time fairly high in an oak tree and regularly indulging in the tail-cocking behaviour - both habits characteristic of this bird. Leg colour was also noticed. It seems likely that others may have been overlooked, but only time will tell!

Olive-tree Warbler *Hippolais olivetorum*

Localized summer visitor from late April to September. Not an easy bird to get to grips with, but at least 2-3 pairs usually nesting in Potamia Valley (especially in the area where olives and oaks intermingle), with 2 seen and heard in mid-May '91, and 3 showing well on 11th May '95.

Also regular around Skala Eressos, where 2 seen on 14th and 16th May '87, and 3 holding territory in orchards behind the village from 24th onwards. Elsewhere, heard singing from the valley west of Vatoussa between early and mid-May '94, and 2 heard and seen at another regular site at Gavathas (next to the taverna!) on 14th, with a single record near Achladeri on 23rd May '95, a singing male in an olive grove near Vatera harbour on 17th May '96 and migrants seen along Kalloni East River 11th and 14th May '97, and singing at 'Devil's Bridge' on 13th and at Faneromeni on 19th. In the north of the island, recorded from Skalochori on 14th May '91, from the road between Petra and Molivos on 28th May '93, near Petri on 29th April '94, and from the area of the Sunset Hotel Petra on 5th May '95, with 2 singing males in olives near Petra on 28th May '96 and 1 singing near Petra on 3rd June that year. Described as fairly common in the foothills behind Petra, and also seen just below Vafios in the first half of May '97. Following on from these records a new breeding area holding at least 7 singing males was discovered in May '98 in predominantly oak woodland a few kms before Skalochori on the minor road from Filia. This may always have been a regular site, as that part of the island is very under-watched. Increased observer coverage in the Potamia Valley that year may, however, have been responsible for the recording of 2 birds there on the exceptionally early date of 13th April. Just away from this site a bird was seen well singing in olives just west of Kalloni East River on 7th June that year, and birds were still singing occasionally in Petra valley during the last few days of July. Obviously much harder to locate when not singing, though single migrants were reported at Petra reservoir on 11th August '96, around Skala Kalloni 29th-30th August '97 and on the dirt track between Sigri and Eressos on 1st September that year. Latest record of 2 birds just west of Anaxos on 4th September '96.

Icterine Warbler *Hippolais icterina*

Passage migrant from mid-April to late May (occasionally early June) - peaking early to mid-May and early or mid-August to late September (peaking early September). A few pairs may breed, though this possibility is largely discounted in *The Birds of Greece*. First recorded at Skamioudi on 18th April '98 and the Kruper's site near Achladeri next day, with 2 seen between Messotopos and Eressos on 30th April that year, 1 in Petra olive groves on 10th May and 1 at Ipsilou on 13th May (following 2 singing birds on 11th). Described by an observer in May '93 as : 'fairly common from 10th in all suitable habitat, including a pair in tamarisk bushes on Petra beach'. Seen regularly on migration around the Skala Eressos area, with sightings mid-month in May '87 and '90, and a total of 4 at Sigri on 15th May '91, with a single there on 17th. In May '91, 1 was singing near Kalloni West River on 11th, 2 were seen below Andissa on 14th and others were at Skala Eressos on 19th and 21st. Spring '95 saw 1 in the Sweet Chestnut Forest above Agiassos on 10th May, in the Potamia Valley on 16th, and another near the Sigri-Eressos junction the next day. A bird was also seen in fig trees at Faneromeni on 7th May. On 11th May '96 one was seen near Kalloni Salt Pans, with another on 14th seen chasing a Wood Warbler at Ipsilou monastery. In spring '97 a bird was seen at Faneromeni from 24th-25th April, with singles along Kalloni East River and above Petra on 26th April, 2nd, 3rd and 11th May (with 2 on 12th), up to 5 west of Eressos on 4th (with 2 there on 12th), 2 at Sigri on 5th, up to 5 there on 11th and 3 on 19th - clearly major falls. Three birds north-east of Petra on 10th May '94 included 2 singing males, with another 2 near Petri the next day, 5 singing from olives between Anaxos and Petri on 26th May '96, and 2 singing betwen Petra and Molivos on the even later date of 3rd June that year. In the light of these records, the observer suspected breeding, but *The Birds of Greece* points out that late migrants often sing, and that there is no concrete evidence of breeding other than occasional pairs in northern Greece. Only autumn records of 1 at Achladeri on 10th August '96, 2 on Molivos beach 2 days later, 1 at 'Vicky Studios' Skala Kalloni 2nd September '97, near Sigri on 3rd September '94, along the East River on 22nd September '94 and 28th September '98, 1 between Petra and Pelopi on 23rd, 1 at Skala Polichnitos Salt Pans on 30th, and 1 at Skala

Eressos on 7th-8th August '89 and 5th October '94 (the latest record); with 3 at Haramida Marsh on 8th September '95, and a further 3 the next day - with 2 there on 12th September '98. Singles recorded near Petra reservoir on 26th July '96 (still present 3rd August) and near Parakila on 29th July '97 may have been exceptionally early autumn migrants, but still probably provide the best evidence yet of possible breeding.

Spectacled Warbler *Sylvia conspicillata*
Scarce and irregular passage migrant, most likely between April-May and August-October and proven breeding on Corfu in '91 (see *The Birds of Greece*).

Subalpine Warbler *Sylvia cantillans*
Widespread summer visitor from March to September. Common amongst scrubby and maquis covered hillsides, this bird attains particularly high densities in the north, east and south-east corners of the island, with the areas between Thermi and Molivos and Petra, Vafios and Skala Sikimmia, the coastal scrub around Achladeri, and the pine woodland above Agiassos seeming especially favoured. Scarcer in the less vegetated hillsides to the west, though present in small numbers around Skala Eressos. First recorded 30th March at Gavathas and 4th April '97 along Kalloni East River and already by far the commonest warbler between Molivos and Eftalou on 8th April '95. Still described as 'very frequent' in occurrence in the first week of August '98, but by mid-August mainly juveniles remaining, though a late adult was seen around Skala Kalloni on 16th August '95. Otherwise 2 first-year birds were trapped at Haramida Marsh on 19th September '94 and 9th September '95 - the latest records.

Sardinian Warbler *Sylvia melanocephala*
Rather thinly distributed resident, and sightings not helped by skulking behaviour. Records of 1 behind Molivos Castle and another near Eressos in mid-May '90. Two were reported at Skala Eressos on both 23rd and 26th October '92. A juvenile was also seen near Stipsi on 3rd August '94 and a few were sighted around Haramida Marsh mid-September '94 and '95. Several sightings were also reported between Kalloni East River and Salt Pans in mid-April '95 and mid-June '97, with 2 seen near Assomatos on 5th May '95. Much more obvious however from autumn onwards (eg several at Skala Eressos on 20th October '95 and 5 just south of Mytilini airport on 18th September '97), when birds were regularly heard and seen along Kalloni East River, at Tavari ford, near Agios Stephanos, by the entrance to Potamia Valley and around both Potamia and Petra reservoirs in January '98. A particularly confiding male was observed actually feeding in the road alongside Kalloni Pool on 24th March '98!

Ruppell's Warbler *Sylvia rueppelli*
Localized summer visitor from mid or late March to September. Although the clifftop site between Petra and Molivos is the best known (with a minimum of 8 males and 6 females recorded in the area in mid-May '94 and 4-6 singing males on 9th April '95). In spite of a fire destroying most of the vegetation in the first lay-by (opposite the disco) in the summer/autumn of '97, some bushes were already starting to green up by late April '98 - when there were at least 6 birds (including 3 males) in the area. Breeding pairs were also present on the hillside just inland from here and also around the next 2 clifftop lay-bys a few hundred metres further on towards Molivos - at least 5 singing males were present in the area on 21st April. A pair also bred in a low gulley above Eressos town on the road to Sigri in '86 and '87, (and were still doing so in '95-7 at least). In spring '95 2 were regularly seen at the top of East River throughout May, and the strip of coastal scrub on the east coast between Misstegna and Aspropotamos also seemed particularly favoured (with several singing males on view in mid-April). Also recorded breeding (carrying nesting material) at the picnic cum bandstand site north of Kalloni on 1st June '96, and on the Bogat headland just west of Nifida in May '97.

First recorded 25th March '97 (a male) above Kalloni East River, and last record of at least 2 males, 2 females and 3 juveniles at the Molivos site on 6th August '96, with 2 males and several juveniles there on 8th August '94 and 3 males and a female / juvenile present on the same date in '98. However, one was ringed at Haramida on the late date of 31st August '96.

Orphean Warbler *Sylvia hortensis*
Localized summer visitor from late March to September. First recorded singing in the Potamia Valley on 1st April '86, and near Vatera on 3rd April '98. Somewhat sparsely distributed, but a good number of records from the north of the island, where located between Molivos and Petra on 9th April '95, with 1 between Thermi and Madamados on 21st, a pair between Skala Sikimmia and Molivos (near Argennos) on 29th, 1 on the Skoutaros road on 11th May, and another pair north-east of Petra from mid-May (on the rough track leading to Molivos close to Petra reservoir - where at least 4 present on 10th May '98). Apart from 2 between Parakila and Agra on 7th May '95, at least 3 between Messotopos and Eressos on 22nd, 1 above Kalloni East River on 26th, a few records from the Potamia Valley (eg 2 singing there 10th April '87), and above Agiassos, pairs also reported most years from the area east of Skalochori, near Andissa and beyond Faneromeni ford, where a pair observed on 23rd April '95. Otherwise, main concentration around Skala Eressos, where up to 3 birds singing by 17th May '87, but found more regularly along eastern side of Skala Eressos valley in May '91, when 4 singing males on 24th joined by a female on 26th. One seen in the Potamia Valley on 30th July '94, with a family party recorded near Filia on 6th August. In May '96 from 10-12 territories were located in the Vatera area, and a singing bird was again showing well at the cliffside Ruppell's site between Petra and Molivos on 20th. Elsewhere, autumn sightings include a bird at Ampelia on 4th September '96, and 1 logged at Haramida Marsh on 8th September '95, with a further 3 on 10th and 1 on 15th (the latest record).

Barred Warbler *Sylvia nisoria*
Scarce passage migrant between April and May and August-September. Two birds were seen in a fig tree at Sigri on 26th April '84, whilst a minimum of 3 birds were located around open

deciduous woodland east of Skalochori on 9th and 18th May '93, with 1 near Lisvori on 12th and 1 north-east of Petra on 13th. More normal records concern 1 on the river near Keramia on 19th April '95, and 1 at the top of Kalloni East River on 10th May that year, a bird at Skala Polichnitos on 21st April '97, west of Kalloni Inland Lake next day (and again on 2nd May), inland from East River on 27th April, north of Petra and also between Molivos and Argennos on 30th, in the Potamia Valley on 1st May, south of Vassilika then next day, near Malemi hotel on 3rd May, with single females just west of Eressos the next day, and beyond Faneromeni ford on 11th-12th May that year. That particular location also held no less than 4 birds (and possibly more) on 27th April '97 and at least 1 on 3rd May '98 (when singles were also seen in oaks between Skalochori and Vatoussa on 18th April and in bushes opposite the Kruper's site at Achladeri on 25th) and on 18th May that year. Lack of autumn records not surprising for such a skulking bird, though the ringing party located 1 at Haramida Marsh on 12th and 18th September '95 (the latest record) and 1st-2nd September '96 (2 birds). One was also seen at Ipsilou monastery 4th August '96, 2 were located in fields close to Mytilini airport on 16th August '97 and 1 was present at Faneromeni on 7th September '98.

Lesser Whitethroat *Sylvia curruca*
Passage migrant from late March to early May and mid-August to mid-October. According to *The Birds of Greece* breeding is probable in upland or mountainous areas. First recorded at Gavathas and Kalloni East River in late March '86, whilst 2 were seen at Kalloni Inland Lake on 3rd April '97 and 3 were at Vatera river mouth on the same date in '98. 'Considerable numbers' were reported at Sigri on 20th April '84, and also during a 'fall' at Perivoli monastery on 25th April '97, with 30+ present in another 'fall' at Faneromeni on 27th April '98 and 'hundreds' reported from Ipsilou monastery next day. Two late migrants or possible breeders were noted at Skala Eressos on 16th May '87, 2 at Petra on 11th May '93, around Skala Kalloni to 21st May '91, and to mid-month in '94. Two were still being seen around Skala Kalloni on the late dates of 7th and 9th June '97 - again suggesting breeding. Earliest autumn migrant seen above Agiassos on 8th August '94, with 2 still at Skala Eressos on 24th September, 1 at Kalloni Inland Lake on 6th October, and 1 on the West River on 13th. Fourteen were ringed at Haramida Marsh between 7th and 19th September '95. Late record of 1 around Kalloni Inland Lake 24th October '96 and 6 at Skala Eressos on 25th October '92.

Whitethroat *Sylvia communis*
Largely a passage migrant from late March to mid-May (peaking mid-April) and mid-August to late October (peaking early to mid-September), with a few pairs breeding. First recorded 23rd March '97 at Tavari ford, 26th March March '86 on Kalloni East River, 30th March at Gavathas, 2nd April '98 at Faneromeni ford, 6th April '85 in the Potamia Valley, and 11th April '95, when several birds in bushes alongside track between Kalloni East River and Salt Pans. (One or two birds were still singing, and appeared to be holding territory here in May, with breeding proven there in early June '96). Two pairs were also on breeding territory along tracks between Papiana church and East River in June '98 - with 1 pair watched feeding young from 1st-5th and possibly another pair nearby. Several migrants still noted Faneromeni ford 23rd April '95 (after a major fall there involving 3 figure numbers on 17th - reducing to 10 by 19th), and seen in first half of May that year above Petra, near Anaxos, between Skoutaros and Skalochori, west of Skala Sikimmia, near Filia, on the Eressos to Messotopos road, above Agiassos and around the Potamia Valley. Two pairs breeding in the Skala Eressos area in May '87, but 4 in one bush on 21st May '91 were more likely to be migrants. Seen on Kalloni East River 10th August '94, and around Skala Kalloni and Sigri in September in hedges bordering olive groves (all first winter birds). Sixty-two were ringed at Haramida Marsh between 7th-19th September '95, and 18 were seen on 8th (suggesting a peak in the autumn migration

around this time). Several sightings also above Agiassos in late September and early October, and last recorded 8th October at Kalloni Inland Lake.

Garden Warbler *Sylvia borin*
Passage migrant in small numbers from April to May and late August to early October. An early migrant seen at Kalloni East River on 28th March '86, and at Gavathas 2 days later. Only records of singles at Skala Eressos on 16th May '87, at the ford between Sigri and Eressos on 9th May '96, 1 near Vatera on 1st May '97, 2 at Ipsilou monastery with other migrants on 11th May that year, 2 west of Eressos the next day, and another at Faneromeni on 19th May '98, with the latest spring record of a bird at Kalloni Inland Lake on 23rd May '98. Obviously under-recorded, since good numbers trapped at Haramida Marsh around mid-September '95, '96 and '98 (including 26 in September '98). An early autumn migrant was seen around Skala Kalloni on 10th August '95 and in the middle 2 weeks of August '96, whilst 2 were around Kalloni Inland Lake on 1st September '97, with singles at Molivos and again around Kalloni Inland Lake on 7th, near Achladeri on 13th September '98 and last recorded at Skala Eressos on 23rd September '94.

Blackcap *Sylvia atricapilla*
Widespread passage migrant and winter visitor (especially amongst olive groves) from September to May (peaking late September and late March to mid-April). Proven breeding on nearby Samos (see *The Birds of Greece*) and may breed locally on occasions - eg pair with 2 young seen at Ipsilou monastery on 18th May '98. However, some birds seen in late May may simply be late migrants. Reported above Agiassos from mid-September '94, and regular there throughout the autumn period, with birds present also at Kalloni Inland Lake at this time. No real record of wintering numbers, but 82 ringed at Haramida Marsh between 7th-19th September '95 (with a peak of 15 on 16th), and 10 seen between Filia and Skalochori on 23rd. Then seen with increasing frequency by October, and large numbers present at Faneromeni ford the following April (23rd onwards) possibly suggesting the beginning of northerly return passage (though not easy to separate from newly arrived migrants). Gathering of 5 at Skala Eressos on 21st April '98, 6 there 23rd May '87, 5 at Faneromeni on 19th May '96, 20+ at Ipsilou monastery the same day and 5 there on 16th May '98 - with good numbers present at Perivoli monastery during a 'fall' of common migrants on 25th April '97. A late record of a male between Petra and Molivos on 28th May '93.

Eastern Bonelli's Warbler *Phylloscopus orientalis*
Probable breeder and scarce passage migrant from late March to late April/early May and more rarely from mid-August to early October. First records of singles at Gavathas on the early date of 30th March '86, and between Petra and Molivos on 6th April '98, with 2 reported near Achladeri (at the Kruper's site) 2 days later. A few pairs almost certainly breed (area above Agiassos most likely - where 2-3 birds singing in Sweet Chestnut Woodland from at least 8th-12th May '95, 2 on 1st June '96 and again up to mid-May '97). *The Birds of Greece* says it 'has possibly bred', and would favour areas of deciduous forest of oak or beech etc, but also mixed or pure pinewoods at an elevation of circa 800-1200 metres. Two or three birds were also present in open oak woodland near Skalochori on 20th April '84, with at least 1 still seen on 26th, and also reported with other migrants at Ipsilou monastery on 11th May '97 and 18th May '98, and in the Potamia Valley on 14th April '98. In autumn recorded above Agiassos on 1st August '98, at Sigri 2 days later, near Parakila on 7th August '94, 2 birds at Vatera on 21st August '93, a single bird near Potamia reservoir 4th-5th September '97 with several in an oak tree at Skala Eressos on 8th September '89, 1 at Kalloni Salt Pans on 15th September '98, and birds last seen above Agiassos on 18th October '95 and along Kalloni East River the next day. Birds of this eastern race (following its recent split) are quite distinctive

because of their greyish and silky-white plumage and most frequently heard call - a Crossbill-like 'chip' (see *The Birds of Greece*).

Wood Warbler *Phylloscopus sibilatrix*
Common passage migrant (though in variable numbers) from early April to mid-May (peaking mid-late April), but scarcer in autumn - from late August to early October. First record of 1 singing at Achladeri on 11th April '98, with 2 birds present in the Potamia Valley on 13th and at Perivoli monastery on 14th April '87 and again in '97. Initially only a few records; of 'several' at Skala Eressos on 23rd April '84, 1 there on 15th and 16th May '87, 1 near Andissa on 21st May '91, singles in the valley west of Vatoussa on 10th May '94, and on East River 2 days later, with 1 there again on 3rd May '95, 6 at Faneromeni on 19th April that year, 1 being chased by an Icterine Warbler at Ipsilou monastery on 14th May '96 and odd birds in the Potamia Valley 2nd-4th May '97, with 2 seen at Achladeri on 2nd, Faneromeni on 5th and around Skala Kalloni on 11th. However, evidence of a more major movement in April '92, when 'large numbers' were reported at Skala Sikimmia from 15th-16th and the species was described as 'abundant' in the oakwoods above Skalochori on 21st, and present 'in substantial numbers' at Gavathas on 24th. Also more regular in occurrence in spring '97 and '98 - eg 15+ at Haramida on 18th April '97 (at which time there was also a large fall at Perivoli monastery and Faneromeni up to at least 25th) 30+ at Faneromeni during a 'fall' on 17th April '98 and 'hundreds' at Ipsilou monastery during another big 'fall' on 28th. Eight autumn records - of singles seen near 'Derbyshire' on 25th August '97, at Skala Eressos on 29th and in a puddle near Potamia reservoir on 31st August that year. Singles were also at Haramida Marsh on 15th-16th September '95 and 8th and 11th September '98, Kalloni Salt Pans on 11th September '98 and near Achladeri two days later, whilst the latest autumn records are of singles seen at Petra on 29th September '94 and the Potamia Valley on 30th September '98.

Chiffchaff *Phylloscopus collybita*
Fairly common winter visitor from mid-October to late March or early April. A few pairs may breed sporadically - eg above Agiassos. Especially numerous around Kalloni Inland Lake during the second half of March '97, and also much in evidence around Kalloni Pool at this time, and during a January '98 visit. Also evidence of return passage in the Faneromeni area on 3rd April '98, when at least 15 birds present. Not recorded during ringing at Haramida Marsh in either early or mid-September trips, but seen in small numbers above Agiassos in late September and early October, and present daily around Skala Kalloni in roadside weed clumps at the same time. Apparently much larger numbers had been seen around Sigri from mid-September '86, and Skala Eressos from mid-September '89. Three unusually late spring records; of singles above Agiassos on 13th and 15th May '95, and 1 singing at Skala Eressos on 25th May '87 and a further 2 singing in the Sweet Chestnut Forest above Agiassos on the very late date of 1st June '96 (with birds singing there on 4th May '97, 10+ singing on 6th May '98 and 3+ still singing on 16th) - suggesting likely breeding in the area. At least 1 record (at Gavathas on 24th April '92) of the northern race *P.c. abietinus* - said in *The Birds of Greece* to occur especially in late March and April. This species is descibed as being greyer, with a characteristic call. *P. c. tristis* is also possible, though there may be only two records so far for the whole of Greece!

Willow Warbler *Phylloscopus trochilus*
Passage migrant from April to May and August to October. Small numbers in spring (when first recorded in song at Kalloni Salt Pans on 3rd April '98, with 5 present at Skamioudi 2 days later), but far more widespread in autumn. In May '87, a few records from Skala Eressos mid-month, with 1 north of Skalochori on 9th May '93, and 1 or 2 around the East River ford on 9th and 10th of May '94, and finally, larger numbers between Parakila and Eressos on 23rd

April '95, with 2 around the Sunset Hotel Petra on 5th and 8th May. In spring '97 a large fall was evident on 29th April, when at least 30 were feeding around Ipsilou monastery (where at least 6 were still present on 13th May '98). In autumn '94 especially large numbers were to be seen everywhere, with a staggering 190 ringed at Haramida Marsh between 29th August-10th September (peaking at 48 on 6th September). Autumn passage around Molivos in September '97 peaked with at least 25 birds around the castle on 17th. Moreover, on 3rd October '94 at Faneromeni a huge concentration was observed on roadside wires and bushes (in company with large numbers of Chiffchaffs) feeding on the emerging caterpillars of the Clouded Yellow Butterfly! Still being recorded daily in small numbers around Skala Eressos in the last week of October '92. Also described as 'abundant throughout' in the first half of September '97, and in the second half of September '98 possibly as many as 1000 birds were feeding in alfalfa fields between Kalloni East River and Salt Pans!.

Goldcrest *Regulus regulus*
Localized winter visitor from October to mid-March, especially to pinewoods. Only recorded from Skala Eressos area in last week of October '92, when present most days, with a noticeable 'fall' on 26th. Outside of this period, several were seen and heard at the Kruper's site at Achladeri on 20th March '97, with at least one still present on 16th April. Moreover a male singing near Vassilika on 21st April '97 and singing birds in the pine forest above the picnic-'bandstand' site north of Kalloni on 7th May that year raise the likelihood of occasional breeding.

Firecrest *Regulus ignicapillus*
Largely a winter visitor from October to February in upland pinewoods, but likely to breed locally (see *The Birds of Greece*). Absence of records hardly surprising at this time, but possibility of breeding should not be discounted until a lot more fieldwork has been done (especially in the light of a record of 3 seen in the pinewoods above Agiassos in August '91 and a single there on 31st August '97). Of particular significance was a male seen and heard singing in pines just outside Molivos on 10th May '94 - which would seem to finally confirm breeding.

Spotted Flycatcher *Muscicapa striata*
Widespread passage migrant from early or mid-April to late May (peaking late April to early May) and usually in larger numbers late August to mid or late October (peaking late September onwards - when weather likely to be more variable). A few pairs may breed, and certainly seen regularly at the Kruper's site at Achladeri up to early June '98. First recorded 7th April '97 at Kalloni East River and 18th April '98 at Faneromeni, peaking by mid-May '95 with a maximum of 50 in the Sigri area on 11th. However, numbers are variable from year to year. Spring '87 produced hardly any migrants at Skala Eressos until 22nd May, though 6 were there on 25th; whilst spring '91 was very quiet. May '93, however, produced exceptional numbers till mid-month (especially in the favoured 'catchment area' between Faneromeni and Eressos). Spring '94 was uneventful, but that autumn (certainly from mid-September) birds seemed to be everywhere, especially around Skala Kalloni and the Potamia Valley, where double-figure numbers were present most days, with birds recorded until at least 11th October. The spring '97 passage peaked in late April - with hundreds present in the Kalloni area on 27th and good numbers at Faneromeni 2 days later, and peak passage in spring '98 was at a similar time (25th April-16th May) - with 20 birds in Petra olive groves on 10th May and 50+ around Ipsilou monstery on 16th! Latest records 2 at Kalloni Inland Lake 22nd October '96 and one 24th October '92 at Skala Eressos. Few summer records (eg just 1 bird reported - near Stipsi - on a 2 week trip in July '98, and 1 seen in Petra Valley on 29th July), but probably fairly localized in more upland areas at this time, and reported as 'frequent in the forests

around Agiassos' in the first week of August '98, when 3 birds were also seen just north of Andissa.

Red-breasted Flycatcher *Ficedula parva*
Rare passage migrant from mid-April to mid-May and mid-August to mid-October. First records of a female at the Kruper's site near Achladeri on 27th April '98 and at Ipsilou monastery with a 'fall' of Pied and Spotted on 29th April '97. One was seen near Molivos in mid-May '90, 1 behind the Villa Yannis Skala Kalloni on 11th May '91, and another was seen mid-month in an olive grove around Skala Eressos fields, with 2 together on the dried-up section of the Chalandra river on 15th. One was also seen near Sigri on 13th May '93 and around 'Derbyshire' on 8th May '94, and a rather dull male was seen around Faneromeni ford with other flycatchers on 4th May '95, with it or another bird around Sigri beach 2 days later. An obvious 'fall' was apparent in mid-May '97, when 10th May produced 2 birds at Ipsilou monastery (with 3 next day and a female still present on 13th), a female behind Petra, 1 at Sigri and 3 more between there and Faneromeni on 12th. One was reported from Sigri beach on 25th April '98, and also near 'Derbyshire' during the fall of *ficedula* flycatchers from 24th-28th April that year. A male was also present at Ipsilou monastery as part of this 'fall' on 28th, with a female beyond Faneromeni ford on 7th May; and one seen in the Potamia Valley on 30th May '98 being the latest spring record. One early autumn record concerns a bird on Kalloni East River 6th August '89, and late sightings include 1 at Haramida Marsh on 12th and 17th September '95, 12th September '98 and one at Limonas monastery on 30th September '97 (the latest record).

Semi-collared Flycatcher *Ficedula semitorquata*
Regular but scarce passage migrant from late March to early May, possible from late August to late September. Largely because of earlier lack of observer coverage at this time, very few earlier records - though a male was identified at Faneromeni on 17th April '95. Thereafter, this species was again reported from olive groves between Achladeri and Vassilika on 12th April '97 (a male) - with another near Eressos a few days later. Also present with a substantial 'fall' of Pied, Collared and Spotted Flycatchers around Ipsilou Monastery between 24th-28th April '98 (including one bird picked up dead). At least 3 males and 3 females were identified by one observer. During this 'fall' a female and 2 males were also positively identified at the nearby Sigri-Eressos road junction on 25th, with a male there and near Faneromeni ford next day. Three birds were also claimed from 'Devil's Bridge' on 2nd May that year - the latest date recorded. No autumn records as yet.

Collared Flycatcher *Ficedula albicollis*
Passage migrant in reasonable numbers from late March to mid-May (peaking mid-April), scarcer from late August to late September. First record of 2 males at Achladeri on 4th April '97, a male around Mytilini castle on 5th April '95, 4 males at Faneromeni ford on 10th April '97, with a single between Kalloni East River and Salt Pans on 11th April '95, and between Parakila and Agra on 13th. Thereafter, not seen till 5 males were located at Faneromeni ford on 16th (rising to circa 20 in the area next day and 14 still on 19th). At least one male was still present on 23rd, and it (with possibly another male and up to 2 females) was seen again on 27th April, and 4th and 5th May, in company with Pieds, a few Spotted, and briefly (on 4th) a Red-breasted! A male and 3 females were seen again near Sigri on 11th. In April '92 'large numbers of eastern race birds' were reported at Gavathas on 24th, whilst in May '93 birds were recorded near Petra on 5th (a male), with a female west of Skala Kalloni on 7th and near Molivos on 8th. At least 10 males were reported at Faneromeni ford during a 'fall' on 17th April '98, whilst at least 20 males were present at Ipsilou monastery on 24th April '98 during the big 'fall' of *ficedula* flycatchers, and reasonable numbers were still being recorded both

there, between Ipsilou and Sigri (15+ on 24th), at Faneromeni ford (10+ on 25th), and along Chalandra River Skala Eressos until 28th. There were also large numbers reported from Skala Vassilikon on 25th. The latest spring sighting was of a male on 23rd May at Skala Eressos, but 2 were also claimed briefly around Skala Kalloni beach in mid-June '97 (following thunderstorms on 11th). The only autumn record is of 2 at Skala Eressos on the late date of 5th October '94.

Pied Flycatcher *Ficedula hypoleuca*
Passage migrant in small numbers from late March to early May (peaking mid-April) and late August to early October (peaking early September). Earliest record of several males and a female at Sigri on 5th April '85, a male at Perivoli Monastery on 5th April '97, with 'several' at Gavathas on 14th April '87 and 15th April '95 (when a large 'fall' of *ficedula* flycatchers was noted), 5-10 at Sigri on 21st-22nd April '92, 3 at Eressos the next day, 2 females and a male at Plomari on 17th April '95, at least 7 in the Faneromeni ford area on 19th-23rd, where seen, sometimes together with a female, on and off to 28th. (Just to complicate things, male and female Collared were also present at this time!) One was also seen above Agiassos on 6th May, with a female around Kalloni Inland Lake on 3rd. In May '94, a single was again around Faneromeni ford on 6th, and 1 was recorded in the valley west of Vatoussa on 10th. Following a 'fall' at Perivoli monastery from 25th-29th April '97, single females were seen in the hills north of Petra on 2nd and 3rd May '97, along the Chalandra River Skala Eressos next day and at Ipsilou monastery on 6th May (apparently a favourite date!). Up to 10 had been present at this site during the above mentioned 'fall' on 29th April - following 2 there on 24th and 4 in the Skala Kalloni area on 21st. This species was initially estimated by one observer to comprise about 60% of the pronounced 'fall' of *ficedula* flycatchers at Ipsilou monastery from 24th-28th April '98 - which would mean that over 100 were present on 24th. At least 20 birds were reported along the Chalandra River Skala Eressos on 27th, whilst only 5+ were seen at Ipsilou monastery next day, and a similar number were noted at Faneromeni on 27th April and 3rd

May. The latest spring record was of a bird at Skala Eressos on 26th May '94. No great autumn influxes documented, and only records concern 1 at Ipsilou monastery on the early date of 4th August '96, 1 at Kalloni East River 4th September '97, 1 at Faneromeni on 7th September '98, 1 between Eressos and Sigri on 8th September '97, 1 at Skala Polichnitos on 12th September '98, singles near Achladeri and at Kalloni Pool next day, at Potamia River Bridge on 14th and 1 north of Plomari on 21st September '94, with another above Agiassos the next day, 2 at Skala Eressos on 2nd October that year, and another near The Petrified Forest on 3rd October '98 - the latest date recorded.

Long -tailed Tit *Aegithalos caudatus*
Scarce and localized resident, mainly in upland pinewoods. The grey-backed Asia Minor race *A.c. tephronotus* occurs. Three to four were seen in the pine forest north of Kalloni on 14th May '93, with 3 on the road to Achladeri (3 kms north-east of Vassilika) on 25th May '95 and 16th and 21st April '97, and 3 pairs reported there on 20th April '92. Four were also seen at the nearby picnic site on the Agiassos to Polichnitos road close to the Vatera turn-off on 5th, with a family party there on 23rd, and parties of circa 10 and up to 20 seen nearby on the respective dates of 3rd and 13th May '97. Also seen in the area en route to the old Kruper's site on 20th May '92, and later found to be fairly regular both around Mikri Limni and also the new Kruper's site at Achladeri in April-May '98, where parties of up to 12 recorded. Away from these areas 'several' were reported near Vatera on 22nd April '92, a pair was seen in open oak woodland near Skalochori in late April '84, just west of Anaxos on 9th May '94, near Anemotia on 20th October '95, and in Petra valley on 29th July '98. Once again, this species seems likely to have been under-recorded in the past.

Sombre Tit *Parus lugubris*
Localized resident in both lowland and upland areas, tending to prefer more open habitats than other tits and avoiding dense woodland. Dry hillsides with scattered oaks, olives and tall bushes are most favoured, especially to the north and west of the island. Seen well above Eftalou, Skala Eressos and the Potamia Valley especially, and anything from 1-4 located above East River between 10th and 20th May '95, and family parties regularly observed by the month's end and in most subsequent years. In spring '98 birds were found nesting both around Kalloni Inland Lake, Potamia Valley, near Parakila and even amongst rocks in the rugged area between Apothikes and Makara. According to *The Birds of Greece*, those occurring on Lesvos belong to the Asia Minor form *P. l. anatoliae*, which to quote ' has a very dark cap and bib, relatively white underparts, dark mantle and small body'.

Coal Tit *Parus ater*
Scarce and localized resident; distribution much as for Long-tailed Tit. Only records of a few feeding in pines above Agiassos on 6th May '95, a pair there on 1st June '96 and the odd single seen around Skala Eressos on 23rd and 25th October '92, between Sigri and Eressos in early September '97, and near Achladeri on 1st and 14th August '96 and 9th May '97 - with at least 2 near Vassilika on 21st April '97. Unlike Sombre Tit, this is not a bird that too many people actively seek out, so most sightings tend to occur by accident - eg whilst waiting for Krupers Nuthatch to appear!

Blue Tit *Parus caeruleus*
Widespread resident around both upland pinewoods, oakwoods and trees at lower elevation.

Great Tit *Parus major*
Widespread resident, as likely to be seen on Kalloni East River as upland pinewoods. On 22nd March '97 a pair was watched nest-building in an upturned urn in the garden of Malemi Hotel!

Kruper's Nuthatch *Sitta krueperi*
Scarce and localized resident, confined largely to upland pinewoods above Agiassos, perhaps spreading westwards as far as Vassilika and south-west to Ambelikon and more recently north-west towards Achladeri. Has been recorded just north-east of Kalloni, but breeding away from main strongholds is not easy to prove. At least 3-4 males were singing beyond the Sanatorium above Agiassos in early spring '95, and a total breeding figure of as many as 50-100 pairs + throughout the island would not seem unreasonable (see *The Birds of Greece*). A family party was watched above Agiassos on 27th May '94, and an adult was seen feeding a juvenile opposite the Ambelikon turn-off on 23rd May '95. Since the discovery of a breeding pair or two near the army camp at Achladeri in May '96 breeding has now been proven there every year since - with one pair often giving very close views round the car park. Proof of no less than 3 successful breeding pairs was obtained when a visit on 9th May '97 produced 2 broods out of the nest and 1 still being fed! The earliest fledging date in '98 was 7th May - coincidentally the date the first charters arrived! Because birds are now so easy to see there in spring, the old site at Agiassos tends to be rather neglected, though 3-4 birds were seen well a few hundred metres opposite the drinking trough and small chapel close to the Achladeri and Agiassos-Vassilika road junction (and were regularly drinking from the trough in mid-August '98); and also at another 'new' site to the right of the main Kalloni-Mytilini road near the burnt-out area before Lambou Mili. The area is about 15 minutes walk from the road up a track opposite a lay-by, and is very close to the ruins of the old Roman aqueduct marked on the island map. The placing of nestboxes in the vicinity of Mikri Limni (previously lacking in suitable nest sites) may also make for more frequent sightings there in the future, and a party of at least 4 was seen in a mixed feeding flock around the nearby picnic site in late September '98, and around the edge of Megali Limni that January. (For further info see P283-7).

Nuthatch *Sitta europaea*
Scarce and very localized resident. Only a handful of records originally appeared to offer reasonably conclusive proof of this bird's existence on the island. First of all, 5-6 specimens were 'obtained' sometime in the 60's by one G. Watson, who wrote in his Ph.D. that he located them in the scattered oak woodland to the west, around Skalochori and Andissa - but not in the island's pinewoods, nor in the Sweet Chestnut woodland above Agiassos. (These specimens are, incidentally, now on display at the Smithsonian Institute in America). A nesting pair was apparently located in an oak near Skalochori on 24th April '84, and a pair was again present in that area in early April '85. It also appears in Marjorie Williams' *Birdwatching in Lesbos*, where it is listed as having occurred around Molivos in spring. Even more conclusive is a mention in Bob Husband's '87 birding report of a pair nesting in a hole in a fig tree behind Skala Eressos that year. Furthermore, 1 was seen at Gavathas on 30th March '86 and singing there on 14th April '87 and during April '92 (when also seen at Skala Sikimmia and the oakwoods above Skalochori), in an oak tree in the valley west of Vatoussa on 17th May '94, and 2 birds initially associating with Kruper's were observed at close range above Agiassos on 25th August. Three birds were also seen around Skala Eressos on 24th October '92, a group of 8 just north-west of Skoutaros on 9th May '94, with a a single record of a pair reported in the Potamia Valley on 19th May '95 (with a male singing there on 3rd and 4th June '96), 2 birds between 'Devil's Bridge' and Parakila on 29th August '97, a bird near Molivos (just up the Vafios road) on 5th and 8th September that year, and near Skalochori in both May '97 and '98 (the former a family party of 4-5). Whilst these sightings appear somewhat erratic, it is likely that a small but viable population of this bird must occur, with regular breeding probable most years, centred in the scattered oak woodland to the west of the island between Skalochori and Skala Eressos (where breeding was proven again by the Chalandra river in May '98 - I have pictures!), but with wandering birds occurring from time to time elsewhere (eg around Molivos) - though largely absent from the seemingly ideal Sweet Chestnut Forest

above Agiassos (except for a few isolated records - including 1 observed in chestnuts along the Agiassos-Plomari road on 10th May '97). Were regular breeding to occur so close to the Kruper's area, there would surely be more records of birds both seen and heard in spring. As a largely non-migratory bird, there is only a small chance of regular immigration from the mainland swelling the numbers. Any further records would be appreciated!

Western Rock Nuthatch *Sitta n. zarudnyi*
Widespread resident in all suitable upland habitat with rocky hillsides. Breeds as close to Kalloni as the upper part of the Potamia Valley and the inland section of East River. In fact the distinctive dome shaped nest with a funnel-shaped entrance is often quite visible once familiar with its favoured sites - usually a large steep rock with a slight overhang to offer some protection, and often decorated with old sweet wrappers, paper or chicken feathers! One such site exists on the rock face behind Kalloni Inland Lake, and another near the Upper East River on the track beyond the grain silos just past the goat-pen on the right! Family parties often encountered in May, when they can be extremely confiding - e.g. on cliffs around Ruppell's site, near Apothikes and Makara and near Skalochori. Other nests found near Pelopi, between Agra and Messotopos, near Eressos and Sigri.

Wallcreeper *Tichodroma muraria*
Vagrant, though quite possibly underrecorded. Apart from sporadic mainland breeding records due west of Lesvos, there are a number of records for this species outside the breeding season (especially October to March) from several of the islands, including nearby Chios - see *The Birds of Greece*. At such times birds can occur at much lower altitudes (perhaps down to 500 metres or less), so the claimed sighting in mid-May '96 of an individual from the small sheer rock-face on which Petra Chapel stands may not be as unusual as one would think. The other fact to be considered is that this bird is so distinctive that the chance of confusing it with any other species must be zero! Nevertheless, any further precise records would be welcomed.

Short-toed Treecreeper *Certhia brachydactyla*
Localized resident in upland pinewoods, Sweet Chestnut woodland, olive groves etc. Regularly seen in same area as Kruper's above Agiassos, where adults were observed feeding 2 juveniles on 11th and 18th May '94, and 6 were seen on 10th May '95. Also reported from the picnic spot near Vassilika (with 12 birds recorded between Keramia and Vassilika on 5th May '95), from olive groves in the Potamia Valley, near Skoutaros, and from the road between Kalloni and Petra. Several pairs also nest around the kruper's site at Achladeri, and a walk amongst the surrounding pinewoods can often prove productive for this species - often located first by sound. Also seen in woodland near the airport on 29th October '94, and 6 were trapped at Haramida between 16th and 18th September that year. These records would suggest that it is actually a much commoner bird on the island than was generally thought. Anyone who can turn one of them into Common Treecreeper is a better man than I am, and should be congratulated!

Penduline Tit *Remiz pendulinus*
Vagrant - but undoubtedly under-recorded. Though recently found breeding on Crete (as well as Corfu) only 3 records currently exist for Lesvos: of one heard calling over Mytilini 17th October '97, one seen well by the Chalandra River Skala Eressos on 10th April '98, and another seen later in the month at Dipi Larssos.

Golden Oriole *Oriolus oriolus*
Passage migrant from early April to late May (peaking late April/early May) and in smaller numbers from mid-August to early October. A few pairs may breed in more open areas of deciduous woodland where oak predominates - though poplars and cherries are also favoured at this time (see *The Birds of Greece*). Scattered records, usually of 1-2 birds at a time, throughout the island, but especially in steep-sided valleys of olive and oak woodland from Kalloni westwards. First recorded on 9th April '95, when 3 birds flying from tree to tree just north-east of Skala Polichnitos Salt Pans (coinciding with a 'fall' of Cuckoos). Also seen the next day near Keramia, with a male between Messotopos and Eressos on 28th, and another singing male in the same area on 5th May. A pair also recorded above Agiassos on 11th May '94, with a female in the Potamia Valley 2 days previously and several birds daily seen between Kalloni East River and Salt Pans from 19th-25th April '96 and '97. Biggest spring concentrations concern 'a considerable fall' in the pinewoods above Vassilika on 20th April '92 (with groups of at least 12 seen on several occasions), 15 together (including 4 males) in the Potamia Valley 2nd May '97, 20+ there 26th April '98 and 40+ at Sigri perched on hedges and feeding in open fields on 26th April '84. Although males regularly sing on passage, several in full song near Skala Sikimmia on 4th May '97 led the observer to believe that they may perhaps nest thereabouts, and singing males were heard above Agiassos and in the Potamia Valley on 6th May '98, whilst one was heard at the Kruper's site at Achladeri as late as 28th May that year. Autumn records include a single in Skala Kalloni fields on 24th September '94, 10th August '96, and sightings of ones and twos at Haramida Marsh between 12th and 18th September '95, with 6 there on 15th and single males at Faneromeni on 8th September '97 and 7th September '98 and at Megali Limni on 12th September '97, Alikoudi Pool on 12th September '98 and Kalloni Inland Lake on 17th September '98 (mobbing a Roller!). The latest record is of a female in orchards near Parakila on 30th September '98 - nine days after a male with a broken wing (presumed shot) was taken to the Lesbian Wildlife Hospital. This would seem to suggest a bigger autumn passage than previously thought, peaking about mid-September.

Black-headed Bush Shrike *Tchagra senegala*
Exceptionally rare vagrant. With no previous records from Greece and possibly only one from Europe this bird's occurrence is bound to be controversial. Nevertheless, on 10th May '98 (after two unsettled days with adverse winds and prolonged showers led to a 'mini-fall' of several more unusual migrants like Thrush Nightingale, Blue-cheeked Bee-eater, Desert Wheatear and Isabelline Shrike, a female identified as this species was observed at close range from a car on the tracks between Kalloni East River and Salt Pans. The four observers obtained brief but clear views of this bird on the ground (just after it had been bathing in a nearby puddle) even down to the spotting on the tail as it flew off when flushed by a passing car. Ideally further confirmation would have been desirable, but in view of the close views, the fact that the observers were familiar with this bird in Africa, and the full written description and identification features received I thought the record worth including.

Isabelline Shrike *Lanius isabellinus*
Vagrant. In spite of several earlier non-specific and unconfirmed reports (eg of 4 birds claimed in the Skala Kalloni area between mid and late September '94 - see under Red-backed Shrike below), the first confirmed record came from Faneromeni on 19th April '95 - after which 2 reliable reports were received- of an immature bird on the Vafios road beyond Petra between 8th-10th May '98, and a full adult male on the rough track between Sigri and Eressos (near the ford) on 14th May. There was also an unconfirmed report of a female at Faneromeni on 27th April that year. Clearly with so many Red-backed Shrikes passing through the island in spring

and autumn, identification of this species can be problematical, and several must be overlooked - witness a mere 3 Greek records in *The Birds of Greece* (of which 2 were subsequently rejected through lack of details).

Red-backed Shrike *Lanius collurio*
Largely a passage migrant, in considerable numbers, from mid or late April to late May (peaking early May) and September to mid-October (when extremely common). Also breeds in modest numbers (mainly to the west of the island), and a pair seen feeding young in June '91 between Kalloni and Eressos - with an adult male seen between Petra and Molivos on 23rd July '96 also likely to be a local breeder. Moreover, a male was seen with 3 juveniles just north of Achladeri in the first week of August '98 - at which time a pair with 2 juveniles was seen at Sigri. First recorded between Tavari and Messotopos on 12th April '98 (with 3 round Kalloni Inland Lake 5 en route to the Potamia Valley next day), with a male near Keramia on 19th April '95, and large 'falls' noticed near Achladeri (with double-figure numbers on 16th May '92) and the river valley between Eressos and Sigri, which held three-figure numbers the next day! A smaller 'fall' was noticed in the same area on 11th May '93, and between 30 and 50 (mostly males) were seen between Eressos and Kalloni on 16th May '87. In spring '96 no birds were seen after singles 24th and 26th May in the Potamia Valley, but breeding birds are often easily overlooked. The spring '97 passage had appeared to peak between 25th-29th April (when 20+ were near Faneromeni beach) and to be virtually over by 30th, but observers travelling on the rough track between Eressos and Sigri on 11th May reported an estimated 400 birds - part of an even larger fall! Smaller but still impressive numbers were present in that area on 1st May '98, with over 100 birds regularly recorded along the tracks beyond Faneromeni ford and between Sigri and Eressos from 1st-7th May. Autumn numbers can also be huge, with juvenile birds especially abundant from mid-late September '94 around both Skala Eressos and Skala Kalloni, outnumbering adults by far. (Only four adult males seen around Skala Kalloni between 16th and 29th, with 4 in the Skala Eressos area on 23rd). At this time there were also unconfirmed reports of up to 4 of the Eastern race *L. c. isabellinus* in the latter area. In September '98, 125 (mainly juveniles) were trapped at Haramida Marsh between 6th-16th, with a peak of 28 on 16th. Juveniles were regularly seen to at least mid-October '94, with latest records of 5 birds seen near Petra on 21st October '95 and 3 birds seen at Skala Eressos on 24th October '92.

Lesser Grey Shrike *Lanius minor*
Localized summer visitor and passage migrant from April to May and August to September. A few pairs breed in the area of Kalloni Salt Pans. First recorded near Kalloni Pool on 11th April '98 and at Faneromeni 2 days later, though near Parakila Marsh and at Kalloni Salt Pans on 18th April '98 and 22nd April '97 more typical dates - with at least 2 birds frequenting the track between the East River and Salt Pans between 29th April and 2nd May '95, and up to 5 seen on 5th May '98. Elsewhere, odd singles seen around West River (where 1 on 12th and 21st May '91), 'Derbyshire', Skala Eressos (where at least 3 in the second half of May '87), Sigri to Faneromeni beach (which holds the earliest record of a bird on 13th April '98) and Molivos area (where described by one observer as 'fairly common and widespread' in mid-May '90). Otherwise nowhere very common, and a maximum of 4 along Sigri beach road on 15th May '91, and 3-4 seen in a big 'fall' of shrikes near Sigri on 11th May '93, with a minimum of 4 on Kalloni Salt Pans next day and 5 the day after. Few sightings after mid-month (except odd singles at 'Derbyshire' and the Salt Pans), though 1 around Skala Eressos beach for several days from 18th May '91, at Kalloni Salt Pans on 30th May '94, and between Sigri and Faneromeni on 23rd May '95. Clearly not as rare in autumn as originally thought, and up to 6 birds were seen in the Kalloni area in the first week of August '98 (with 2 seen near irrigators at Faneromeni on 3rd), 2 west of Eressos on 12th August '89, whilst an adult and 3 juveniles

were together at Kalloni Salt Pans on 11th August '96 (with up to 4 birds present on 12th August '98). Five were seen together near Achladeri on 25th August '97, singles were seen at Petra reservoir on 4th September '96 (with another at Skala Polichnitos next day). 'Several' were also seen in company with other shrikes at Skala Eressos on 7th September '89, and the species was described as 'abundant' in the Kalloni area in the first half of September '98 (with 1 seen at the Salt Pans on 13th September '95 and 3 birds there on 13th September '97). One was at Kalloni West River mouth on 16th September '94, 1 in olive groves at Sigri on 17th September '86, 4 again around Kalloni Salt Pans on 18th September '98, a juvenile present there from 23rd-25th September '94 and up to 28th September '98, (with 1 between Petra and Molivos 2 days earlier). Another late record of 28th September '94 from Skala Polichnitos Salt Pans, with a single juvenile bird still being seen near the Aegean hotel Skala Kalloni up to 2nd October '97 (the latest recorded).

Great Grey Shrike *Lanius excubitor*
Scarce vagrant, known to be declining (see *The Birds of Greece*). Only 9 definite records - of a bird seen above Agiassos on 6th May '95, 1 in fields adjoining Kalloni West River on 8th September the same year, one seen well on wires along the Chalandra River (close to the Messotopos road) on 4th May '97 and another at Kalloni West River on 6th August that year, with a further sighting near Madamados on 23rd August. One was then seen near Achladeri on 25th (in the same field of view as 3 Lesser Grey! - see above). It or another bird was seen at the Kalloni Salt Pan headland 2 days later, along Kalloni East River the next day and West River on 2nd September '97. Clearly the possibility exists that all the autumn '97 records could relate to one bird. In short, there are scarcely enough records to form any real pattern, though the possibility remains that the odd bird seen briefly at a distance may be confused with the much commoner Lesser Grey (especially juveniles seen in autumn). Also the seemingly most favoured period of late August-early September is when there are usually few birders on the island. Either way, more records are needed!

Woodchat Shrike *Lanius senator*
Common and widespread summer visitor and passage migrant from late March to September. Certainly the commonest breeding shrike on the island (and described by one observer staying in Eressos in May '87 as : 'abundant, probably more common than Red-backed'. First recorded 4th April '97 around Kalloni Inland Lake , 5th April '85 and 7th April '98 at Faneromeni and 8th April '95 between Molivos and Eftalou, with 1 on 12th between Kalloni East River and

Salt Pans, but not again till 23rd and thereafter seen in all suitable habitat throughout (with sizeable fall on coast road between Sigri and Eressos on 26th). Numbers declining somewhat by mid-May as migrants give way to breeding birds. Probably commonest to west and north of the island, but quite regular also around the Kalloni - Achladeri area. Both adults and juveniles were seen regularly throughout the island in late July and early August '94 and '98. However, by autumn juveniles more difficult to come by, though 1 still seen by Kalloni West River on 19th September '94 and an adult seen at Eftalou on 27th. The latest records concern singles at Petra on 17th and 19th October '95.

Masked Shrike *Lanius nubicus*
Localized summer visitor from early or mid-April to late August or early September. Birds favour olive groves, small fields with tall hedges and trees, and generally more enclosed areas than other shrikes, where (because of their habit of perching quite low down) they are not always that prominent - see *The Birds of Greece*. First recorded 8th April '98 along the tracks between Kalloni Inland Lake and the Potamia Valley (where several pairs were regular from 18th) and 10th April '87 at Papiana and the Upper Potamia Valley. Although known to breed at Faneromeni, and at least 3 were regular in the Skala Eressos area in the second half of May '87, other breeding strongholds would appear to be the valley west of Vatoussa (where a pair was regularly seen on roadside wires from mid-late May '95), the areas to the west and east of Molivos (where a pair seen east of Eftalou mid-May '93, with singles north of Petra and south-west of Skoutaros at the same time, and a pair regularly just west of Anaxos in May '95 - with up to 6 nests found in nearby olive groves mid-month). In the Potamia Valley pairs have been found breeding most years since at least '91, with 2-3 pairs likely in May '95, and odd sightings around Parakila Marsh and East River (where 2 observed by the bridge on 21st May '91). Pairs also regular in the Achladeri area near the Kruper's site, and in the olive groves approaching Skala Polichnitos from that direction - with breeding pairs seen collecting nesting material between Lambou Mili and Pigi on 2nd May '98. Later in the year, an adult and juvenile were seen near Parakila on 31st July 94, with a pair and a juvenile up the Potamia Valley about the same time. Described as 'widespread' and often encountered in family groups throughout the north and west of the island in the first week of August '98, when 2 adults with 4 juveniles were showing well just outside Anaxos village. Last recorded dates between Skoutaros and Anaxos on 27th August '96, with 2 birds around Potamia reservoir on 25th August '97, 1 near East River next day and 1 round Kalloni Inland Lake 30th August. Three late birds were seen near Alikoudi Pool on 12th September '98 and a juvenile was seen at Faneromeni ford on the exceptional date of 23rd September that year.

Jay *Garrulus glandarius*
Widespread resident in orchards and woodland, especially oaks - common but secretive. Birds on the island are of the black-crowned form *G. g. atricapillus* (see *The Birds of Greece*).

Magpie *Pica pica*
Vagrant. Six records only - near Kalloni on 18th October '95 and around the Petra area on 27th June '97 and in late September and early October the same year. There is also a report from somewhere on the island in May '98 which for some reason the observers were not prepared to elaborate on! Finally one was seen near The Petrified Forest on 3rd October '98. The fact that 3 of these records are from the north coast (the shortest distance from Turkey) and also that 3 are in October (a likely time for vagrancy) ties in with this bird's current status. Slightly more puzzling is the fact that the June bird was described as a juvenile! There are also other odd unconfirmed reports of birds thought to be this species, but not checked out because the observer simply wasn't aware of its very scarce occurrence on the island!

Nutcracker *Nucifraga caryocatactes*
Vagrant. One record only (from a reliable source) of a bird seen well in mid-May '93 flying directly in front of the car on the road between Vafios and Argennos (coincidentally the prime Hawfinch site!). *The Birds of Greece* shows a small breeding nucleus in the north of the country, with a few scattered records further south (one in May). In the light of this, such a record gains a little more credence.

Chough *Pyrrhocorax pyrrhocorax*
Vagrant. Though confirmed as breeding on the nearby island of Chios in '71 and as resident on Crete (see *The Birds of Greece*), this species has true vagrant status on Lesvos, with just one record of a bird near Dafia on 8th June '96.

Jackdaw *Corvus monedula*
Localized resident,with small flocks often to be seen around Kalloni, Skala Eressos, Molivos, Petra, Gavathas, Apothikes and Sigri (where *c*60 were seen on 11th May '95 and *c*50 on 30th May '96), with breeding likely on small offshore islands in the latter two cases. In late May and early June '96 up to 60 were seen daily around Anaxos commuting to 'Rabbit Island' (where breeding seems likely). Elsewhere quite scarce, with biggest gathering *c*250 feeding around an irrigator at Faneromeni beach on 3rd October '94, and 140+ near Kalloni on 5th August '98.

Rook *Corvus frugilegus*
Scarce and irregular winter visitor. Two birds were seen at Faneromeni on 8th April '86. Then followed a 10 year gap before a wandering adult and immature were seen at both sets of salt pans and at Faneromeni once again between 22nd April and 11th May '96 (coincidentally the same date that one was seen flying east along Vatera beach). It would seem likely, therefore, that this sighting involved the same adult bird. Undoubtedly some are likely to have been overlooked at this time of year.

Hooded Crow *Corvus corone*
Widespread and abundant (but wary) resident throughout the island in virtually all habitats. Often seen drinking from areas like Kalloni East River or Chalandra River Skala Eressos, and also regular along the shoreline between Eftalou and Skala Sikimmia. Just to give some idea of numbers, a pre-roost gathering near Achladeri on 28th September '94 held close on 500 birds!

Raven *Corvus corax*
Localized resident in small numbers. Usually seen in ones and twos above Agiassos, between Filia and Andissa, the mountain approaches to Sigri, the cliffs east of Skala Eressos, the Potamia Valley, and area east and south of Molivos. Maximum numbers 4 at Argennos in late May '95, 4 near Skala Sikimmia in the first week of August '98, 4 at Molivos rubbish tip on 8th August that year, 4 at Vatoussa on 7th September '98, 6 over Faneromeni beach on 1st September '97, 8+ between Skoutaros and Filia on 5th August '96, 10 near Filia on 6th August '94, 4 there on 13th August '98, and 10+ over the rubbish tip east of Skalochori on 22nd October '96. It would seem that early autumn is a good time for producing the most sightings of this rather elusive species - presumably when family parties are most visible. A knowledge of local rubbish tips is also an advantage!

Starling *Sturnus vulgaris*
Winter visitor in good numbers from October to late March or early April. *The Birds of Greece* points out that the species is not as common in winter as one would expect, knowing its liking for olives, which are abundant on the island at this time. First recorded 12th October '94, when a flock of 4 was located near Kalloni East River, with another 6 at 'Derbyshire' the

same day. Odd records of lingering birds in spring, like the single seen between Kalloni East River and Salt Pans on 24th April '98 and around Skala Eressos from 14th-15th May '87. One was also reported sporadically from Kalloni Salt Pans between early and mid-May '95. Several thousand were roosting at Dipi Larssos Reedbed in January '98 and were regularly attracting the attentions of local Marsh Harrier, Peregrine, Sparrowhawk and Buzzard! Birds were seen feeding in local wet pastureland in reasonable numbers up to late March (when still 100+), with a few lingering into early April and 1 still present between Kalloni Salt Pans and East River on 24th April.

Rose-coloured Starling *Sturnus roseus*

Passage migrant from mid-May to June in varying numbers (usually in flocks of between 5-40 birds - see *The Birds of Greece*). Earliest records of a single behind Kalloni Salt Pans on the exceptional date of 4th May '98, with 2 there on 12th May '97 and the next just west of there on 13th May '93 and 20th-21st May '91. In May '87, a single adult at Skala Eressos on 16th was followed by a roosting flock on 18th, with *c*90 counted the next day, and an incredible 500 on 20th! Thereafter migrant flocks were seen daily until 27th. In May '92, a flock of 8 overflew the East River on 21st, and 50+ were seen in a tree by the Salt Pans on 28th. In May '94, small flocks were noted from 17th, with 12 together at East River the next day, 50 in the area on 22nd, 50 at Skala Eressos on 23rd and 100 at Eressos the same day, though with none seen after 25th. In spring '95, passage was observed from 19th May, with 7 birds near East River on 20th and 14 the next day. Much larger numbers were seen around Molivos on 20th, and a sizeable flock was watched feeding in a mulberry tree between Kalloni Salt Pans and 'Derbyshire' from 23rd-24th. Four birds seen over East River on 25th, and *c*15 were seen at Eftalou the next day, with the final group of 10 or so over East River on 27th. A flock of 35 was seen near Petra on 26th May '96 (with 20 over Kalloni the same day) and a further 6 reported at Anaxos on 31st May. As late as 3rd June that year 26 birds were counted feeding on rapidly ripening mulberries near East River ford. As the observer commented, when feeding in the midst of mulberry trees, birds can be surprisingly elusive, and are sometimes best located by sound! Enthusiasts could try rising at dawn and checking out the East River ford for the regular parties of bathing and drinking birds! More recently the large field at the back of Kalloni Salt pans has been favoured, and 2 summer plumage birds there on 13th May '97 had grown to 16 by 15th - obligingly perched along the perimeter fence when not feeding in the field! East River produced a flock of 20 on 17th and 25+ were at 'Derbyshire' on 20th May. Spring '98, by contrast, was a poor one for observing this species, with the only sizeable flocks consisting of 20+ near Vatera on 22nd May and a maximum of 60 between Kalloni East River and Salt Pans on 15th, with 2 late birds at the Kroussos River ford near Tavari on 27th May.

47)	**Great Reed Warbler -**
	Noisy songster in wetland areas

48)	**Olivaceous Warbler -**
	Commonest breeding warbler around wetlands

49) **Olive-tree Warbler -**
Localized and much sought after summer visitor

50) ♂ **Ruppell's Warbler-**
Star bird of the Molivos area!

51) ♂ **Collared Flycatcher -**
Early spring migrant

52) **Sombre Tit -**
Localized resident in more open areas

53) **Western Rock Nuthatch -** Common in rocky habitat

54) ♂ **Red-backed Shrike -**
Numerous in spring and autumn

55) **Lesser Grey Shrike-**
A few pairs breed around Kalloni Salt Pans

56) **Masked Shrike-** Regular breeder in olive groves

57) **Rose-coloured Starling-** Latest spring migrant

58) **Rock Sparrow-**
Listen for nasal call in western uplands

59) **Serin-**
More obvious in winter and early spring

60) **Hawfinch** - Winter visitor and likely
breeder in northern oak woods

61) ♂ **Ortolan Bunting** - Peaks in mid to late April

62) ♂ **Cretzschmar's Bunting** - Common in rocky
terrain

63) ♂ **Black-headed Bunting-**
Widespread from early May

64) **Kalloni Inland Lake**-A tranquil setting
65) **Kalloni Plain** - Fertile lowland area
66) **Kalloni East River** -
Productive both for migrants and breeding birds
67) **Kalloni Pool** - Excellent viewing potential
68) **Kalloni Salt Pans** -
Easy access for close wader views
69) **'Derbyshire' from above** - Semi-tidal wetland
70) **Kalloni West River saltings in winter flood** -
Levels can fluctuate dramatically

71) **Dipi Larssos** - Island's main reedbed
72) **Parakila Marsh** - Always worth a look!
73) **Parakila to Agra** - Gateway to the western uplands
74) **Ipsilou monastery** - Spectacular migration 'falls' likely
75) **Sweet Chestnut Woodland above Agiassos -** A unique habitat
76) **Molivos and castle viewed from coast road -** Picture postcard scenery
77) **North coast above Eftalou -** Closest point to Turkey

House Sparrow *Passer domesticus*
Widespread and abundant resident in towns and villages. Particularly large flocks seen around Skala Kalloni in September '94, and also around the tracks to Kalloni Inland Lake and surrounding fields and hedgerows - where at least 100-150 birds were regular in mid-April '98.

Spanish Sparrow *Passer hispaniolensis*
Common resident (tending to occur in more fertile areas than House Sparrow), but with a noticeable passage evident from early April to early May and late September to late October - eg 300 at Sigri on 12th April '87, up to 5000 at Skala Kalloni on 15th and 600 at Ancient Andissa on 17th, with up to 400 at Kalloni Salt Pans on 22nd - all heading north. Up to 2000 were also present at Faneromeni on 20th April '92. In spring '98 a gathering of 20+ birds along Kalloni East River on 12th April was followed by 70+ round Kalloni Inland Lake next day, 80+ at Faneromeni on 14th and 210+ there on 17th! Certainly flocks more noticeable (and audible!) from mid-April onwards, when nesting colonially in tamarisks around both Skala Eressos and Skala Kalloni beaches, where 30-40 not unusual. Also a thriving (and extremely noisy!) colony in the grounds of the nearby Malemi Hotel, and another pine-nesting colony at Arisvi. A large colony also found at Vatera in May '97, and further smaller colonies regularly to be found in the base of occupied storks' nests! (eg Papiana church). Birds often seen bathing and drinking at Kalloni East River and ford at Skala Eressos. Large post-breeding flocking is likely in autumn (especially from September to October), when some birds are less easy to identify out of breeding plumage - see comments at end of ringing data tables P134! In the first week of August '98 birds were described as 'frequent only at Kalloni' - apart from 2 males and 12 females/immatures at Skala Eressos on 5th. Otherwise several were seen with House Sparrows near Anaxos on 26th September that year, but a shortage of winter records suggests possible dispersals and short range movements at this time.

Tree Sparrow *Passer montanus*
Localized resident and accidental visitor (as on the neighbouring island of Chios - see *The Birds of Greece*). Outside the breeding season odd birds may appear amongst flocks of House Sparrow, finches or buntings; and most reports are from this period. In fact only 4 records exist, of a single bird at Skala Eressos on 28th October '92, a report of small parties between Molivos and Skala Sikimmia on 10th April '94 and near Anaxos (with a party of House Sparrows) on 11th August '96. There is also an unconfirmed record of a single bird in the Kalloni area on 8th May '96, but given the number of birders present in the area at this time it seems surprising that no further sightings have come to light.

Rock Sparrow *Petronia petronia*
Locally distributed resident in suitable rocky areas, particularly to the west of the island, where small breeding colonies occur between Agra and Messotopos, on the coastal route between Eressos and Sigri, on an almost tunnel-like steep-sided roadside rock-face on the road above Eressos leading to the Sigri junction, and on rocks just below Ipsilou Monastery, where a pair were feeding young in an old Rock Nuthatch nest on the monastery wall 27th May '98! Usually best seen in spring and prior to breeding, when distinctive 'nasal' call often gives away their presence on roadside rocks or posts. Eight were seen between Andissa and Eressos, and 12 between Andissa and Sigri on 8th May '95. They tend to form loose flocks outside the breeding season - though these can often be difficult to locate. A party of *c*20 birds seen between Sigri and Eressos on 26th September '94 was eclipsed by 40+ seen feeding on roadside rocks near the Sigri-Eressos road junction on 6th April '98. However, the most impressive gathering concerned no less than 200 birds seen at a construction site on a small hill near Skala Eressos on 26th September '94! A group of 37 was also seen on screes just north of Eressos on 5th August '98.

Chaffinch *Fringilla coelebs*
Widespread resident, especially in pinewoods, with numbers augmented by the arrival of winter visitors from mid to late October - see *The Birds of Greece*.

Brambling *Fringilla montifringilla*
Scarce winter visitor in variable numbers from late October to early March. Numbers, as throughout Greece, are governed by the success of the beech-mast crop - see *The Birds of Greece*.

Red-fronted Serin *Serinus pusillus*
Scarce winter visitor from October to March to suitable scrub-covered hillsides, especially with wild roses. Only records of a pair in just such habitat west of Andissa on the rather late date of 15th May '94, though 2 birds seen briefly at Perivoli monastery in late April '97 were thought likely to be this species. A juvenile was also seen well feeding with Serin above Agiassos on the Megalochori road 18th September '98.

Serin *Serinus serinus*
Resident in suitable pinewoods, particularly to the east of the island. Seen especially in pine trees around Mytilini and Molivos Castles, and regularly heard 'jangling' along the pine-covered banks of the Vouvaris River near Achladeri (where 20+ were recorded on 9th October '94), and also around the Kruper's Nuthatch site above Agiassos (where up to 25 were counted in May '95), the pine woods near Achladeri and the woodland between Keramia and Vassilika. A more unusual record of 2 in tall weeds between Papiana and the East River on 26th September '94, with a few reported from Skala Eressos in late October '92. Birds are generally more easily seen in winter and early spring, when they tend to flock more with other finches and feed at lower elevations, often on the ground. Good numbers were feeding with finches and buntings in a weedy area at the head of the Potamia Valley in January '98 and also on seeds alongside Kalloni East River in the same period. They were still doing so up to the end of March in both '97 and '98 - after which the flocks tended to disperse prior to breeding.

Greenfinch *Carduelis chloris*
Widespread resident, but not as common as Goldfinch, and found more often around stands of conifers.

Goldfinch *Carduelis carduelis*
Widespread and abundant resident in lowland areas. Regularly seen bathing and drinking around Kalloni East River and Chalandra River ford especially, and also feeding on early maturing Thistle heads from May onwards (especially along East River and around Kalloni Inland Lake and approaches).

Siskin *Carduelis spinus*
Irregular winter visitor from mid-October to early April. First recorded 18th October '96, when a small flock of circa 10 birds was noted in the Potamia Valley. A late record of a female at Perivoli Monastery on 10th April '97, where also seen in January '98.

Linnet *Carduelis cannabina*
Fairly common resident on open hillsides, but not numerous. Reasonably regular above Eressos, and seen drinking from puddles in Potamia Valley, above Agiassos etc. Can also be seen flocking to feed at lower elevations in winter - ie mid-October to mid-April.

Twite *Carduelis flavirostris*
Irregular winter visitor from October to March. An unusually late sighting of 2 birds of the Turkish race at Kalloni Salt Pans on 5th May '94 constitutes the only known record for the island.

Crossbill *Loxia curvirostra*
Irregular vagrant most likely between June and February. Apparently the particular species of pine that grow on Lesvos are not ideal for Crossbills, in that their cones can usually only be prised open in these months! Nonetheless, it is almost certain that with an irruptive species like the Crossbill (breeding as it does so close to the island) some 'invasions' must occur, and there is one intriguing record of a pair feeding a fledged youngster above Agiassos in the third week of April '97. Coincidentally the pines by the nearby sanatorium also hosted a party of between 4-8 birds on 1st August '98. Otherwise *The Birds of Greece* cites reports of possible breeding both on Lesvos and nearby Samos.

Scarlet Rosefinch *Carpodacus erythrinus*
Rare passage migrant from April to May and again in September. Only 4 records - of a singing (non-pink) male at Molivos on 22nd May '91, a juvenile ringed at Haramida on 1st September '96, a pair seen at Faneromeni ford on 10th May '97 and a singing male north of Petra four days later.

Bullfinch *Pyrrhula pyrrhula*
Scarce and localized winter visitor. With only 2 records (of singles in upland olive groves north of Kalloni on 17th April '84, and in the Potamia Valley on 27th March '86) this bird's status apparently borders on the side of vagrancy. However, as *The Birds of Greece* states, its secretive habits and preferred montane habitat may lead to many being overlooked, especially at this time of year.

Hawfinch *Coccothraustes coccothraustes*
Largely a winter visitor from October to April, more recently suspected of breeding. *The Birds of Greece* cites a record of 1 or 2 birds seen in June '82 (location not recorded), and also mentions their attraction to cherry trees in the breeding season. Otherwise most often seen in areas of oak woodland (eg a single bird seen in this habitat between Skoutaros and Skalochori on 10th May '95, with a pair there on 13th May '98). Also seen near Eressos on 8th May '96 and up to 3 very confiding birds (a female and 2 males) frequenting a puddle between Vafios and Sikimmia from mid to late May that year. They were observed both drinking and apparently collecting mud, and were at the same site in early April to at least early May '97 (when 3 possible first-summers were seen on 6th May), with 2 seen there again on 20th April and the first week of May '98 - with an earlier sighting of a pair betwen Petra and Molivos on 6th April. This spate of late sightings in both the Skalochori and Vafios areas would seem to substantiate evidence of long-suspected breeding. A more typical wintering record concerned a flock of 25+ feeding in plane trees at the head of the Potamia Valley on 29th March '97, which had reduced to about 12 by 31st, to 6 by 4th April and only 1 on 8th. However, 1 was seen alongside the road out of Parakila town on 22nd April and 2 were present again along the Potamia river on 28th. The only autumn sighting is of a single bird around Kalloni East River on 21st October '96.

Yellowhammer *Emberiza citrinella*
Irregular winter visitor in small numbers from November to March to lowland areas. Apart from singles seen at 'Derbyshire' (a male) on 15th March '97, and Faneromeni (a female) on 12th January '98, there is one very unusual record of 3 seen at point blank range in a puddle by

Potamia reservoir on the strange date of 30th August '97! Oddly, (considering the lack of records from other Aegean islands) this species is listed as being a common autumn migrant on nearby Chios between September and October (Spinthakis *et al* 1993). If this were true, the last record may not be quite so unusual - though *The Birds of Greece* casts some doubt on an autumn passage.

Cirl Bunting *Emberiza cirlus*
Widespread resident, common on hillsides with small trees and shrubs. Perhaps commonest to the north-east of the island, and between Kalloni and Molivos (where 8 singing males recorded on 8th May '95). A similar number were recorded between Molivos and Sikimmia and also between Kalloni and Andissa at this time, with 6 between Messotopos and Eressos. More skulking than other buntings, however, and not always easy to locate when not singing, though family parties regularly observed in Potamia Valley, East River and elsewhere by mid-May most years. More locally distributed in autumn, when (like most buntings) they gather in flocks. In late September '94 small flocks were encountered in upland areas to the west of the island, but also above Agiassos and around Kalloni Inland Lake, where birds regularly drank.

Rock Bunting *Emberiza cia*
Rare winter visitor from November to March (usually occurring just above the treeline), and scarce resident, with breeding most likely in the area of Mount Lepetimnos, but also above Agiassos. A pair was seen just north-east of Sigri on 17th September '86, with records from the Eressos area on 2nd and 4th June '88, and several seen around the same area in September '89. A bird was also seen between Molivos and Eftalou in August '91, with a more recent record from the Potamia Valley on 13th May '95. More interesting was a record of 2 adults and 3 juveniles above Agiassos on 11th September '96, with a male (and possibly a female also) nearby along the Agiassos-Plomari road on 10th May '97. Elsewhere one was also recorded on 27th April '98 beyond Faneromeni ford, below Ipsilou monastery on 3rd May '98 and inland from West River on 10th May. A pair were also seen well around 'Devil's Bridge' from 26th April to the month's end.

Cinereous Bunting *Emberiza cineracea*
Localized but not uncommon summer visitor from early April to early or mid-August to the sparsely-vegetated, boulder-strewn upland areas to the west of the island. In recent years, it has been discovered that the breeding population, thought originally to be mainly centred on the area around Eressos, actually extends east as far east as Parakila, and even the inland section of Kalloni East River. Birds have been recorded here in several recent years, and a male was singing close to the inland ford on 24th April '98 - whilst a singing male was also present for a while on the ridge at the back of Kalloni Inland Lake in the third week of April '97 (though successful breeding could not be proved), and a male was watched drinking from a stream in the Potamia Valley on 10th May that year. Moreover, in mid-May '95 at least one male was heard singing in the north of the island, just east of Stipsi (see P82). These additional breeding season records, however, are more likely to be due to an increase in observer coverage than an expansion of range. Peter de Knijff, for example, found up to 38 occupied territories between Andissa and Sigri in May '95 and as many as 45 between Parakila and Agra in May '96, but only 6 between Eressos and Sigri in the same period (see P83). Those feeling a little more lazy, however, now only need to go to the 'Devil's Bridge' Chapel west of Parakila in April or May - where birds recorded from 23rd April '97. Otherwise first records of a singing male below Ipsilou monastery on 6th April '98 and then not till 20th April '84 on a hilltop near Skalochori. Clearly the species can be easily overlooked in its breeding areas if not actually singing. Autumn records include up to 8 birds east of Eressos from 10th-13th August '89, and 6 above Eressos on 1st August '94 - with a male between Agra and Messotopos on

7th. Later in the month, 2 birds were still to be seen above Eressos on 23rd August, with several others nearby (mainly juveniles). On 24th an adult male was present with a juvenile, with another male and juvenile nearby and 2 further birds just outside the village. Two very washed-out birds seen by a water trough in a cultivated area near Eressos on 30th were almost certainly this species. Likely to be reported away from usual sites during this dispersal period (both north and south), when it has been recorded in the Loutra area. A female was flushed from a ditch just south of Petra on 7th May '94, but more interesting still was the discovery of 2 singing males on the Bogat headland just west of Nifida on 5th May '97 - though this is directly opposite Apothikes (where they are known to occur). In addition a party of 8 was seen for several days on the headland just east of Anaxos beach up to at least 24th August '96. Following a party of 1 male and 3-6 females/immatures near the quarry just north of Eressos in the first week of August '98, and up to 5 birds together just west of the Sigri-Eressos road junction on 17th August '97, a migrant was seen near West River road bridge on 22nd August, with 2 also seen along the coast near Vatera on 28th, and an extraordinary record of 8 together in a puddle by Potamia reservoir on 30th August that year! However, a calling female was opposite the Ruppell's site between Petra and Molivos on 7th September '97, 2 were seen at Faneromeni on 7th September '98, and a male was still present between Sigri and Eressos on 8th September '97 (the last recorded date).

Ortolan Bunting *Emberiza hortulana*
Fairly scarce passage migrant from early April to mid-May (peaking around mid-April) and again in September. A few pairs may breed in upland areas. Earliest record of males at Achladeri and Limonas monastery 16th April '98, a single at Parakila Marsh outlet on 17th April '97 and a pair near the Petrified Forest at Sigri on 21st April '84, with a male east of Eftalou on 17th May '93, east of Petra on 14th May '95 and another between Kalloni and Sigri on 29th May '93. Elsewhere counts of 6 on a stream-bed near Molivos 25th April '97, 13+ near Skala Polichnitos and an impressive 50 odd between Pedi and N. Kidonas on 21st April that year, with 3 females along Faneromeni beach road on 24th April '98 and at least 6 birds feeding in a recently mown hayfield near Skamioudi with pipits and wagtails next day. One was around Skala Kalloni on 9th August '94, and 2 were along East River on 5th August '98, but the best proof of breeding rests with the record of a female and 2 juveniles in the Potamia Valley on 4th (seen by several observers) and a bird near Anaxos on 11th August '96, with 2 juveniles seen between Petra and Molivos on 19th July '97 and an adult at Petra reservoir on 5th August the same year. A bird was also in fields by the Malemi Hotel Skala Kalloni in late July '94, when 3 or more were also seen near Sigri, where 1 was present on 3rd August '98. Also of interest was at least 2 males present at a culvert between 'Devil's Bridge' and Agra on 7th May '97. Late records of 1 at Molivos on 6th and 7th September '97, 1 at Faneromeni on 7th September '98, near water at Molivos castle on 10th September '97 and overflying Haramida Marsh on the same date in '95. There were still later gatherings of 6 at Kalloni Salt Pans on 11th September '98, 2 near Achladeri 2 days later and the last autumn record of a single from Potamia River Bridge on 18th September that year.

Cretzschmar's Bunting *Emberiza caesia*
Widespread summer visitor from late March or early April to late August or occasionally early September, favouring rocky hillsides with scattered vegetation. Commonest to the west and north-east of the island (where had already arrived in good numbers on the coastal maquis slope east of Eftalou by 8th April '94). First records, however, of a male at Tavari ford on 23rd March '97 and 2 at East River mouth on 26th March '86. Up to 60 singing males recorded between Parakila and Agra on 6th May '95, with at least 40 between Andissa and Sigri, and a similar number between Andissa and Eressos - whilst at least 10 pairs were present between Eftalou and Skala Sikimmia on 20th May '98. A bird located in the south of the island

(in orchards in Kato Stavros near Vatera) in early May '97 was somewhat outside its normal breeding range. Twenty + were still above Eressos on 1st August '94, with several birds at lower altitude by then (eg 4 on Kalloni East River 29th July, and 3 on 9th August). In the first week of August '98 this species was described as 'very numerous in arid scrub habitat and farmland fringes', where 34 were recorded drinking together around irrigators at Faneromeni, and no less than 46 were seen at the clifftop Ruppell's site north of Petra on 2nd. Numbers thinning out by the month's end, and only September records of an immature at Eressos on 4th September '94, a party of 6 between Anaxos and Ampelia up to at least 4th September '96, 15 at Kalloni Inland Lake on 5th September '98, 3 there on 7th September '97, with a male at Skala Eressos on 7th September '89, 12 at Faneromeni on 7th September '98, 1 at East River on 14th September that year, 2 still around the Skala Kalloni area 15th September '97 and the last record near Andissa on 22nd September '94.

Little Bunting *Emberiza pusilla*
Vagrant. Only record of a juvenile trapped and ringed at Haramida Marsh on 17th October '97.

Reed Bunting *Emberiza schoeniclus*
Common winter visitor from mid-October to mid or late March around suitably vegetated wetland areas. However, only recorded from Kalloni Pool, Parakila Marsh and Dipi Larssos in mid-January '98. Last recorded at the latter site on 25th March '98. Two late records - of singles at Sigri on 11th May '97 and near Kalloni the next day.

Black-headed Bunting *Emberiza melanocephala*
Abundant summer visitor from late April or early May to early or mid-August. Certainly the latest bunting to arrive, but soon widespread throughout the island in virtually all habitat. Males usually arrive first, and are easier to see, singing as they do from virtually every exposed perch! A single male first recorded at Kalloni Salt Pans on 23rd April '98 and on East River 24th April '95 (the same date in '98 that 4 males were seen together at Faneromeni ford), with a more general arrival from 29th April '95. A flock of 50-60 newly arrived birds at Kalloni Salt Pans on 25th April '98 was particularly impressive, as was 50+ around the roadside pool at Faneromeni on 2nd May that year. First female seen on 2nd May '95, and several migrant flocks then recorded (especially from the area between Sigri and Faneromeni, where 20-30 females were drinking from the roadside pool on 6th May). Another flock of 17 reported from Skala Eressos on 16th May '87. Between 50 and 60 singing males were recorded between Andissa and Sigri and Andissa and Eressos on 7th and 8th May '95! No birds seen after August, and maximum of 8 near Parakila on 30th July '94, with 1 at East River on 6th August and 1 south of Molivos on 10th - nearly all were juveniles. However, a fine male was seen with 2 juveniles in an orchard just south of Sigri village on 3rd August '98, and this was followed later in the day by no less than 77 birds gathered around trackside pools by the irrigated fields at Faneromeni! Though mostly juveniles, another male and several females were located, as were 3-4 females and a moulting male amongst a flock of up to 30 at the Chalandra River mouth Skala Eressos on 5th August. Two juveniles were also seen around Kalloni Pool next day. One juvenile was present at East River on 11th August '94. It was in company with a number of other juvenile buntings, but all had departed by the next day. However, 3 juveniles were seen together in the Potamia River Valley on 16th August '98 and the latest ever autumn record refers to a juvenile between Polichnitos and Achladeri on the exceptional date of 14th September '98.

Corn Bunting *Miliaria calandra*

Widespread resident, abundant in farmland, lowland areas with scattered trees and bushes and even open hillsides. Especially common between Kalloni East River and Salt Pans (where regularly singing from almost every bush and post in April and May, and flocks of *c*60 were seen on 11th August '97 - with 100+ not unusual by early October), and also around Potamia Valley, Skala Eressos etc, where flocking observed by early August, building up to 50 along the Chalandra River in late September '94. A large roost of 130+ was also discovered in a small reedbed at the end of the large flooded field behind Kalloni Salt Pans in the second half of September '98. Resident birds may be joined by further numbers in winter, and large flocks were noted near Skala Polichnitos in January '98.

COMMENTS ON SYSTEMATIC LIST

Although the preceding list is the most comprehensive it was possible to put together from the information currently available, its limitations should be recognized. The island has only really been open to tourism since 1985, and then only on a very localized basis. In consequence its birdlife remained a well kept secret for some time, and most records in the original *Birding In Lesbos* therefore related to a fairly short period (mainly from '91 to '95) and were obviously biased in favour of certain time periods when birders habitually visit the island (ie spring and autumn). Following my own extended early spring visits (and one in January), together with a steady stream of new records (many relating to the summer and autumn periods when records were previously sparse) and a growing interest in the island, the overall picture has now become much clearer. Moreover, several of these 'new' records actually go back as far as '84, when certain pioneering individuals were already visiting (like myself) in early spring. Special thanks are due here to John Bowers for sending me a fascinating selection of early spring records spanning eleven years.

Hopefully the resulting fourteen year period (up to autumn '98), together with certain earlier records and a wealth of other information gleaned from the excellent *The Birds of Greece* should make for a far more accurate picture regarding status and occurrence of species than could otherwise be hoped for. Though still lacking precise information on winter influxes and other hard weather movements, it has at least been possible to get an idea of typical wintering species - which really represent the final pieces of the jigsaw.

Of course, there is always going to be 'the one that got away', and one or two hoped for records (usually verbal) either never arrived or were inconclusive or unsubstantiated. Clearly it is not an easy task in sifting through so many to decide just which ones to accept and which ones to preclude, and obviously some have to be taken on trust. Thankfully, with increasing coverage of the island over the last few years, many are now duplicated by other observers or confirmed by my own experiences. One also has to remember that Lesvos (situated where it is on a migration route so close to the Turkish coast) has the potential to turn up almost anything - even, perhaps, the occasional species not recorded elsewhere in Greece. For this reason it may sometimes be necessary to keep an open mind. Ultimately, however, by including or not including particular records I have to accept a certain responsibility for any errors. I am especially obliged to all those who were kind enough to send me their notes and records, and a full list of contributors appears at the end of this book. Please remember that more unusual records (or those relating to rare breeding birds) can be sent direct to - **The Hellenic Ornithological Society, 53 E. Benaki St, 10681, Athens, GREECE.**

Regrettably lack of space precludes mentioning all those who were good enough to record their sightings in the log-books I placed in several of the hotels at Skala Kalloni in spring '98. I would also like to thank Dawn Balmer for proof reading, constructive criticism and moral support! I only wish it were possible to elaborate on the wealth of other attractions which Lesvos has to offer - plants and dragonflies for example. What I can do, however is to list, by way of conclusion, some of the mammals, reptiies, amphibians and butterflies one is most likely to encounter on this magical island (leaving aside status and distribution). I am indebted to Dr Makis Axiotis (author of *The Fauna of Lesbos* - 1995) for help with the reptile and amphibian list and to John Grearson for his input on the butterfly section.

MAMMALS OF LESVOS

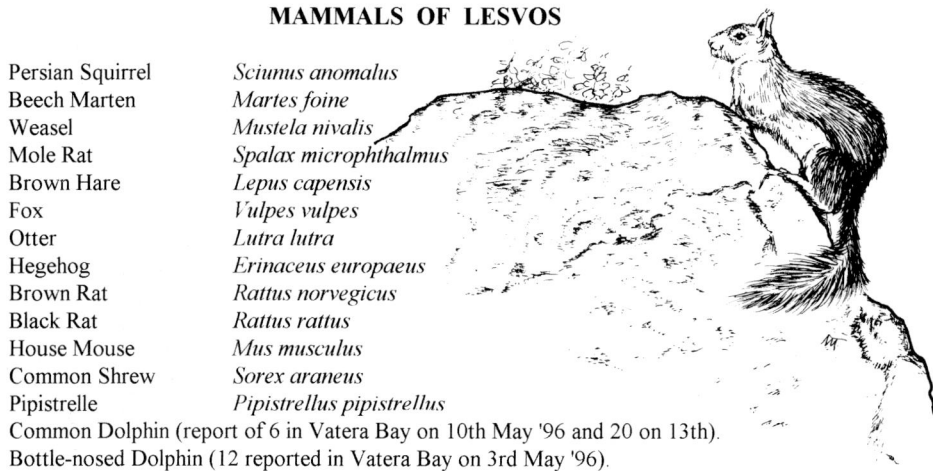

Persian Squirrel	*Sciunus anomalus*
Beech Marten	*Martes foine*
Weasel	*Mustela nivalis*
Mole Rat	*Spalax microphthalmus*
Brown Hare	*Lepus capensis*
Fox	*Vulpes vulpes*
Otter	*Lutra lutra*
Hegehog	*Erinaceus europaeus*
Brown Rat	*Rattus norvegicus*
Black Rat	*Rattus rattus*
House Mouse	*Mus musculus*
Common Shrew	*Sorex araneus*
Pipistrelle	*Pipistrellus pipistrellus*

Common Dolphin (report of 6 in Vatera Bay on 10th May '96 and 20 on 13th).
Bottle-nosed Dolphin (12 reported in Vatera Bay on 3rd May '96).

In addition, there is a fair selection of bats, mice and shrews - one of which, *Crocidura lasia*, is an Asian species whose distribution throughout Greek territory is confined solely to Lesvos. There is also a small population of the Rabbit *Oryctolagus cuniculus* and of the Fallow Deer *Dama dama* from recent introduction schemes - the latter centred on the Agiassos area.

I have seen a good number of these mammals myself - excluding dolphins that is. Certainly **Persian Squirrel** is widespread in olive groves, and especially in the Sweet Chestnut Woodland above Agiassos. **Beech Marten** is also common, and occasionally seen during the day -though sadly more often as a road casualty. I have regularly seen them in the Kalloni area at night (and several times close to the hotels in Skala Kalloni in winter and early spring). **Weasel**, too. is not an unfamiliar sight, and I have occasionally recorded family parties in drystone walls amongst the olive groves. **Mole Rat** is quite unmistakeable if seen - I have only seen one once in the west of the island attempting to cross the road! Normally, of course, they remain underground. **Brown Hare** is very scarce (mainly I suspect because of shooting pressure). I have only ever recorded one sighting - surprisingly in an olive grove to the south of the island. **Foxes** are not uncommon, though again regularly shot and sometimes hung from trees! I have seen several crossing the road at night. The **Otter** is clearly much rarer, though a road casualty was observed at Dipi Larssos during the '96-7 winter and one was also seen chasing birds at Faneromeni ford one evening in mid-May '98! **Hedgehogs** are certainly widespread, though again often end up as road casualties. I cannot comment on the small rodents, except to mention the **Shrew** colonies at sites like the mouth of Kalloni West River and the back of the two salt pans, where many holes are visible and the occupants quite often seen - and heard (rather like a child's squeaky toy!). Although I have seen a few **Rabbits** near Molivos (obviously escapes from captivity) I have never seen **Fallow Deer** - though I have reports of them near the picnic site on the main Polichnitos to Agiassos road.

COMMONEST REPTILES AND AMPHIBIANS

Spur-thighed Tortoise	*Testudo graeca*
Stripe-necked Terrapin	*Mauremys caspica*
European Pond Terrapin	*Emys orbicularis*
Agama Lizard	*Agama stellio*
Balkan Green Lizard	*Lacerta trilineata*
Snake-eyed Lizard	*Ophisops elegans*
Balkan Wall Lizard	*Podarcis taurica*
European Glass Lizard	*Ophisaurus apodus*
Turkish Gheko	*Hemidactylus turcicus*
Large Whip Snake	*Coluber jugularis*
Balkan Whip Snake	*Coluber gemonensis*
Dahl's Whip Snake	*Coluber najadum dahlii*
Ottoman Viper	*Vipera xanthina*
Dice Snake	*Natrix tessellata*
Leopard Snake	*Elaphe situla*
Four-lined Snake	*Elaphe quatorlineata*
Cat Snake	*Telescopus fallax*
Sand Boa	*Eryx jaculus turcicus*
Worm Snake	*Typhlops vernicularis*
Montpellier Snake	*Malpolon monspessulanus*
Marsh Frog	*Rana ridibunda*
Common Tree Frog	*Hyla arborea*
Green Toad	*Bufo viridis*
Eastern Spadefoot Toad	*Pelobates syriacus*

(Largely confined to temporary ponds to the west of the island).
For further information on the above I would recommend *A Field Guide to the Reptiles and Amphibians of Britain and Europe* (Arnold, Burton and Ovenden - ISBN 0 00 219318 3).

COMMONEST BUTTERFLIES

Swallowtail	*Papilio machaon*
Scarce Swallowtail	*Iphiclides podalirius*
Eastern Festoon	*Zerynthia cerisyi*
False Apollo	*Archon appollinus*
Large White	*Pieris brassicae*
Small White	*Pieris rapae*
Southern Small White	*Artogeia mannii*
Bath White	*Pontia daplidice*
Small Bath White	*Pontia chloridice*
Eastern Dappled White	*Euchloe ausonia*
Orange-tip	*Anthocharis cardamines*
Clouded Yellow	*Colias croceus*
Cleopatra	*Gonepteryx cleopatra*
Holly Blue	*Celastrina argiolus*
Nettle-tree Butterfly	*Libythea celtis*
Plain Tiger	*Danaus chrysippus*
Southern White Admiral	*Limenitis reducta*
Peacock Butterfly	*Inachis io*
Red Admiral	*Vanessa atalanta*
Painted Lady	*Cynthia cardui*

Southern Comma	*Polygonum egea*
Silver-washed Fritillary	*Argynnis paphia*
Knapweed Fritillary	*Melitaea phoebe*
Spotted Fritillary	*Melitaea didyma*
Lesser Spotted Fritillary	*Melitaea trivia*
Marbled White	*Melanargia galathea*
Balkan Marbled White	*Melanargia larissa*
Southern Grayling	*Hipparchia aristaeus*
Eastern Rock Grayling	*Hipparchia alcyone syriaca*
Meadow Brown	*Maniola jurtina*
Small Heath	*Coenonympha pamphilus*
Small Copper	*Lycaena phlaeas*
Scarce Copper	*Heodes virgauraea*
Grecian Copper	*Hoedes ottomanus*
Lesser Fiery Copper	*Lycaena thersamon*
Brown Argus	*Aricia agestis*
Small Skipper	*Thymelicus sylvestris*
Mediterranean Skipper	*Gegenes nostrodamus*

All the above species and their ranges are covered in the Collins Field Guide *The Butterflies of Britain and Europe* (Tom Tolman and Richard Lewington - 1997). For further information on the many and varied plant species try specialist books such as *Flowers of Greece and the Balkans* (Oleg Polunin 1997), *Flowers of the Mediterranean* (Oleg Polunin and Anthony Huxley - ISBN 0 70112284 6) and *Field Guide to Orchids of Britain and Europe* (Buttler - ISBN 1 85223 591 8). *Flowers of Greece and the Aegean* (Huxley and Taylor - ISBN 9 7011 228 5) may now be out of print. There is also a useful book by Lance Chiltern (Marengo Publications) called *Lesvos Plant List* (Phone 01485 532710 to order).

ACKNOWLEDGEMENTS

I am indebted to the following for their records, and I apologise to any whose names I may have omitted.

Dr Filios Akriotis
David Allison
Jonathan Anglios
Colin Antrobus
Kevin Armitage
Terry and Mandy Atkinson
John Austin
Dawn Balmer (BTO) and Dr Jeremy Wilson
Peter and Margaret Bancroft
Peter and Anne Barratt
Bill Baston
Michael D Bell
L Benson
Mr and Mrs A Blamire
Robert Boreham
John, Anne and Simon Bowers and AC Spence
J Bowler
Neil Bowman
Dennis K Buisson
Bob Bullock
P Cadman
Chris R Christie
JD and AD Clarke
K and M Claydon
Ranon Baucells Colomer
Mike Crewe (*Limosa* holidays)
Simon Davidson
Alan and Jane Dean
Grant Demar

Paul Denning
R Dokter and PL Franeker
Bob Duckhouse
Karl Dutton *et al*
ECO Tourist Services
Stephen Edwards
John Fairfax-Ross
Peter Feltham
Les and Margaret Finch
John Fife
Joan Fine
Stewart Foster (Lincoln RSPB)
K Garrett
Simon Gillings and Su Gough (BTO)
Tony Goddard
Chris Gooddie
Mike and Olga Gould
John and Josie Grearson
Peter Greenstreet
Robert Grimmond
CL Grimshaw
Russell Haywood
Michael Hemingway
Brian Hewitt
Brian Hicks
Brian Hillcoat
Mike S Hodgson
Clive Hope, Chris Fox and John Newnham
Tom Howard-Jones

The late David Jackson
Colin Jakes and Linda Hayward
Wim Jautze
John Jennings
Eddie and Nica Jones
Graham Jones
Juha Juutinen
Andy Kane
Nicky Kardakari
Drs Peter de Knijff and Mariette Hoffer
CG Knox
Phil Langston
Mathew, Peter and Margaret Latham
John and Mark Lewis
Derek Lister
Eric J Locker
Anders Magnusson
Derek Marsh
Nigel A May
Doug and Carole Mayes
Tony and Sausa Mead
John and Brenda Mighell
Gordon Mills
John Lovat Mole
Paul and Sue Murfitt
Tony Murphy and Peter Wolstenholme (*Birdguides*)
JS Nadin
Mark Newsome
Russell G Nisbet
Geoff Norman and Nicola Airey
Vivien and Dave O'Connor
Peggy Page
Clairie Papazogloie
John Parish (Croydon RSPB)
Andy Pay
Nigel Peace
Alan and Lou Petty
Granville Pictor

Peter Pinnock
JW Piper
Alastair Rae and Anne Feltham
Nick Ransdale
Steve Riley
Ian Roberts
Lieven de Schamphelaere
Mick Shepherd
John Silcock
R Simpson
JR Smith
RS Smith
Ian Stewart
Mike and Pat Strickland
Ray Sturgess and Pearl Edgeworth
Hohn Sweeney
Graham Todd and Ray Sargeant
Ralph and Brenda Todd (*A&K Travel*)
Keith Temple
WH Truckle
George Turnbull
D Waldridge
FJ Walker
RV and GV Walker
Andy Wallis
David Walsh (*Gullivers Travels*)
J Ward
Rod Ward
Prof WE Waters
Heather and Jonathan White
Steve White
Raymond Whittam
Mike and Margaret Wilkes
Mick Wilson
Keith Wimbush
David Wright
Graeme Wright
John Wright

I am very grateful to Dawn Balmer for kindly compiling and making available ringing data from her four trips between September '94 -'98 - it is reproduced on P240. Peter de Knijff was also good enough to furnish me with updated information on breeding Cinereous Bunting (with the result that the '95, '96 and '98 seasons are now covered). This data appears on P83. Thanks, too, to both Dennis Buisson and Major Gilbert for additional proof reading, and to my mother for her unstinting support throughout! Further thanks are due to my friend George of Hotel Malemi Skala Kalloni for his visionary outlook, hospitality and for making everyone so welcome - whilst his wife Effy's friendliness, excellent cooking and packed lunches are legendary! Just ask anyone who stayed there in any of the recent early spring trips!

I would also like to thank Ernest Leahy for his two evocative colour paintings reproduced on the inside front cover, and a further two reproduced in black and white in the text. He has a good selection of similar spectacles captured on his visits, and often exhibits at both *The Wildlife Photofair* at Tamworth and *The British Birdwatching Fair* at Rutland. He can be contacted at :- 32 Ben Austins, Redbourn, Herts AL3 7DR - Phone 01582 793144. My thanks also to Steve Cale for his fine black and white bird illustrations. (He can be reached for commissions at :- Bramble Cottage, Westwood Lane, Gt. Ryburgh, Fakenham, Norfolk NR21 7AP - Phone 01328 829589). I am indebted to my neighbours, Kelvin and Mary Thatcher, for additional sketches capturing the essence of the island and for completing the maps to such a high standard against all the odds! Barbara Martin also helped me with some tricky translation.

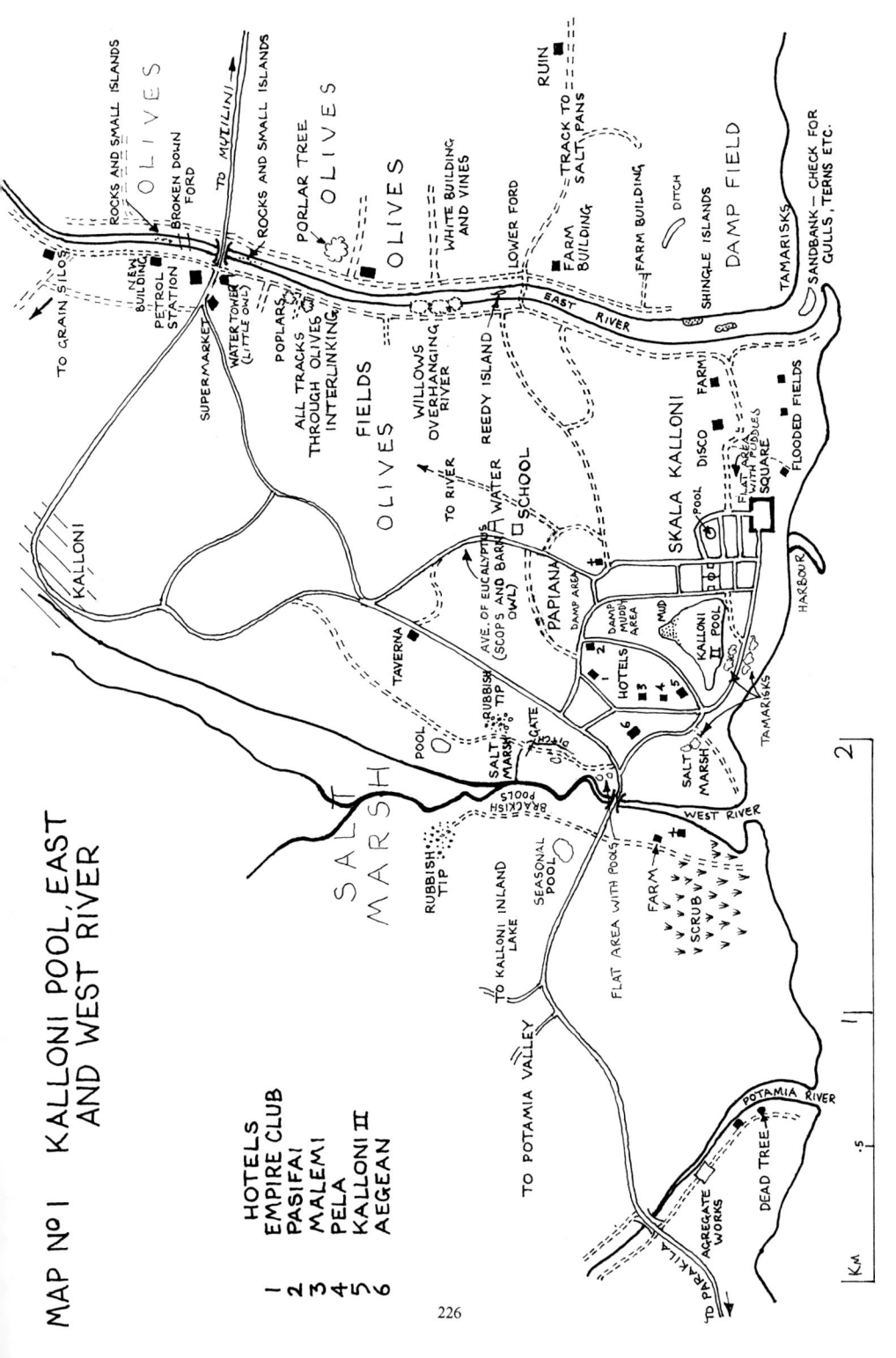

MAP Nº I KALLONI POOL, EAST AND WEST RIVER

HOTELS
EMPIRE CLUB
1 PASIFAI
2 MALEMI
3 PELA
4 KALLONI II
5 AEGEAN
6

226

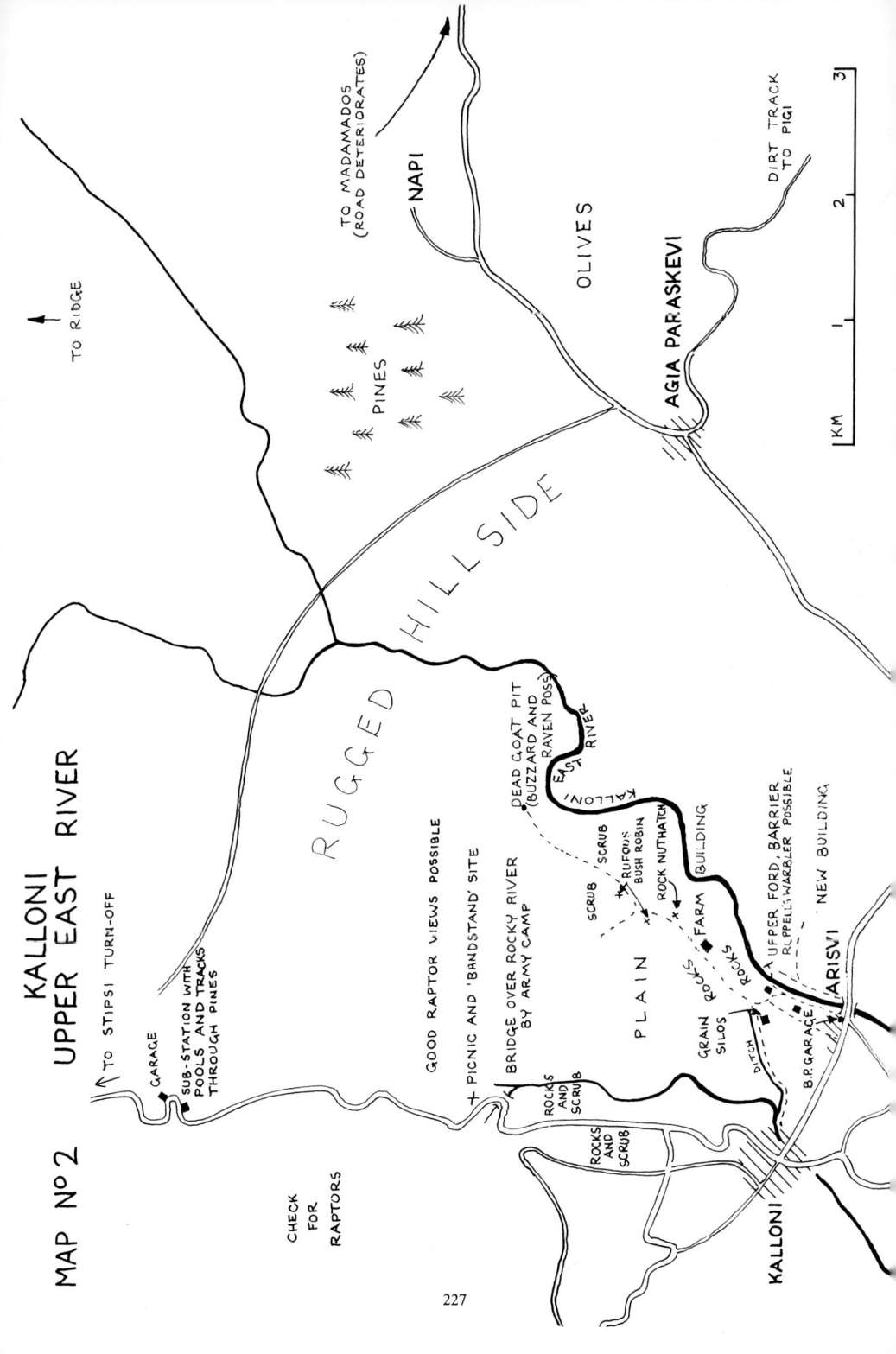

KALLONI
UPPER EAST RIVER

MAP Nº 2

TO RIDGE

TO STIPSI TURN-OFF

GARAGE

SUB-STATION WITH POOLS AND TRACKS THROUGH PINES

CHECK FOR RAPTORS

GOOD RAPTOR VIEWS POSSIBLE

PICNIC AND 'BANDSTAND' SITE

BRIDGE OVER ROCKY RIVER BY ARMY CAMP

ROCKS AND SCRUB

ROCKS AND SCRUB

PLAIN

GRAIN SILOS

ROCKS

ROCKS

DITCH

B.P. GARAGE

NEW BUILDING

KALLONI

ARISVI

FARM BUILDING

ROCK NUTHATCH

RUFOUS BUSH ROBIN

SCRUB

SCRUB

DEAD GOAT PIT (BUZZARD AND RAVEN POSS)

EAST RIVER

KALLONI

UPPER FORD, BARRIER RÜPPELL'S WARBLER POSSIBLE

RUGGED HILLSIDE

PINES

OLIVES

AGIA PARASKEVI

NAPI

TO MADAMADOS (ROAD DETERIORATES)

DIRT TRACK TO PIGI

KM   1   2   3

227

MAP Nº3 POTAMIA VALLEY AND INLAND LAKE

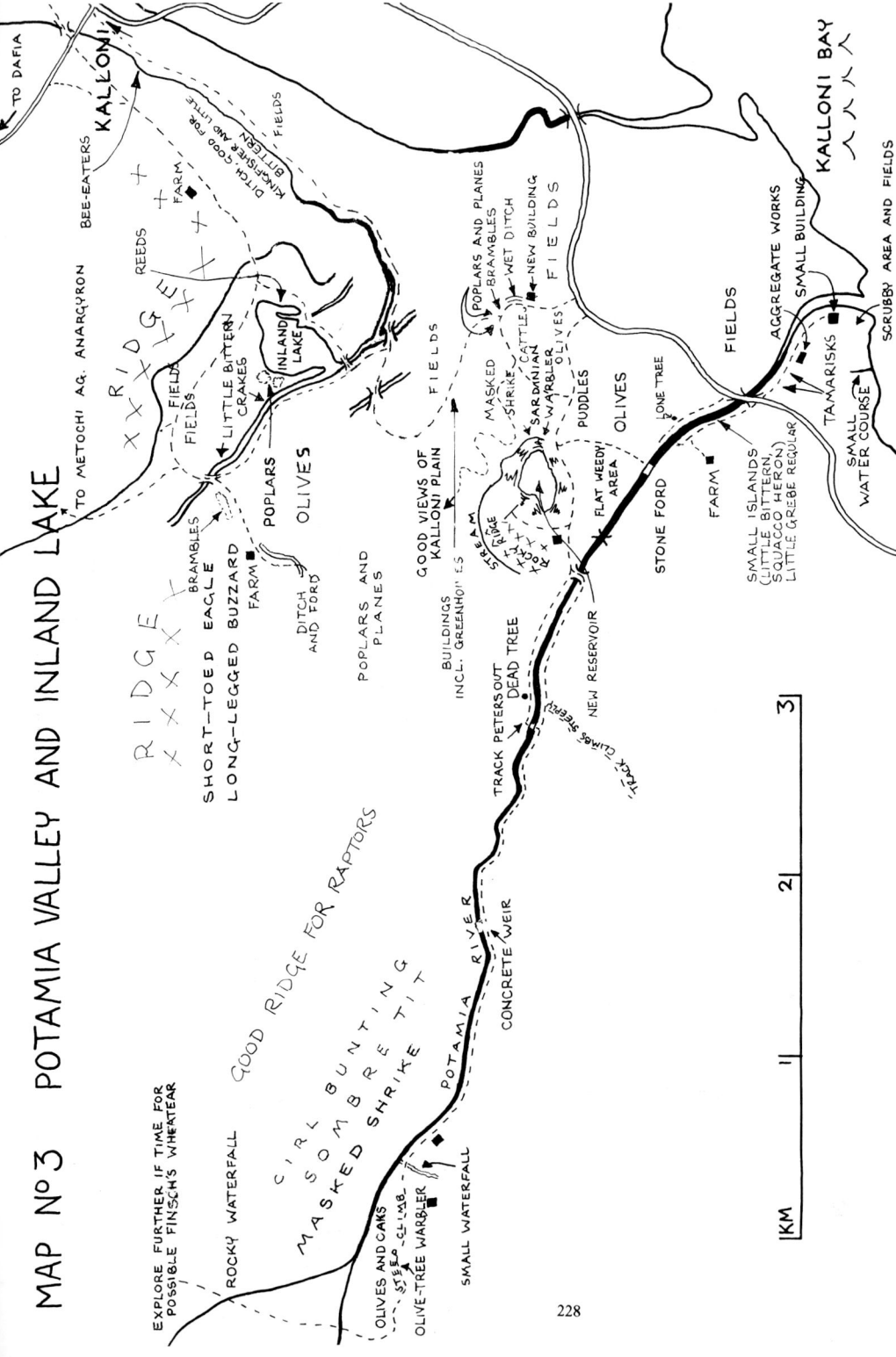

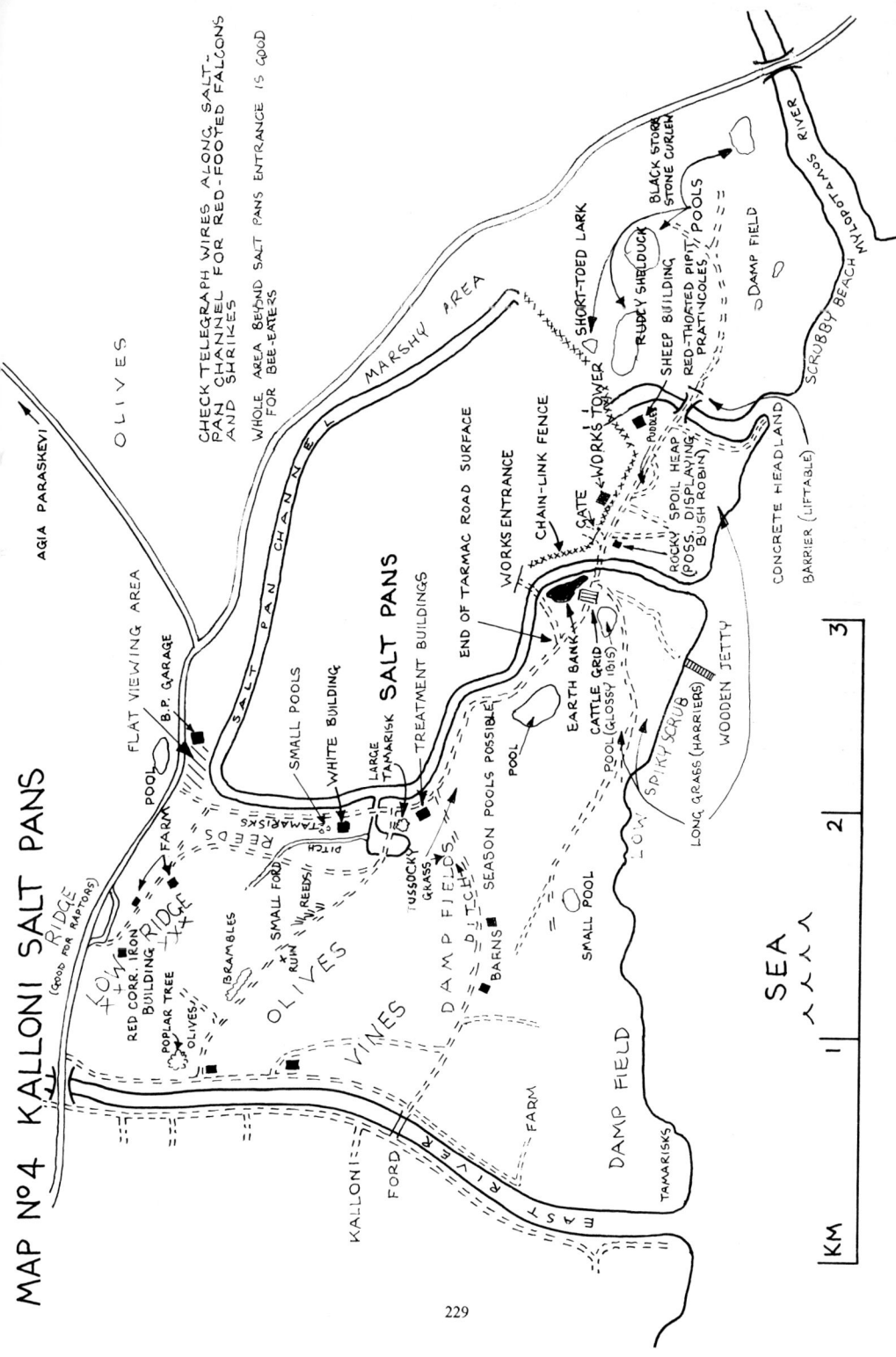

MAP Nº4 KALLONI SALT PANS

SEA

KM 1 2 3

229

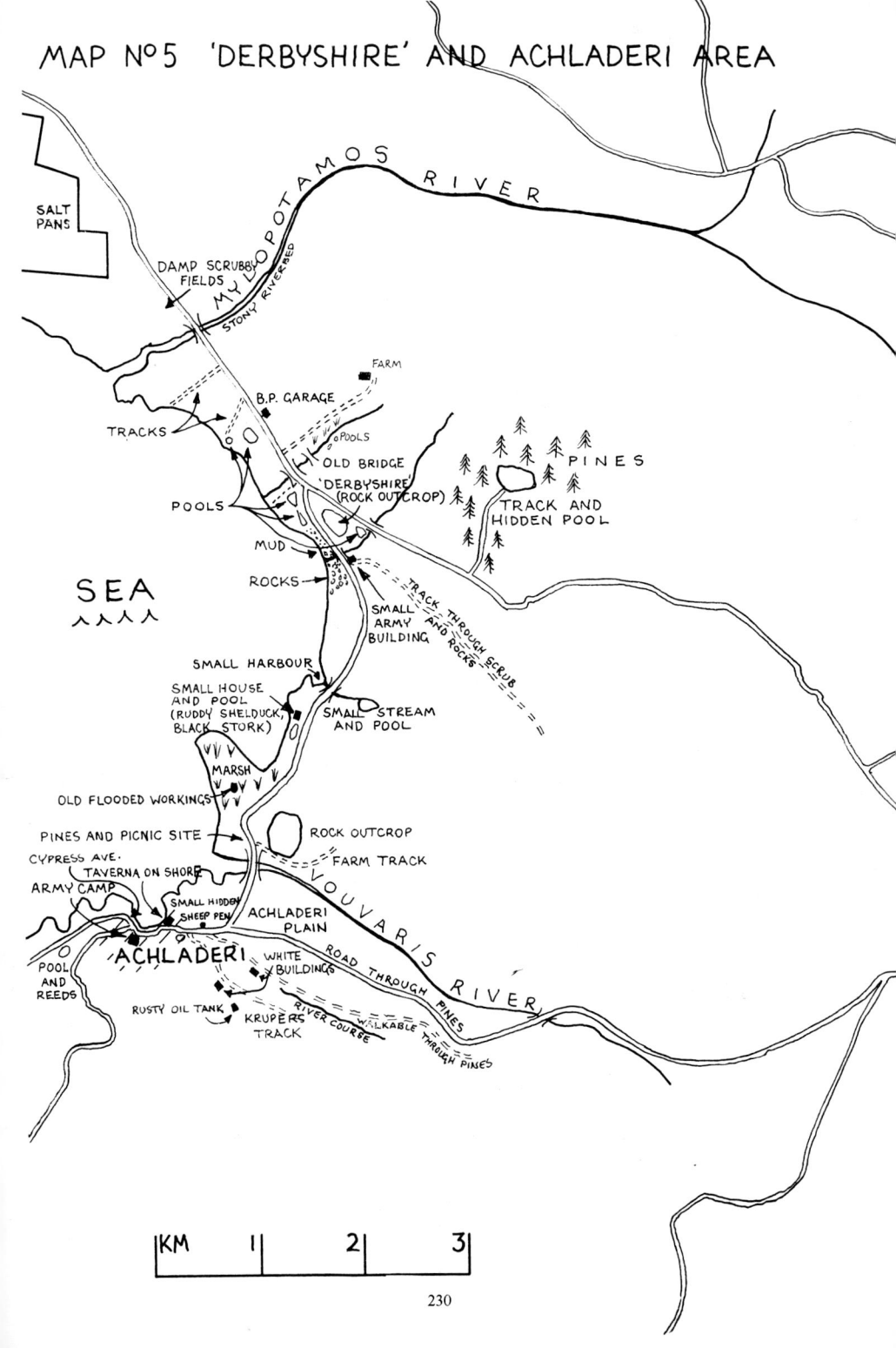

MAP Nº5 'DERBYSHIRE' AND ACHLADERI AREA

SALT PANS

MYLOPOTAMOS RIVER

DAMP SCRUBBY FIELDS

STONY RIVERBED

FARM

B.P. GARAGE

TRACKS

POOLS

OLD BRIDGE

'DERBYSHIRE' (ROCK OUTCROP)

PINES

TRACK AND HIDDEN POOL

POOLS

MUD

ROCKS

SEA

TRACK THROUGH SCRUB AND ROCKS

SMALL ARMY BUILDING

SMALL HARBOUR

SMALL HOUSE AND POOL (RUDDY SHELDUCK, BLACK STORK)

SMALL STREAM AND POOL

MARSH

OLD FLOODED WORKINGS

PINES AND PICNIC SITE

ROCK OUTCROP

CYPRESS AVE.

FARM TRACK

TAVERNA ON SHORE

ARMY CAMP

SMALL HIDDEN SHEEP PEN

ACHLADERI PLAIN

VOUVARIS RIVER

POOL AND REEDS

ACHLADERI

WHITE BUILDINGS

ROAD THROUGH PINES

RUSTY OIL TANK

KRUPER'S TRACK

RIVER COURSE

WALKABLE THROUGH PINES

KM   1   2   3

230

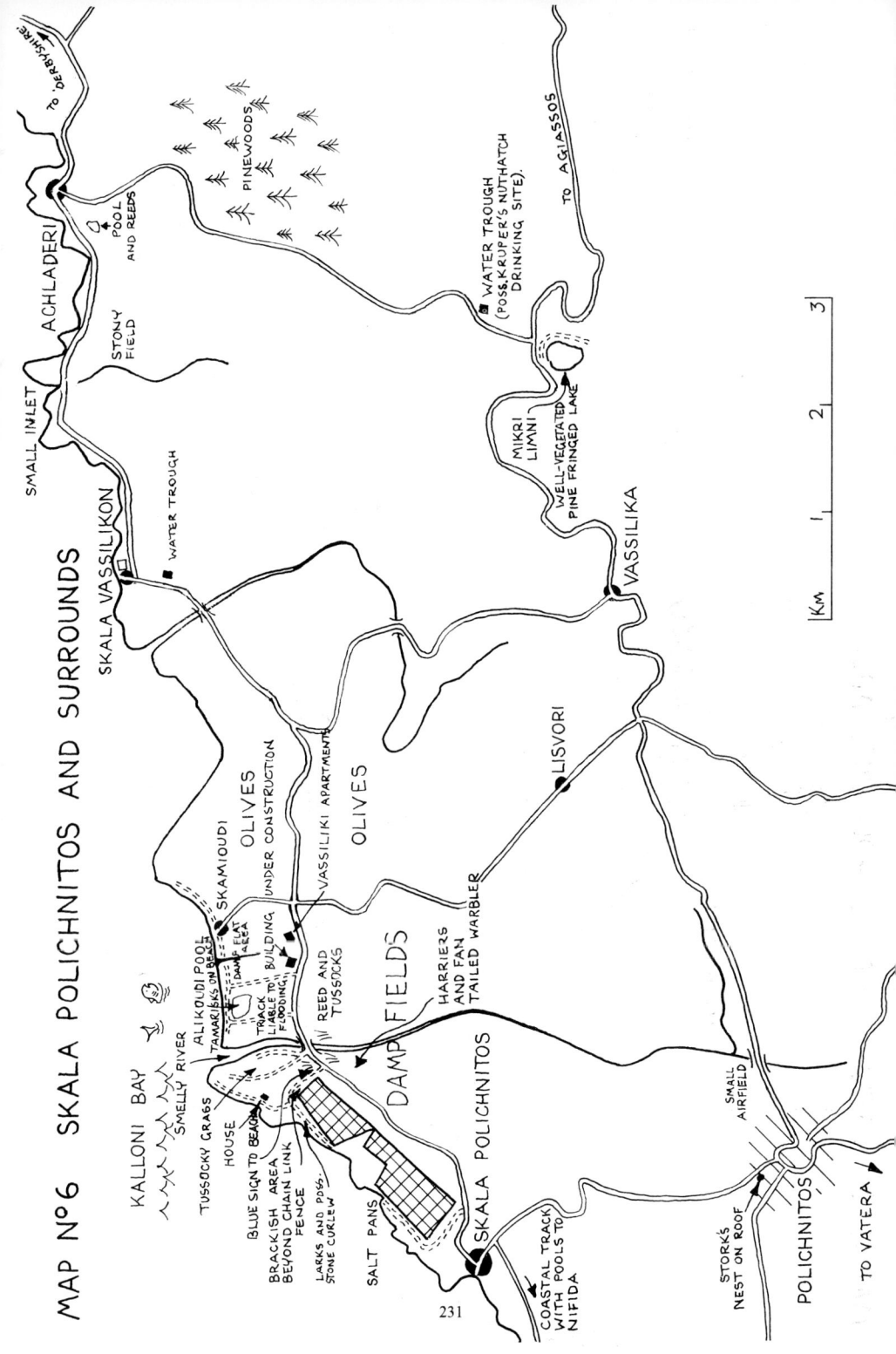

MAP Nº6 SKALA POLICHNITOS AND SURROUNDS

TO DERBYSHIRE

TO AGIASSOS

PINEWOODS

ACHLADERI

SMALL INLET

POOL AND REEDS

STONY FIELD

WATER TROUGH (POSS. KRUPER'S NUTHATCH DRINKING SITE).

MIKRI LIMNI

WELL-VEGETATED PINE FRINGED LAKE

VASSILIKA

Km   1   2   3

SKALA VASSILIKON

WATER TROUGH

LISVORI

OLIVES

OLIVES

VASSILIKI APARTMENTS

SKAMIOUDI

UNDER CONSTRUCTION

DAMP FLAT AREA

BUILDING

TRACK LIABLE TO FLOODING

REED AND TUSSOCKS

HARRIERS AND FAN TAILED WARBLER

DAMP FIELDS

KALLONI BAY

SMELLY RIVER

ALIKOUDI POOL TAMARISKS ON BEACH

TUSSOCKY GRASS

HOUSE

BLUE SIGN TO BEACH

BRACKISH AREA BEYOND CHAIN LINK FENCE

LARKS AND POSS. STONE CURLEW

SALT PANS

SKALA POLICHNITOS

COASTAL TRACK WITH POOLS TO NIFIDA

SMALL AIRFIELD

STORK'S NEST ON ROOF

POLICHNITOS

TO VATERA

231

MAP Nº 7 VATERA AND SURROUNDING AREA

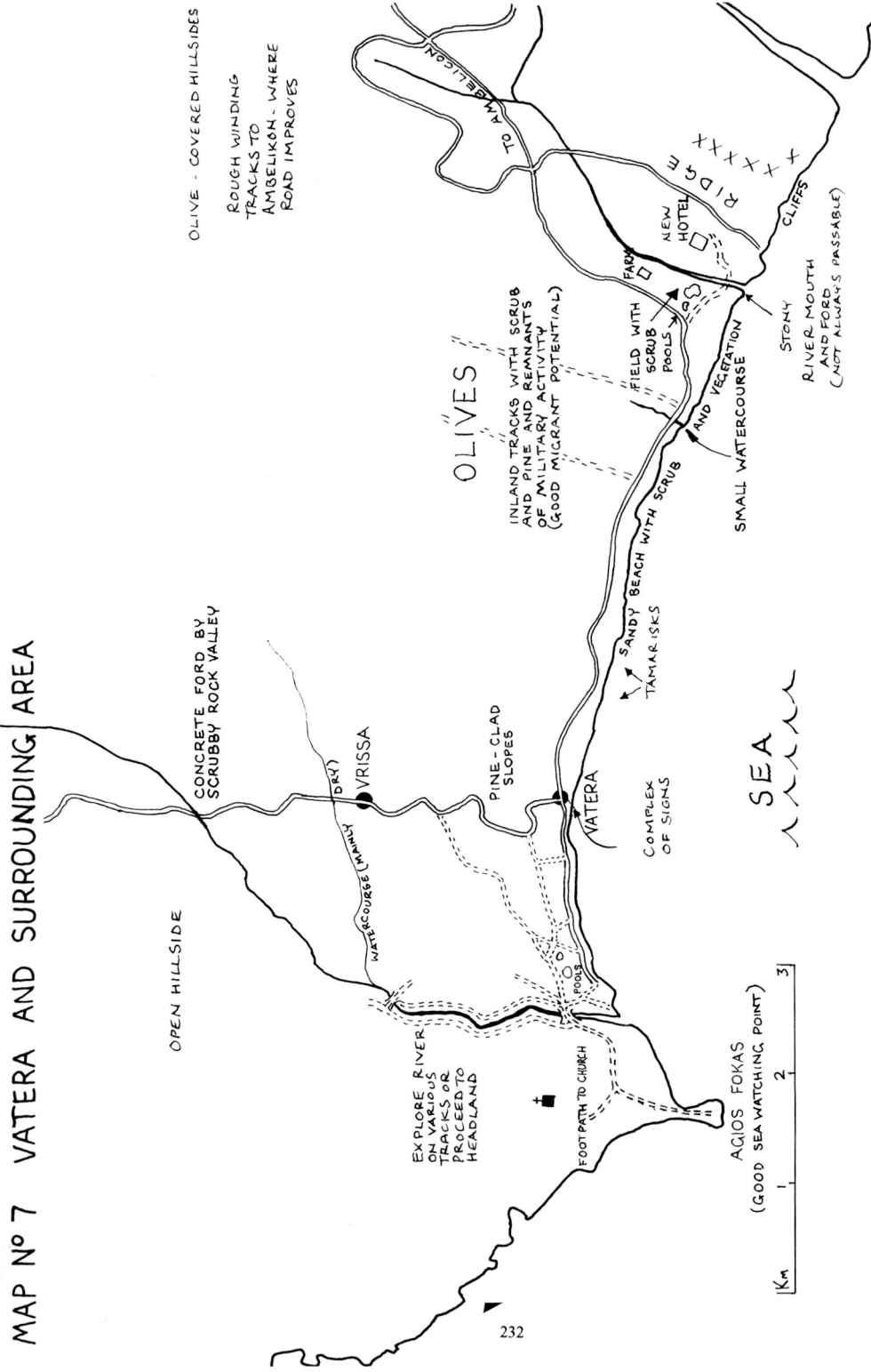

OLIVE - COVERED HILLSIDES

ROUGH WINDING TRACKS TO AMBELIKON - WHERE ROAD IMPROVES

TO AMBELIKON

RIDGE
×××××
NEW HOTEL
FARM
CLIFFS

FIELD WITH SCRUB POOLS

OLIVES!

INLAND TRACKS WITH SCRUB AND PINE AND REMNANTS OF MILITARY ACTIVITY
(GOOD MIGRANT POTENTIAL)

STONY CLIFFS

RIVER MOUTH AND FORD (NOT ALWAYS PASSABLE)

SMALL WATERCOURSE

AND VEGETATION

SANDY BEACH WITH SCRUB

TAMARISKS

CONCRETE FORD BY SCRUBBY ROCK VALLEY

VRISSA

WATERCOURSE (MAINLY DRY)

PINE - CLAD SLOPES

VATERA

COMPLEX OF SIGNS

SEA

OPEN HILLSIDE

EXPLORE RIVER ON VARIOUS TRACKS OR PROCEED TO HEADLAND

POOLS

FOOT PATH TO CHURCH

AGIOS FOKAS
(GOOD SEA WATCHING POINT)

Km   1   2   3

232

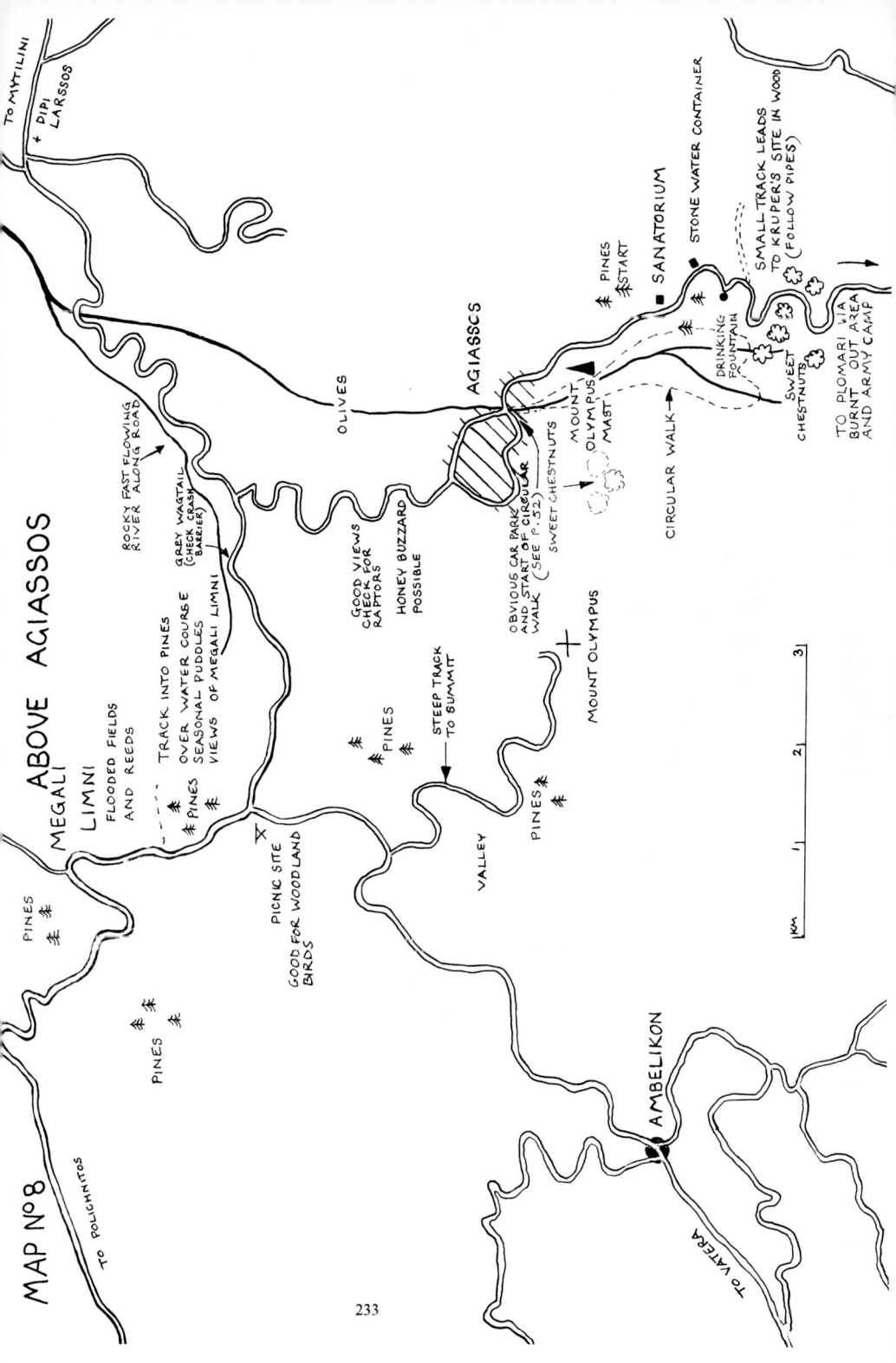

ABOVE AGIASSOS

MAP N°8

TO MYTTILINI
+ DIPI LARSSOS

MEGALI LIMNI

PINES

TO POLICHNITOS

PINES

PINES

FLOODED FIELDS AND REEDS

PICNIC SITE
GOOD FOR WOODLAND BIRDS

TRACK INTO PINES

OVER WATER COURSE
SEASONAL PUDDLES
VIEWS OF MEGALI LIMNI

ROCKY FAST FLOWING RIVER ALONG ROAD

GREY WAGTAIL
(CHECK CRASH BARRIER)

OLIVES

GOOD VIEWS
CHECK FOR RAPTORS

HONEY BUZZARD POSSIBLE

STEEP TRACK TO SUMMIT

PINES

VALLEY

PINES

MOUNT OLYMPUS

AGIASSOS

OBVIOUS CAR PARK AND START OF CIRCULAR WALK
(SEE P.52)

SWEET CHESTNUTS

MOUNT OLYMPUS MAST

CIRCULAR WALK

PINES START

SANATORIUM

STONE WATER CONTAINER

SMALL TRACK LEADS TO KRUPER'S SITE IN WOOD
(FOLLOW PIPES)

DRINKING FOUNTAIN

SWEET CHESTNUTS

TO PLOMARI VIA BURNT OUT AREA AND ARMY CAMP

AMBELIKON

TO VATERA

KM 1 2 3

233

MAP Nº9 DIPI LARSSOS REEDBED AND SURROUNDS

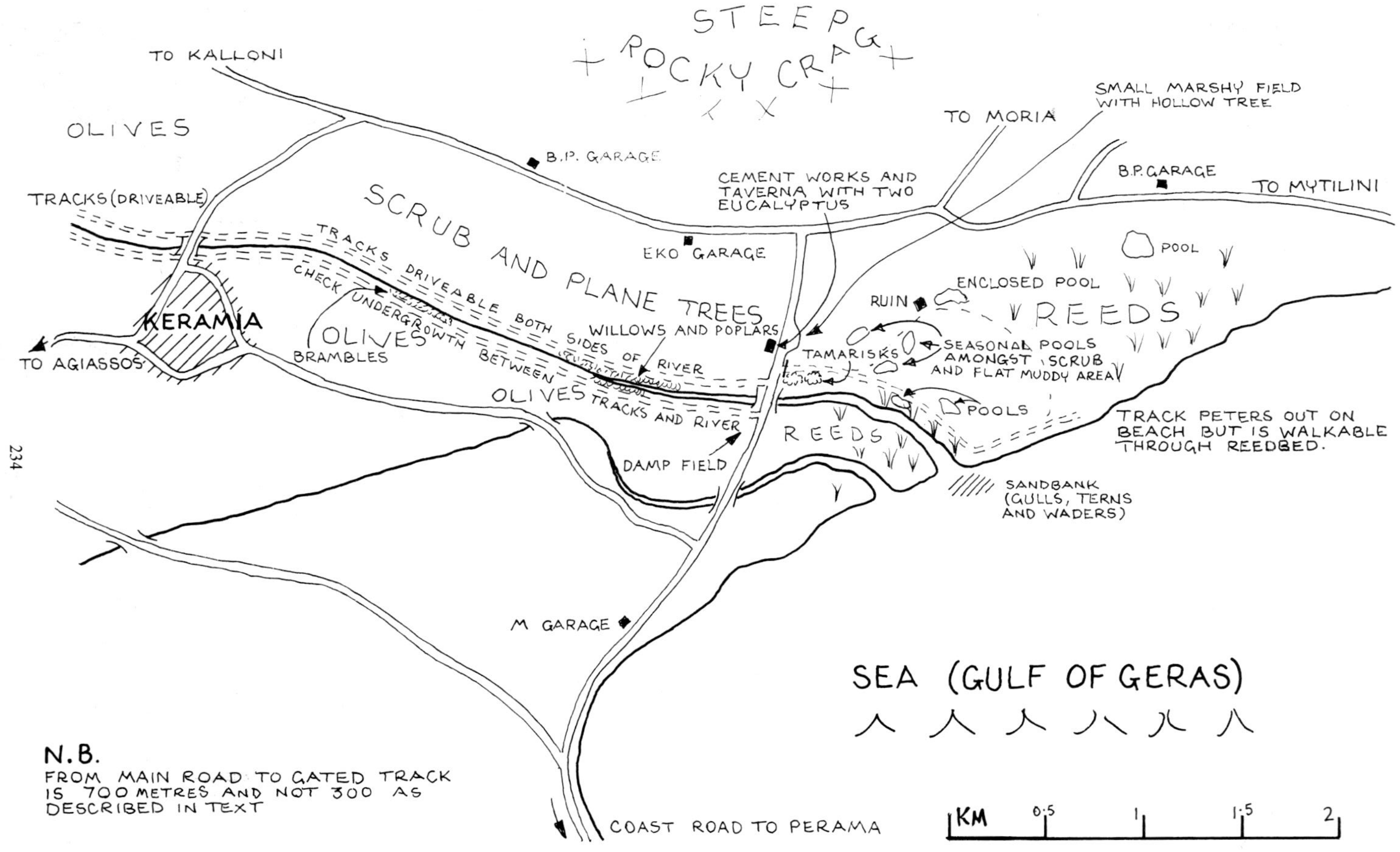

TO KALLONI

OLIVES

TRACKS (DRIVEABLE)

KERAMA

TO AGIASSOS

STEEP & ROCKY CRAT

B.P. GARAGE

CEMENT WORKS AND TAVERNA WITH TWO EUCALYPTUS

EKO GARAGE

SCRUB AND PLANE TREES

OLIVES

BRAMBLES

CHECK UNDERGROWTH BETWEEN

TRACKS DRIVEABLE BOTH SIDES OF RIVER

OLIVES TRACKS AND RIVER

WILLOWS AND POPLARS

DAMP FIELD

M GARAGE

TO MORIA

TO MYTILINI

SMALL MARSHY FIELD WITH HOLLOW TREE

B.P. GARAGE

POOL

RUIN

ENCLOSED POOL

REEDS

TAMARISKS

SEASONAL POOLS AMONGST SCRUB AND FLAT MUDDY AREA

POOLS

REEDS

TRACK PETERS OUT ON BEACH BUT IS WALKABLE THROUGH REEDBED.

SANDBANK (GULLS, TERNS AND WADERS)

SEA (GULF OF GERAS)

COAST ROAD TO PERAMA

KM 0·5 1 1·5 2

N.B.
FROM MAIN ROAD TO GATED TRACK IS 700 METRES AND NOT 300 AS DESCRIBED IN TEXT

234

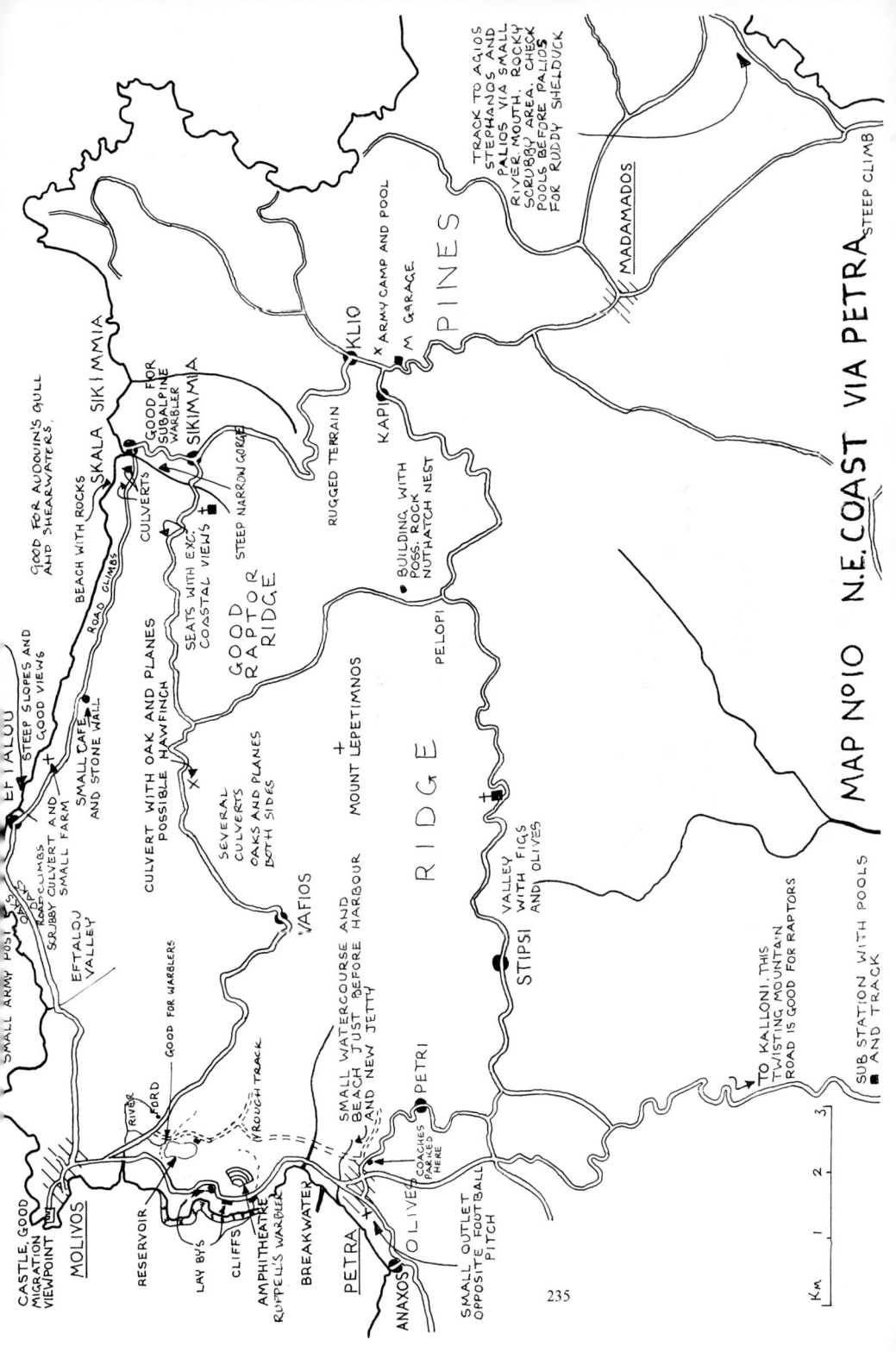

MAP Nº 10 N.E. COAST VIA PETRA STEEP CLIMB

235

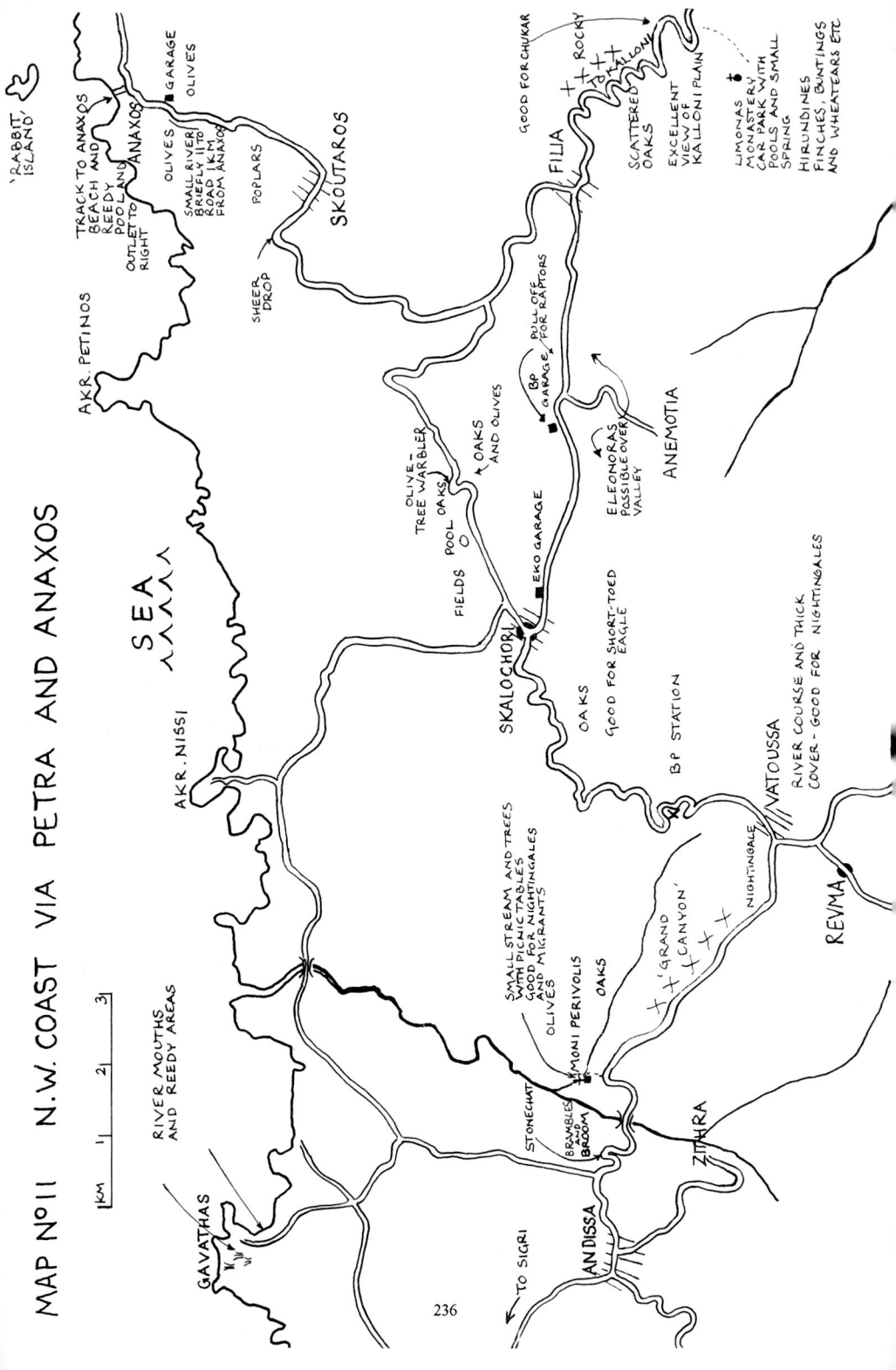

MAP N°11 N.W. COAST VIA PETRA AND ANAXOS

'RABBIT ISLAND'

SEA

AKR. PETINOS

AKR. NISSI

KM 1 2 3
RIVER MOUTHS AND REEDY AREAS

GAVATHAS

AN DISSA
TO SIGRI

ZITHRA

REVMA

VATOUSSA

STONECHAT
BRAMBLES AND BROOM
MONI PERIVOLIS
OLIVES
OAKS
SMALL STREAM AND TREES WITH PICNIC TABLES GOOD FOR NIGHTINGALES AND MIGRANTS

NIGHTINGALE
'GRAND CANYON'
RIVER COURSE AND THICK COVER - GOOD FOR NIGHTINGALES

BP STATION
GOOD FOR SHORT-TOED EAGLE
OAKS

SKALOCHORI
EKO GARAGE
FIELDS
POOL
OAKS
OAKS AND OLIVES
OLIVE-TREE WARBLER

ANEMOTIA
ELEONORAS POSSIBLE OVER VALLEY

BP GARAGE
PULL OFF FOR RAPTORS

FILIA

GOOD FOR CHUKAR
ROCKY
SCATTERED OAKS
'SWALLOW'
EXCELLENT VIEW OF KALLONI PLAIN
LIMONAS MONASTERY CAR PARK WITH POOLS AND SMALL SPRING
HIRUNDINES FINCHES, BUNTINGS AND WHEATEARS ETC

SKOUTAROS
SHEER DROP
POPLARS
OLIVES
OLIVES GARAGE
ANAXOS
TRACK TO ANAXOS BEACH AND REEDY POOL AND
OUTLET TO RIGHT
SMALL RIVER BRIEFLY ROAD 1KM FROM ANAXOS

236

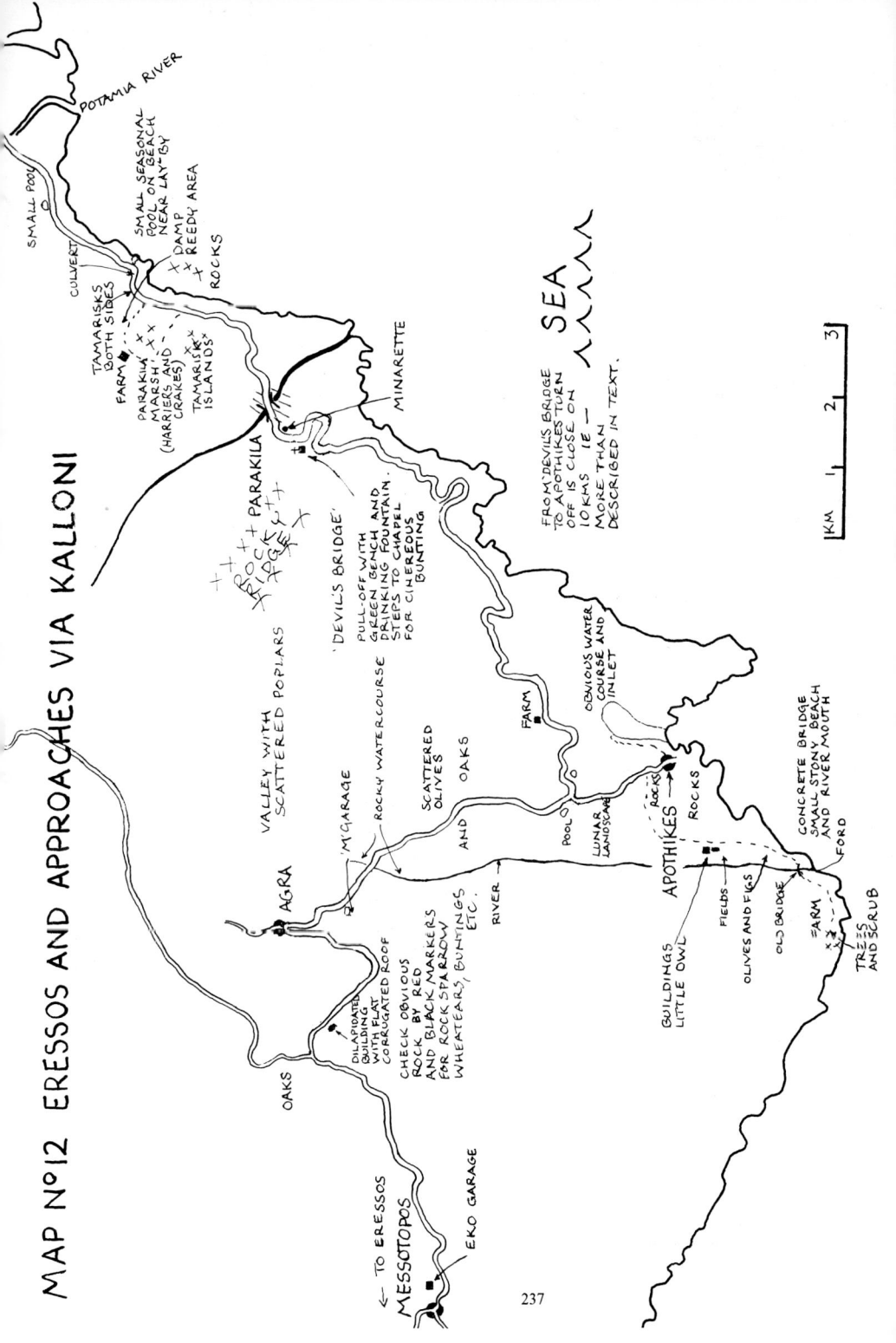

MAP N°12 ERESSOS AND APPROACHES VIA KALLONI

POTAMIA RIVER

SMALL POOL

SMALL SEASONAL POOL ON BEACH NEAR LAY-BY

DAMP REEDY AREA

× × × ROCKS

CULVERT

TAMARISKS BOTH SIDES

PARAKILA FARM

PARAKILA MARSH (HARRIERS AND CRAKES)

TAMARISK ISLANDS

MINARETTE

ROCKY RIDGE

PARAKILA

'DEVIL'S BRIDGE'

PULL-OFF WITH GREEN BENCH AND DRINKING FOUNTAIN STEPS TO CHAPEL FOR CINEREOUS BUNTING

VALLEY WITH SCATTERED POPLARS

ROCKY WATERCOURSE

'M' GARAGE

SCATTERED OLIVES AND OAKS

FARM

POOL

LUNAR LANDSCAPE

OBVIOUS WATER COURSE AND INLET

SEA

FROM 'DEVILS BRIDGE' TO APOTHIKES TURN OFF IS CLOSE ON 10 KMS IE — MORE THAN DESCRIBED IN TEXT.

KM 1 2 3

RIVER

AGRA

DILAPIDATED BUILDING WITH FLAT CORRUGATED ROOF

CHECK OBVIOUS ROCK BY RED AND BLACK MARKERS FOR ROCK SPARROW WHEATEARS, BUNTINGS, ETC.

OAKS

ROCKS

ROCKS

APOTHIKES

BUILDINGS LITTLE OWL

FIELDS

OLIVES AND FIGS

OLD BRIDGE

FARM

TREES AND SCRUB

CONCRETE BRIDGE SMALL STONY BEACH AND RIVER MOUTH

FORD

MESSOTOPOS

← TO ERESSOS

EKO GARAGE

237

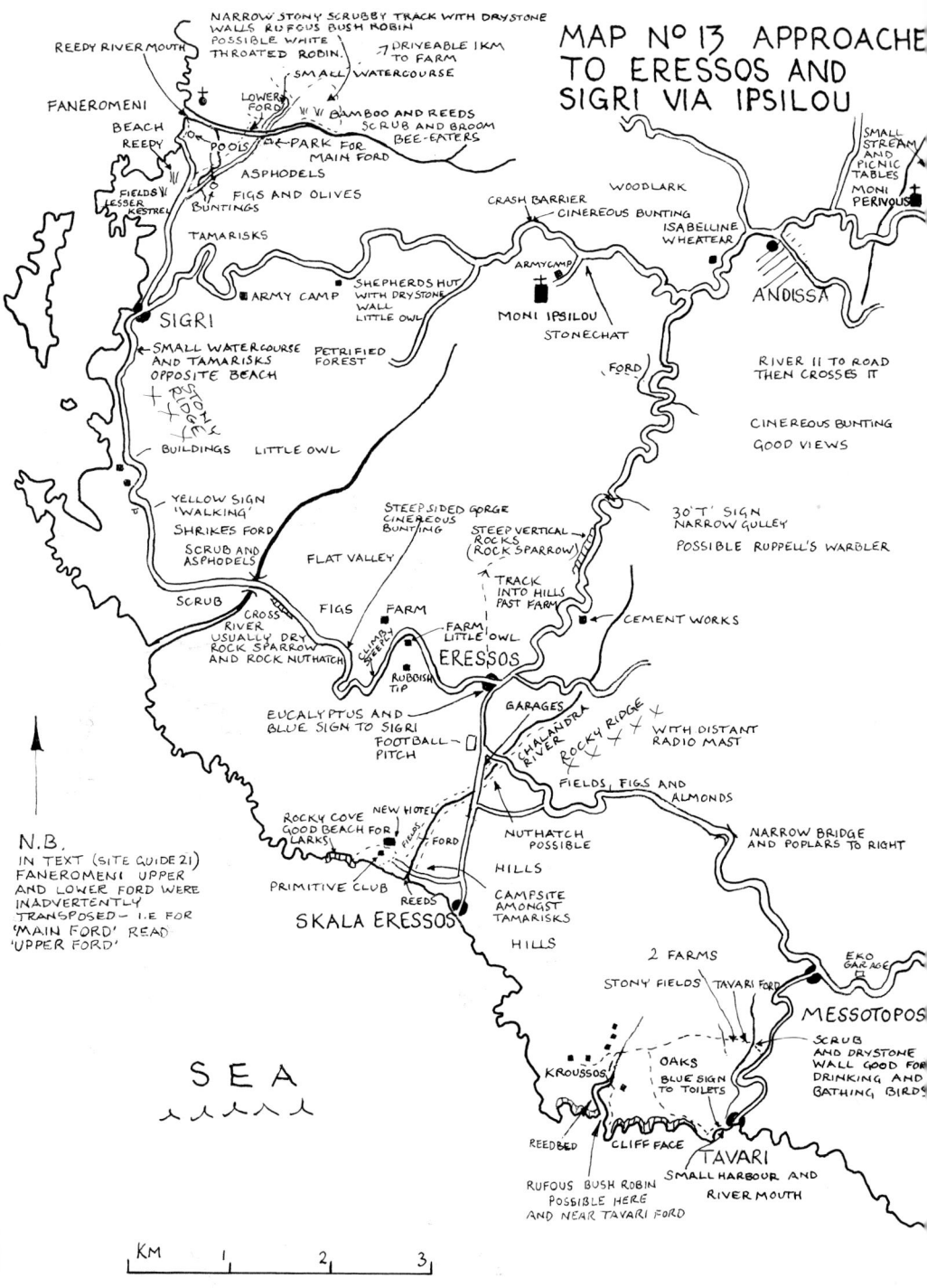

REEDY RIVER MOUTH

NARROW STONY SCRUBBY TRACK WITH DRYSTONE WALLS RUFOUS BUSH ROBIN POSSIBLE WHITE THROATED ROBIN.

DRIVEABLE 1KM TO FARM

SMALL WATERCOURSE

FANEROMENI BEACH REEDY

LOWER FORD

BAMBOO AND REEDS SCRUB AND BROOM BEE-EATERS

PARK FOR MAIN FORD

POOLS

ASPHODELS

FIELDS LESSER KESTREL

FIGS AND OLIVES BUNTINGS

SMALL STREAM AND PICNIC TABLES MONI PERIVOUS

WOODLARK

CRASH BARRIER

CINEREOUS BUNTING

ISABELLINE WHEATEAR

TAMARISKS

ARMY CAMP

SHEPHERDS HUT WITH DRYSTONE WALL LITTLE OWL

ARMY CAMP

MONI IPSILOU

ANDISSA

SIGRI

STONECHAT

SMALL WATERCOURSE AND TAMARISKS OPPOSITE BEACH

PETRIFIED FOREST

FORD

RIVER 11 TO ROAD THEN CROSSES IT

CINEREOUS BUNTING

GOOD VIEWS

BUILDINGS

LITTLE OWL

YELLOW SIGN 'WALKING' SHRIKES FORD

SCRUB AND ASPHODELS

STEEP SIDED GORGE CINEREOUS BUNTING

STEEP VERTICAL ROCKS (ROCK SPARROW)

30 'T' SIGN NARROW GULLEY

POSSIBLE RUPPELL'S WARBLER

FLAT VALLEY

SCRUB

FIGS

FARM

TRACK INTO HILLS PAST FARM

CEMENT WORKS

CROSS RIVER USUALLY DRY ROCK SPARROW AND ROCK NUTHATCH

SLIGHT SEEPS

FARM LITTLE OWL

ERESSOS

RUBBISH TIP

EUCALYPTUS AND BLUE SIGN TO SIGRI FOOTBALL PITCH

GARAGES

CHALANDRA RIVER

ROCKY RIDGE

WITH DISTANT RADIO MAST

FIELDS, FIGS AND ALMONDS

NARROW BRIDGE AND POPLARS TO RIGHT

ROCKY COVE GOOD BEACH FOR LARKS

NEW HOTEL

FIELDS

FORD

NUTHATCH POSSIBLE

PRIMITIVE CLUB

REEDS

HILLS

CAMPSITE AMONGST TAMARISKS

SKALA ERESSOS

HILLS

2 FARMS

EKO GARAGE

N.B.
IN TEXT (SITE GUIDE 21) FANEROMENI UPPER AND LOWER FORD WERE INADVERTENTLY TRANSPOSED – I.E FOR 'MAIN FORD' READ 'UPPER FORD'

STONY FIELDS

TAVARI FORD

MESSOTOPOS

SCRUB AND DRYSTONE WALL GOOD FOR DRINKING AND BATHING BIRDS

KROUSSOS

OAKS BLUE SIGN TO TOILETS

SEA

REEDBED

CLIFF FACE

TAVARI SMALL HARBOUR AND RIVER MOUTH

RUFOUS BUSH ROBIN POSSIBLE HERE AND NEAR TAVARI FORD

KM   1   2   3

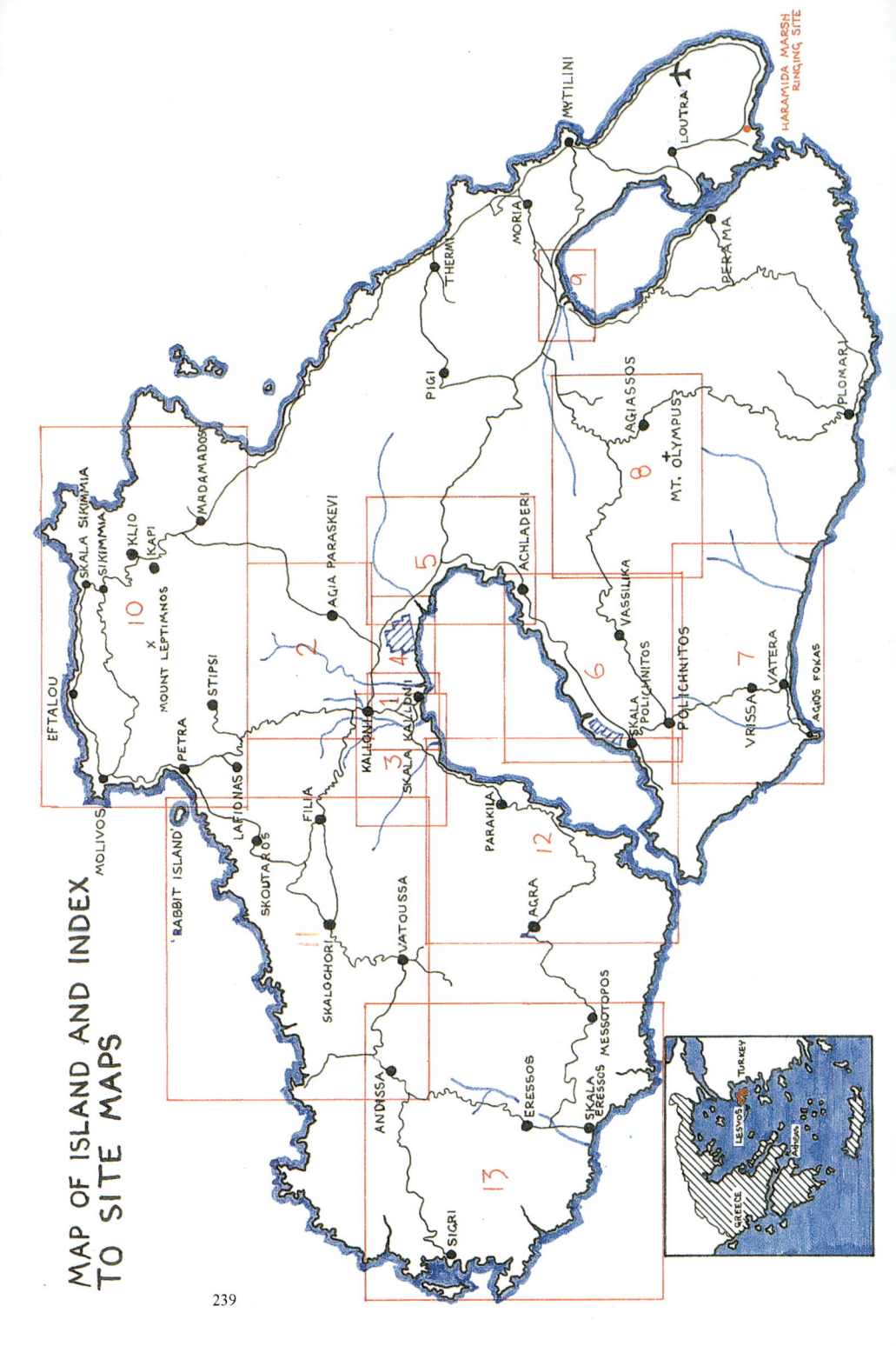

MAP OF ISLAND AND INDEX
TO SITE MAPS

239

HARAMIDA MARSH RINGING TOTALS

SPECIES	1994	1995	1996	1997	1998	TOTAL
Little Bittern				2		2
Spotted Crake				1		1
Corncrake					1	1
Ruff*				2		2
Wood Sandpiper				4		4
Scops Owl				1		1
Swift				4		4
Alpine Swift				1		1
Kingfisher	1	1	1	1	1	5
Bee-eater		2	1		4	7
Hoopoe					1	1
Wryneck	1	1			1	3
Middle Spotted Woodpecker	7	4	5	1	1	18
Short-toed Lark					1	1
Crested Lark	2				2	4
Woodlark			2			2
Sand Martin	1	9	5	232	30	277
Crag Martin				2		2
Swallow	24	38	51	402	92	607
Red-rumped Swallow	1	17	100	28	68	214
House Martin				78		78
Tawny Pipit					1	1
Tree Pipit	1	1	6		2	10
Yellow Wagtail**	1	125	197	13	74	410
White Wagtail		1				1
Wren				1		1
Robin				1		1
Thrush Nightingale	2	1	5		15	23
Nightingale	1	1	1	7	1	11
Redstart		2				2

SPECIES	1994	1995	1996	1997	1998	TOTAL
Whinchat	4	17	27	7	29	84
Wheatear				4		4
Black-eared Wheatear		1	3			4
Blackbird	31	14	20	12	16	93
Song Thrush				1		1
Cetti's Warbler	1	10	6	3	10	30
River Warbler			1			1
Savi's Warbler		3	4	1	7	15
Sedge Warbler	5	13	58	24	69	169
Marsh/Reed Warbler[***]	18	116	109	8	124	375
Great Reed Warbler	4	14	15	14	24	71
Olivaceous Warbler			2			2
Icterine Warbler	1	9	7		3	20
Subalpine Warbler	1	1	7	5	3	17
Sardinian Warbler	2	4	7	1	9	23
Rüppell's Warbler			1			1
Orphean Warbler		5			1	6
Barred Warbler		2	2			4
Lesser Whitethroat	7	14	7	9	7	44
Whitethroat	18	62	29	1	38	148
Garden Warbler	4	19	14		26	63
Blackcap	20	82	50	55	54	261
Eastern Bonelli's Warbler					1	1
Wood Warbler		1	1	11	2	15
Chiffchaff				5		5
Willow Warbler	89	82	190		170	531
Spotted Flycatcher	3	5	3	2		13
Red-breasted Flycatcher					1	1
Collared Flycatcher				2		2
Pied Flycatcher				4		4
Blue Tit	30	45	56	4	25	160

SPECIES	1994	1995	1996	1997	1998	TOTAL
Great Tit	35	46	34	4	25	144
Short-toed Treecreeper	6		3	1		10
Red-backed Shrike	35	85	70		125	315
Lesser Grey Shrike		2			1	3
Woodchat Shrike		1		1		2
Masked Shrike				1	1	2
Jay			3			3
House Sparrow	21	30	58	3	22	134
Spanish Sparrow	11	61	15			87
Sparrow *sp* (females)[****]	22	80	66		29	197
Chaffinch	3	5	12	16	1	37
Serin				2		2
Greenfinch	5	11	5	13	8	42
Goldfinch			9	4		13
Scarlet Rosefinch			1			1
Cirl Bunting	3	6	17		13	39
Corn Bunting		10	3		4	17
TOTALS	421	1057	1291	999	1143	4911

Ringing Dates
1994:   15 - 21 September   (6 days ringing)
1995:   7 - 19 September   (10 days ringing)
1996:   29 August - 10 September   (10 days ringing)
1997:   14 - 20 April   (5.5 days ringing)
1998:   6 - 16 September   (8.5 days ringing)

Note
[*]   Caught at Kalloni Saltpans.
[**]   Total for 1996 includes birds caught at Dipi Larssos Reedbed.
[***]   Separation of first-year Marsh and Reed Warblers is problematic in the population passing through Lesvos in the autumn. Conclusive identification of these birds awaits full analyses of biometric data.
[****] Identification of female House and Spanish Sparrows could not be achieved with certainty.

Haramida Ringing Group
Filios Akriotis, Dawn Balmer, Christine Bourne, Greg Conway, Les Hatton, Antonios Kyrkos, Shirley Millar, Jeremy Wilson. Assistance also from Environmental Science students at the University of the Aegean, Mytilini.

Dawn Balmer & Jeremy Wilson

(FOR LOCATION OF HARAMIDA MARSH SEE ISLAND MAP P239)

SITE GAZETTEER AND MAPS

The figures in bold type refer to the map number and page where appropriate.

LIST OF PICTURES

FIRST COLOUR SECTION

1. Black-necked Grebe
2. Little Bittern (male)
3. Bittern
4. Squacco Heron
5. Black Stork
6. White Stork
7. Great White Egret
8. Greater Flamingo
9. Garganey (male)
10. Ruddy Shelduck
11. Marsh Harrier (male)
12. Montagu's Harrier (female)
13. Long-legged Buzzard
14. Lesser Kestrel (male)
15. Hobby
16. Red-footed Falcon (male)
17. Eleonora's Falcon.
18. Spotted Crake
19. Little Crake
20. Stone Curlew
21. Collared Pratincole

SECOND COLOUR SECTION

22. Spur-winged Plover
23. Curlew Sandpiper
24. Marsh Sandpiper
25. Wood Sandpiper

26. Whiskered Tern
27. Little Owl
28. Scops Owl
29. Middle Spotted Woodpecker
30. Kingfisher
31. Bee-eater
32. Great Spotted Cuckoo
33. Calandra Lark
34. Woodlark
35. Crag Martin
36. Red-rumped Swallow
37. Red-throated Pipit
38. Tawny Pipit
39. Black-headed Wagtail (male)
40. Citrine Wagtail (male)
41. Rufous Bush Robin
42. Black Redstart (male)
43. Nightingale
44. Black-eared Wheatear (male)
45. Isabelline Wheatear
46. Blue Rock Thrush (male)

THIRD COLOUR SECTION

47. Great Reed Warbler
48. Olivaceous Warbler
49. Olive-tree Warbler
50. Ruppell's Warbler (male)

51. Collared Flycatcher (male)
52. Sombre Tit
53. Western Rock Nuthatch
54. Red-backed Shrike (male)
55. Lesser Grey Shrike
56. Masked Shrike
57. Rose-coloured Starling
58. Rock Sparrow
59. Serin
60. Hawfinch
61. Ortolan Bunting (male)
62. Cretzschmar's Bunting (male)
63. Black-headed Bunting (male)
64. Kalloni Inland Lake
65. Kalloni Plain
66. Kalloni East River
67. Kalloni Pool
68. Kalloni Salt Pans
69. 'Derbyshire'
70. Kalloni West River
71. Dipi Larssos
72. Parakila Marsh
73. Parakila to Agra
74. Ipsilou monastery
75. Above Agiassos
76. Molivos
77. North coast above Eftalou

243

INDEX OF BIRD SPECIES

The figures in bold type refer to the numbered photos, and those in standard type to the main text.

REFERENCES

Chilton, L. *Walks in North Lesvos* - Marengo Publications (ISBN 1 900802 48 1)

Eleftheriadis, M. (1986) *Lesvos (History, Art, Folklore, Modern Life)* - Toubis, Athens.

Handrinos, G. and Akriotis T. *(1997) The Birds of Greece* - A and C Black - London. (ISBN 0 7136 3929 6).

Harrap, S. (1993) Corsican and Kruper's Nuthatches - *Birding World* (Vol 6 No 3).

De Knijff, P. (1991) Status and distribution of Cinereous Bunting - *Birding World* (Vol. 4 No.11).

Lesbios, P. (1989) *Lesbos (History, Folklore, Archeology, Touring)* - Moliviati Brothers, Mytilini.

Miles J. (1994) *Lesbos* (Great Guides to Greece) - Domboli, Athens.

Tucker, G.M. and Heath, M.F. (1994) *Birds in Europe : their conservation status* - BirdLife International.

Various authors *Lesbos Compilation* - Whitehouse, S.

Williams, M. (1992) *Birdwatching In Lesbos* (ISBN O 9519629 06).

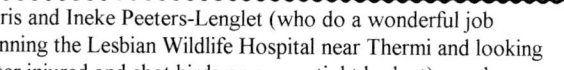

Joris and Ineke Peeters-Lenglet (who do a wonderful job running the Lesbian Wildlife Hospital near Thermi and looking after injured and shot birds on a very tight budget) are always pleased to welcome visitors - and of course donations!

If you find an injured **wild animal or bird** please call : (0251) 71076 or 093833022

LESBIAN WILDLIFE HOSPITAL

STOP PRESS! - ADDITIONS TO SYSTEMATIC & SPECIES LIST + ERRATA

Black-throated Diver *Gavia arctica* (P103) - A party of 8 seen offshore from Achladeri on 24th March '99 was impressive.

Storm Petrel *Hydrobates pelagicus* - Two unspecified petrels seen over Sigri harbour together with 20 Mediterranean Shearwaters during a violent thunderstorm on 2nd April '99 were thought most likely to be this species and would represent a first for the island. Described in *The Birds of Greece* as a 'rare and local summer visitor' it is admitted that this bird's migration patterns are still poorly known.

Pygmy Cormorant *Phalacrocorax Pygmeus* (P105) - A flock of c45 observed at Haramida Marsh on 31st October '99 ranks as a new island record.

Bittern *Botaurus stellaris* (P106) - An exhausted individual found in the middle of an olive grove near Petra in late December '98 was taken into care and later released.

Little Bittern *Ixobrychus minutus* (P106-7) - An adult seen from 5th-7th July '99 near Kalloni East River Lower ford may suggest breeding in the area.

Night Heron *Nycticorax nycticorax* (P107) - An impressive flock of 33 over Kalloni East River on 13th April '99, and an adult flushed from there on 6th July '99 was even more unusual.

Cattle Egret *Bubulcus ibis* (P108) - Two seen at Kalloni West River on 16th April '99 constitute only the island's third record.

Grey Heron *Ardea cinerea* (P109) - A gathering of c90 at Kalloni Salt Pans on 28th March '99 was an island record!

Black Stork *Ciconia nigra* (P110-111) - A gathering of 32 feeding on a rapidly drying out Potamia reservoir on 31st August '99 was an island record!

Spoonbill *Platalea leucorodia* (P112) - An oversummering pair lingered around Kalloni Salt Pans throughout June and July '99.

Greater Flamingo *Phoenicopterus ruber* (P112-3) - The increasing occurrence of summering individuals was responsible for a count of 122 birds on 8th June '99, rising to 237 on 5th July, 380 on 30th July and 500+ from mid-August!

Mute Swan *Cygnus olor* (P113) - Six birds wintering on Kalloni Pool in December '98 reduced to 3 by January '99, with 1 remaining till at least mid-May.

White-fronted Goose *Anser albifrons* (P113) - Seven geese flying high SSW over Kalloni Pool on 27th April (with 2 a couple of days later over Kalloni Inland Lake) were thought most likely to be this species, but the great height involved precludes positive identification.

Tufted Duck *Aythya fuligula* (P116) - A retrospective record concerns a pair seen to touch down briefly on Kalloni Salt Pans on 19th May '98.

Egyptian Vulture *Neophron percnopterus* (P118) - A bird seen over Napi Valley on 7th May '99 was only the fifth island record.

Montagu's Harrier *Circus pygargus* (P120) - Evidence of possible wintering concerns a female (regrettably a shooting casualty) taken to the Wildlife Hospital in late December '98.

Imperial Eagle *Aquila heliaca* (P123) - A sub-adult heading north at Vatera on 29th March '99 was followed by a bird near Skala Sikimmia commuting from Turkey on 3rd May that year, a pair near Vatoussa coming in low from the south-west and heading east on 17th May and 2 birds seen by several observers between Agra and Eressos at the end of May '99.

Red-footed Falcon *Falco vespertinus* (P126) - A flock of c120 seen over Kalloni East River on 6th October '99 was exceptional for autumn.

Hobby *Falco subbuteo* (P126-7) - An unusual record of a pair apparently nesting in a stunted tree growing out of a small stone ruin between Kalloni East River and Salt Pans in August '99!

Corncrake *Crex crex* (P130-1) - One was calling around Kalloni Salt Pans on 19th April '99.

Crane *Grus grus* (P132) - A bird seen briefly circling Kalloni Salt Pans on 23rd April '99 constitutes only the fourth confirmed island record.

Black-winged Pratincole *Glareola nordmanni* (P134) - A late individual was present at Kalloni Salt Pans on 8th June '99.

Little Ringed Plover *Charadrius dubius* (P134-5) - A concentration of 45 in a field at Faneromeni on 2nd April '99 was a good number.

Ringed Plover *Charadrius hiaticula* (P135) - A gathering of 22 birds at Kalloni Salt Pans on 4th May '99 (rising to an impressive 31 next day) was unusual for spring.

Greater Sand Plover *Charadrius lescenaultii* (P135) - A winter-plumaged bird which put in a brief appearance at Kalloni Salt Pans channel on 9th May '99 was possibly present earlier.

Dotterel *Charadrius morinellus* (P136) - A single seen near Sigri on 23rd April '99 was the island's first documented spring record.

Spur-winged Plover *Hoplopterus spinosus* (P137) - Three seen together along the track bordering Kalloni Pool on 31st March '99 was an island record.

Knot *Calidris canutus* (P137) - A single at Skala Polichnitos Salt Pans on 23rd April '99 was only the fourth for the island.

Broad-billed Sandpiper *Limicola falcinellus* (P139) - A bird first seen at Kalloni Salt Pans on 4th May '99 and then relocated at Parakila Marsh from 9th-11th May (and thankfully photographed by me!) was seen again at the Salt Pans up to 15th May. Though regular in August this constitutes the island's first spring record.

Great Snipe *Gallinago media* (P140) - An individual was both videoed and photographed along Kalloni East River from 24th-28th May '99 (though regrettably not by me - having left the island the day before!).

Marsh Sandpiper *Tringa stagnatilis* (P143-4) - The 8th April '99 saw an all-time record count of 110 birds in flooded fields at Kalloni Salt Pans!

Red-necked Phalarope *Phalaropus lobatus* (P146) - A female seen at Kalloni Salt Pans during a large wader passage between 7th-10th May '99 was only the second for the island.

Arctic Skua *Stercorarius parasiticus* - A single bird off Agios Fokas on 29th March '99 and a further 2 together (both a light and dark phase) harassing terns off Kalloni Salt Pan headland on 15th April that year constitute the first ever island records!

Caspian Tern *Sterna caspia* (P149) - Three birds at Kalloni Salt Pans on July 7th '99 was unusual for the time of year.

Arctic Tern *Sterna paradisaea* (P150) - A single at Kalloni East River mouth on 16th April '99 was only the fourth island record, while only 8 records exist for the rest of Greece up to '97.

Black Tern *Chlidonias niger* (P159-60) - A flock of c50 (an island record) was present over the flooded sheep field at the back of Kalloni Salt Pans amongst a general influx of marsh terns on 7th May '99.

Stock Dove *Columba oenas* (P161) - Further long overdue sightings concern a bird over Kalloni Pool on 20th April '99 and a pair which flew in off the sea from Turkey over the Petra-Molivos headland on 3rd July '99.

Great Spotted Cuckoo *Clamator glandarius* (P162) - A pair first seen on 16th April '99 spent several days in the Achladeri area.

Eagle Owl *Bubo bubo* (P163-4) - A male found shot near Moria in December '98 was taken into the Wildlife Hospital, where it sadly died. More encouraging were reports recently received from a reliable source of a pair both seen and heard in the nearby area of Pyrgi (just west of Mytilini on the Bay of Geras) - where breeding was thought likely.

Tawny Owl *Strix aluco* (P164) - Heard near Petra on 3rd July '99 and near Achladeri on 5th.

Long-eared Owl *Asio otis* (P164) - One again flushed near the Kruper's site at Achladeri on 5th July '99.

White-breasted Kingfisher *Halcyon smyrnensis* - A bird was watched down to 20 ft sitting in a dead tree near Molivos harbour on 26th and 27th August '99 before heading off inland. This constitutes a first for the island and only the fifth for Greece!

Blue-cheeked Bee-eater *Merops superciliosus* (P167) - Following a retrospective record of one perched on overhead wires at Skala Eressos with common Bee-eaters on 19th September '98, a fourth record concerned a bird seen and videoed by Malcolm Rymer at Kalloni Salt Pans on 19th April '99.

Syrian Woodpecker *Dendrocopos syriacus* (P169-70) - A pair was watched in olive groves between Skala Polichnitos and Polichnitos on 5th April '99 by a couple familiar with the species.

Calandra Lark *Melanocorypha calandra* (P170) - Apart from sightings on Skala Kalloni beach 8th April '99 and at 'Derbyshire' on 24th April, spring '99 also produced some late records - from Kalloni Pool surrounds on 27th May and along Kalloni West River on 7th June.

Sand Martin *Riparia riparia* (P172) - An unusual record of five along Kalloni East River on 7th July '99 may suggest local breeding.

Richard's Pipit *Anthus novaeseelandiae* (P174) - A bird was seen once again at the back of Kalloni Salt Pans on 13th April '99.

Desert Wheatear *Oenanthe deserti* (P183) - A suspected female of this species was watched at close range at 'Derbyshire' on 9th May '99 during an unsettled spell of weather. This was backed up by a full written description, which would constitute only the second island record.

Finsch's Wheatear *Oenanthe finschii* (P184) - A male seen in the Upper Potamia Valley and at 'Devil's Bridge' on 19th April '99 and a pair observed at Ipsilou monastery on 24th April that year are respectively the third and fourth island records.

Ring Ouzel *Turdus torquatus* (P184) - At long last a sequence of sightings in spring '99 involved a male in the Potamia Valley on 16th April, one near Achladeri on 23rd April and another male at Ipsilou monastery on 23rd May.

Grasshopper Warbler *Locustella naevia* (P185-6) - A bird heard in song from a scrubby coastal gulley just east of Molivos on 29th May '95 is the most up-to-date record.

Upcher's Warbler *Hippolais languida* (P188) - A bird seen well by several observers at Ipsilou monastery on 16th May '99 confirms its vagrant or scarce migrant status.

Firecrest *Regulus ignicapillus* (P195) - A bird singing above Parakila on 7th April '99 constitutes only the fourth island record.

Kruper's Nuthatch *Sitta krueperi* (P199) - Last line of text should read 'For further info see P83-7.'

Nuthatch *Sitta europaea* (P199-200) - A new breeding site was confirmed by several sightings of a nesting pair in the Napi Valley between mid-May and June '99.

Penduline Tit *Remiz pendulinus* (P200) - Two birds observed flying over Dipi Larssos Reedbed calling on 27th March '99 were the fourth documented record for the island.

Great Grey Shrike *Lanius excubitor* (P203) - A bird seen well between Kalloni Salt Pans and East River on 28th September '99 was definitely identified as this species.

Spanish Sparrow *Passer hispaniolensis* (P215) - Comments at end of ringing data tables are on P242, not P134.

Tree Sparrow *Passer montanus* (P215) - A retrospective record concerns a small flock seen along the coastal approaches to Sigri in the third week of May '98.

Hawfinch *Coccothraustes coccothraustes* (P217) - Flocks a hundred or more strong were a regular feature of the island in the last few days of March '99, when they were seen (especially to the south-east around Dipi Larssos) feeding on the copious seeds of the pistachio tree.

Rock Bunting *Emberiza cia* (P218) - Three males were reported (including one singing) between Molivos and Vafios on 17th April '99.

To the mammal list (P222) should be added the **Monk Seal** *Monachus monachus*, which is thought to still frequent the rugged west coast - though no positive sightings have been reported for about 5 years. The **Striped Dolphin** *Stenella coeruleoalba* is now considered to be more widespread than the **Common Dolphin** *Delphinus delphinus*. Reports were also received of a dead **Badger** *Meles meles* on the Madamados around mid-May '99. Although the body was partly decomposed it would be difficult to misidentify this species, so it is possible that isolated pockets could still occur and that it is not, after all, extinct on the island.

New additions to the butterfly list (P223-4) include :- **Berger's Clouded Yellow** *Colias australis*, **Purple Hairstreak** *Quercusia quercus*, **Ilex Hairstreak** *Nordmannia ilicis*, **Large Blue** *Maculinea arion*, **Baton Blue** *Pseudophilotes baton*, **Common Blue** *Polyommatus icarus*, **Cardinal** *Pandoriana pandora*, **Freyer's Grayling** *Neohipparchia fatua*, **Dusky Meadow Brown** *Hypnonephele lycaon*, **Oriental Meadow Brown**, *Hypnonephele lupina*, **Gatekeeper** *Pyronia tithonus*, **Southern Gatekeeper** *Pyronia cecilia*, **Oberthur's Grizzled Skipper** *Pyrgus armoricanus*, **Lulworth Skipper** *Thymelicus acteon* and **Essex Skipper** *Thymelicus lineola*.

My apologies to Lance Chilton for misspelling his name on P224, and also to John Sweeney and Duncan Walbridge (P225), and to Andrew Clarke, Phil Langston, Andrew Steed and Steve Woolnough for omitting them from the list of contributors. Other contributors are credited in my Lesvos Spring '99 Update, except for recent records from MS Backhouse, John Bannon, Paul Bowley, Pam and Cliff Gibson, Tony Gill, Dr M Griffin, Dave Hardaker, Roger Hewitt, Alan Hudson and Carol Davies, Paul Pearsall, JC Sutherby and Stuart Thompson - my thanks to all.

Changes to maps

In **Map 2** (P227) the discovery of a new site known as **Napi Valley** is worth mentioning. It is accessed via the Agia Paraskevi to Napi road, remembering to bear right in Agia Paraskevi square, taking the sign for Napi and Madamados and following straight on at the next road sign and taking a left at the Greek sign on the wall for Madamados. On approaching Napi keep to the left of the village (without doing a sharp left) and follow a yellow or blue sign to Madamados and then another similar sign, which leads you on to a surprisingly good road with an open, rocky vista, which eventually deteriorates somewhat after skirting a river, but which leads eventually to Madamados (and here most of the island maps are inaccurate). The predominance of oaks makes for some excellent birding (Masked Shrike, Sombre Tit and Olive-tree Warbler especially) and the area around the large radio mast to the left looking seawards proved in spring '99 to be one of the best raptor fly-throughs on the island. **Further details on this and other sites, changes to sites, species counts and status and spring '99 migration highlights are available in my 'Lesvos Spring '99 Update' - available from me for £4.50 with postage.**

In **Map 6** (P231) the locations of Skamioudi and Alikoudi Pool have been juxtaposed - ie the latter lies east of Skamioudi and not west of it, approx 3kms before the salt pans are reached. In addition, the 'half-finished buildings' on the corner of the approach track are now completed and the approach tracks inland from Skala Vassilikon to Polichnitos are now largely tarmacked and possess new blue and white signs, which together make my original instructions to 'bear right onto the tarmac road' now redundant - though the 'rusty Greek sign' mentioned later currently still survives.

In **Map 8** (P233) the car or bus park and start of the circular walk has been positioned at the wrong end of Agiassos. Approaching from the Polichnitos road simply park in the obvious area to the right just before the road splits to the left (signposted *center*).